The Gift by H.D.

University Press of Florida

Gainesville · Tallahassee · Tampa · Boca Raton
Pensacola · Orlando · Miami · Jacksonville

The Gift
by H.D.

The Complete Text

☙

Edited and Annotated
with an Introduction by

Jane Augustine

Copyright 1969, 1982 by the Estate of Hilda Doolittle

Copyright 1998 by Perdita Schaffner

Notes, annotations, and introduction Copyright 1998 by the Board of Regents
of the State of Florida

The full text of *The Gift* is published with the permission of H.D.'s daughter,
Perdita Schaffner, through her agents, New Directions Publishing Corporation,
the publishers of an abridged version of *The Gift*.

Printed in the United States of America on acid-free paper

03 02 01 00 99 98 6 5 4 3 2 1

Library of Congress Cataloging-in-Publication Data
H.D. (Hilda Doolittle), 1886–1961.
The gift : the complete text / by H. D. : edited and annotated,
with an introduction by Jane Augustine.
p. cm.
Includes bibliographical references and index.
ISBN 0-8130-1644-4 (hardcover : alk. paper)
1. H.D. (Hilda Doolittle), 1886–1961—Childhood and youth.
2. Women poets, American—20th century—Biography.
3. Bethlehem (Pa.)—Social life and customs.
4. Moravians—Pennsylvania—Bethlehem.
5. Creative ability. 6. Peace. I. Augustine, Jane. II. Title.
PS3507.0726Z464   1998
811'.52—dc21
[b]   98-26236

The University Press of Florida is the scholarly publishing agency for the State
University System of Florida, comprised of Florida A & M University, Florida
Atlantic University, Florida International University, Florida State University,
University of Central Florida, University of Florida, University of North Florida,
University of South Florida, and University of West Florida.

University Press of Florida
15 Northwest 15th Street
Gainesville, FL 32611–2079
http://nersp.nerdc.ufl.edu/~upf

To Perdita,
for her continuing generous interest,
and to the memory of
the Reverend Henry Williams,
historian, hymnologist, kind guide
to Moravian wisdom

Contents

A Note on the Text and Its Arrangement : ix

List of Abbreviations : xv

Introduction : 1

The Gift

I. Dark Room : 33

II. Fortune Teller : 55

III. The Dream : 81

IV. Because One Is Happy : 107

V. The Secret : 145

VI. What It Was : 183

VII. Morning Star : 207

VIII. Notes

I. : 228   II. : 232   III. : 250   IV. : 255
V. : 258   VI. : 269   VII. : 274

Editor's Notes : 279

List of Works Cited : 289

Index : 295

A Note on the Text
and Its Arrangement

This text reproduces the third and final typescript of *The Gift,* including unpaginated title pages with epigraphs. It can be considered definitive. In December 1949 in Switzerland, H.D. reread this typescript carefully because Norman Holmes Pearson, her literary agent and executor, had suggested possible revisions. She wrote to him that she could not revise, as it was "impossible to go back emotionally" (*BHP,* 93). Although she then suggested that her Moravian-based short story, "The Death of Marin Presser" (1943), could serve as an ending and thus accomplish what he wanted in revision, she did not instruct him to place it with the original typescript of *The Gift.* Later, in 1957, she approved of his effort to have the story published separately (*BHP,* 202). Writing the final draft during World War II, she had not chosen the fictional work to end the "almost autobiographical" *Gift,* although the story was at hand. This text adheres to her original conception, the 1944 version. It was conveyed by Pearson to the Beinecke Rare Book and Manuscript Library at Yale University, New Haven, Connecticut, and is held there along with the first two drafts, which have been occasionally consulted on difficult points.

The typescript has two main parts. The first contains the seven chapters of the memoir itself. Its title page carries a note in H.D.'s handwriting: "From H.D. Aldington, Croce Bianca, Lugano," and its final typewritten lines read "London—1941–1943." The second part is the 94-page set of "Notes," comprised of seven sections corresponding roughly to the seven chapters. It was completed, according to internal dating, in July 1944. H.D. composed these "Notes" in sections separated by line spaces, each of which opens with an underlined phrase from the main text indicating the passage to which the particular note refers. The "Notes" have a separate title page, on which is handwritten "From: H.D. Aldington, Villa Verena, Küsnacht, *bei* Zürich," and a final typewritten line "London—1940–44." These dates spanning the composition of the entire book offer evidence that H.D. intended the "Notes" as a coda to and completion of *The Gift*.

No changes have been made in H.D.'s wording or in a few characteristic and unusual (but correct) spellings—e.g., *hypatica, swathe*—or in her sometimes idiosyncratic punctuation, including her hyphenations. This principle accords with Robert Spoo's reasoning in his note on the text of *Asphodel:* "To grant H.D. her punctuation is to respect her syntax, the special rhythms and 'voices' of her text" (*A*, xviii). British typographical conventions, e.g., punctuation outside of quotation marks and a single hyphen for a dash, have been altered to American style. The five dashes that indicate a break in the text have been replaced by line spaces, as H.D. apparently desired. Spoo has pointed out that on page 151 of the typescript of *HER*, H.D. jotted the word "Space" in the margin opposite the five dashes, indicating that the compositor should interpret the dashes as meaning extra spacing, not the insertion of dashes or some other distinguishing mark (letter to the editor, March 31, 1993).

When a quotation begins within a sentence, H.D.'s policy of using a lowercase letter after the quotation mark has been retained, although the American convention requires a capital letter. British spellings have also been retained, as characteristic of the milieu in which she was writing. The frequent run-on and comma-spliced sentences have also been retained, because they have the intended effect of signaling a rush of thought, emotional urgency, and overflow of boundaries appropriate to the content. The New Directions abridged edition (*NDG*) extensively regularizes the punctuation, altering this effect. *NDG*'s chapter 6, for example, has only two minor changes in wording from H.D.'s original but 245 changes of punctuation, a figure approximately true for the abridged chapters as well.

Despite adherence to the editorial principle of minimal intervention with H.D.'s text, a few changes were necessary. Although no words in the typescript are illegible, a number of them, chiefly proper names and foreign words, are misspelled or lack the appropriate accent marks. These have been silently corrected.

H.D.'s pagination has necessarily been changed. In the typescript, she renumbered each chapter's pages, starting with number one; here they are paginated sequentially. The "Notes" sections were paginated sequentially to form a unit; here they follow the page sequence after the chapters. She titled the chapters but did not number them one through seven. In the "Notes," she did the reverse: she numbered but did not title the seven sections. The first through fifth chapters have corresponding "Notes" sections, but the last two "Notes" sections dilate on themes in chapter 5 and do not correspond specifically to chapters 6 and 7. For clarity of general correlation, the chapters have been given roman numerals in brackets above the titles, and the "Notes" sections have the corresponding chapter titles in brackets below their roman numerals, except for the last two.

H.D. did not interfere with the flow of the main text by inserting into it any signals, such as superscripts, to indicate which phrases are keys to sections in her later "Notes." An editorial decision was made to follow her lead and refrain from annotating the main text in the few places that might require it. In H.D's "Notes," however, the editor has inserted superscript numbers referring to endnotes that cite titles and page numbers of works quoted by H.D. and that supply additional information where necessary. The index headings refer to both the main text and the "Notes."

Acknowledgments

I would like to thank Perdita Schaffner, H.D.'s daughter and executor of H.D.'s estate, and the New Directions Publishing Corporation, agents for the estate, for permission to publish this original full-length version of *The Gift*. I wish also to thank Mrs. Schaffner and the Yale Collection of American Literature, Beinecke Rare Book and Manuscript Library, Yale University, for permission to quote from unpublished H.D. material in the introduction and appendices. I am grateful to Beinecke Library for the H.D. Fellowship in American Literature to complete this project and to Mrs. Schaffner for permitting me to work in the Bryher Library at her home in East Hampton, New York, where I first read the privately printed memoir "A Moravian Heritage" by Francis Wolle, H.D.'s first cousin, containing material relevant to *The Gift* and unavailable elsewhere. Photographs are reproduced by permission of the Moravian Archives and the artist Fred Bees in Bethlehem, Pennsylvania, the Historical Society of Pennsylvania in Philadelphia, the Yale Collection of American Literature, Beinecke Rare Book and Manuscript Library, Yale University, New Haven, Connecticut, and the Archiv der Brüder-Unität, Herrnhut, Germany.

Every edition is a collaborative effort; this one is especially so. I want to acknowledge and express my deep gratitude to those who did important prior work on *The Gift*—Diana Collecott, Rachel Blau DuPlessis, Susan Stanford Friedman, Adalaide Morris, and the late Norman Holmes Pearson—and to the publications in which portions of the full original version appeared. L. S. Dembo, the editor of *Contemporary Literature,* who early recognized H.D.'s importance, published chapter 3, "The Dream," in issue 10, no. 4 (Autumn 1969, 605–26), accompanied by an interview with Pearson (436–46). Chapter 1, "Dark Room," edited by Susan Stanford Friedman and Rachel Blau Du-Plessis, including H.D.'s "Notes" to that chapter, was published in *Montemora* 8 (1981, 57–76). Chapter 2, "Fortune Teller," appeared in *Iowa Review* 16, no. 2 (1986, 14–41), with an introduction by Adalaide Morris, editor of this H.D. Centennial issue. Diana Collecott performed a special service by placing the editor's name, Griselda Ohannessian, on the title page of the abridged New Directions edition brought out in England by Virago in 1984. The title page of the American *NDG* lacks this information; abridgment is mentioned only in the introduction by Perdita Schaffner (xiv).

Thanks for technical, moral, and literary-critical support also go to many others: Louis L. Martz for invaluable editorial advice and professional assistance; Robert Spoo for his example of meticulous editing of H.D.'s *Asphodel* and careful reading of this text; Donna Hollenberg for information from the H.D.–Norman Holmes Pearson correspondence related to *The Gift;* Louis H. Silverstein, H.D.'s chronologer and the cataloger of her materials; Patricia Willis, curator of the Yale Collection of American Literature; Steven Jones and the staff of the Beinecke reading room; the Reverend J. Thomas Minor, head librarian, Bonnie Falla and Linda LaPointe, reference librarians, at Reeves Library, Moravian College, Bethlehem, Pennsylvania; the Reverend Vernon Nelson and the Reverend Albert Frank, archivists at the Moravian archives, Bethlehem, Pennsylvania, and Esther von Ungern, assistant at the Archiv der Brüder-Unität, Herrnhut, Germany; the late Reverend Henry Williams, former head librarian, Reeves Library, Moravian College, and an authority on Moravian hymns, Bethlehem history, church doctrine, and genealogy of H.D.'s Philadelphia cousins, the Bells, for research aid and his indispensable information on complex issues in Moravianism; A. S. Bell, head librarian of the London Library; Alice S. Creighton, head of special collections, Nimitz Library, United States Naval Academy, Annapolis; Monica Crystal, secretary of collections, and Pamela Webster, rights and reproductions coordinator, at the Pennsylvania Historical Society, Philadelphia; Rose-marie Zagarri, professor of American history, George Mason University; Sherri Williams, University of California at San Marcos; the staff of the gene-alogy room and the Center for the Humanities of the New York Public Library; Mark Norbeck at the General Theological Seminary Library, New York; Margot Karp and Josephine McSweeney of Pratt Institute Library, Brooklyn, New York, and Joseph M. Cahn of Denver Public Library, Denver, Colorado, who are special friends as well as skilled librarians; the staff of the Cañon City Public Library, Cañon City, Colorado; Jennifer Tolpa of the Massachusetts Historical Society, Boston; Carol Shivvers of St. Aidan's Church, Boulder, Colorado; and Geoff Chester and Whitney Treseder, histo-rians at the U.S. Naval Observatory, Washington, D.C.; Margaret Gordon and Alan Ritch of the McHenry Library, University of California at Santa Cruz; and Robert Tilton, University of Connecticut at Storrs. I am also very grateful to Felicia Bonaparte, Jane Marcus, Charles Molesworth, and the late Alfred Kazin, of the City University of New York Graduate Center, for en-couraging my initial research into H.D.'s Moravianism.

Much material on Charles Doolittle and the Flower Observatory was sup-plied by Professor Emeritus William Blitzstein of the Department of As-tronomy and Astrophysics at the University of Pennsylvania and his daugh-ter, Sybil Csigi, former secretary in that department and now secretary in the Department of Classics and Ancient History. I am especially indebted to them for their lasting interest and wonderful archival capacities.

As this project was beginning, the Mellon Fund of the School of Liberal Arts and Sciences, Pratt Institute, Brooklyn, New York, and its administra-tor, Dean Richard Perry, provided a grant to cover the cost of transcribing the typescript to computer disks. I thank them for this early assistance. Many thanks as well to Elise Snyder, M.D., for housing in New Haven during Bei-necke research trips and for insights relevant to issues in H.D.'s psychoanaly-sis, and to Patricia Hampl, Regents Professor of Creative Writing at the Uni-versity of Minnesota, for inviting me to lecture on a portion of this text in her graduate seminar. Finally, I thank the editors at the University Press of Florida for their enthusiasm and especially Jacqueline Kinghorn Brown for her valued support, as well as Sharon Damoff for her meticulous copyedit-ing, in bringing to completion the complete text of *The Gift by H.D.*

Abbreviations

A	H.D. *Asphodel.* Ed. Robert Spoo. Durham, N.C.: Duke University Press, 1992.
AGS	August Gottlieb Spangenberg. *The Life of Nicholas Lewis Count Zinzendorf.* Tr. with abridgment by Samuel Jackson, with an introduction by the Rev. P. La Trobe. London: Holdsworth, 1838.
BHP	*Between History and Poetry: The Letters of H.D. and Norman Holmes Pearson.* Ed. Donna Krolik Hollenberg. Iowa City: University of Iowa Press, 1997.
CN	Henry Rimius. *A Candid Narrative of the Rise and Progress of the Herrnhuetters . . . .* London, 1754.
CP	H.D. *Collected Poems, 1912–1944.* Ed. Louis L. Martz. New York: New Directions, 1983.
DAB	*Dictionary of American Biography.* Allen Johnson and Dumas Malone, eds. New York: Scribner, 1928– .
DNB	*Dictionary of National Biography.* Sir Leslie Stephen and Sir Sidney Lee. London: Oxford University Press, 1921–22.
G	H.D. Third ts. of *The Gift.* H.D. Papers, Beinecke Library, Yale University, New Haven, Connecticut.
GN	H.D.'s "Notes" in the third ts. of *The Gift.* H.D. Papers, Beinecke Library, Yale University, New Haven, Connecticut.
HB	Joseph Mortimer Levering. *A History of Bethlehem, Pennsylvania, 1741–1892.* Bethlehem, Pa.: Times Publishing Co., 1903.
HDDA	"H.D. by Delia Alton." *Iowa Review* 16, no. 3 (1986): 174–221.
HE	H.D. *Helen in Egypt.* New York: New Directions, 1974.
HMM	Joseph Edmund Hutton. *A History of Moravian Missions.* London: Moravian Publications Office, 1923.

JA *Mys*   "*The Mystery:* H.D.'s Moravian Novel Edited and Annotated." Ed. and intro. Jane Augustine. Ph.D. diss., City University of New York, 1988.

LTDZ   Edmund de Schweinitz. *The Life and Times of David Zeisberger.* Philadelphia: Lippincott, 1870.

MA   Harriette Augusta Curtiss and F. Homer. *The Message of Aquaria.* Washington D.C.: Curtiss Philosophic Co., 1932.

MH   Francis Wolle. "A Moravian Heritage." Boulder, Colo.: Empire Reproduction and Printing Co., 1972.

MR   H.D. *Majic Ring (1943–44).* Ts. H.D. Papers, Beinecke Library, Yale University, New Haven, Connecticut.

NDG   H.D. *The Gift.* Abridged by Griselda Ohannessian. New York: New Directions, 1982.

NDG-V   British edition of *NDG.* Intro. Diana Collecott. London: Virago, 1984.

NEH & GR   *The New England Historical and Genealogical Register.*

NTV   H.D. *Notes on Thought and Vision.* Edited and introduction by Albert Gelpi. San Francisco: City Lights Books, 1982.

PIT   H.D. *Paint It Today.* Ed. and intro. Cassandra Laity. New York: New York University Press, 1992.

PW   Susan Stanford Friedman. *Penelope's Web: Gender, Modernity, H.D.'s Fiction.* New York: Cambridge University Press, 1990.

SN   H.D. "Séance Notes." Ts. H.D. Papers, Beinecke Library, Yale University, New Haven, Connecticut.

T   H.D. *Trilogy.* Foreword by Norman Holmes Pearson. New York: New Directions, 1973. Also in *CP.*

TF   H.D. *Tribute to Freud.* Foreword by Norman Holmes Pearson. New York: New Directions, 1984.

ZN   "Zinzendorf Notebook." Ms. H.D. Papers, Beinecke Library, Yale University, New Haven, Connecticut.

The Gift by H.D.

Introduction

The original full-length version of *The Gift* by H.D. (Hilda Doolittle, 1886–1961) is presented here complete as she wrote it and wanted it read, nearly a third longer than the New Directions abridged trade edition (*NDG*). This full-length version, H.D.'s "final copy,"[1] includes her own "Notes" section, punctuation preserving her syntax, and all the excised passages, many of them related to Moravian history and mystical religion. It is an essential sourcebook for enriched understanding of H.D. as a major modernist writer, an innovator in both prose and poetry, no longer limited to the label "Imagist poet." It is particularly important as a locus classicus of her visionary and revisionary woman-centered poetics, her "Moravian gyno-poetics."[2]

Written in London during the blitz of World War II, this narrative of female empowerment embodies H.D.'s belief in an eternal creative feminine spirit continually manifesting as the living bearer of peace to the world. Incarnate in her, it is a spiritual gift bestowed through her reinvocation of the female Holy Spirit celebrated by her maternal Moravian Christian ancestors.

The New Directions edition, however, emphasizes "the gift" as primarily artistic giftedness, evidently in accordance with a note on the typescript's first page, handwritten apparently by Norman Holmes Pearson—certainly not by H.D.—quoting a line from chapter 1: "The Gift / Artists are people who are gifted."[3] The New Directions editing process produced this shift of emphasis, probably to make the text conform to a familiar marketable genre, the memoir of childhood.

But the edited version is rather problematic for scholarship. In her review of *NDG* in *Sulfur* 9 (1984), Rachel Blau DuPlessis points out the fact of abridgment and warns that it alters H.D.'s intentions:

In her work, H.D. parses a gift: more than creativity, more than heritage, more than talent, it is some visionary capacity of profound social and historical use in a redemptive drama. . . . the individual, apparently the subject here, is an instrument of, a conduit for this spiritual politics: "a vision of power and peace" ([*NDG*], 135). *The Gift* is, therefore, an intentionally religious and prophetic text. Cuts that remove this dimension of the text have changed its basic premises. (179)

Diana Collecott in her introduction to the British edition (Virago, 1984) echoes DuPlessis and adds that, as a "religious and prophetic text," *The Gift* has a "crucial position in the development of H.D.'s poetics": "The book's spiritual politics are no less significant than its sexual politics to a critique of H.D. that recognizes in her writing a feminism that displaces hierarchies of gender, race and creed" (*NDG-V,* x). The full-length version is required for this critique. Scholars therefore have not used the abridged one, although access to H.D.'s previously unpublished prose[4] has led to expanded interest in her life and oeuvre, and studies are proliferating.[5]

Prominent among these studies is *Penelope's Web: Gender, Modernity, H.D.'s Fiction* by Susan Stanford Friedman. Friedman comprehensively examines H.D.'s fiction through psychoanalytic lenses from the early Madrigal cycle to the late wartime work, revealing its intimate involvement with autobiography and gender concerns. In contrast to H.D.'s early poetry that conformed to modernism's poetic doctrine of "impersonality," her fiction is personal and relational, often in the form of a roman à clef, re-creating her own experience set within history, overriding genre boundaries, and conspicuously gendered (*PW,* 6). Her themes and methods, allied with those of Gertrude Stein, Virginia Woolf, and Dorothy Richardson, create a "gendered modernism," revising canonized concepts (*PW,* 3). In her final chapters Friedman discusses *The Gift*—that is, the full-length version presented here—as intertextual with *Trilogy.* Her conclusion reinforces Rachel Blau DuPlessis's assertions of *The Gift*'s spiritual intentions. Together the poem and the prose form "a redemptive drama" that enacts "the poet's gyno-vision of (re)birth for a world caught in the death spiral of war" (*PW,* 354).

War both occasioned and motivated *The Gift,* virtually forcing it into existence. It came, H.D. said, with the "daemonic drive . . . released by ps-a [psychoanalysis] . . . and the Second World War."[6] German bombs fell almost every night for nearly nine months between September 1940 and May 1941, destroying buildings close by the 49 Lowndes Square flat that she shared with the novelist Bryher (Annie Winifred Ellerman, 1894–1983). Obsessed by fear of death and in very real danger of being killed, H.D. began to write to save her sanity. Not to escape from the present reality but to find its meaning, she reentered in memory her peaceful childhood in the Moravian community of Bethlehem, Pennsylvania, founded in 1741.

The Gift thus represents an act of courage. In it H.D. confronts her war terror, making a journey of descent into the past and into her unconscious mind as she had done earlier during psychoanalysis with Freud in Vienna in 1933–34. She becomes again the child Hilda who seeks her particular heritage from the Moravians, the mystical Gift underlying her artistic gift. She intuits that the Gift provides access to an all-important secret—the way to end war. Clues to the secret arrive through affinities with her mother and grandmother, whose ancestors, Matthias and Margaret Catherine Weiss, had come from Europe in 1742 with the second large group of Moravians to settle in Bethlehem.[7]

The Gift, then, is primarily the record of a religious quest, although its mixed genre presents aspects of autobiography, childhood memoir, *Kunstlerroman,* mystical meditation, psychoanalytic reconstruction, rites of initiation, and myth.[8] The writing of it constituted a spiritual practice deeper than recollection, genealogical curiosity, or literary gesture and devoid of nostalgia. It recapitulated the commitment made by her Moravian forebears. Their church, officially called *Unitas Fratrum* (United Brethren) had from its beginnings espoused universal peace, racial tolerance, and understanding among hostile cultures, including the native tribes whom the Europeans encountered upon arrival in the North American wilderness. H.D. reentered her past to bring about this universal peace and tolerance, "world unity without war," as she described it, through recovery of the secret at the heart of the Gift.[9]

In the keystone chapter 5, the child Hilda is depicted as hearing hints of the secret from the garbled speech of her grandmother, Elizabeth Weiss Seidel Wolle, the great-granddaughter of Matthias and Margaret Catherine Weiss. The child has been asking questions about the mysterious years of 1745 to 1750, the "Sifting Time,"[10] in which it seems to her that certain Moravian missionaries and Indian chieftains possessed and shared that secret, "a secret that, properly directed, might have changed the course of history, might have lifted the dark wings of evil from the whole world" (*G*, V, 40).

To change the course of history, to expunge suffering and pain from a world radically divided between good and evil, as in Gnostic thought—these are H.D.'s motives for writing *The Gift*. She wrote in order to rebuild the world of her childhood, guaranteed by the piety and high purpose of eighteenth-century Moravianism. The values of the Moravian Church define the good that she summons up against the evil of World War II. Robert Spoo has written:

> *Unitas Fratrum* thus bequeathed to H.D. a moving counter-image to place against the shattered Europe of the 1940s—one meaning of "the gift" in this many-layered work. In these pages H.D. created what T.S. Eliot called a "mythical method," a means of ordering the anarchy and futility of contemporary civilization. But the "mythical method," as she conceives it—"completion in another dimension"—is no abstract fiction, no self-consciously manipulated parallel; rather it is a set of profoundly spiritual experiences and memories rooted in childhood. H.D. found the clue (as she might put it); her Moravian heritage could be called upon to make bearable the nightmare of modern history.[11]

H.D. was born into that heritage in Bethlehem on September 10, 1886, the middle child and only living daughter of Charles Leander Doolittle, professor of astronomy at Lehigh University, and Helen Eugenia Wolle Doolittle, daughter of Francis Wolle, principal of the Seminary for Young Ladies, and his wife Elizabeth Weiss Seidel, the young widow of Henry A. Seidel, who had a daughter, Agnes, from her first marriage. These grandparents are the Papalie and Mamalie (also called Mimmie) on whom much of the memoir focuses. H.D. refers to *The Gift* as "a series of family-portraits,"[12] but this generic description is inadequate to account for the interrelations between her childhood experiences and the events of World War II.

Those interrelations, the ground of her "mythical method" and redemptive goal, were made possible through the symbolic methods of Sigmund Freud, which H.D. encountered in her psychoanalysis with him in Vienna in 1933 and 1934. She credits Freud in her description of the genesis of *The Gift* in "H.D. by Delia Alton" (1949–51):

I assembled *The Gift* during the early war-years, but without the analysis and the illuminating doctrine or philosophy of Sigmund Freud, I would hardly have found the clue or the bridge between the child-life, the memories of the peaceful Bethlehem, and the orgy of destruction, later to be witnessed and lived through in London. That outer threat and constant reminder of death, drove me inward, almost forced me to compensate, by memories of another world, an actual world where there had been security and comfort. But this was no mechanical intellectual trick of mind or memory, the Child actually returns to that world, she lives actually in those reconstructed scenes, or she watches them like a moving-picture. (192)

Her living "actually" in the Moravian world occurs because the psycho-analysis stimulated a strong re-involvement with the image, memory, and influence of her mother. H.D. accepted Freud's view that she had come to him "hoping to find my mother," as she notes in *Tribute to Freud,* her account of the analysis, the first section of which was completed in 1944, a few months after *The Gift* was finished (*TF,* 17; *PW,* 364). There Freud and her mother are shown as parallel and equally important to the basic grounding of her confidence and well-being:

I felt that to meet him [Freud] . . . and to be accepted by him as analysand or student, seemed to crown all my other personal contacts and relationships. . . . I had come home, in fact. And another poem comes inevitably to prompt me:

> *On desperate seas long wont to roam,*
> *Thy hyacinth hair, thy classic face,*
> *Thy Naiad airs, have brought me home*
> *To the glory that was Greece*
> *And the grandeur that was Rome.*

This is, of course, Edgar Allan Poe's much-quoted *Helen,* and my mother's name was Helen. (*TF,* 44)[13]

This reference to her mother and association with her home immediately precedes her account in *Tribute to Freud* of one of the most important among her several "visionary or supernormal experiences" (*TF,* 64), called the "Writing on the Wall." It occurred while she was traveling in Greece with Bryher in 1920. She named it in allusion to the supernatural intervention—the "hand of God"—in the biblical story of Belshazzar's feast.[14] In her summary of Freud's interpretation, her wording echoes the Poe poem: "The professor translated the . . . picture-writing on the wall of a hotel bedroom in Corfu, the Greek Ionian island, that I saw projected there in the spring of 1920, as a desire for union with my mother. I was physically in Greece, in Hellas (Helen). I had come home to the glory that was Greece" (*TF,* 44).

H.D. wrote a letter to Bryher during the analysis, explaining Freud's expanded interpretation of her desire for "union" with her mother: "F. says mine is the absolutely FIRST layer, I got stuck at the earliest pre-OE [pre-oedipal] stage, and 'back to the womb' seems to be my only solution. Hence islands, sea, Greek primitives and so on. . . . hence you and me in Corfu (island = mother). . . . and apparently I am of a good 'life' vibration as I went on and on, repeating, wanting to give life or save life, never in that sense, to destroy life . . ." (March 23, 1933; *PW,* 319).

The desire "to give life or save life," an underlying motive for this book, pervades the interlocked associations of the mother, Greek islands, the sea, and Helen of Troy. Bryher is a "mother" as well, because she had nurtured the influenza-weakened H.D. through childbirth in 1919, and together the two women raised H.D.'s daughter, Perdita. These associations derive from H.D.'s transference to Freud as mother after her transference to him as father. The mother-transference is alluded to in "Advent," the second section of *Tribute to Freud* (136, 175), which H.D. completed in 1948 from a reconstruction of her 1933–35 notes.[15]

This mother-father-Freud nexus of transferences remained in H.D.'s mind from the 1930s, but in a fluid state, since she also viewed her self-psycho-analysis as an unending process. As she began to write this memoir, the associations to the mother took ascendancy and again prompted her to quote Poe's poem in the dedication of *The Gift:*

To
HELEN
who has
brought me home
for Bethlehem Pennsylvania 1741
from Chelsea London 1941
L'amitié passe même le tombeau.[16]

Both Freud and Helen Wolle brought H.D. "home," but "home" extends its limits beyond the domestic to become an eternal religious realm transcending death, yet beginning within time and history in Bethlehem and in the Moravian Church. In "Advent" the entry dated March 9 records a dream and a session with Freud, establishing the associations of Freud with religion, psychoanalysis, and the mother:

> I dream of a Cathedral. . . . Inside the Cathedral we find regeneration or reintegration. This room is the Cathedral.
>
> The Professor said, 'But you are very clever'. It is not I who am clever. I am only applying certain of his own findings to my personal equation. The house is home, the house is the Cathedral. He said he wanted me to feel at home here.
>
> The house in some indescribable way depends on father-mother. . . .
>
> Yes (I repeated), the Cathedral of my dream was Sigmund Freud. 'No,' he said, 'not me—but analysis'. (*TF,* 145–47)[17]

Another passage in "Advent" strengthens this set of associations linking her mother, her hometown, and Christianity. H.D. had recounted to Freud an experience, with uncertainty as to whether it was "dream, fantasy or reality" (*TF,* 120), set in Bethlehem and also recounted in *The Gift,* of the Old Man who gave the child Hilda a white lily and would send his sleigh whenever she wanted it. Freud asks her: "'You were born in Bethlehem? It is inevitable that the Christian myth—' He paused. 'This does not offend you?' 'Offend me?' 'My speaking of your religion in terms of myth,' he said. I said, 'How could I be offended?' 'Bethlehem is the town of Mary,' he said" (*TF,* 123).

Applying Freud's findings to her "personal equation," she did not always accept his conclusions, particularly that her supernormal experience of the Writing on the Wall showed "dangerous" symptoms indicative of megalomania (*TF,* 41, 51). These experiences, dream-like but occurring while she was awake, signified to H.D. an altered state of consciousness, an eruption from that "great ocean underground," not a danger but a blessing from "beyond."

Did she want to be the founder of a new religion, Freud had asked her, after she reported "the Princess Dream," in which she saw Pharaoh's daughter finding the infant Moses in the bulrushes (*TF,* 36–37, 41). She wonders if she is that baby. Freud's question implies that such a desire would be grandiose and inappropriate, perhaps especially so for a woman. However, her "strange experiences," as she also called them (*TF,* 41, 45–56; *NTV,* 18–21), convince her of a spiritual vocation. She sees herself as an initiate in the hermetic sense, one capable of undergoing the tests and trials inherent in an exalted quest and of opening up to higher consciousness. Freud's view of the unconscious is the ground of this connection, reinforcing her belief that dreams are the source of biblical prophecy, the Delphic oracle, and symbolic systems of divination, all revelations of the universal and eternal truths that underlie every religion.

In a significant passage in *Tribute to Freud,* she asserts that Freud "had dared to say that the dream came from an unexplored depth in man's consciousness," which "ran like a great stream or ocean underground" uniting all people: "And he dared to imply that this consciousness proclaimed all men one; all nations and races met in the universal world of the dream. . . . in the dream, man, as at the beginning of time, spoke a universal language, and man, meeting in the universal understanding of the unconscious or subconscious, would forgo barriers of time and space, and man, understanding man, would save mankind" (70–71).

The Gift is fundamentally based upon this view of a universal unconscious mind unifying all peoples of the world and manifesting in sensitive persons, especially those in Bethlehem's history labeled "gifted," with whom H.D. identifies. The imagery of a "great stream or ocean" also links the unconscious to the mother, since the maternal and feminine in psychoanalytic tradition are associated with water and the sea, and in H.D.'s "personal equation" with Helen Wolle, her family, and home in Moravian Bethlehem.

Since the unconscious is coterminous with the higher consciousness that exists in "another dimension," eternity (*TF,* 23), H.D., the initiate, becomes a conduit by which that consciousness may descend, bringing light to our dark, dense, material world. In this context, she might have wanted at least unconsciously to "found a new religion," not a patriarchal institution but an instrument of peace and enlightenment in the hands of a matriarchal lineage.

Count Zinzendorf's revival of the ancient church of Bohemia amounted to the creation of a "new religion." Although he had no intention of deviating from Christian orthodoxy—he was an ordained Lutheran clergyman as well as a bishop in the *Unitas Fratrum*[18]—he strove in his sermons for linguistic freshness, inventing vivid and unusual metaphors to inspire a heartfelt connection between his listeners' beliefs and their everyday lives. In one significant invention he spoke of the Holy Spirit as a Comforter, a "Mother."[19] This concept was embraced by John Christopher Frederick Cammerhof (1721–1751),[20] a Moravian missionary whose "enthusiasm" disturbed some of his contemporaries but impressed H.D. Cammerhof had had a verse carved on a stone laid in the wall of the Single Brothers' House (now concealed by new construction of Moravian College buildings), which is quoted in chapter 5 by Mamalie as having been told to her by her first husband, whom she calls by the name Christian:[21]

[Christian] felt that the Church had lost the thing that the meetings in the Sanctuary [on Wunden Eiland] had held together. . . . The thing was symbolized by the star that Cammerhof had had designed and cut into one of the lintel-stones of the new Brothers' House that they were building. The carved words

> *Father, Mother, Dearest Man*
> *Be honoured with the Young-Men's Plan*

or

> *Vater, Mutter, Lieber Mann*
> *Habt Ehr vom Jünglings Plan*

meant more than just the words. *Mutter* wasn't just the Holy Ghost. It was a special Spirit that some of the Crusaders had worshipped. . . . and *Plan* didn't mean, Christian said, just *plan* or even company, but referred to some secret-society or organization (*G*, V, 16–17).

This verse reflects both Zinzendorf's vivid language and his Christ-centered theology. He created an unorthodox trinity that replaces the traditional creedal formulation "Father, Son, and Holy Ghost" with an hierogamy. "Mutter" (Mother) is the Holy Spirit, equal to the Father and Bride of God, bringing forth the "dearest" or "supreme" man, Jesus Christ.[22] Jesus loves every soul *(anima)* so deeply that he unites with it as a husband unites with a wife, and their "child" is the Christian soul embodied, the true Christian person. This view is not entirely unorthodox; the collectivity of Christian souls, the Church, has been traditionally called the Bride of Christ because Christ loves it as a husband loves a wife. Zinzendorf vigorously pursued this analogy, preaching that the sexual union of wife and husband should be regarded as a sacramental enactment of the union of the soul with its Savior.

Orthodox or not, these ideas nevertheless gave great offense to Zinzendorf's enemies, not only because he was frank in his allusions to sexuality but also, it seems, for his elevation of the feminine principle. The most outspoken of these enemies, Henry Rimius, wrote in 1752 a diatribe titled *A Candid Narrative of the Rise and Progress of the Herrnhuetters . . .* , a copy of which H.D. owned. Evidence of heresy occurs in Zinzendorf's *Natural Reflexions*, according to Rimius, who, in *A Candid Narrative,* quotes the heretical idea: "The Holy Ghost is called by the *Herrnhuetters* the eternal wife of God, the Mother of Christ, the Mother of the Faithful, the Mother of the Church" (45–46). H.D. read this passage while doing research early in the war. She also read lines from Zinzendorf's 1896th hymn addressed to the Holy Ghost, which she then copied into her "Zinzendorf Notebook" (*CN,* 41; ZN, 8 [39]). Translated, these lines read: "God, thou Mother of the Church, eternal Wife of God the Father."

But those views most repulsive to Zinzendorf's enemies are precisely the ones most attractive to H.D.—that the Holy Spirit is a mother, and every soul, whether a woman's or a man's, is feminine, as in the gender of the Latin word *anima.* This sanctifies her attachment to and desire for "union" with her Moravian mother. It is a mystical union with the Holy Spirit, as becomes clear in the final chapter of *The Gift.*

Because both Zinzendorf and Freud expressed opinions unacceptable to conventional minds, particularly concerning sexuality, H.D. regarded both as men ahead of their times, highly evolved spiritually. A comment in her "Notes" to chapter 5 indicates how she used Zinzendorf's theology to support her vision of valorized womanhood and redeemed sexuality: "Count Zinzendorf himself was much criticised for a series of poems or hymns, dealing for the most part, with the mystery of love or marriage. He is said to have offended many by regarding every woman as a symbol of the Church, as literally Christ's Bride. There is beauty and poetry in many of these mystical ideas but undoubtedly, the world at large, then as now, is not ready for this revelation" (*GN,* 68).

Zinzendorf's emphasis upon every Christian soul as feminine and his marital and familial symbolism—his spelling-out in explicit language "the mystery of love or marriage"—were decisively abandoned by the Moravian

Church after his death in 1760, but their effects remained, fostering the intimate familial quality of Bethlehem that H.D. experienced as a child. In the Christmas season particularly, the community came together as a family imbued with Zinzendorf's "heart religion" and his sense of mystical communion with Jesus, his Savior.

Speaking later to Freud about Bethlehem's sense of family as an extension of her own family, particularly of her mother, H.D. steps back into the child's mind, signaling the child's perspective through word choice and use of the present tense: "Everyone knows our mother so we are never sure who is related and who is not—well, in a sense everyone is related for there is the church and we all belong together in some very special way, because of our candle service on Christmas Eve which is not like what anyone else has anywhere, except some places in Europe perhaps" (*TF,* 33).

The child Hilda was greatly impressed by the Moravian Christmas with its unique customs of the *Putz*—a gigantic crèche in the Central Church, richly draped with fresh-cut fir boughs, emulated by a smaller *Putz* at home—and the candle-lighting ceremony in the church on Christmas eve reenacting December 24, 1741, when Zinzendorf named the new settlement for the town in which Mary gave birth to Jesus, the founder of a new religion. H.D.'s reassembled memories add another dimension to her historical home. It is an internalized mental environment that "depends on father-mother," the male and female elements joined in profound union as in Zinzendorfian thought.

H.D.'s sense of a cosmic Mother united with the Godhead received reinforcement when she discovered that the "New Age," the Aquarian Age thought to have dawned when Halley's comet appeared in 1910, is said to be a "Woman's Age." This declaration, which impressed her so much that she repeated it in a letter to her friend Viola Jordan,[23] appears in a book that H.D. owned, annotated, and read probably in 1936 or shortly after, titled *The Message of Aquaria,* by the Christian theosophists Harriette Augusta and F. Homer Curtiss, M.D.[24] The Curtisses assert that the new age is a "Woman's Age," and they add the logical corollary that the preceding Piscean age had been a man's age. But now, they declare, "the Father may be said to be growing old" (*MA,* 407).

H.D. accepted this view. The patriarchal mythos of a universe ruled by an external father god-figure is being replaced by a female mythos centered on a mother goddess-figure, the Comforter, an eternal refuge and home. An analogue of this situation is suggested in chapter 3 of *The Gift*, in which H.D. relives a childhood Christmas with her maternal grandfather, Papalie, making the animals for the *Putz*, as God made the creatures of the world. Helping him, H.D. feels the awakening of a sense that she too is a cocreator with him. Chapter 4 brings her through subsequent awakenings overseen by her father, but in chapter 5, the focus of her concentration returns to the maternal Moravian lineage, centering on her mother's mother, Mamalie, and Mamalie's power to reveal through her trance-like utterances the lost secret of the Moravian Sifting Time, the Gift that must be restored.

By associating Zinzendorf with her grandparents, H.D. sees him as a liberating, creative *ur*-father united with the maternal Holy Spirit, and Freud as a kind of reincarnation of both father and mother, based upon her double transference. The parallelism of the father figures Zinzendorf and "Papa" Freud is made clear in "H.D. by Delia Alton":

> Zinzendorf's father was an Austrian, exiled or self-exiled to Saxony, because of his Protestant affiliations. . . .[25]
>
> From the actual family of Bethlehem, Pennsylvania, the scientific "Pastor," the part-German or Slavonic grandfather . . . , from a legend of a new way of life, a Brotherhood, dedicated to peace and universal understanding, it is not really such a far cry to Vienna and to Sigmund Freud.
>
> Count Zinzendorf was an Austrian, we were called Moravians, Professor Freud was an Austrian, born as it happened in Moravia. (188–89)

The palimpsestic overlay of Freud upon the figure of Zinzendorf affiliates both men with the cosmic Father who is "growing old" but who is far-seeing, ready to make way for the new dispensation, which will come through the mothers.

That coming occurs in a dream visitation recorded in the middle volume of H.D.'s poem *Trilogy*. Intuitively prepared by her discovery of Zinzendorf's description of a female Holy Spirit and by Freud's praise of her skill at interpreting dreams, H.D. receives in a dream a visitation by a lady, the "Poet's Lady,"[26] who carries in her arms not the traditional Christ child but the "unwritten book of the new," that is, the book of the new age and a resurrected world.

Trilogy, originally called *The War Trilogy*, was written at almost the same time as H.D. was finishing the third typescript of *The Gift*, whose main text is dated "London / 1941 / 1943" with the final dateline for the whole, after the "Notes": "London—1940–44." The first book of *Trilogy, The Walls Do Not Fall,* was finished in 1943, and the second book, *Tribute to the Angels,* came speedily in the last two weeks of May 1944 (*T,* vi–ix). In the midst of her invocation and giving thanks to the seven angels—"regents" or "ruling spirits" of the seven planets,[27] but also the seven angels at the foot of God's throne in the Book of Revelation (8:2)—the Lady appears to her.

Who is this Lady? Not the Roman Catholic Virgin Mary, asserts H.D. as she explains to Norman Holmes Pearson the Lady's non-Christian roots: "I distinctly link the LADY up with Venus-Annael, with the Moon, with the pre-Christian Roman Bona Dea, with the Byzantine Greek church Santa Sophia and the SS of the Sanctus Spiritus. . . . The Venus name, I believe is Anael but I spelt it ANNAEL; it didn't seem to 'work' until I did—it links on too with Anna, Hannah or Grace" (*T,* ix–x).[28]

The name Anna also belongs to Anna von Pahlen, the "gifted and pious young Livonian baroness" who was John Cammerhof's wife.[29] She is the Moravian pioneer of the Sifting Time with whom H.D. most identifies, envisioning her as the Gift's chief bearer who unites in peace the Native Americans and the European settlers. The dream Lady is therefore linked with the Moravian woman. Both figures signify Grace, the evidence of God's healing love by which human pain is transformed into triumph. In section 8 of *Tribute to the Angels,* this transformation is accomplished by an invocation in an alchemical-poetic ritual:

> Now polish the crucible
> and in the bowl distill
>
> a word most bitter, *marah,*
> a word bitterer still, *mar,*
>
> sea, brine, breaker, seducer,
> giver of life, giver of tears;
>
> Now polish the crucible
> and set the jet of flame
>
> under, till *marah-mar*
> are melted, fuse and join

and change and alter,
mer, mere, mère, mater, Maia, Mary,

Star of the Sea,
Mother. (*T,* 71)

Thus, the figure of the mother is also joined with the Lady and the early
Moravian women as a conduit of Grace. *Trilogy*'s ritual invocation of the
mother has a parallel in chapter 4 of *The Gift,* in a passage omitted from the
New Directions edition. Here H.D. records another dream, a nightmare of
herself as a child being bitten by a huge snake and comforted by the black
servant "dark Mary":

> Mary, Maia, Miriam, Mut, Madre, Mère, Mother, pray for us. Pray for us,
> dark Mary, Mary, mère, mer; this is the nightmare, this is the dark horse, this
> is Mary, Maia, Mut, Mutter. This is Gaia, this is the beginning. This is the
> end. Under every shrine to Zeus, to Jupiter, to Zeu-pater or Theus-pater or
> God-the-father, along the western coast of the Peloponnesus, there is an
> earlier altar. There is, beneath the carved super-structure of every temple to
> God-the-Father, the dark cave or grotto or inner hall or cella to Mary, mère,
> Mut, Mutter, pray for us. (*G,* IV, 10)[30]

The power of the primal Mother, the female Holy Spirit, Grace, to enter the
poet-initiate and shape her into an instrument of new life, peace, and unity
is symbolically articulated throughout *The Gift.*

It appears, however, that H.D. wanted to anchor this symbolic and theological vision in history, her own and that of Moravian Bethlehem, to draw
parallels with her immediate wartime situation. She therefore added her
"Notes" to the typescript. These seem to have begun in research and note-
taking in 1940, but she reworked them later, probably intermittently, and
completed them in July 1944.

The seven sections of the "Notes" correlate at first with the chapters of the
main text, but soon they deviate from the tidy norm of quasi-footnotes to
serve larger purposes. These deviations gave her an opportunity to incorporate subtexts, to solidify the factual milieu, and to add a historically grounded
finale to the visionary main text. H.D. had clear motives for this unconven-
tional ending. She wanted to be seen as part of the "real world," not as an
ivory-tower escapist or a "poetess" overly involved in feminine subjectivity.[31]

The "Notes" enlarge the scope of the main text and enrich its meanings in three principal ways.

First, H.D.'s "Notes" clarify and authenticate names and places alluded to in the main text, stressing their historical accuracy and relevance. These data reinforce her intention to place her individual spiritual experience within the powerful mystical and ecumenical tradition of the Moravian Church so that it is not perceived as purely self-invented, neither a poetically contrived dream nor a private imaginative excursion—not solely an "autobiographical fantasy," as she later referred to it (HDDA, 189).

Second, the "Notes" reveal those aspects of Moravian history and theology, their origins, motives, and heroes, that particularly influenced H.D. to see her own experience in terms of a legacy from those early "gifted" communal ancestors. Of special importance for her was the Moravians' establishment of uniquely peaceful and non-exploitative relations with Native Americans based on common religious understandings. The "Notes" verify that this peace among races and nations actually existed; the Moravians made it happen. She can therefore believe that her own spiritual Gift, legacy of the Moravians and expressed in writing, may contribute to its happening again on a larger scale among the races and nations of the entire world.

Third, the "Notes" enlarge the scope of *The Gift* by providing further insight into the evolution of H.D.'s creative processes and the interrelations of this memoir with her other writings of the wartime period. While the method of the "Notes" appears in part scholarly, quoting sources, it is also largely dictated by free association, as in psychoanalysis. Thus, details appear that might be perceived as irrelevant. In "Notes" section 4 she justifies a remark about a "fan-maker in London," although it is not related to chapter 4. The passage describes both her compositional and editorial methods and shows that the "Notes" are integral to her conception of this book. It is worth quoting at length:

> In assembling these chapters of *The Gift* during, before and after the worst days of the 1941 London Blitz, I let the story tell itself or the child tell it for me. Things that I thought I had forgotten came to light in the course of the narrative and although, for instance, I had a vague recollection of having heard of this fan-maker or having read of him, the actual fan-maker had nothing to do with our story. Yet I tried to keep "myself" out of this, and if the sub-conscious bubbled up with some unexpected finding from the

depth, I accepted this finding as part of the texture of the narrative and have so far, in going over these chapters (to-day is July 2nd 1944) changed very little. Instead of tidying up the body of the narrative, I thought it better to let things stand as they were (as the story was written under stress of danger and great emotion) and where indicated, confirm certain statements or enlarge on them in these Notes.

Actually, I have been greatly indebted throughout to J. M. Levering's *History of Bethlehem*. . . . But in recalling my own childhood, I approach the subject from a different angle, not critically but emotionally. There was a fan-maker. He gave the Bethlehem community a spinet in the very early days and it is not at all unlikely that one of old Jedediah's ancestors touched the keys of that spinet for the first time, as it was joyously acclaimed and set up in one of the assembly room or *Gemein* houses.

Hence the spinet and the fan-maker become personal matters and of interest to me. (*GN*, 56–57)

Her project in the "Notes" is explicit: to "confirm" and to "enlarge." They permit her to dilate on one "personal matter" of supreme interest to her—the origin of her Gift in the rapport achieved between eighteenth-century Moravians and Native Americans.

A passing mention in chapter 2 of James Fenimore Cooper's *The Last of the Mohicans* enables her in "Notes" section 2 to inform the reader that the historical model for Cooper's character Chingachgook was a Native American who became a Moravian Christian named John Wasamapah, called Tschoop. She follows up this information with a lengthy and beautiful fictional account, virtually a short story, of Tschoop's conversion by the Moravian missionary Christian Henry Rauch.[32] She is eager to emphasize the Moravians' compassion, self-sacrifice, and genuine concern for Native Americans because these qualities stand directly opposed to the crimes and deceptions practiced on them by typically racist, land-grabbing European settlers, the eighteenth-century analogue of twentieth-century Nazis.

But the historical rapport was destroyed by deceit and complications over which the Moravians had no control during the French and Indian Wars on the 1750s frontier. "Notes" section 5 explains the loss of the Gift alluded to by Mamalie in chapter 5 by relating the story of the Gnadenhuetten massacre of 1755 in which Moravians were scalped, shot, and burned to death by angry

Delaware tribesmen incited by false propaganda. While Moravians would know of this hideous episode, non-Moravian general readers would not, and it is a vital piece of information, adding an atavistic dimension to H.D.'s fear of death by fire, the theme introduced in the book's first paragraph. In "Notes" section 6, H.D. balances against this picture of "bad Indians" a dramatic account of "bad white men," the monstrously cruel slaughter in 1782 of peaceful Christian "Moravian Indians" by roving soldiers at another Gnadenhuetten in Ohio.[33]

The "Notes" make clear H.D.'s preoccupation with Native American and Moravian relations. Why, in war-beset England, was she so concerned? An answer appears in her unpublished prose work *Majic Ring* (1943–44),[34] which she was composing simultaneously with *The Gift* and *Trilogy*. During that time she was involved in spiritualist séances[35] almost weekly with the medium Arthur Bhaduri, who had a Native American called Kapama, or K, as his principal "control" or "spirit guide"—that is, the spirit in the "beyond" who contacts other spirits and who speaks to and through the medium.

During a séance, Kapama presented to H.D. another more powerful Native American, Zakenuto.[36] This name doesn't make sense to "Ben Manisi," as Bhaduri is called in *Majic Ring,* but "Delia Alton," the H.D. figure, understands it. She says: "It was because I had been reading, in connections actually with Moravian missions, some details of the Mohicans, that I was in a position to say that Z-a-k-e-n-u-t-o was not nonsense. For I had written down, rather painfully, that very morning, a name given to one of the Moravian brothers, by his friends the Mohicans. The name was Z'higochgoharo" (34). *Z'higochgoharo* is the Mohican name of Christian Henry Rauch, and H.D. had copied it from page 242, note 7, in Levering's *History of Bethlehem*. Factuality connects with mysticism; she believes that *Zakenuto* "came through, on the vibration of that name" (*MR,* 34). Thus the information in H.D.'s "Notes" to *The Gift* amplifies her intellectual autobiography and suggests an interesting direction for intertextual studies of her wartime oeuvre, which has its fertile if irregular basis in her involvement with the spiritualist tradition.

In that tradition the principal spirit guide is very frequently a Native American, because Native Americans are regarded as a "psychic race" with higher spiritual consciousness.[37] H.D., however, believed that the Native Americans came through the medium with the specific intention to communicate with her because she was American, baptized Moravian, and gifted with her maternal great-grandmother's legacy of "second sight." The "Notes" provide her with the opportunity to tell this family story at the end of section 5, corresponding to chapter 5, in which Mamalie passes on the Gift to her granddaughter. This story of the "gifted" great-grandmother, Mamalie's mother, is vital to H.D.'s sense of her own giftedness and her mission, but it could not be fitted into the main narrative as she "let the child tell it" for her.

In "H.D. by Delia Alton," H.D. at first uses her spiritualist nom de plume, "Delia," to indicate separation from the child Hilda, but these identities later work together as "we" in the construction of *The Gift:*

Dec. 18 [1949]

What it is, is that she was not a God-less child. I mean, she was possessed in a serene, protected way, by his Idea. Or Him, the Idea. There is a book . . . called *The Gift.* This book was written in London, during the days of the bombardment. It is autobiographical "almost." The author has the privilege of . . . concentrating or expanding, where it will suit him [*sic*]. . . . We worked on and off at *The Gift* during the first years of War II, and finally assembled it in 1943. . . . *The Gift* is a story of *Death and Its Mystery* and we quote from this book of Camille Flammarion, on the title-page of the first section, "Dark Room." (HDDA, 187–88)

The psychic sensitivity established in the dual authorship is next connected to the Moravian mother and grandmother, and then to Zinzendorf and the Moravian Church:

The Gift is a family-portrait or a series of family-portraits, but more particularly of the Child's mother and the grandmother. In the fifth section, "The Secret," the grandmother tells the Child, in dream or half-trance, of a memory of her own grandmother's or a fear based on the community memory. The community had been settled by Count Zinzendorf. It was originally known as the *Jednota,* from the Bohemian word meaning association or society. The Latin *Unitas* was later substituted and the remnant of the old Bohemian Church became known as the *Unitas Fratrum.* This *Unitas Fratrum* was eventually called the Moravian Church. (HDDA, 188)

The child Hilda is fascinated by the name of the long-lost "Isle of Wounds," an island once located in the Monocacy River at Bethlehem, which was named *Wunden Eiland* during the Sifting Time of 1745 to 1750.

This period of misbehavior and scandal caused persistent damage to the church's reputation, largely through gossip circulated in screeds composed by the Prussian lawyer Henry Rimius and Protestant clergy such as Bishop Lavington.[38] But neither the gossip nor the history read by H.D. is reflected in what the child hears in the fragmented speech of her grandmother. She hears only of the "*Plan*":

> Bethlehem, Pennsylvania was named by Count Zinzendorf on Christmas-eve, 1741. It was one of a number of Moravian settlements, having to do with a mysterious *Plan* of "peace on earth." The Child, only half a "Moravian" and mystified by inscriptions on some of the oldest tombstones, perceives a strange affinity in the tiny, dark creature who is her mother's mother. Mamalie is not like anyone else. She is very old but she plays games with them and answers all their questions.
>
> Through Mamalie, the Child traces back her connection with the *Jednota* in Europe and with the vanished tribes of the Six Nations in America, with whom Zinzendorf had made a curious, unprecedented treaty. In fantasy or dream, the grandmother tells the story of *Wunden Eiland,* an actual island which was later actually and symbolically washed away in the spring-floods.
>
> On this island, certain of the community met delegates of the Six Nations, who planned together to save the country (and the world) from further bloodshed. Through the grandmother's submerged consciousness, runs the fear and terror of the arrow that flieth,[39] torture and death by burning.
>
> This terror was in our conscious minds in London, while assembling *The Gift.* (188–89)

Thus, although her mother's Bethlehem appears a refuge of peace, H.D.'s mental reentry into it under wartime conditions arouses again her fear of death by burning. She puzzles over the female relatives whose graves she visited and decorated with flowers, especially the dead girls. But almost greater than her fear of death is her fear of mediocrity and helplessness. She had been quite hurt when she heard her mother speak, to visitors, of her children as "not gifted." "Gifted" seemed an epithet reserved only for her father and for her uncle Fred, her mother's younger brother, John Frederick Wolle, whose great musical abilities won him worldwide fame as the founder of the Bach choir and festival of Bethlehem.[40]

The connection of H.D.'s artistic gift to her Moravian background is made through her highly personal interpretation of events in the Sifting Time. Because it was controversial and had generated highly conflicting views and long-lasting effects, she researched it extensively. She read in the *History of Bethlehem* a relatively balanced and accurate account of what happened then in Bethlehem and in the two Moravian communities of Herrnhaag and Marienborn in the Wetterau region near Frankfort, Germany. But she also read the inflamed anecdotal accounts by Zinzendorf's attackers, such as Heinrich Rimius, as well as the judiciously abstract record in A. G. Spangenberg's otherwise detailed *Life of Nicholas Lewis Count Zinzendorf.*

The Sifting Time was a period of religious enthusiasm and fanaticism, which overtook the Moravians in the German congregations in particular through a kind of fundamentalist literalism regarding the "Blood and Wounds" theology. J. E. Hutton in his *History of the Moravian Church,* which H.D. also read, quotes Zinzendorf's declaration on this theme: "We stick to the Blood and Wounds Theology. We will preach nothing but Jesus the Crucified. We will look for nothing else in the Bible but the Lamb and his Wounds, and again Wounds, and Blood and Blood. . . . We shall stay forever in the little side-hole, where we are so unspeakably blessed" (275–76).

Levering asserts that in the course of adhering to this principle, Moravians lost track of adult common sense. He says that while Zinzendorf[41] intended "to propagate a more emphatically Christ-centered teaching, he neglected for a time the proportions of essential doctrine. . . . In his desire to foster a genial conception of spiritual life over against the austere type of pietism, and, at the same time, to encourage a child-like clinging to the Saviour of sinners, as opposed to both legalism and perfectionism, he unwittingly occasioned a peculiar species of careless self-complacency in the direction of antinomianism" (186).

Evidence for H.D.'s having been impressed by Levering's comment occurs in chapter 5, where she puts the word "antinomianism" into her grandmother's mouth. H.D. glosses this technical term in her "Notes," confessing that she had to look it up: "Chambers' English Dictionary says antinomianism is 'the belief that Christians are emancipated by the gospel from the obligation to keep the moral law—a monstrous abuse and perversion of the Pauline doctrine of justification by faith'. The word is from the Greek *anti,* against and *nomos,* law" (*GN,* 67).

The antinomian inclination worsened in the Wetterau because Zinzendorf, who traveled incessantly, had left the two communities there in the care of his immature 18-year-old son, Christian Renatus. A "rage for the spectacular" took over,[42] resulting in constant celebrations of officials' birthdays and other feast days by lavish parties with the castle adorned by pine boughs and thousands of candles at night.[43] Dioramas of Jesus' side-wound were constructed, painted red and illuminated by candlelight from behind, large enough for a person to crawl into, and devout persons did so, as an act of piety.

Both neighbors and Protestant clergymen reported in shocked tones these expensive parties as close to orgies, involving wine, music, dancing, and, by inference from Zinzendorf's enemies' quotations, considerable sexual activity. In 1750, the itinerant Zinzendorf came back to Europe, repentantly understood his responsibility for the damage, paid all debts personally, and over three years entirely disbanded both Herrnhaag and Marienborn. He revoked the twelfth appendix to the hymnal of 1752, whose hymns, many composed by him, had overly literalized the "Blood and Wounds" imagery. The "evil" eventually "through the efforts of Zinzendorf, Spangenberg, and others . . . was totally suppressed," asserts Bishop de Schweinitz.[44]

Before the suppression, however, the symbolic view of the Holy Spirit as a comforting mother was introduced into Bethlehem by the young bishop John Cammerhof, who imported from Europe an exuberant and good-hearted version of the "Herrnhaag extravagances."[45] As H.D. researched these, she saw their damaging and foolish aspects, but overall she was attracted to the errant Moravians' "enthusiasm" and celebratory attitudes. Even when taken to extremes, or perhaps because taken to extremes, these attitudes signified mystical insight and an entrée to the unconscious, the shared inspired condition that, to H.D.'s distress, disappeared from later Moravianism. She saw joy and celebration of the union of human beings—sexual, social, and religious—as part of the "*Plan*" that she wished to see renewed and carried out in the modern world.

In the seventh and last chapter of *The Gift*, H.D. draws on mysterious hints dropped by Mamalie in chapter 5 to envision that renewal. She re-creates a scene of mystical union and transfiguration in the Sifting Time centered on Anna von Pahlen, who in 1747 had arrived with Cammerhof in Bethlehem. She initiates the renewed "*Plan*" of "world unity without war" through her exchange of names with Morning Star, wife of the Delaware chief Paxinosa (or Paxnous), when the Native American woman was baptized at Bethlehem on February 17, 1755.[46] Thus the Native American woman, member of one of the lost tribes of Israel according to Zinzendorf's belief,[47] becomes the German aristocrat, who in turn becomes Morning Star. Their separate identities intermingle; the women are sisters or more than sisters, "spirit-doubles," inseparably united in one indivisible tribe or family.

Through her new name, *Morning Star,* Anna von Pahlen also becomes identified with the Bethlehem star carved beside the verse declaring "Mutter" as the Holy Spirit and with Hesperus, the planet Venus, whose various associations appear in sections 10, 11, and 12 of *Tribute to the Angels,* following the "mer, mere . . . / Star of the Sea / Mother" passage in section 8. As Morning Star, she is further linked to the Virgin Mary, one of whose appellations is *Stella Maris,* Star of the Sea; to Venus-Aphrodite-Isis, the Greco-Roman and Egyptian versions of Mary; to the "dark Mary" of H.D.'s dream, who is both the sea and the Mother; and of course to her own Moravian mother, Helen Wolle, artist and musician. "This Isis takes many forms," said H.D. in explaining her women characters (HDDA, 182, 221).

Christ is also called the Morning Star, Star of Morning, the "bright and morning star" (Rev. 22:16), herald of a "new day" and new life for the Christian, his birth having been signaled by a brilliant, theretofore unseen star. This Star of Bethlehem, the annunciatory light, led the magi, the occultists of their day, to find the savior. For H.D. it symbolizes the vision of eternal life universally available to all peoples of all religious persuasions because of the "great ocean underground," the unconscious that is also the higher consciousness coterminous with the Holy Spirit, the Comforter and Mother.

"Morning Star" is the title and theme of *The Gift's* final chapter, set in the Lowndes Square flat during a bombing raid. In this threatening situation, H.D. suffers uncertainty that she is spiritually gifted. But a key passage, omitted from *NDG,* shows her recovered confidence in her legacy of second sight. By means of that clairvoyance and by recalling the former Moravian custom of making decisions by drawing lots,[48] she has a vision, as if in a trance, in which Anna von Pahlen appears as the guiding presence of wisdom, the embodiment of the Holy Spirit and the Moravian *anima:*

> I blinked my eyes and I saw in the dark; I could see, when the waves of planes
> went over the roof, a meeting of various people; Anna von Pahlen, the Santa

Sophia or Holy Wisdom or the Holy Spirit of the gatherings, had given her name Angelica (which was my Aunt Agnes' name, too) to the wife of Paxnous, and this was his only wife, his beloved and they drew out the written texts from a bowl or basket. Why, I could see the writing on the slips of paper. . . . (*G*, VII, 9)

In the darkness when H.D. had been learning of the secret *"Plan"* from Mamalie, her grandmother called her Agnes (lamb) and Lucy (light), so the name choice Angelica (angelic)—not the name that Paxnous' wife was given historically, but indeed the middle name of H.D.'s aunt Agnes[49]—brings about a transcendent "union" of all of H.D.'s spiritual mothers with herself, shaping her own "message of Aquaria," an Advent for the birth of the Aquarian Age.

These foremothers are unorthodox; they are not mild Madonnas. The spiritual powers they possess are intimidating; they incorporate qualities of the Primal Mother and the "phallic mother."[50] The young initiate Hilda had been both frightened and fascinated by her grandmother's resemblance to a witch, powerful and heretical in her mysterious incantatory speeches. H.D.'s fears are reactivated in the final chapter as the bombs fall closer. She feels utterly deprived of the power of vision, convinced that she is indeed "not gifted" and therefore will not be able to restore the Gift.

But by going to the rock bottom of her terrors, both those in the child's past and in the adult's present, she finds release. In a passage also omitted from *NDG*, she describes the paradox that liberates her into joyful transcendence:

> The gate that opens to let out the Old-Witch serves, this is the odd thing, to release Saint Nicholas and the Princess with the Star on her forehead who was Mamalie's Morning Star whose name was Angelica and Aunt Agnes' name was Angelica, so when Mamalie called me Agnes, I was Morning Star or I was Anna von Pahlen who had been a sort of Princess in Europe. So Europe and America had at last been reconciled in the very depth of my subconscious being. (*G*, VII, 20)

H.D. becomes one with "Anna, Hannah or Grace," bearer of the Gift of peace and love, which has not been lost and which the Indian priest hails in his own language: "*Kehelle.*"[51]

The Europeans and Americans together, led by the women, also cry,

"Hail," a sign of their union under the Great Spirit, Manitou,[52] "who is the God of the Brotherhood," the Christian God, and "the God of the Initiates," the hermeticist's God, who is one God with many names and forms. Therefore there is one Church, the secret church uniting all branches of contemporary Christianity with the Gnostics, Albigensians, spiritualists, psychic researchers, Freud, and others with minds in quest of truth since the beginning of time, in whose company H.D. counts herself.

This secret church "ran underground," she hears Mamalie say, evoking the same image in almost exactly the same words that H.D. uses in *Tribute to Freud* to describe the unconscious, which runs underground and gives rise to the universal language of dream, which all people can understand. The imagery of water, conqueror of fire, closes in full circle the past, the present, and the future.

H.D.'s greatest fear had been that her death by fire in a bombing raid would mean loss to the world of the legacy for which she was responsible, the divine Gift of peace, tolerance, and understanding. In the coda of the "Notes," she unifies the mothers' legacy with that of her fathers by applying to her own work the intentions expressed in the last words of a treatise composed by her ancestor, the English Puritan clergyman Thomas Doolittel: "In all which, if thou findest any thing profitable to thy Soul, and tending to promote the work of Grace wrought in thy Heart ... give God the Glory; but where thou findest any thing that favoureth of the weakness of the Author, do not censure, but pray for him, who is willing, according to his own Talent he has received from the Lord, to further thee in thy way to Heaven and Eternal Life" (*GN,* 94).

This intention seals and delivers the revelation brought to H.D. in the final lines of the main text. The "all-clear" sounds, announced by Bryher, the companion who has confirmed and continually supported the poet's mission, who is her present-day "mother" and therefore also an agent of grace and peace. It is the all-clear of H.D.'s own mind, the initiate's enlightenment, the fulfillment of her role in the cosmic "*Plan.*" She did not lose the Gift. She found it and passed it on. It is a victory gift, finished a few weeks after D-Day, June 6, 1944, when—as she desired—America joined Europe to end the nightmare of war and make way for the dawn of a peaceful world.

NOTES TO THE INTRODUCTION

1. Diana Collecott quoting H.D., *NDG-V,* x.

2. This phrase is Susan Friedman's in *Penelope's Web: Gender, Modernity, H.D.'s Fiction,* 352.

3. Donna Hollenberg, who edited the H.D.–Pearson correspondence (*BHP*), verifies this handwriting as almost certainly his (letter to the editor, November 9, 1994).

4. Notable publications of H.D.'s prose since the early 1980s are *HERmione,* intro. Perdita Schaffner (1981); *Notes on Thought and Vision,* ed. Albert Gelpi (1982); *Paint It Today,* ed. and intro. Cassandra Laity (1992); *Asphodel,* ed. and intro. Robert Spoo (1992). Black Swan reprinted *Hippolytus Temporizes* (1927 verse drama) in 1985; *Hedylus* (1928 novel) in 1980; and *Ion* (1937; "a play after Euripides") in 1986; these contain afterwords by John Walsh. New Directions reprinted *Nights* (1934 novella; intro. Perdita Schaffner) in 1986 and *Kora and Ka* with *Mira-Mare* (1930 novellas; ed. and intro. Robert Spoo) in 1996.

5. Recent book-length publications include *H.D. and Hellenism* by Eileen Gregory (1997); *Between History and Poetry: The Letters of H.D. and Norman Holmes Pearson,* ed. Donna Krolik Hollenberg (1997); *H.D. and the Victorian Fin de Siècle* by Cassandra Laity (1996); two-volume letter collection *Richard Aldington and H.D.: The Early Years in Letters* (1992) and *The Later Years in Letters* (1995), edited by Caroline Zilboorg; and *Out of Line: History, Psychoanalysis and Montage in H.D.'s Long Poems* by Susan Edmunds (1994).

6. *NDG-V,* ix, quoting H.D.'s letter to Norman Holmes Pearson, October 14, 1959.

7. Joseph Mortimer Levering, *A History of Bethlehem, Pennsylvania, 1741–1892,* 166–70.

8. Friedman relates this generic mélange to the conditions giving rise to gendered modernism: "H.D.'s prose is *outré.* Its shape is outside the patterns of conventional readability. . . . [It] inscribes a feminine metanarrative" (*PW,* 19).

9. Jane Augustine, "*The Mystery:* H.D.'s Unpublished Moravian Novel," 213.

10. The phrase "Sifting Time," also called the "Time of Sifting," was taken by Zinzendorf from Luke 22:31–32, in which Peter's denial of Christ is predicted: "And the Lord said, Simon, Simon, behold, Satan hath desired to have you, that he may sift you as wheat: But I have prayed for thee, that thy faith fail not . . ." (King James Version).

11. Letter to the editor, March 15, 1993; cf. Adalaide Morris, "Autobiography and Prophecy: H.D.'s *The Gift,*" 235.

12. H.D., "H.D. by Delia Alton," *Iowa Review,* ed. Adalaide Morris, 188.

13. The poem's title is actually "To Helen."

14. Daniel 5:24–31.

15. Friedman supplies details of this double transference in *PW,* 303–56.

16. "Friendship passes even beyond the grave." H.D. said that this motto appeared on an old seal belonging to Mamalie's first husband's family, the Seidels (*G,* V, 24). The seal's present location is unknown.

17. Collecott also alludes to this passage and the theme of regeneration (*NDG-V,* xi).

18. *HB,* 86–91.

19. Ibid., 199. Beverly Smaby in *The Transformation of Moravian Bethlehem from*

Communal Mission to Family Economy verifies that "Mother" or "Dear Mother" was a common appellation for the Holy Ghost in the years 1741–60 (178).

20. *HB*, 185. Levering and de Schweinitz spell the name "Cammerhoff," but the portrait of this missionary reproduced in *HB* is labeled "Cammerhof." The historian J. E. Hutton, whose books H.D. also refers to in these "Notes," uses the spelling "Cammerhof." It appears that the original records are inconsistent. H.D. chose "Cammerhof," and that form is retained here.

21. Mamalie's first husband's name was actually Henry A. Seidel, but H.D. "inspirationally" renames him "Christian" (*GN*, 63) to link him with the early Moravians Nathanael Seidel, Christian Seidel, and Christian Renatus, Zinzendorf's son.

22. Cf. *HB*, 199.

23. H.D. wrote to Viola Jordan on July 2, 1941: "The Aquarian age that is coming with such agony, as was always predicted, is a woman's age and we must stick together. . . ." Pearson also quotes H.D.: "'I wish Aquarius would get born before we perish,' she wrote to a friend" (*T*, vi).

24. The Curtisses, American students of Madame Blavatsky, between 1912 and World War II wrote and self-published nine large volumes and six or more smaller volumes elucidating their amalgamation of Christianity and theosophy. H.D. owned copies; they are now in the Bryher Library. In the margin on page 45 of *The Message of Aquaria*, "1936" is penciled in H.D.'s handwriting.

25. Not Zinzendorf's father but his grandfather was an Austrian who emigrated to the German state of Bavaria, not to Saxony. H.D. evidently misremembers P. La Trobe's introduction to A. G. Spangenberg's *Life of Nicholas Lewis Count Zinzendorf*: "The grandfather of the Count, Maximilian Erasmus, emigrated from his native land and settled at Oberberg, near Nuremberg, esteeming the loss of all his estates counterbalanced by the superior liberty of conscience which he thus obtained" (vi, n.). Zinzendorf's estate, Herrnhut, is in Saxony, not in Bohemia, as stated in *PW* (346). Moravians got their name because they fled from Roman Catholic Moravia and Bohemia to avoid persecution as Protestant followers of the principles of Jan Hus, the early fifteenth-century Bohemian church reformer. They went over the mountains to Protestant Germany's nearest bordering province, Saxony, and there found religious sympathy and refuge on Zinzendorf's estate (*HB*, ch. 1; cf. *NDG-V*, xvii). See p. 234.

26. Pearson's introduction to *Trilogy* cites a letter from H.D.: "she is the Troubadour's or Poet's Lady; anyhow, she put in an appearance—in a dream" (*T*, ix).

27. The "Curtiss Book," titled *The Key of Destiny*, owned and annotated by H.D. and in 1934 (Silverstein, 9) read by her, speaks of the "Elohim" who rule the planets (26, n. 4). These spirits are also called "Angelic Rulers of the Hours of the Heavens," a concept that has affinities with her later poem *Hermetic Definition*. See also *Tribute to the Angels*, sections 28, 34.

28. In *Majic Ring* (1943–44) H.D. gives another explanation of the dream of the Lady. She originally appeared during a séance as a "picture" like a white statue, "the snow-queen certainly. Yes, she was snow and cloud-queen. . . . I thought of her or now think of her as a moon-goddess. . . . Yes, she was the moon certainly" (98–100).

29. *HB*, 185.

30. The word "cella" in this significant passage is correct, not one of H.D.'s famous misspellings. It is an architectural term meaning "the body of the temple, as distinct

from the portico etc." and therefore is synonymous with the words "inner hall" that immediately precede it. Friedman quotes this passage (*PW,* 345) and changes "cella" to "cella[r]," a conjectural emendation that has led to frequent misquotation as "cellar."

H.D.—or her typist—did not capitalize "Mutter" in the last line, or perhaps mistook it for the English word *mutter.* Capitalized, it is the German word for *mother,* which better fits the context and alludes to the Cammerhof verse "Vater, Mutter, Lieber Mann." *Mut* is the German word for *courage.* This prayer during a bombing raid is thus an appeal for courage to come from the support of the divine Mother.

31. Susan Friedman, in an H.D. Society discussion on the Internet, pointed out that "the 'real world' of history is everywhere a part of the subjectivities of writers like H.D. and [Virginia] Woolf. People have always understood that about [James] Joyce . . . but it has been all too easy to assume that the subjectivist writing of women is escapist. Even *Sea Garden* ends with the long sequence 'Cities'" (c. July 11, 1995; cf. Friedman, *Psyche Reborn,* 102, 309–10, n. 31).

32. *HB,* 113; *HMM,* 85–88.

33. Grisly details of this "act of inhuman barbarity" are given in Edmund de Schweinitz's *The Life and Times of David Zeisberger,* 537–57, although it appears that H.D. did not read this account. However, she did read in Levering that the "deliberate butchery of a lot of defenseless, submissive, praying Christian men, women and children" should be "classed with the most inhuman deeds that men professing to be civilized have even been known to commit in warfare" (523), an observation that certainly resonated with H.D.'s wartime experience.

34. In *Majic Ring* H.D. sheds light on the way in which *The Gift* is autobiographical "almost" by describing chapter 5's transmutation of a "supernormal" experience on Corfu with Bryher:

> I wrote a story or novel about my grandmother and my mother and I used the psychic experience that Gareth [Bryher] and I had had, but I worked it into a sequence of reconstructed memories that I made my grandmother tell me, as if in reverie or half-dream or even trance.
>
> I worked last winter [1943] on that book and finally finished it. I called the book *The Gift.* It was in fact a real story, there was a Gift in our family, taken out in music for the most part. . . . I worked the story of myself and Gareth into my own family and made my grandmother reconstruct a strange psychic experience to me, a child.
>
> The story held, it rang true. (118–19)

Helen Sword discusses *Majic Ring's* connections with *Trilogy* and *The Gift* in her essay "H.D.'s *Majic Ring*" in *Tulsa Studies in Women's Literature.*

35. Barbara Guest, *Herself Defined: The Poet H.D. and Her World,* 260–62. H.D.'s "Séance Notes" (ts. Beinecke) outline the contents of sessions with Arthur Bhaduri dramatized in her autobiographically based mythic reconstructions *Majic Ring* and *The Sword Went Out to Sea* (1946–47).

36. Zakenuto is introduced on October 29, 1943 (SN, 3).

37. Interview with Tim Haigh, editor, *Psychic News,* London, August 29, 1995. Estelle Roberts and Grace Cooke, two well-known mediums living in London in the 1930s and 1940s had Native American "controls," Red Cloud and White Eagle,

respectively. Through White Eagle's guidance, Grace Cooke founded White Eagle Lodge, a still-active spiritualist church.

38. George Lavington, Anglican Bishop of Exeter, accused the Moravians of being Papists in his pamphlet "Moravians Compared and Detected" (London, 1755). H.D. owned and read this pamphlet. Cf. *LTDZ*, 143.

39. Psalm 91:5 (King James Version).

40. *HB*, 764, 770.

41. H.D. misattributes this statement to Cammerhof when she quotes it in her "Notes."

42. *HB*, 187.

43. J. E. Hutton, *A History of the Moravian Church*, 277.

44. *LTDZ*, 143.

45. *HB*, 186; Hutton, *Church*, 279. *HB*, 185, and *LTDZ*, 143, confirm Cammerhof's virtues as well as his faults.

46. *HB*, 300. Neither the native name of the woman whom H.D. calls Morning Star nor her baptismal Christian name is recorded by Levering. William Reichel reports that she was baptized Elizabeth (*Memorials of the Renewed Church*, 109).

47. *HMM*, 90; cf. Reichel, *Memorials*, 18–20.

48. *HB*, 102, n. 7. For examples of use of the lot, see *HMM*, 15, 21, 38, 190.

49. Francis Wolle, "A Moravian Heritage," 21.

50. H.D. sees the "phallic mother," according to Friedman, in the dream of her mother holding a lighted candle (*TF*, 174–75). Helen Wolle is thus linked not only with the Moravian Christmas Eve candlelight ceremony but with the "maternal deities of the past," especially the "Cretan Snake Goddess" (*PW*, 318), and thus with "dark Mary" and H.D.'s snake-bite dream. These figures coalesce in the ascendant divine feminine principle that will rule the coming Aquarian Age.

51. *HB*, 300.

52. Moravians and Native Americans mutually agreed that *God* and *Manito* or *Manitou* refer to the same Great Spirit, the over-arching power in the universe. See G. H. Loskiel, *History of the Mission of the United Brethren Among the Indians in North America*, pt. 1, 39–40, and Lewis Spence, *The Myths of the North American Indians*, 114. H.D. read both of these books and quotes a long passage from part 2 of Loskiel at the beginning of her "Notes" to *The Gift*.

The Gift

To
H E L E N
who has
brought me home

for Bethlehem Pennsylvania 1741
from   Chelsea   London   1941

L'amitié passe même le tombeau.

Contents

Dark Room : 33

Fortune Teller : 55

The Dream : 81

Because One Is Happy : 107

The Secret : 145

What It Was : 183

Morning Star : 207

Dark Room

The brain comes into play, yes, but it is only the
tool . . . the telephone is not the person speaking
over it. The dark room is not the photograph.

Death and Its Mystery, Camille Flammarion

Dark Room

There was a girl who was burnt to death at the Seminary, as they called the old school where our grandfather was Principal.

We were for a long time, under the impression that we had two fathers, Papa and Papalie, but the children across the street said, Papalie was our grandfather. "He is not," we said, "he is our Papalie." But Ida, our devoted friend, who did the cooking and read Grimm's tales to us at night before we went to sleep, said yes, Papalie was our grandfather, people had a grandfather, sometimes they had two. The other grandfather was dead, he was Papa's father, she explained. But the girl who was burnt to death, was burnt to death in a crinoline. The Christmas-tree was lighted at the end of one of the long halls and the girl's ruffles or ribbons caught fire and she was in a great hoop.

The other girls stand round. There is Mama who is a tiny child and Aunt Laura, who Mama said was the pretty one, two years older and Aunt Agnes in her long frock, who in the daguerreotypes and old photographs looked like the young mother of the two little girls and the three boys, the uncles.

Mamalie had married twice; there was a picture of one of Aunt Agnes' family in a wig with a sword; he had been at the Court of Czar Alexander, in Russia; that was a long time ago. Aunt Agnes' children were young men, almost like uncles, there had been eight altogether, five grew up. There had been a little girl; and in our own plot at Nisky Hill, there was a little girl who was our own sister and another little girl who had been the child of the Lady who had been Papa's first wife. But the girl in the crinoline wasn't a relation, she was just one of the many girls at the Seminary when Papalie was there and she screamed and Papalie rushed to her and Papalie wrapped a rug round her but she is shrieking and they can not tear off her clothes because of the hoop.

"Why are you crying?" This is Mama and her younger brother, little Hartley. Mamalie finds them crouched at the turn of the stairs under the big clock that Mamalie's father had himself made.

"It is a grandfather-clock," we said proudly, "and it was made by Mamalie's father."

"Ah, so it is *really* a grandfather's-clock," one out-of-town visitor remarked; we felt indifference, even irreverence in her unfamiliar low drawl. Wasn't it a thing to be proud of, that Mamalie's father made clocks? We were very proud of it. Mamalie's father had even been asked to Philadelphia to sing in a great choral-service; he kept bees and he played the trombone at the Easter services in the old grave-yard when we went out and said *the Lord is risen indeed* and watched the sun come up over the graves.

But "why are you crying" was Mama and little Hartley, it was not Hilda and little Harold. Hilda and little Harold did not creep under the clock and cry but it was the same clock.

"Why are you crying?"

Mama, who was older, said, "we are crying because Fanny died." Mamalie laughed when she told us the story of Mama and Uncle Hartley crouching under the clock, which was our clock in our house now and our great-grand-father had made it and kept bees and been asked to Philadelphia to sing, even at a theatre or an opera-house.

"They were crying," Mamalie explained when we wondered why she laughed about it, "because Fanny died."

"But why is it funny?"

"Well, you see they couldn't possibly remember Fanny, Fanny died before Hartley was born and your own mama was just a baby, how could she re-member Fanny?"

I wondered about that. Mama was crying about Fanny. Why did Mamalie think it funny? Mamalie did not seem to think of Fanny, Mama did not speak often of little Edith, and the other little girl was not mentioned; Ida said it was better for us not to share Edith's flowers on her April birthday, with the other graves, with the Lady and with Alice. We felt somehow that this was not right but there were things we did not understand.

We had spread Edith's pansies, equally on Alice's twin-grave and then borrowed from both of them for the Lady who was not our mother but the mother of the two (to us) grown men, our brothers, who were finishing their work at the University across the river; their names were Eric and Alfred. But Ida said the flowers were meant for Edith and "your mama would feel hurt"—we did not follow this but had been sent with the basket of pansies and pink-and-white button-daisies for Edith's grave, so we collected the pansies and daisies from the flat tops of the other graves and gave them back to Edith. And then there was Fanny, difficult to find in the crowded plot where Mamalie's and Aunt Agnes' other children were. There was Elizabeth Caroline for instance, who had been Aunt Agnes' and Uncle Will's first baby. But Fanny, among them all, had become a myth, she was a family byword. "Why so sad, Helen?" Mamalie might say, then Mama would answer, perhaps too suddenly, too swiftly forcing the expected "Mimmie, of course, you know why. I'm crying because Fanny died." And they would both laugh.

I seemed to have inherited that. I was the inheritor. The boys, of whom there were so many, the two brothers and later, the baby-brother, the two half-brothers, the five grown Howard cousins, not to mention the small-fry, Tootie, Dick and Laddie (who lived with their parents, our Uncle Hartley and Aunt Belle in the house next ours, on Church Street) could not really care about Fanny; little Hartley had cried only because his tiny older sister was crying. I cared about Fanny. And she died. I inherited Fanny from Mama, from Mamalie, if you will, but I inherited Fanny. Was I indeed, Frances come back? Then I would be Papalie's own child, for Papalie's name was Francis; I would be like Mama; in a sense, I would be Mama, I would have important sisters, and brothers, only as seemly ballast. Why was it always a girl who had died? Why did Alice die and not Alfred? Why did Edith die and not Gilbert? I did not cry because Fanny died, but I had inherited Fanny. Mama cried (although I had seldom seen her cry) because Fanny died, so Mama had cried. I did not cry. The crying was frozen in me but it was my own, it was my own crying. There was Alice, my own half-sister, Edith, my own sister and I was the third of this trio, these three Fates, or maybe Fanny was the third. The gift was there but the expression of the gift was somewhere else.

It lay buried in the ground; in older countries, fragments of marble were brought to life again after long years. On those altars, flowers had lain, wild-pansies, mountain-laurel, roses. So we placed, in their season, daisies, roses and peonies on those altars in the old grave-yard where the stones lay flat, or in the new grave-yard where the more worldly-minded newcomers to our town, erected columns, artificially broken, around which, carved-ivy clung. They walled off their own personal little plots with white stones or low iron-railings with chains, for to those newcomers to our town, death was a per-

sonal and private matter, not like the first Moravians who rested, more or less
in the order of their going, under small stones that lay, even and symmetrical,
like dominoes on a green baize cloth.

There was Miss Helen at school. There was the Beaver lesson; the chart of
the Beaver was hung on the wall beside the black-and-white drawing of the
Eskimo and the Eskimo snow-house. The Eskimo lived in a snow-house,
rather like the ones we tried to build, though we never succeeded in round-
ing them off neatly or, if they were any size, getting the roof to stay on. There
was Miss Helen. There was the map she cut out of brown paper and the
offering of a camel of mine, pasted on. We brought pictures, cut out from the
advertisements at the backs of magazines; Miss Helen chose those suitable
for her brown-paper map of Africa; she pasted the animal or the palm-tree
where it belonged on the map. There was an oasis which was, she said, an
island in the desert.

There were the Egyptians who lived along the river. They built little
houses to live in when they were dead. In these underground houses they
piled up furniture, chairs, tables, boxes, jars, food even. Some wheat taken
out of a tomb (it had been buried thousands of years) grew when it was
planted. The grain grew like the kernels of yellow corn we laid on a piece of
mosquito-netting, tied over a kitchen-tumbler. We broke off the bare twigs
of the chestnut-trees, and the leaves came out, long before any green showed
on the branches. The trees outside lined the brick-walk that led up the slope
from Church Street past the Church and the Dead-house (as we called the
Mortuary) to the school.

Florence said one of the Sisters was lying in the Dead-house, but we could
not see her. The Dead-house had little windows, too high up but Florence
said Melinda had said that Nettie had said, there was a Sister in the Dead-
house. She would lie there until they carried her to the old grave-yard or
more likely to Nisky Hill, as the old grave-yard was very crowded. Along the
fence of the old grave-yard, there were mounds without stones, which were
the soldiers, grey and blue, who had died in the old Seminary, when Papalie
was there, during the Civil War. They were being taken in wagons to Philadelphia to the hospitals but if they were too weak or going to die, they were
left in the Seminary on Church Street where they lay in rows in the beds
where the girls had been, before they broke up the school to make a hospital

of it, for the soldiers from Gettysburg. There had been wounded soldiers there too, during the War of Independence.

Papa had been a soldier and Florence's father, too. Papa was only seventeen, he told them he was eighteen. He and his brother Alvin had gone off and Alvin had died of typhoid fever. Papa had had typhoid, too. He said his mother cried when she saw him come back; she said, "O, I thought it was Alvin, coming back." Papa never told us much about himself except that his mother had been disappointed when she found it was Charles and not Alvin, who had come back from the Civil War.

Papa went out to look at the stars at night. He measured them or measured something, we didn't know quite what. We could see what Papalie was doing with his microscope on his study-table. But when Papa took us into his little domed house—with a dome like the Eskimo made of ice over their snow-huts—and we asked to look into his telescope, he said that we would see nothing; you could not see what he was looking at or looking for, in the day-time. Papa looked at the thermometer and opened or closed a shutter (that opened with ropes that pulled) in the curved roof or dome of his little house, which was built higher up the mountains, above the University buildings, the other side of the river. When we kept on asking him to let us see, he did let us see, but it was as he had told us; there was only a white glare and nothing to be seen and it hurt your eyes. It would be too late to go over there at night, he said, and anyhow at night, he was busy.

I can not say that a story called *Bluebeard* that Ida read us from one of the fairy-tales, actually linked up in thought—how could it?—with our kind father. There was a man called *Bluebeard,* and he murdered his wives. How was it that Edith and Alice and the Lady (the mother of Alfred and Eric) all belonged to Papa and were there in the grave-yard? No, of course I did not actually put this two-and-two together.

"But why did they call him Bluebeard?" I asked Eric, who had time to answer questions that other people could not or would not answer. "His beard, was blue, was it?"

"No," said Eric, "it was just a way of saying that he had a very black beard."

Papa had a black beard. (A few years after, it was to turn white, almost overnight, but that comes later.) There was a man with a black beard and a dead wife or dead wives and there was Edith and there was Alice and there was the Lady whose name written on the stone, was, Ida told us ("but do not ask your mother questions") Martha. The name Martha was written on a stone and Alice was written and Edith. My name was Hilda, Papa found the name in the dictionary, he said. He said he ran his finger down the names in the back of the dictionary and his finger stopped at Huldah and then went back up the line to Hilda. What would I have been, who would I have been, if my initial had come at the beginning and he had put his finger on Alice? Had he put his finger on Alice?

Papa went out of the house "like a thief" as he used to say, "or an astronomer," every evening if the stars were shining. If the stars were shining—O God of stars, let the stars shine—then Mama would lift the lamp from the centre round-table in the sitting-room and fold up the embroidered table-cover and say to Gilbert or Harold or Hilda, "just take this pile of books, don't drop them, and put them on the piano, no, the piano is open, you can't reach up, not the floor, you don't put books on the floor, no, not the chair—here—" and she would take them back and pile them on top of other books on the book-case in the corner.

There was the cuckoo-clock that would strike (too soon) eight, to-bed. There was the desk in the corner, in one of the compartments of which there was a little box with some sort of eggs, we were not sure what kind of eggs, "but they won't hatch now," Papalie had said. Mama thought they might be dangerous, be snake's eggs.

"But if they won't hatch, Mama, why don't you throw them away?"

"O—give me that box, I told you not to touch that box."

"But you said, Papalie said, they wouldn't hatch, can't I throw them in the garden?"

"No—no."

"Why not?"

"They might hatch."

"I thought you said, Papalie said, they wouldn't hatch now."

"He said, he *thought* they wouldn't hatch now."

"Then they might hatch—they might hatch here in the desk."

"No, no, no—put that box down. Don't shake it."

"But I thought you said . . ."

Papalie had an alligator in their attic, in a tank with thick netting but anyhow, "you children must not go up there any more."

"But the alligator is asleep."

Mamalie would tell us how someone who knew Papalie had sent him two alligators, as small as very large lizards, in a cigar box from Florida. They were wrapped in Florida-moss. Their names were Castor and Pollux, one had died and was varnished and mounted on a board and hung over the slippery horse-hair sofa in Papalie's study. Once a tarantula had dropped out of a bunch of bananas at Mr. Luckenbach's, the grocer's on the corner.

Mr. Luckenbach had caught it in a shoe-box and rushed across the street to ask Papalie what it was. Everyone brought things like that to our grandfather, because he had a microscope and studied things and drew pictures of branches of moss that you could not see with your eyes. He put them on a glass-slide or pressed a drop of water from a bottle (that he had brought back from trips to the mountains) between two glass-slides. That (in time, it was explained) was fresh-water *algae,* a sort of moss, invisible for the most part, to the naked eye. The apple of my eye. He was the naked eye, he was the apple of God's eye. He was a minister, he read things out of the Bible, he said, *I am the light of the world,* when the doors opened at the far end of the Church and the trays of lighted beeswax candles were brought into the Church by the Sisters in their caps and aprons, while Uncle Fred in the gallery at the organ, was playing very softly, *Holy Night.*

When Mama folded the embroidered table-cover and put it on top of the books, she might get out the jack-straws or she might get out a box with a horse-shoe that was a magnet and drew little bits of specks of iron in patterns after it. But she might turn over the card-board box of yellow squares and say, "we will have some anagrams, Gilbert, you must help now."

There was not one single word that I could spell, not one, not c-a-t even, but if I shouldered over to Gilbert and clutched the edge of the table, I could from time to time select a letter; sometimes it was the right one, not very often.

"Mimmie, he's spelt a word," says Mama very proudly to Mamalie, our grandmother, or if it's Aunt Jennie, "Jean, look he's spelt dog," but Jean will push it back and say, "d-a-g doesn't spell anything that I know of, Sister would know an *a* from an *o* if you don't, Gibbie," and it might even be perceived that miraculously, a round shape in black, on the yellow square of card-board was somehow alone and staring at me, by Aunt Jennie's elbow.

It was a game, it was a way of making words out of words, but what it was, was a way of spelling words, in fact it was a *spell*. The cuckoo-clock would not strike, it could not, because the world had stopped. It was not frozen in time, it was like one of Papalie's water-drops that he had brought down from the mountains or from a trip to the Delaware water-gap, in a jar. It was a drop of living and eternal life, perfected there; it was living, complete, not to be dried up in memory like pressed-moss—Papalie had pressed-moss, too. But there was a difference between Papalie's pressed-moss and the things that shone in the crystal-lens of his microscope, on the glass-plate that a moment ago had been empty and just two pieces of glass, like small empty magic-lantern slides, stuck together.

When Papalie lifted us, one by one in turn, to kneel on the chair by his work-table, we saw that it was true what he said, we saw that where there is nothing, there is something. We saw that an empty drop of water spread out branches, bright green or vermilion, in shape like a branch of a Christmas-tree or in shape, like a squashed peony or in shape, like a lot of little green-glass beads, strung on a thin stem.

In these flashes of flash-backs, we have the ingredients of the Gift.

They had so much to give us, Papa and Papalie and old Father Weiss, as the whole town had affectionately called our grandmother's father. There were the others before these, who went back to the beginning of America and before America, but the Gift seemed to have passed us by. We were none of us "gifted," they would say.

"How do you mean—what?"

"O—I don't mean—I don't mean anything."

But they did mean something. They didn't think any of us were marked with that strange thing they called a Gift, the thing Uncle Fred had had from the beginning, the thing Papalie (they said) wasn't sure about, so Uncle Fred was put in a drug-store. An errand-boy who crawls under the counter and hides there with stolen fragments of church-music, was not much good in a drug-store. So Papalie made sure of the Gift that Uncle Fred had. We hadn't any Gift to make sure about.

But where did he get the Gift, just like that? Why didn't Mama wait and teach us music like she did Uncle Fred when he was a little boy? Mama gave all her music to Uncle Fred, that is what she did. That is why we hadn't the Gift, because it was Mama who started being the musician and then she said she taught Uncle Fred; she gave it away, she gave the Gift to Uncle Fred, she should have waited and given the Gift to us. But there were other Gifts, it seemed.

"What—what do you mean, Uncle Hartley?"

"People draw, if a person draws or writes a book or something like that; a gift isn't just music. Artists are people who are gifted."

"Is Uncle Fred an artist?"

"Well, yes, I suppose so. Yes, of course Fred is an artist."

"But an artist is someone with a paint-box and a big hat?"

"No, an artist is someone who—well—he can draw or paint or write a book or even do other things."

"Like what?"

"Well, I don't know—well—to be *artistic*—I suppose you might say your Aunt Belle was *artistic*—"

"Then can ladies be just the same as men?"

"Just the same what?"

"I mean what you said—about writing a book?"

"Why, yes, ladies write books of course, lots of ladies write very good books."

"Like Louisa M. Alcott?"

"Yes, like Louisa Alcott and like Harriet Beecher Stowe."

"Who is that?"

"That's *Uncle Tom's Cabin,* you know, you saw the procession and the play, didn't you?"

We saw Uncle Tom. He sat on a bench before a wooden hut that was drawn in a cart. The wooden hut was his cabin and they told us that the book was called *Uncle Tom's Cabin* and that the play we were going to be taken to see, in a real theatre, on the other side of the river, was called *Uncle Tom's Cabin* but it was the book that started it or it was the real story, in the beginning, that started it, because Uncle Tom was a real darkie on a real plantation, *Way down upon the Swanee river.*

That was before the Civil War; that happened a long time ago when Papa was seventeen, though he told them he was eighteen, so that he could run away with his brother Alvin in Indiana, and help free the slaves.

The slaves were roped together and they walked along tied together like that, in torn trousers and old shoes or no shoes, and a man in a big hat and a whip, slashed round them with the whip but Ida said he wasn't really hurting them, only cracking with his whip like that to show how Simon Legree (that was his name) drove the poor slaves in the cotton-fields, down in the south.

There was someone on the ice with a baby, but the baby, Ida said, was a doll, and the ice was not real ice because it was summer and it would have melted, but Eliza, I think it was, was pulled along with the ice on wheels, like Uncle Tom's cabin. Then there were some horses and donkeys; it was like a circus but there weren't wild animals, only horses and donkeys and then there was the last and the best thing. It was a sort of golden cart or it was a chariot like *Swing low, sweet chariot,* and there was an angel, only it was made of wood and gilded over like the things on the Christmas-tree and it had a wreath in its hands. It was stretching out its wings and it was holding the wreath over the head of Little Eva who was the most important thing in the procession.

There were real dogs pulling on straps, with dollars round their necks. They were very big dogs. Ida said they were blood-hounds, they were to hunt the slaves and the slaves went along and they sang songs out of Uncle Bob's song-book on the top of their piano. They sang *Massa's in the cold, cold ground* or they just hummed and then Simon Legree cracked his whip and they stopped singing. The blood-hounds would chase them through the woods—only now they weren't slaves any more.

"It's only a parade," Gilbert said, "they are as free as you are."

The darkies tied together, were as free as I was, because our father and our Uncle Alvin had fought in the Civil War and now we all had the same flag that Betsy Ross made in a house in Philadelphia, which we have a picture of in school, with the thirteen original States which are the thirteen stripes and all the other States which are the Stars. Our State which is Pennsylvania, is one of the thirteen original States.

Once we had a procession, too; we all waved flags when we met other children from other schools. That was for 1492, I mean it was in 1892 which made 400 years since Columbus discovered America.

We were Americans and so were the darkies who were tied together and so was Simon Legree and so was Little Eva. Little Eva died in a bed, we saw her die. It was a stage, Ida said. You call it the stage and this was our first time at the theatre. We knew it was a stage because we had our school entertainments on the stage in the big hall at school. Now Little Eva died and it was just as if she had died but then she came back again in a long night-gown. Little Eva was not really dead at all. She was the same little girl with the long gold hair who was driven in the chariot down the street, and she would do it all over again in Allentown or Easton, Ida said. They went on to other towns like the circus did, but this was not the circus. Uncle Tom died too and that was when Little Eva came back, after she was dead and she was a dream or a vision, like something in the Bible, that Uncle Tom had, when he died.

That was how it was. Little Eva was really in a book, yet Little Eva was there on the stage and we saw her die, just like the book, Aunt Belle said, though we hadn't read it. Aunt Belle sat in the row back of us with Tootie and Tootie changed places with Gilbert (because he couldn't see very well) between the acts. Tootie liked Topsy best and Harold did too, I think.

Ida and Aunt Belle liked the song, Little Eva's father sang, when Little Eva's mother played the piano. We had to wait for them to finish that before we could see the blood-hounds. The blood-hounds did really chase Eliza on the ice. She screamed and jumped on the pieces of ice and you forgot that it wasn't ice at all. You forgot the people around you and that you were in the theatre, you forgot you were in a town even, that you would have to go home after this. That is how it was. Everybody waited and someone laughed when the blood-hounds sniffed round the lights in front of the stage, and didn't chase Eliza. But I could see that they were not real terrible dogs. I could see that they were really very good dogs, yet at the same time, something else in me, that listened when Ida reads us a fairy-tale, would know that they were terrible and horrible dogs, that they would rush at Eliza and her baby which was only a big bundled-up doll or even only a bundle, and tear at her and bite her to death. I mean, I would know that we were there, that Harold was beside me, and that Tootie had the place on the end that Harold had had, so that he could see down the aisle. Harold was next me, where Gilbert had been.

There were three acts, they said. We had seen the first and second. There were small acts in between when they just dropped the curtain. In between the acts, everything was the same as when we came. There was red velvet on the seats of the chairs, a boy in a round cap went down the aisle selling pop-corn. Tootie said, "could we have pop-corn, Mama?" Aunt Belle bought us pop-corn. But you could tell all the time, even when you were crackling your pop-corn that everything was different. I mean, it went on even after the lights came up in the theatre, even after people turned round in their seats and talked and the boys in the gallery shouted and stamped.

It was the University students in the gallery; Aunt Belle called them boys. They stamped and laughed and clapped and made a lot of whistling noises to the blood-hounds, when they came on the stage.

"Why do they laugh, Aunt Belle?"

"O—well—to them—I mean, lots of them come from big cities or even from New York. I suppose they think it's just a funny little provincial theatre."

"What's provincial, Aunt Belle?"

"Well, a small place, a little town, like ours, I mean to them, to lots of them, it's a funny old-fashioned show, that's why they laugh and have fun like they do, whistling at the wrong time to make the dogs forget to chase Eliza."

It was fun for the University boys to whistle and stamp their feet. But people hushed at them and a man in front turned round and said he'd speak to the manager about this, and in the last act when Uncle Tom died, maybe the man had spoken to the manager, because the University boys seemed to be quiet in the gallery.

The University boys were grown-up young men like our Howard cousins, and Eric and Alfred who were at the University, too. The thing was, it was very exciting and maybe the University boys thought it was exciting, too, but in a different sort of way. They did not understand how it is for some people, they did not understand that when Aunt Belle said, would Gilbert mind coming back with her so Tootie could sit next to the aisle, that *aisle* all at once, was the same as the aisle in Church. They could not understand how some people could sit like that in the chairs with the red velvet in the dark, and it was like being in Church.

The theatre was dark and the lights that Aunt Belle called foot-lights, were like ours in Church, when we sit in rows, grown people and children like this, and the Sisters walk down the aisles to hand the candles to the children.

Lots of people do not know the things we know and that Uncle Tom was seeing a vision like something in the Bible, when he saw Little Eva with a long night-dress and her gold hair, standing against the curtain that had wings painted on it, just where Little Eva was standing, so it made Little Eva look like the Princess in our fairy-book who had long gold hair, only the Princess hadn't wings, only maybe the University boys didn't have that kind of book or maybe they didn't know how to look at pictures, or to see things in themselves and then to see them as if they were a picture.

Anyhow it was over. We went home. But the street would never be the same again, it would always be different, really everything would always be different. This street that we walked along, deliberately dodging ahead to thwart Aunt Belle and Ida, who would prefer we knew, the short way across the bridge and up the hill, was the street down which, only yesterday, Uncle Tom had been pulled, complete with log-cabin; the hounds we had seen, less than an hour ago, chasing Eliza, had snuffled and shuffled their way along these very paving-stones. Here by the Linden House, the procession halted and the slaves pushed together and Simon Legree took off his hat and got out a cigar. I could have wished the parade had got stuck near the end, then I could have looked and looked at Little Eva, I could have pushed forward and touched a gold wheel of her chariot.

Here the donkeys had slowed down, and they had one donkey pulling a log, I suppose to show how the cabin was built. Well, really there had been so much, you kept remembering bits of it; in the light of the play itself, the details of the parade came into different perspective, everything came true— that is what it was. Everything came true.

The street came true in another world, our side-street past the Linden House in our small-town that the University students, Aunt Belle said, would call provincial, was a street across which wheels of a great procession had passed. O well, I know it was only Little Eva in a jerry-built, gold chariot, and yet it was the very dawn of art, it was the sun, the drama, the theatre, it was poetry, why, it was music, it was folk-lore and folk-song, it was history. It was all these things, and in our small-town, on the curb of the pavement, the three children—and maybe Tootie—who stood watching, were all the children of all the world; in Rome, in Athens, in Palestine, in Egypt, they had watched golden-chariots, they had seen black-men chained together and cruel over-seers brandishing whips. It was Alexandria, it was a Roman Triumph, it was a Medieval miracle-play procession with a Devil who was Simon Legree and the poor dark shades of Purgatory, who were the negroes chained together, and it was Pallas Athene in her chariot with the winged Victory poised with the olive-crown, who was coming to save us all.

It was all these things and many more, and the names of many cities could be woven together on a standard to be carried at the head of this procession, and yet you would not have told half the story. It was art or many of the arts, concentrated and maybe consecrated by the fixed game of these same American children, who in the intensity of their naif yet inherent or inherited perception, glorifying these shoddy strolling-players, became one with their visionary mid-European ancestors and their Elizabethan English forebears.

And it didn't stop there because when we got home, everything was like that. If you take down one side of a wall, you have a stage. It would be like the doll-house that had only three walls, and you could arrange the room without any trouble; a bed could be over there by the window instead of drawn up in the corner by the wall; Mama was sitting at the piano and it was still Mama and yet it was Little Eva's mother and if Uncle Fred came in and sang *Last Night there were four Marys,* like he did when Mamalie asked him to, then he would be Little Eva's father.

Papa did not sing of course, and we would not want to change our father for anyone else and Uncle Fred was our uncle anyhow, but that is what you can do.

If Mama sits at the piano and plays *Moonlight,* the room is the same and there is always that difference that *Moonlight* makes when Mama plays it, but there was another difference. There would be someone else who was myself, yet who was the child of the Lady who Played the Piano, then I would be Little Eva and I would have an Uncle Tom who was not really an uncle, but it was like that. It was called a play, it was the first play we had been to. But a play and to play were the same. You could play now without any trouble; you could arrange the sofa that was too heavy to pull on the other side of the room and you could see how the room had only three sides and you could walk across the room and toss your head and say, "O, this is so hot, it's so heavy," and you could carefully push it aside when you sat down on a chair; although anyone could see that you had short hair with, at best, mousy duck-tails at the nape of the neck, yet you could toss your head and the gold curls.

It was the same gold as the Princess had, who had the seven or the nine brothers and I had brothers and could make up more by counting in the cousins. Then, I would be like that. But no one would know about it. Everything was the same but everything was different. You could think about it in bed. Then everyone's house would be open on one side and you would see it all going on. The Williams' family across the street, would be in bed, at least most of them would be, but Olive maybe would be allowed to stay up and help Professor Williams put away the stones that he had in little boxes for his students at the University.

I did not want to think of the University and the students but of the Williams' family across the street, and Papalie and Mamalie sitting in their sitting-room and Ida in the kitchen. I did not tell Gilbert about it, and I laughed when he laughed about how funny it was when the blood-hounds didn't chase Eliza but sniffed and scuffled in the foot-lights. The foot-lights threw shadows, so that faces were different. Now I could see that their faces were different under the lamp in the dining-room so that Mama said, "What's the matter, Sister? Why don't you eat your dinner?"

The dinner was on the table. The lamp was on the side-board. The doors opened from the little hall that led into the kitchen and every time the door opened and Ida came in, you could see how the whole room was different. There was the door that led down steps to the street, that we called the side-door; it was closed now. There was the door that led into the sitting-room. Someone might come in, like they did, maybe Uncle Hartley with a newspaper or Aunt Jennie with a basket or even Mamalie with a plate and a napkin over it, "I know Charles likes my apple-pies," she would say and Mama would take the plate and say, "O, Mimmie you do spoil us," and say, "sit down Mimmie," and Mamalie would say, "but Francis" (that was Papalie) "is waiting for his dinner."

At any moment, someone might walk in the room through that street-door or the closed sitting-room door and you would see now, how they said things, how Mama was sure to say, "O, Mimmie you spoil us," and Papa would look up and get up to find Mamalie a chair and then she would slide out; she is a very little lady; really, soon, Gilbert will be as tall as she is. You could see how pretty Mamalie was, in her lace cap.

It would not always be like that. But because it once had been like that, it would be possible with time and with the curious chemical constituents of biological or psychic thought-processes—whatever thought is, nobody yet knows—to develop single photographs or to develop long strips of continuous photographs, stored in the dark-room of memory, and again to watch people enter a room, leave a room, to watch, not only those people enter and leave a room, but to watch the child watching them.

All this is really very simple. The trouble is, the process of this letting loose or letting flow, continuous images like a moving-picture, is a secret one can not, with the best will in the world, impart. Because one does not quite know how it works, when it will work or how long it will continue to work, once it is started. The store of images and pictures is endless and is the common property of the whole race. But one must, of necessity, begin with one's own private inheritance; there, already the measure is *pressed down and shaken together, and running over.*

Though maybe at times we are motivated by the primitive curiosity of the proverbial tiresome child who "wants to see the wheels go round," yet even so, there must be a beginning, there is a Gift waiting, someone must inherit the Gift which passed us by. Someone must reveal secrets of thought which combine a new element; science and art must beget a new creative medium. Medium? Yet we must not step right over into the transcendental, we must crouch near the grass and near to the earth that made us. And the people who created us. For the mechanism, the very complicated coils and wheels and springs that are brain-matter or the nerves and living tissues of the brain itself, can be unhinged by disassociation, can be broken; shock can scatter the contents of this strange *camera obscura.* That is, to be scatter-brained or worse.

Shock can also, like an earthquake or an avalanche, uncover buried treasure. It is just as it happens. And there is no formula yet discovered that fits all these bone boxes, these *coffres forts* or the *camera obscura* where our living inheritance is stored. Really, you might say there is no single formula that will fit even two of these boxes or cameras or "safes," where indeed the treasure of the individual life and of its racial and biological inheritance is as a rule, far too "safe," hidden, buried under the accumulated rubble of prescribed thinking, of inevitable social pruning and trimming of emotion and imagination. There is no royal road into this kingdom; you just stumble on it; it is one of those things you really do actually find in your Grimm or your Andersen; it is not just glimpsed in a crystal-gazing ball, out of an Arabian Night's story; it does exist.

It does exist moreover, not only in vague generalities or in sentimental musings, it exists, an actual psychic entity, that continent, for the most part buried, of the self, which contains cells or seeds which can be affiliated to the selves of people, living or long dead. Not just Mamalie's father who was our great-grandfather who made clocks, but people in Europe or people in England or people in Egypt. It is like matching beads. A bit of me can really "live" something of a word or phrase, cut on a wall at Karnak. But really "live" it, I mean. Then, I am for a moment (through a picture carved on a wall, tinted with just such bright colours as we had in our own paint-box) Egyptian; a little cell of my brain responds to a cell of someone's brain, who died thousands of years ago. A word opens a door, these are the keys, it is like that little flower that Mrs. Williams called a primula, that Mamalie called *himmelschlüssel* or keys-of-heaven.

That is how it is. A word opens a door or just a few remembered facts doled out, apparently indifferently or received apparently with little or no interest, become later, a clue, a focus, a centre or node for the growing branches of ideas or imaginative speculations. It was not really so very important that Mama had been, for instance, to a fortune-teller. Yet it was important. I do not remember when she first told me about it, yet I remember the strange gap in consciousness, the sort of emptiness there, which I soon covered over with my childish philosophy or logic, when she said, "It's funny, the fortune-teller told me, I would have a child who was in some way especially gifted."

It was that that stuck. We were not any of us "gifted," as if we had failed them somehow. I can not say why we cared, or maybe the others didn't care. But there should have been a child who was gifted. How could I know that this apparent disappointment that her children were not "gifted," was itself her own sense of inadequacy and frustration, carried a step further?

Mama told me how she heard a voice outside one of the empty class-room doors.

"What voice, Mama?"

"O, it was only Papa, it was only Papa; he said, 'who is making this dreadful noise in here?'"

"Who was?"

"Well—I was alone, I went off, I was alone, I was hiding, I was singing—"

"O—I see—didn't Papalie know—"

"Well—I don't think he meant to hurt me, no, I know he didn't mean to hurt me."

"Maybe it was someone else making noise in another classroom."

"No—maybe it was—yes, but anyhow, I was so hurt, I never sang any more, not even in church."

So Mama never sang any more, though her speaking voice had a rare quality, it was low and rich and vibrant. Yet, it couldn't have been just that, that stopped Mama singing, there must have been other things as well. Anyhow, she told me that and she told me how she went to a fortune-teller.

Mama did not tell me that the Spanish Student came into the fortune-telling, but she did tell me about the Spanish Student. I see the Spanish Student, in capital letters like that, like a play or an opera. It was perhaps a play or an opera to Mama, something that might have happened, which did not happen, in which she played a small part, in which she might have played a leading role.

She told me about Madame Rinaldo who had taught singing at the Seminary, and who had been an opera-singer, and the aunts often talked about her and we still had some of the old things that Madame Rinaldo had left Mama—a crown, bracelets, stage properties, veils, and robes in an old chest in the attic. Madame Rinaldo did come into it, but Mama never said she imagined herself in Madame Rinaldo's crown and bracelets, though I often tried them on, and wished I were enough grown-up so they would fit me, and like Mama, I pretended to sing when no one else was around.

The Spanish Student was from South America; he was at the University.

Mama said, "There was a Spanish Student at the University—he—well, he thought that he was very fond of me. I was sorry afterwards." What was she sorry about? Was she sorry he had gone away or that she had not gone with him, or what?

"How do you mean you were sorry afterwards?"

"I mean," she said, "I forgot myself, I might almost have forgotten myself—I mean he was a stranger, he was a Southerner, he did not understand—I mean, I never told Papa about it, I was sorry afterwards."

I waited for more.

She said, "he went away."

Madame Rinaldo died and left Mama her opera-things, the Spanish Student went away, Mama met Papa at the Seminary at German reading-classes they had for older people in the evenings. Mama said the fortune-teller was just like those people, she just happened to say this or to say that, I did wonder what she really did say. But Mama did tell me that the fortune-teller told her that she would have a child who was gifted.

"You know what these fortune-tellers are like," said Mama, "of course we never told Papa."

I did not know what fortune-tellers were like, I had never been to a fortune-teller, though we played fortune-telling games, Hallowe'en with candles floating in a bowl or in a tub of water. We did not "see things," we did not conjure up the dead or see ghosts. But now, through some curious combination of circumstances, distance in time, in space, fever and turmoil of present-day events, certain chemical constituents of biological or psychic thought-processes are loosed—whatever thought is, nobody yet knows—and the film unrolls in my head, and it is impossible not to see how Mama went to a fortune-teller.

[II.]

Fortune Teller

. . . tongues in trees, books in the running brooks,
Sermons in stones, and good in everything.

Fortune Teller

Mama went to a fortune-teller who had set up a tent near her painted-cart between the canal and the river, near Willow Eddy.

Three of them went together. They didn't tell anyone about it. Mama went with cousin Edd and one of his sisters. There was a trail of delicate lavender; little flowers grew like moss in the spring-deposit of sand on the river side. There was a shelf or island of sand beyond the bank, and Mama stood watching the river swirl round the sand-shelf or sand-island.

The bank across the river with its low bushes and shelf of pebbles and sand, was exactly like the shore of the real island further down the river where they had their summer picnics.

There was the round summer-house on the island, with the lattice-work like the one in the Seminary grounds, but the one in the Seminary grounds was covered with jasmine and honeysuckle and small yellow-roses; they were a sort of tea-rose; the girls from Charleston called them cherokee-roses. At one time, there had been many girls from the South; they ran through the halls and whispered and laughed in corners and did dance-steps behind doors, while they waited for a Mademoiselle or a Fräulein or one of the Sisters for a lesson.

In those days, Mama wore a little frock, cut *en bateau* at the shoulders and she would peep from behind a sofa or a big chair or through a crack in a door, at the swirl of lace when they had a party, and the trailing shawls. Once suddenly everything was very quiet and she heard feet moving overhead. She held her spoon in her hand; she listened; her ears were set close to her head and her high forehead contracted with the intensity of her listening. It was not just the footsteps, it was something different. There had been the ringing of church-bells, but Mama had always known the bells and as she grew older, she could tell from the hymn played from the cupola on the church, what had happened; she could tell whether someone was born or someone had died and what sort of person, how old, if it was one of the old Brothers from the Brothers' House or one of the Sisters from the Sisters' House or "Aunt" Carlotta or "Aunt" Maria from the Widows' House.

It was easy to understand the hymns and carols, to interpret their particular message, if almost the first thing you could remember was the sound of the trombone-notes from the cupola that was like a little extra open temple, placed on top of the church roof. There were the four separate clock-faces and eight pillars, something peculiar and special and their own, not like the ordinary steeple of the church across the river, where sometimes a group of the girls went, but mostly the girls wanted to go to the Old Church, as they always called it. It was not the sound of footsteps nor the fact that they had stopped, nor the bumping and scraping of trunks on the upper floor. That happened from time to time, if a letter came or even a special messenger arrived to say that Elsie or Isabella or one of the many Virginia's or Carolina's or Georgina's father was ill, or even that their mother was dead.

Of course Mama did not remember how she had listened, how suddenly the dining-room was empty. She did not remember the oval-mirror facing her, she did not look into it. It was part of her consciousness, she did not think about it. She might remember it now, if she were thinking that the bank opposite looked like the island, because she was thinking of cherokee-roses and those clamboured with the honeysuckle over the lattice of the summer-house down by the creek that, one winter or spring, had so swollen that it had flooded the gardens and the deer that someone had sent Papalie, were drowned.

Maybe, Mama did remember the mirror, if she thought the bank opposite that shelved out with its sweeping branches was like the island summer-house for that would make her think of their own summer-house and that might make her recall the oval-mirror in the sequence, because Papalie had moved it once so that it reflected the grounds or pleasure-grounds, as they called the garden, with the summer-house, and in the convex Claude Lorraine glass, the deer would pass, minute, in exquisite perspective, and a girl would sweep across the lawn, in billowing white like a sail on a green sea and a child would fall down and its hoop would roll on downhill toward the shallow margin of sand that ran along the Monocacy creek, that at times seemed almost like a small river.

But the hoop would not roll in, because there was a fence of woven branches, a sort of pen so that the deer should not wade across the little river, though there was another pen built out so that they could stoop down and drink from the river, and there it was in the glass; the thick green branches, the cone-shaped down-sweep of a large ever-green; maybe a branch of white magnolia or round spots like carefully applied white-blue paint on the bush, that would be hydrangeas or the green-white of the snow-balls, not yet snow-white or the delicate, almost imperceptible specks and flecks that would be the tiny clusters of the flowering-currant.

There would be the burning-bush and plum and apple in their season.

Would Mama remember this? She would remember it like a swirl of notes, that caught in her throat, that would proceed upward by immutable laws and down, and make a sort of graph in the air that was her heart singing. No, Mama was not singing. Really, she never sang, not even in Church with all the others. And she had almost forgotten Madame Rinaldo who had gone away because she could not do justice any more to her pupils, she said, and who had died soon after and left her a chest full of her old stage-properties.

Mama did not think of this. But maybe she did, maybe she was reminded of the box, that she seldom opened; it was hard to get at, in the big Seminary-attic with so many empty boxes; with the girls' trunks, coming and going, their own things were apt to get shoved away into inaccessible corners. The girls had always to be considered first. The older girls who had seemed to Mama like formidable young ladies, not so long ago, were only tall children now; they were her own pupils. She taught drawing and gave piano-lessons, and Miss Helen was the one always to be consulted. It was Miss Helen this, Miss Helen that, everywhere. Mama did not know what had caught her by the throat, it was a change, there was change coming about, not only in the air, because it was spring but she was getting old. Everyone thought it odd that Miss Helen who was so capable, never married.

She would be old; in a few years now she would be thirty. Laura with her rose-damask cheeks, her dark eyes and black hair, had married years ago and Agnes had married brother Will while she and Laura were still school-girls. Of course, someone had to stay with Papa.

Maybe Mama did think of Madame Rinaldo because, standing aside to let cousin Ruth go first into the little tent, she had caught a glimpse of black eyes, long ear-rings, she had thought of a red carnation; maybe she did remember how Madame Rinaldo had been persuaded to dress up in her Carmen costume for one of their New Year's Eve parties or had, at the last minute, found two spangled veils, one white with gold, one black with silver that she said Helen and Laura could wear and be Day and Night, after they had thought it was too late to make up any costumes for Martie Baines' party, because Martie had begged for a party as she had just heard of her sister's engagement in Saratoga.

There were so many parties then, even though Mimmie would say, "I'm afraid I don't care for this new type of girl as much as the old ones, from before the war." Mimmie would not commit herself, no, never, by hinting that for instance, Martie Baines was showy or even common; maybe it was only that things, in retrospect, had seemed gay, seemed bright.

"I am getting old," thought Mama. "What would Papa think of our coming here and we did not even tell any sort of lie, Edd said right out, 'I want to take the girls up the river, maybe even as far as Willow Eddy, the first violets are out or maybe, they will be out,'" but she had seen no violets, only these lavender-mist flowers that sometimes they called quaker-ladies, some people called them bluets, there never seemed a right name for the tiny blossoms, that grew like grass, no leaves, just flowers, *flower of the grass,* what was it? *that withereth and is cast into the fire.*

There was an enormous bonfire when the war was over, she remembered the bonfire, it was in the other part of the town, Papa had not even wanted to ring the church-bells for Victory, though the other part of the town, the new-town had run wild, with a band and speeches.

They were always apart; Papa had taken in the wounded from Gettysburg, making no distinction between the grey and blue; they had even moved out of the Seminary for a time, to leave more rooms free; the army-surgeon had taken over the big reception-room, where now she was always being called to interview parents or to say good-bye to girls who were leaving or to see old-girls who came back. The reception-room had been stripped of its plush curtains, the chandelier had been done up in linen bags and the bell-jars of wax-flower taken down from the long mahogany dresser, in the drawers of which they kept the old photograph-albums filled with pictures of the old-girls.

Many things that were so carefully put away were never brought back, or if they were brought back, they looked different, though Papa had said we must go on, Mimmie had told her afterwards, as if everything were the same; everything must be the same.

But it was never the same after that night, which she could barely remember, which indeed she could not remember, when she faced the Claude Lorraine glass, which had been brought back from the verandah corridor and replaced on their dining-room wall. It had been the night when Papa had assembled the girls, to tell them that there really was war; Helen would not remember but Mamalie or Agnes or even Laura might have told her. Already, before he had officially informed them, one of the more hysterical girls had gone up to the attic, with a lighted candle, to find her trunk labelled Charleston, South Carolina or Richmond, Virginia.

Mama could not remember this, but she had heard the stories so many times; the old-girls, whose crinolines she had just glimpsed in passing, through a crack in a door, were nearer to her, it seemed sometimes, than these "new" Americans from up-state or from Dayton, Ohio even. But we are a small-town, we are small-town people—that was a new idea! The old-girls had said it was almost like going abroad to come to Bethlehem to the Seminary and their fathers would come for them at Christmas and stay at the Inn, and there were coaching-parties and groups of riders along the sand-path that ran beside the canal.

At one time, the town had even been a sort of summer-resort, though that seemed odd, as the summers were really very hot. But people from the South came up and brought their servants and horses, and had boating-parties, up and down the river, even shooting the rapids and exploring the water-gap and sometimes going further down the upper reaches of the Delaware; the Delaware ran into the sea, of course. Mama had never been to the sea.

The river was wide or the spring floods had given it a further dimension, and the sun caught the light and flung it back in a million little lines and dots, ta-ta-ta-*ta* said Mama and not humming but *thinking,* she swung over to the violins in the change-over to the *dolce* following the *adagio* of the opening movement of the Fifth Symphony.

Of course, I am getting old, thought Mama, and more girls were crowding in now; the town was taking on a new lease of life, but it was another sort of life. Another brisk, aggressive Bethlehem was growing up around the steel-mills. Those furnace-fires glowed, crimson at night, between the river and the mountains. Old Cousin Theodore had even said at vespers, the other evening, that he wondered if in time, the smoke and fumes from the mill-furnaces might not affect the trees.

"O, not the trees, surely," said Aunt Lucia, "why, there is that elm that your grandfather, no, your great-grandfather's father, Helen, but no, I forget it was Agnes' father's people who brought those cuttings direct from *Herrnhut,* and that apple in your Aunt Amelia's garden, Elizabeth, I mean Helen, was grafted from one of the original cuttings that Count Zinzendorf himself brought over from his orchards at Berthelsdorf. And Brother de Schweinitz still has—" Mama remembered the conversation going on, she had heard it all so often.

Mimmie had Count Zinzendorf's desk and some bits of cloth and miniatures, but it seemed the chief things really should belong to Agnes, because Mimmie's first husband's father was a brother to a *Chevalier* in Russia, the one whose portrait Mimmie of course, gave over to the Howard boys.

Brother Will was a Howard from Maryland. Agnes had had eight children, with hardly any pause, in about ten years.

The fathers who came to take the girls home now, stayed on the other side of the river or in the new hotel they had put up for the business men who came back and forth now from Pittsburgh and New York. The line of the mills grew daily and there was a whole colony of Poles or Hungarians or Swedes. They came to work in the mill. One seldom saw them, this side of the river.

"What are you thinking, Helen?" Edd had caught up to her. He had waited outside the tent. Now he followed Helen, "I think you'd better come back, it will be your turn, soon."

"Are you going in?" said Helen.

Edd said, "no," it seemed somehow to Edd that it was unmanly to consult a fortune-teller and anyhow Edd, who was one of the younger instructors at the Divinity College, had had his first serious "call." He was not quite sure that he did actually approve of his sister coming here; it was Ruth who had heard from one of the Stenton twins that there was a fortune-teller and Edd had gone out of his way to find out where the gypsy-caravan had moved to; he had really engineered the party for this would be an occasion.

There had been other occasions; it was true that Helen was not, as they say, as young as she once was, but Philadelphia was not so far away and she could make trips back to town to see Uncle Francis and Aunt Elizabeth. He felt it would be suitable, although they were not so distantly related, that was true.

"What do you think of cousins marrying?" he said suddenly now, for he had always been a little shy of Helen though he adored her, she was like her name, what was that poem of Edgar Allan Poe? *Helen thy beauty is to me . . .*

They had had boy-and-girl expeditions to the water-gap and here to Willow Eddy, "really this is my name," he thought, though Edward did not like people to call him Eddy, yet he thought of his mother whenever anyone did call him, even for a joke, Eddy and he had a sincere deep romantic nature.

Well, that was it. They were perhaps too near. He had been one of the family, another of "my boys" as Aunt Elizabeth would say; they had discussed this before.

"Marry?" said Mama.

She was looking at a broken branch that was floating down the river. "If that branch catches in the island of sand, not in the submerged sand," she thought, "then I will marry Edd." She did not want to marry Edd. But she thought she could help him with his work; he was a little helpless, he had had a "call" to Philadelphia. She knew that he was going to ask her for the hundredth time to marry him. Old Hundred. That was the name of the Choral that Papa liked best. She had played Old Hundred from the time she could remember, from the time they had had to find a book to put on the piano-stool and then they had taken away the piano-stool because the book was too heavy, and fitted her into an ordinary chair on top of the book; "now Helen will play Old Hundred," Papa would say, and they would put down their coffee-cups, and even Mimmie and Aunt Lucia would lay aside their knitting or their crochet work that they kept for "company" as Mimmie would say, as if to explain away the fact that maybe it was a little frivolous to do tatting or even woollen baby-coats when there was so much plain-sewing always waiting in a heaped-up basket in the sewing-room or in Mimmie's bed-room.

"If the branch catches in the sand-island, I will marry Edd." But she knew that the branch would not catch in the little island sand-bank. It was rushing straight for the shelf of sand; there was a tuft of dead foliage that the wind would be sure to catch; the wind would be sure to waft the branch out of the current, or the branch would catch in some layer of just submerged sand. Mama could not think this in that time but that is how the thought would have gone, if she had had time to put it into words. For she knew that she would never marry Edd and she knew there was something more than her own thinking, than her own volition, that would keep her from it.

If she thought in a formal pattern, she would be seeing the river ruled like a page of music; they were not perfectly straight lines, it is true, like a sheet of music, but the ripples did suggest music somehow; the specks of sunlight were the notes, so that there really was—what was it?—*books in the running brooks,* music-books, folios like the old parchment-sheets in the choir-loft that someone said should go to some museum, in Boston or Philadelphia; they must start their own museum, they must collect the old things, people were saying now; that would mean Count Zinzendorf's desk and the portraits and the painting of Zeisberger and the Indians and maybe even those old napkins that Agnes had, with the tiny embroidered crown.

What belonged to them? What belonged to the town? They belonged to one another, since the day when Nicholas Louis, Count Zinzendorf, that first Christmas-eve, called the town Bethlehem. But the town was changing now, the girls who came to the school were different and the old-town was growing conscious of its difference to the new-town and in fact, to the rest of the world about it.

She had never been to Philadelphia. There was the new member of their German evenings that Bishop Leibert had every Friday at the Seminary. There was that Professor Charles from the university, they had teased her about. He was not a young man. Papa and Bishop Leibert talked to him about the stars. She would never marry Edd because she was thinking of the young Spaniard who was a student at the University, who had caught her in his arms, at the close of Commencement exercises when she went back to the hall after they had all left, to be sure everything was all right. They were always afraid of something catching on fire.

"What are you thinking, Helen?"
Helen is my name but the whole world is changing.
"I was wondering," she said, "what sort of branch that is."
"What branch?" said Edd.
"That one, just there, it's got stuck or it's just stopped drifting."
"O—there—" said Edd.
"Yes," said Helen.
Now the wind caught the dried tuft that was dead pine-needles or a tuft of withered oak-leaves. Things weren't the same any more. Here, the forest was all around them. But the trees the other side of the river by the mills were burnt and blackened and old Cousin Theodore had said the other evening at vespers, that maybe all their trees, in time, would grow sick and die in the fumes from the steel-mills. Bethlehem Steel. They were already shipping steel

all over the country and there were new rails being laid by the old station and a new bridge was being built over the river. The old covered-bridge was still standing but that would go, someone said, soon. If she thought of a carnation, she was thinking of Madame Rinaldo and she was reminded of Madame Rinaldo, by the ear-rings and the red handkerchief knotted around the throat of a gypsy-woman who was waiting to tell her fortune.

If Edd would leave her alone now, she would see everything. She would not see it in her eyes or even at the back of her head. None of it went into her correct formal drawings and her careful copies in oils; she was a good copyist, they said.

It wasn't seeing exactly, it was something that might happen now, at any moment. With the bright glint and reflection of the afternoon sun on the ripples and whirls and eddies of the river, went some incredible horror, yet the horror and the joy were one. The dull-green cone of a pine-tree ruled (like a formal drawing-board divider) the tangle of bushes and low shrubs of the sand-bank opposite. The floating branch might have broken from one of the trees at the far end of the island-like projection, or from the heavy forest-growth, this side.

The branch had got bogged, it was held in some hidden sand-shelf, it would sink now. It was not important and anyway she could do what she wanted even if the branch floated again and swirled toward the little edge of sand that she had named in her thought as the component part of this game or this oracle. There could be nothing wrong about it. In the old days of the church-beginning, back in Bohemia in Europe, they had chosen the first Bishops or Church-patriarchs by drawing lots, but they had done that too, in the Bible. Or there was pulling daisy-petals, he loves me, he loves me not. What would Edd think of her if she went on gazing at the river?

"I think it's going to sink," she said.

"What?" said Edd again.

"O, that branch."

"But," said Edd, "it's made an eddy of its own, it's made its own whirl-pool."

So it had, already the very texture of the river seemed to change because (above the edge of sand) opposite the cone-shaped evergreen on the bank to their right as they stood there, there was a circling of water round the drowning branch.

"It must have got rooted in some near-surface sand," said Edd, not caring but drawn into this game out of his formal sense of politeness.

"Yes," said Helen.

It would sink, it would be water-logged, it would be bogged, and the river would run past. It was not a live branch on a tree, not even a dead branch rushing down the shallow river-rapids to its predicted end. It was caught, it would sink, it was, she thought now, a branch of pine, the dried tufts of brown foliage, she thought, were evergreen; dry oak or elm or chestnut-leaves would had been water-soaked, out of all recognition. It was like an old sponge, it had absorbed all that the river had to give, uselessly, without any value, a sponge in a little saucer, to rub out sums on slates. That is what she was. She, Miss Helen. What was Edd saying? No, he must not say it.

"Helen—" he was saying.

Helen? That is my name. Brother Will always called me *la belle Hélène* when I was a tiny child and so ugly, everyone else said.

That was one of the "things," the other was that she could not sing.

When Madame Rinaldo singled her out from among all the girls, for the timbre and quality of her rich low-toned contralto voice, she thought it must be another joke; she did not really register the fact at all, that Madame Rinaldo considered her, as it were, a gift from heaven, the answer to her own frustrations and years of work and final breakdown and various yearnings towards the old days and the old ways, in this new America.

New York was indeed new to Madame Rinaldo, Bethlehem was old, and here in the core of its theological and scholastic life was this girl with a . . . face. It was pale, not like the pretty vivacious Laura nor even with the fascination of the Slav-eyed much older, Agnes. It was a little static, a little cold, thought Madame Rinaldo . . . but . . . Mama, of course, did not know that she was beautiful, so when the Spanish Student followed her back to the assembly-hall that June day after the closing exercises and caught her in the dark after she had turned out the last little jet of light, she was not so much surprised as stricken, as if she must explain to the poor boy that he had made a mistake. As if she must say, "I know this is all wrong Mr. Fernandez, I know I have caught you by a trick, because you think it is Estelle here in your arms or Elsie, who led the singing of *Auld Lang Syne* so prettily for the old-girls at the end. Why, Mr. Fernandez," she might have said, disentangling herself from the wild embraces, "I am not even one of the old-girls, though in a sense I am. You have made a mistake," stepping back, "I am—I am the Principal's daughter, one of the teachers here, I teach here, I am Miss Helen."

She did say, "I am Miss Helen." She said now, "I am Helen." Edd gave her that security at least, she would always be what she had been, his Uncle Francis' daughter, if she stayed with Edd. But he was too much part of herself, part of the old Seminary, the wisteria over the lattices, the kitchen-end, the bell-shaped or the cup-and-saucer shaped campanulas and the dark-blue *rittersporn* in Aunt Amelia's garden or the wild-pansies they gathered in the mountains or the mountain-laurel. *Rittersporn?* Larkspur never somehow meant the same thing; there were certain words in German that you could not translate. *Zeige mir den Stern* for instance, in what they called Zinzendorf's hymn (Gregor's 46th Metre, it was) because he had been chanting it that first Christmas-eve, when the cattle, lowing from the adjoining room of the log-shelter, seemed to prompt him, indeed actually to tell him, "this is not only like that town, this is indeed that town, Bethlehem."

"It's all right," she said and when Edd said, "what?" again, she turned to pull at the loose bark of a paper-birch that was leaning toward the river.

If she thought of a carnation, she was not thinking of Madame Rinaldo and her Carmen costume nor the gypsy who was, Edd said, waiting for her. She did not want to go to the gypsy now. They had started out, full of excitement, and Ruth had had one of those giggling fits. They had laughed and laughed and run along the tow-path, pretending to be children again and Ruth had swung her hat over the canal and the streamer gave and the hat fell into the canal, the way hats do on these occasions, it seemed almost a ritual, and Edd got it out with a pronged branch. It was the way picnics started in the old days, and when they shouted and someone could not stop laughing, Mimmie would say, "Louisa (Jean or Bella), you be a little careful. *There's a black rose growing in your garden.*" That meant too much laughter, that full suspense before the laughter came, boded ill, there was sadness mixed with joy, there was something terrible waiting if you were too happy, and she turned round suddenly and said aloud, "it's gone, it's either sunk or it's swirled by itself down the river, I will never know now, but it did not catch in that little sand-bank island."

She went swiftly back the way they had come. This little zigzag path might be one of the old Indian tracks, it would lead with inevitable precision (the way this sort of path did) to a spring, to an old ford across the river, to a clearing in the woods, to a burnt-out deserted plot, where maybe there had once been a collection of farm-houses or one of the early missions, upon which the unfriendly tribes had fallen.

No one remembered those times, of course, but there was something in the air, at the turn of the season, there was a trap-door under her feet some-times when she was happiest; there was a certain corner or a certain turn, a certain slope of the bricks in the side-walk past the old bell-house, that would invariably be associated with that feeling and she would run as a child, across the harmless stretch of bricks or irregular paving-stones as if one particular square of bricks or one particular paving-stone might give suddenly, like a spring-trap set for an animal in the forest, a wolf—were there once wolves here? There were deer, certainly; she would fall down, and the trap would snap shut over her head and she would fall and fall. So it was now, so it was on this path; she must walk very quickly or just there, where the fronds of last year's dried fern made a little mat across the surface of the path, she would step on a hidden spring, even here in the woods, maybe here especially in the woods, the danger lurked. It might have been hearing the older boys talk about *The Pathfinder* or *The Last of the Mohicans* when she was too little to understand that the Indians had long since, left this valley.

She did not herself anyway, at any time care for Fenimore Cooper, though they had a sort of proprietary interest in *The Last of the Mohicans,* for there was his grave actually in their church-yard and there were the other Mora-vian Indians in rows with their names.

They had a list of their tribal marks, a turtle, a lizard, a fox or a weasel, along with their baptismal names, Anton, Daniel, Amos or Michael, written in the church-chronicles, where all their own family names were written, with the dates when they had left Europe or England, and the time of their arrival in America from the church-boat.

Some of them had gone from *Herrnhut* to Rotterdam, to London and then across to Charleston or direct to New York. If she thought of New York, she thought of Madame Rinaldo and the stories she told of the New York Opera House, and now she thought of the box of red carnations that had arrived after Mr. Fernandez had gone.

She must settle this thing, she must step on the mat of dried fern, she must not swerve this side of the path, she must not turn quite out of her way, round the cluster of young larches that blocked escape from her right, as she neared the patch of fern.

Once and for all, she must step right on to the thing that threatened; was she a little crazy? There was Crazy Peter who had run after them, all along the inner side of the new cemetery fence; Nisky Hill would always be associated now with the spectacle of Crazy Peter and even death itself masqueraded as this poor wretch who shouted, "look, look," while she did her best to look away and did at last look away and ran and ran between the rows of grave-stones toward the precipitate far edge, where trees made a natural barricade, yet it was unnatural too, to stand on solid ground and look over the tops of the trees as they went down the embankment to the railway tracks below, to the tow-path, to the river, to the mills that lined the far side of the river.

Even in the day, great sudden bursts of flame would be clear against the sky and there was the terror, the thing pursuing them, "But why did you run away?" said Emily Engel catching her up, "he couldn't get through the fence." She was amazed at the question. Why had she run away? Why had Emily *not* run away? And now they were in a dilemma as they picked their way along the embankment edge. There was the excitement of that danger, too, but even if one slipped off the edge, Emily said, one wouldn't fall far, for the trees grew thick, and their trunks (if you leaned over) showed almost upside-down like tree-reflections in water.

The trees grew flat against the straight wall of rock and stone. But the grass was thick at the top, one could clutch that if one fell, and they wandered along, almost it seemed walking on the tops of those trees, looking for the sparse clusters of green-white flowers that grew in little bunches, wax-white with the wax-green markings and the stem, slightly hollow. They sat on the grass picking the tangled stalks from their hats and fitting them together in neat bunches and Emily said, "We ought to tell." How could they? What would they say? Who would they tell? And Emily Engel said, "but if we do tell, they will lock him up again." Should they tell, shouldn't they? "Someone else will see him," said Emily, "someone else will tell." The flowers were called Stars-of-Bethlehem.

"Helen, Helen, where are you going," said Edd, "that is not the way."
"I know," said Mama, "I know."
She had suddenly stepped aside after saying to herself that she would, this

time, put her feet firmly on what she suspected was a trap. She knew it was not a trap. They flung a baby to wolves in an old steel-engraving in the hall outside Aunt Carlotta's rooms at the Widows' House. Or didn't they? The wolves were chasing the sledge, it was a Russian scene. Or was that a story she and Laura had made up? They made up stories about the pictures. There was the engraving, *Zeisberger preaching to the Indians.* There was *Washington at Mount Vernon.*

There were various prints of the old town and scenes of the Indians. There was the story of Count Zinzendorf and the puff-adders; she could not remember if she had seen an engraving of it, there should have been one. She saw Count Zinzendorf sitting in the tent and she felt Martin Mack's terror as he perceived the two adders making their way under the flap of the tent and Martin Mack called out as his palms slapped down on the earth and moss and dead leaves and jagged stones.

Mama could almost feel her hands now, scarred with the edge of a rock, as if she were Martin Mack.

When Martin Mack lifted the flap of the tent, he saw that the puff-adders were sliding like phantoms or ghost-adders (so light, making so little noise) actually over Count Zinzendorf's scattered papers.

She looked at her hands. They were the hands of Martin Mack; the puff-adders had slipped away, the strong firm fingers were metal-jointed, that was from felling trees, no, why no, that was from practising Czerny and scales with the special pupils. Scales? Scales fall from one's eyes, scales weigh out sugar and cherries, one pound of sugar one pound of cherries, scales are laid in geometrical precision along the puff-adder's back, its puff is filled with venom. Gift? *Gift?* That was the German for poison.

She had been too old to cry, it seemed, from the beginning. Madame Rinaldo had been right when she had thought the features a little cold, frozen even.

She was authoritative, even dictatorial, some of the younger teachers said. Miss Helen was "bossy" even. But she was acting a part. She was Miss Helen, the Principal's daughter, someone had to do these things, arrange lectures, see the old-girls and their parents or even their children when they brought them back to enter the school. She was mechanical; even her playing, they said sometimes, was mechanical. Her drawings were perfect, "I was," Mama used to say, "everyone said, a very good copyist." She was copying something, the original of which was made clear to her, had been made clear to her, from the beginning. I, Helen, am a good copyist. I am copying Miss Helen, the accomplished daughter, the one who stayed at home after the others married, the one who took over part-management of the old school when Papa began to give up a little, in order to make time for him, so that he could finish up the plate-drawings for his *Diatomaceae of North America*.

She did not stand apart from herself and see herself, she did not even see herself as Edd might see her as he stood, a little puzzled on the zigzag path from which she had stepped.

If she saw herself, it would be because of a temporary embarrassment only, which might make her wonder why she had allowed her skirts to get caught in this bramble, or she might wonder if she could stoop, without Edd lunging precipitately forward to kneel and embarrass her with tugging at the caught fringe of her petticoat. She had always been embarrassed when he offered in the old days, to fasten her skates.

She did not analyse any of her feelings. She did not look back, except in vague generalisations . . . she did not stand apart from herself and see herself with her silver spoon lifted like a baton, instinctively to beat time, ever so delicately to the inflected rise and fall of a voice above her head. Even if her mind had stood apart and seen herself with the criss-cross plaid frock, cut with square bodice like a doll's dress and the full long skirt, she would only so far have seen herself, old enough to tie her own petticoat-tapes, old enough to fasten the two buttons on her cross-strap heelless slippers.

She would not allow herself to see herself like reflections in double-mirrors, getting smaller and smaller. Even, if possibly she had seen all this, she would have said to herself, "I couldn't possibly have remembered. What was it Mimmie had said? 'They were crying because Fanny died, but they couldn't possibly, either of them, have remembered Fanny'."

Now the forest was quite still. How could there be Indians prowling in it, how could there be the flash of a tomahawk? There was nothing of the kind. Just beyond the clump of larches around which the path curved, was the tent where Ruth would be waiting for her. They had not been very far, it was only a short walk really to the river. Yet Mama had been very far. Mama would never know, not with her mind, how far she had been. She put out her hand

and she knew that she would draw it back again because of the sharp sting of the edge of the stone which would cut across her hand when she fell forward. But that was Martin Mack's hand, that was Martin Mack in an old engraving, no not in an engraving, in a sort of series of pictures like the pictures that showed in the slats of the gyroscope, that round box like a hat-box that turned like a top on its pivot. You folded the strips of coloured sheets inside it. A dog jumped over a barrel, a lady leapt through a hoop, a pony jumped over a gate, something of that kind. The colours were bright, crude magenta, blue, vermilion, smudged black shadows. It made her eyes blur as a child, when she had lain on the floor and watched the boy roll his hoop or watched the girl in the bright yellow skirt and tight red jacket, jump the rope. She had watched the flash of the pictures which became almost continuous as the whirling gained momentum and there was no longer the interruption of the brown squares of pasteboard between the slats in the box, that was like a hat-box with slats cut in it like a shutter.

She knew it was a branch of larch now, not a real Christmas-tree that she was touching and she knew that she had only for a second thought of Martin Mack because of the gypsy-tent, set up the other side of the larches, off the main road, that they had had a little trouble finding.

She could not possibly have felt the sharp edge of a stone as Martin Mack slapped his palms, hard on the ground to smack the adders to death, to smack possibly himself to death with that gesture. They were crawling over Count Zinzendorf's papers.

The Indians said he had a charmed life, they were an unfriendly tribe, far up the valley, surely much further than this, but they let Martin Mack and the Disciple go back again and even helped them with corn for their provisions.

They said the Great Spirit had taken Brother Johanan under His protection because, sly and sinister and expectant, the Indians had allowed Martin to choose that very spot to set up the tent though they knew the place was an old burying-ground, hallowed or bewitched by their sorceries and that the soft earth-mound at the back (which they had, with such diabolic cunning led Martin to, foreseeing that he would, in this waste of tangle and green, look upon the flattened ground and the mound behind it, in the light of a little clearing) was a well-known hide-away of a colony of adders.

Brother Johanan who was in God's hand, did not himself question the decision of Martin to set the tent there; the bank at the back would afford shelter against the wind, and leave an extra fold for enlarging the tent or for extra protection against rain.

The Disciple's hand was poised with its quill-pen. We can not know what the Disciple was thinking. Was he comparing some hunting-expedition or outing of his childhood with this scene around him or was he remembering in this desolation, the halls of the great, even whispering a passing blessing on his wife Erdmuth Dorothea's ancestor who, as King of Bohemia, more than two and a half centuries before, had been "the first lordly patron of the Brethren." Or was he pondering one of his poetic strophes as he still poised his pen in his hand, not putting word to paper?

The serpents passed over the paper and his hand held steady.

"Did you see a snake?" said Edd.

"Snake—no—why—" said Mama, startled back now to the actual present, to the sun slanting across the down-sweeping branches of the dog-wood trees that made a background for Edd's round face, to the sassafras saplings that ran along the path beyond the dog-wood.

She felt that Edd had been reading her thoughts; although her thoughts had been in a sense, vague, sweeping, yet she had been thinking of that incident that Cousin Theodore was speaking of again the other evening at vespers, which Martin Mack had recorded in his diary. Mama was proverbially afraid of snakes and the boys would laugh at her and tease her, "look out, Helen, there's a rattle-snake," they would say and watch her jump.

"No," she said and she stepped out of the patch of bramble, giving a decisive jerk to her skirts.

Her skirts brushed free of the blackberry tangle and she stood on the path again.

"No, she said, "but actually I was thinking of that story of Count Zinzendorf and the puff-adders, you remember."

Edd remembered.

"Why were you thinking of that?" said Edd, "they're only little grass-snakes in this part of the valley, I'm always telling you."

Mama said, "well, I don't know, I was watching that branch, it looked like a snake's head looming out of the river."

"O, that branch," said Edd.

They went on along the zigzag path and this time Mama stepped firmly on the path of dead fern and no trap-door opened and the wood was full of fragrance and she stooped to some flat evergreen hypatica leaves, wondering if she would find the first buds to take home to Papa.

She did find the buds, just tipped with blue; a cluster of that particular blue, there was really no word for it, one of the New Orleans girls had once called it *pervenche,* but that was myrtle, what they called periwinkle, and that wouldn't be out until the dog-wood was in flower.

"I must take this home," she said; she was kneeling on the path now regardless of the double flounce of her puce-coloured over-skirt and the moiré facings of the petticoat beneath it. She was kneeling on the ground and her hand, cupped over the evergreen leaves of last year's growth, was the same hand that had lifted a silver spoon, that had kept time instinctively to a rhythm that rose and fell above her head, as she stood in her doll-dress by the empty dining-room table, facing the Claude Lorraine glass that was fastened above the wide sofa, exactly in the middle of the wall.

There was the hand that year after year as the season came round, bore the flame of the beeswax-candle that was given her at the special service.

If they got the candle home and put it on their tree, or got it as far as the tree or as far, some said, as the room the tree stood in, or as far even as the front door, then . . . then . . . she did not remember that there was any special formula for this carrying of the light-of-heaven back through the Church, across Church Street to their own front door. It was a feeling, *Stimmung,* sentiment, it was again something not quite defined.

But this was another sort of fire though the cluster of leaves, growing close to the ground was not unlike the frill of paper that was cut every year by the Sisters as Christmas drew near, to wrap round the base of the beeswax-candles, to keep the wax from dripping. It was a candle, not yet lighted, the tiny points of woollen buds almost hid the clear blue of the flowers that would come out, Mama calculated, in a few days' time, now, if Papa put them in the flat dish with the maidenhair fern that he kept in the little window-space that they called his conservatory, in the alcove where his work-table stood.

Sometimes he had the aquarium full of specimens that he was watching, sometimes the square glass-tank was empty.

Now Mama visualised the tuft of buds as already flowering in the sun through the double windows of Papa's study-alcove.

"Get a stick," she said to Edd, "or something, I want to grub up this root."

Edd knelt beside her and tugged gently at the leaves while she unfolded the clean handkerchief that she had tucked into the opening of her dress between two of the many little cut-steel buttons, that relieved the severity of the straight-seamed bodice, that decorated and "gave body" as Sister Giering had said when they planned this dress together.

Mama folded the square of her clean handkerchief around the roots of the blue hypatica.

Now she saw Ruth wandering across the field looking lost.

"We're late," Mama said; she knew they were late and that Ruth was re-proving them or else she would have come this way to meet them, as they had told her they would stop just out of ear-shot, down the path in the direction of the river.

"You're late," Ruth called across the stretch of grass when Edd hallo-ed at her.

Now Ruth was trailing toward them and Mama said, "I'll be quick, then," and dodged into the tent.

She found herself seated on the folding-stool that was placed to the right of the tent-opening. She saw the white handkerchief. Now she put it down on her lap and opened her palm as the woman told her to, and bent forward with the handkerchief and the root in her lap. She had not wanted to come here really, Ruth didn't want to come alone, she had come with Ruth. Now Mama wished she had waited to hear what the gypsy had told Ruth; some-thing seemed to have annoyed Ruth; it might have been what the woman told her.

Now she wished she had waited outside, the tent was stuffy and small and the woman was too large. "Now the other hand," said the woman.

There was a dark square or patch, said the gypsy, but Mama didn't care. She had decided that this was simply fortune-telling like the games they played, hallowe'en. They scooped out the kernels from walnut-shells and lighted tiny candle-ends and set candles on the shells afloat on the water of the tub, in which the boys had been bobbing for apples. No, it wasn't any-thing important.

The gypsy said again, "there is a dark patch," she drew with her finger, a square on the table as if she saw the patch there, "and a rose," she said. Mama thought, "that is what Mimmie says when we laugh or scream suddenly with some joke, a special sort of laughing that gets out of hand." Mama simply thought, it's as if she could read my mind, not actually what I am thinking at this moment, but the things I may have been thinking while I was waiting by the river and by the paper-birch and in the blackberry-brambles by the clump of larches.

Mimmie would say, *there's a black rose growing in your garden* and that is what this was, the black patch that the woman drew and the rose inside it.

The gypsy still poised her finger, she said, "a star." There was a black rose and a star but Mama thought, "really, I was thinking of Nisky Hill and how I ran, I couldn't have been more than six, I remember because it was the first year I actually went to school and Emily was one of the day-girls and they had a house near Nisky Hill and they moved soon after, across the river but Emily still came to the Seminary to school. This gypsy is remembering what I remembered," thought Mama who would not have run back in her mind to these thoughts, if the woman had not, as it were, recalled them for her.

"Carnations," said the gypsy and she made a great sweep of her arms above what Mama presumed was a heap of carnations on the table. This was thought-reading too, thought Mama, though that didn't really explain anything. She was not trying to explain this, really, it was only that the woman's images and ideas seemed to pick up the thread of what she had been thinking, though even so, Mama would not have re-constructed her thought if the images of the gypsy had not recalled them to her.

The carnations were there piled up and the gypsy swayed in her low chair, her chin tilted back, her eyes closed. She breathed out suddenly, a full deep breath, as if the deep bliss of the inhaled fragrance could not be endured any longer, and then she sank forward again.

Mama did not catch any scent of carnations but she supposed the gypsy was indicating their fragrance by her gesture.

The woman was acting something, or did she really see the carnations? They would be red of course, and why carnations?

"Of course," Mama thought, "yes, I was thinking of Madame Rinaldo, I don't know why, yes, because I thought of Carmen when I first saw the gypsy and how we persuaded Madame Rinaldo to dress up in her Carmen costume for a party and she gave me and Laura long veils and we were Night and Day. And the star—it might be that I was thinking of the veils and how Laura's had the moon sewn on it, lots of little silver crescents, and my gold trimmings looked like stars but we said it would do for the sun."

Then she knew that was not the reason the carnations were heaped on the

table, not real carnations of course, but . . . of course, Mama did not in the
least consider that carnations were there. That would be superstitious, irreli-
gious. But there was some sort of hidden meaning in all this. This was more
than a stray tent set up on the edge of the woods by the clump of larches.
This woman belonged to the superstitions and magic of the old Indian legends. She belonged, did she, to the old, old wisdom, that had led the very
Magi to a star? Star? That is what she had said, there was a black patch, a rose,
there was a star. Or else, she indicated by her curious gesture of abandon as
she slumped forward in her chair with her eyes half closed, there was completion in another dimension, shall we say in one dimension. Mama did not
work this out, it is not easy to work it out for her, but it seems as if the rose
in the dark square was one dimension, the star another. The carnations were
of themselves complete and prophesied rich, magnificent life.

Carnations? Now she saw it. No wonder poor Ruth was angry. What had
this gypsy done to Ruth? "Where is my purse," thought Mama, "I must put
the money on the table, I left my purse with Edd, he stuffed it in his pocket.
Now I must get out and get Edd. This is just a silly game and maybe not
right, maybe sorcery, maybe witchcraft. It is like the games we played
hallowe'en. We threw an apple-peeling over our left shoulder, standing before a mirror, a lighted candle in one hand. *A candle on a candle-stick. The
light of the world.* The apple-peeling might or might not make a letter, S as
likely as not or nothing. It was just for fun.

"I will not have her talking about carnations. It was all over, what there
was of it, there was nothing of it. I, Miss Helen, met Mr. Fernandez in the
summer-house after dark, I, Miss Helen, who had charge of the girls and
Papa was always so very careful and even once almost expelled one of the
Lovatt girls from New York, because she lowered a little basket out of her
window and one of the University boys put letters in it, for her and from
other boys to other girls and I am Miss Helen and I met Mr. Fernandez in the
summer-house.

"The summer-house was veiled in flowering jasmine and it was dark and
we were together, enclosed and there was a wreath of jasmine in his hand,
which he had been making and he wanted to put it on my head. I, Miss
Helen, and he was younger and I only went to the summer-house because he
said he would make a scene, he would stop me on the street, he would go
straight to Papa, he would simply take me away, how could he do that?

"—and then—and then—it was terrible, because I was melted away, why something dreadful might have happened. His kisses were—but I must not think of his kisses because I thought it all out and I got him to go away and he sent me red carnations, but I wrote and told him if he would promise not to send me any more flowers, I would think it over, I would let him know, though I had told him he must go away and I could not think about it.

"Why, he was from South America and he was a Catholic, I knew because he said I was like their Lady of the Carnations, he said, then he said it in Spanish, carnations; it might have been roses, but he said carnations. He said they had a festival when all the girls carried carnations to the Madonna, but carnations in Spanish scenes, are the flowers, girls in lace mantillas wear in their hair, and their lovers serenade them and that is all ridiculous like Nita Juanita, a silly song, a castle in Spain.

"Why," thought Mama, "no wonder Ruth was angry."

She thought now, only about getting away. She heard Edd and Ruth moving around outside, there was a voice and then feet scuffling a little as if someone were kicking dead leaves. The thought of dead leaves reminded her of the matted fern on the path and the thought of a trap-door; it was happening now, under her feet as if the folding-stool she sat on, like the stools they carried on their sketching-trips, might simply drop through a hole in the floor, a hole in the earth, like that Greek myth in the *Tanglewood Tales* that they used now as a reader in some of the special classes; there was a girl who was raped away—raped, yes, the word somehow sounded like something out of the Bible—by the darkness, by Dis, by Death.

That was the feeling; suddenly, she knew it, she recognised it, it was the black-rose that Mimmie would speak of, that black-rose of despair when one was happiest (that was it); if one were happy, swept quite, quite away, melted away so that even your name was forgotten . . . when someone sounded words from a deep-sea shell, in another language that sounded like the sound of the sea when you first heard it—Mama had never been to the sea—in a deep-sea shell. So far away, she had gone, the summer-house was wreathed in fragrant sea-weed and the jasmine-flowers were froth and pearls from the sea, and she who was a mermaid, ageless, timeless, with a whole set of poetical and biological emotions that there were no names for, that were things having to do with the Tree of the Knowledge of Good and Evil and that were not right.

How much did one give this old-witch? That is what she was. She was talking about a gift. Ruth had explained that one did not pay her but crossed one's palm with silver. She had not asked to have the palm crossed, and now Mama clenched her hands in her lap, ah, here was the handkerchief, here was the little plant.

Papa was given a great pot of calla-lilies, by some of the old-girls who came back for the Easter service. He had planted the tall stalks already among the rocks by the edge of the creek where he had his rock-garden. He would plant the blue flower there. How much did one give? This gift. But this was another gift, here was a gift, the Gift would come to a child who would be born under a Star.

A child born under a star? But that didn't mean anything. Why, every child was born under a star. Hadn't Bishop Leibert said at little Fred's christening—she could remember as if it were yesterday—that every child was born under the Star of our Redemption.

There was a star, there was a black patch, there was a gift, there was a great swathe of carnations . . .

But the carnations were gone now and Mama was standing with the blue flowers pressed against her heart. She opened the flap of the tent and she stepped out. Everything was just as she had left it. Nothing had changed. She had not fallen through the earth, she had not been raped away by darkness. "Edd," she said, "Edd, will you put fifty cents (there is a half-dollar in my purse) on the gypsy's table."

The Dream

The *Ram,* the *Bull,* the heavenly *Twins,*
And next the *Crab,* the *Lion* shines,
The *Virgin* and the *Scales,*

The *Scorpion, Archer* and the *Goat,*
The *Man* who bears the watering-pot,
The *Fish* with shining scales.

Zodiac nursery-rhyme

The Dream

The dream escaping consciousness, is perceived. In one vivid moment, it may be held, circled in a ring of complete understanding. Then it leaps the rope of the tightening lasso, and we are almost glad to see it has gone. The dream is gone now, it is running wild in the pastures of the mind's *hinterland.* It may come back some day lured into consciousness by another related dream, or a pack of them may rush forward and drag the ego, senseless, back with them. This is madness, or is it inspiration?

If you wish to relate the dream, you press it carefully between the pages of the mind's memories and associations. There it is, there it is perfect in con-tour, related to this section of the mind, to that event in the life, to variously associated remembered moments of emotion, joy or pain. The dream? But this is not the dream, there is no life in it, it is really not even the shape of the dream, for the dream is four-dimensional, you can not relegate it to a collec-tion of dried memories and relate it to this one, to that one, just because it has a blade-shaped leaf or a clover-like leaf or a leaf that is cut like a little saw along the edges.

The emotion occasioned by the dream, by that trampling of wild horses, however, may be indelibly stamped on the memory forever.

Now thought wedded or welded inviolably to the word and that word the right word, may give no true expression of the emotion or of the dream-picture. The dream-picture focussed and projected by the mind, may per-haps achieve something of the character of a magic lantern slide and may "come true" in the projection. But to "come true," it must not aim at the outline of a masterpiece, it must not set up Gothic cathedrals or Brunelleschi doors, it must not photograph flying buttresses and bronze gates. It must photograph the very essence of life, of growth, of the process of growing. Therefore we must not strive to compose the picture, this is no formal garden with clipped-yew and paved-walks between box-hedges.

The dream, the memory, the unexpected related memories must be allowed to sway backward and forward, as if the sheet or screen upon which they are projected, blows and is rippled in the wind or whatever emotion or idea is entering a door, left open. The wind blows through the door, from outside, through long, long corridors of personal memory, of biological and of race-memory. Shut the door and you have a neat flat picture. Leave all the doors open and you are almost out-of-doors, almost within the un-walled province of the fourth-dimensional. This is creation in the truer sense, in the *wind bloweth where it listeth* way, in the way the snow falls, in the way a branch of mock-orange blossom runs askew out of its frame, against a high wooden-fence or along a shed where there are rabbits or hens or a kennel where there was once a dog.

The dog is now a myth, for that reason he appears in dreams, unmistakably and in the most satisfactory manner. He wallows in snow-drifts, his ears are like the knitted mittens on that long tape that ran through the sleeves of our winter-coats; he carries, of course, the barrel strapped to his collar and as I fling my arms about his neck—he is larger than a small pony—I am in an ecstasy of bliss. The snow gives back whatever an anaesthetic may have once given.

Mythology is actuality, as we now know. The dog with his gold-brown wool, his great collar and the barrel, is of course none other than our old friend Ammon-Ra, whose avenue of horned sphinxes runs along the sand from the old landing-stage of the Nile barges to the wide portals of the temple at Karnak. He is Ammon or he is *Amen forever and ever.* I want you to know he is as ordinary as the cheap lithograph that used to hang in nursery bed-rooms, he is even as ordinary as the coloured advertisement sheets, bearing his effigy, tacked to telegraph poles that one passed in the old days, along the reaches of the *Bernese Oberland.* You see him on a post-card in a window along the lake of Lucerne. There is a monk standing beside him, we may whisper Saint Bernard. Or, depending on what particular line or telegraph-pole, our particular wire of approach to the eternal verities is strung, we may actually be reminded of our own or a friend's dog or we may know that we have seen in the flesh, the Lion of Saint Mark's or the Lion of Saint Jerome or we may recognise our indisputable inheritance, Ammon, *Amen* from time immemorial, later Aries, our gold-fleece Ram.

Our Ram however, had not gold-fleece, his fleece came from Mamalie's medicine-cupboard. It was pulled off in tufts from a roll of cotton for making bandages or for stuffing pillows or for putting in ears with a little oil or for borrowing to make a quilt for the new bed for the doll-house. Cotton? Was this from a bush that grew in the south or was it from a sheep? I do not think we knew or asked, greater issues were at stake, greater questions though unasked were being answered.

It would be near Christmas again, because Papalie had a great lump of clay on his table, the microscope was put away on top of the book-case and the tray of pens for his red and green and black ink was pushed aside and he had just said, "Elizabeth" (which was Mamalie) "will you keep an eye on these ink-bottles." There was not a breath of a suggestion that any of us might upset the ink-bottles, there was nothing of that in his voice. He wanted room for the lump of clay that was wrapped in a damp cloth and the cotton-wool and the roll of fine wire and the match-sticks.

You may wonder what mysterious occult ceremony requires cotton-wool from Mamalie's medicine-cupboard, a knot of wire and the gardening-shears which did not belong on his desk, match-sticks, a lump of clay. You yourself may wonder at the mystery in this house, the hush in this room, you may glance at the row of children on the horse-hair sofa and at the plaque of mounted butterflies, or at the tiny alligator, who is varnished and looks like a large lizard and whose name is Castor or whose name is Pollux, the children can not tell you for no one has been able to answer that question for them.

Castor and Pollux are, you may know, stars shining in the heavens but though two or three of the children seated on this sofa, watch their father go out of the house on clear evenings to look at the stars in his little observatory across the bridge up the side of the mountain, this Castor and Pollux are not thus Greek, they are not stars in the sky, they are not even a myth out of a later more grown-up fairy-book called *Tanglewood Tales.*

They have not yet read the *Tanglewood Tales;* Ida reads Grimm to some of them at night after they are in bed, temporarily three in a row in the same bed.

Castor and Pollux are two alligators, one is dead, true to the Greek myth which after all, came from the older Egyptian layer of thought and dream. Castor is, shall we say, hibernating in the attic in his tank behind the wire-netting. Pollux shall we say, is mounted on an oval of beautifully varnished wood, a talisman, a mascot, an image—an idol even. Men worshipped crocodiles in the day when men's minds were not more developed than the minds of this row of children.

Papalie is leading them out of Egypt but they do not know that. He is leading them to the Promised Land which is just around the corner, only a week or a few days off, for this is part of Christmas. You may wonder what a lump of clay and match-sticks has to do with Christmas but if you are a stranger in our town, you will be told if you will wait quietly in the other room, under the picture of Jedediah Weiss who is Mamalie's father, who is dead. If you belong to the town, you will know all about Christmas, I mean the real Christmas with a *putz* under the tree. If you are a stranger you will say, "what a funny word, I mean, I don't understand," and Mamalie will say, "O it's German but we never found another word for it"; if you are well informed you may say, "I suppose it derives from something"—"*putzen*" Mamalie may say, "to decorate or to trim."

It is part of the tree, the most important part, the children think. "It is what you put," says Tootie, "I think; I think *putz* is what you *put* on the moss" and they all laugh, for Tootie is very quick and clever they say, not like the Professor's children who are so quiet, but the Professor's children do talk sometimes. Gilbert the oldest who is two years older than Hilda, talks quite a lot and makes jokes. Once walking on the mountains with Papalie, he saw an old goat that belonged to some of the shanty-people, as they called them, behind the mills. "Look, Papalie," he said, "look at that goat, it looks like you, Papalie."

Everybody told that story often, Gilbert was rather bored with it. He had said it when he was only a little boy, younger than Tootie even, who now said things they thought were quick and clever and cute. Papalie came back and told them the story. Hilda who is the only girl, sitting between Gilbert and Tootie, wondered a long time about it. "Does he look like a goat, Mamalie?" Mamalie laughed and said, it was just his white beard and maybe the way his hair curled over his ears. But Papalie's hair is not like goats' horns but if you look and look at him, maybe he is like a goat. Hilda never thought it was so funny, though they always laughed and kept on telling it, though now Tootie said the funny things, like "*putz* is a place where you *put* things under the Christmas-tree."

What he did was, he took his ivory paper-knife and cut off an edge of the lump of clay. The clay lay on the damp cloth, like the dough Ida mixed in our kitchen. He turned back the edges of the cloth around the clay. He took the clay in his hands and rolled it, like Ida makes a biscuit, he pulled at one end and you knew exactly that it would not look like a sheep. But when he jabbed two points in the face and drew a line for a mouth with the handle of his pen you knew exactly what it was, it was eyes and a sheep-mouth though it would not show very much until he had finished several sheep and put them aside to dry.

Afterwards, he would ink in the eyes with black ink and draw a little line in red ink for the mouth. What he did was, he made several sheep like that in a row, like Ida's biscuits on the kitchen-table.

He pulled the cotton-wool into little puffs and stuck the puffs of wool on the sheep. But first he stood them up on legs, that is what the match-sticks were for, and the burnt-out end of the match-stick was the sheep's hooves. He made small sheep too, those were the lambs, and at the end, he made one large sheep. This was the special moment. He cut off bits of wire from the small coil of wire, he bent the wire into shape, he stuck in the wire-horns. All this time, we were sitting on the sofa. The sheep stood up on their match-stick legs but he would not put in their faces until they were quite dry.

He also had little pointed bits of stiff paper which he had inked red for their ears. That is what he did. Later, before we went to bed, when we were a bit older, say, two years older, Mama would get down the old boxes of Christmas-tree things from the attic and open them on the dining-room table. From inside the crinkled faded tissue-paper that a glass-ball was wrapped in, there would come a sort of whisper and a sprinkling of tiny old dead pine-needles would fall on the table, from last year's tree.

We carefully unwrapped the balls, not remembering, hardly remembering anything of what happened last Christmas but already the joy would seep into the room, it would creep somehow under the carpet, it would be impossible even if you wanted to, to shut out the "thing" that the fallen pine-needles on the table conjured up; there was the moment, when it began to happen, when indeed it had happened; that was not the exact moment when the boxes were set down on the table, not even the moment that Mama unknotted the old bit of red ribbon fastened round the flat somewhat battered cardboard box that had cardboard compartments for the separate glass-balls. The compartments were not full for some glass-balls were always broken, but we would go to the five-and-ten and get some more balls, some more silver or gilt lengths of trimming, as we called it, though it was all trimming.

On the table, we made separate heaps of the things; the glass-balls, in their open box were gone over, like toys in a toy-hospital. It was this special moment when Mama said, "see if you can find the end of an old candle, Sister, among the paper cornucopias," that the "thing" began.

The "thing" could not begin if there were not an old end or several almost burnt-out stumps of last year's beeswax candles. Whoever untrimmed the tree, never forgot those candle-ends. It had to be the beeswax candles, the special candles that were used for the children's Christmas-eve service; the red and pink and blue and green five-and-ten boxes of candles could be seen all the year round, at home or anywhere, on anybody's birthday cake.

But this was another sort of birthday; it was, of course, exactly the birthday of the Child in the manger, in whose honour we had arranged the sheep on the moss, yet it was something else, indefinable yet deeply personal, something our perception recognized though our thought did not then relate our Child to the other Holy Children, His racial or spiritual or mythological predecessors. We arranged the sheep on the moss but we did not think of Amen-Ra or the Golden Fleece, or even Abraham and Isaac. We gathered the moss ourselves, on trips to the mountains, or Uncle Hartley or Uncle Bob would make an excuse to get the moss for us. "Helen, all the thick moss has been pulled off the rocks for miles around, it's too far for the children—" or if it were a snowy December, the aunts and uncles might hire a sleigh and go off together and come back, screaming and laughing, with bunches of mountain-laurel. *Fir tree and pine and the laurel bough, We are twining in wreaths to greet thee now.*

It was not only a small Child in a manger, in a stable, in a town that had the same name as our town. It was not only those wooden Wise Men that Aunt Millie had on their *putz* or the star that was clipped onto the highest single upstanding top-spray of the tree. It was not only the smell of the moss, it was not only the smell of the spiced ginger-dough that was waiting under a cloth in the biggest yellow bowl on the pantry-shelf, and yet it was all these; it was all these and the forms of the Christmas-cakes, the lion, the bear, the lady with no arms, like Mrs. Noah, the oak-leaf, the round circle we called the moon, the actual star, the other animals.

The "thing" was that we were creating. We were "making" a field under the tree, for the sheep. We were "making" a forest for the elk, out of small sprays of a broken pine-branch. We ourselves were "making" the Christmas-cakes. As we pressed the tin-mould of the lion or the lady into the soft dough, we were like God in the first picture in the Doré Bible who, out of chaos, created Leo or Virgo to shine forever in the heavens. "We" were like that, though we did not know it. Our perception recognised it, though our minds did not define it. God had made a Child and we children in return now made God; we created Him as He had created us, we created Him as children will, out of odds and ends; like magpies, we built him a nest of stray bits of silver-thread, shredded blue or rose or yellow coloured paper; we knew our power. We knew that God could not resist the fragrance of a burning beeswax candle!

There was the prickly sting of the pine-needles under the rope that fastened the branches. The tree was standing on the back-porch, looped round so that it stood up thin and stiff; at this moment, a child's very ribs and diaphragm would be changed for a whole year with that deep in-take of breath, as Ida or Mama or even the new gardener cut the thick cord that bound the limbs; living limbs were bound and cramped in their rope-cage.

There was that actual in-take of breath (and the almost unbearable out-breathing of joy bordering on ecstasy) when the cord fell on the floor and nobody cared, nobody stopped to pick it up, though later Ida might call through the swing-doors from the dining-room, "will one of you children, undo these knots for me, this is good twine, and put it in the kitchen-drawer."

No; we will not undo her knots for her. We have other things to do, we are busy. Mama has bought a new pot of paste, "unscrew the top, Gilbert, will you. There is a brush too, where have I put it? Harold, run out to the kitchen and fill a glass with water. Where are my scissors? What a lot of old needles this year—take care—here, spill them out on this—" and she spreads out a piece of brown wrapping-paper—"we'll put all the scraps on this. That tinsel looks pretty dull but perhaps we can use it once more at the back of the tree, for filling in. Maybe, you'll find the top of this ball among the papers, Sister, if not, you can fasten a lump of wax to stick the hook in, you know how to do it. Here—" she finds the little candle-stump.

There is still a frayed edge of the original red-paper around the base, stuck to the wax. "I wonder whose candle this was, did you have a green or red one last year?" Hilda can not remember. Last year is a very, very long way off. Last year just after Christmas, they moved from the old-town and the old-house, to this new big house that was built with the new Transit House and the new Observatory that wasn't yet finished, for Papa, when they asked him to come to the University in Philadelphia. Philadelphia even, is quite a long way off, Papa goes in to teach his students at the classes there. Papa is out now at his Transit House, he may come in at any moment in his high boots and his fur cap, like a Russian in that picture they had at the Widows' House that Mama said she and Aunt Laura made up stories about.

Zeisberger preaching to the Indians is hanging in the sitting-room, *Washington at Mount Vernon* is in the hall, the same clock is ticking in the hall that Mamalie's papa himself made. It is a grandfather's clock, it was made by Mama's grandfather.

Everything is the same, yet in the great tide-wave of moving everything is different. What fun to move, "Papa is going to a bigger university, they are building him a Transit House." "What's a Transit-House?" "I don't know, it's something important." They felt alienated but important before they left and the last Christmas-tree was not quite like the others but the reason for that—Papalie was dead, there was a new baby.

There was the painful wrench from the school but that pain too was mitigated; Miss Helen was leaving to get married, anyway. She gave each of her children a *carte-de-visite* photograph as Aunt Jennie called them, the reason Aunt Jennie said, was that the photograph was not much larger than a visiting-card. There were visiting-cards from the Philadelphia ladies who came to call. There were many visiting-cards on the Dresden platter on the table in the hall.

Rosa Bonheur's *Horse Fair* was set on an easel in the front room, there were two rooms with big folding-doors; there had been two rooms with folding-doors in the old house. We folded the doors and pinned up a sheet for the magic-lantern or for pinning on the donkey's tail. There had been parties like that with the children up and down the street, now the children, the nearest, were two miles away. The school was a public-school, "the children are too young," Mama would explain to the University ladies, "to send in to town yet." The new school was horrible.

There was something horrible about the school. We took lunch in a basket and did not get back until four. At the old school we went home at noon for lunch and did not go back to school until two, and then home at four. There were hours which were torture, it was too far to walk home in that noon-hour and back. There was twelve to one for lunch. Now time included a new factor, a school-clock in a public-school ticked differently from the church-clock in the old town. There was no doubt about it. There was nothing to do because Gilbert didn't seem to mind and ran off and played base-ball with the other older boys, but Harold was lonely with no child to play with.

Hilda felt Harold's pain and loneliness but could not translate it into words. Later, she learned to get through the hour by skipping rope with the other girls, children from the near farms and from the small village. "It's not that they're *common*." There were no words for it. They were different, they were younger in mind and reasoning; "don't think I will make any distinction with your children," one of the teachers had said to Mama. It was a funny way for anyone to talk to Mama. We go to a public-school; that is not what is wrong. It isn't that the room *smells* differently, it's the way the clock ticks on the wall.

Now there were sounds. There was the sprinkling of the paper as Mama swept aside the pieces from the old box; there had been the rustle of the old pine-needles, yet it was very quiet. Ida was opening the stove-lid, she was pouring in coal from the coal-scuttle. She would lock the back door. It was dark outside. There was a big maple-tree in front of the house; they had built the house just there because of the three big maple-trees. There were no other trees. The ground had been ploughed up, it had been an old corn-field. There would be a lawn, they would put up the sun-dial that was now in the empty room in the wing that was to have the University books later.

The wing was empty. There were three rooms upstairs in the wing and an extra bath-room, and downstairs, the big empty library and the hall with the wing-door, as we called it. Papa was expecting an assistant to live there, and maybe Eric would come too. Eric and Mr. Evans, whom we had just met, would move into the wing later; then the wing would be full. Now the wing was empty. Ida had a big room over the kitchen. There was Annie, too, but Annie was sitting upstairs with the baby.

There was a farm beyond, fields and cows in a shed. The wind blew through the maple-branches and Ida had put down the coal-scuttle. Harold had brought back the glass of water for the paste-brush. "Here, give it to me, Gilbert," Mama said, for Gilbert had not been able to unscrew the top of the new paste-pot. In a minute, maybe Papa would come in with his beard and his fur-cap and his high boots, then maybe Mama would send us all to bed. This minute must last forever. It would last forever.

The clock in the hall ticked off this minute, so this minute belonged to the clock in the hall, it belonged to Mamalie and to Papalie who was dead. The clock in the hall would strike but even if it struck, it would not matter. Now Mama did not send us off to bed so early. Mama was unscrewing the top of the new paste-pot. She set it down on the table and put the sticky lid on the brown-paper. All around us, were the table, the dining-room chairs, the side board and the china-cupboard with dishes that Aunt Mary (who wasn't a real aunt) had painted for Mama's wedding, with bluebells and daisies and wild-roses.

The University ladies would say, "but aren't you afraid, cut off like this miles from a doctor?" Then they would hush their voices and whisper but behind the folding-door, you could almost hear what they said. The folding-door might be shut but even so, there was a large crack; "now run along Hilda" or "run along Sister," Mama would say and I would go out, maybe possibly to ask Ida to bring in tea on a tray; it was different here, the ladies had to hear everything over and over, maybe even, one had not heard of the Moravians or the Bach choir, or else like Mrs. Schelling, they would talk about Vienna and where they had gone.

Mama had been to Europe on her honeymoon, there were the pictures, *Paul Potter's Bull* was over the bench in the hall that had a lid and was a box really for our leggings and our over-shoes. The *Venus de Milo* was in the sitting-room, there were those two rooms and now here, the dining-room. There was a narrow hall with two swing-doors from the dining-room to the kitchen. There was a hen on the chest across the table. It showed just over Harold's head. It was a white hen. It was sitting on a china basket, if you picked it up, you saw that it was hollow, the china-nest was for boiled eggs.

Mamalie had one too, hers was grey and speckled. The hen sat on the dresser opposite the table. It was the same hen that had sat on the same dresser in the old dining-room.

Aunt Jennie brought Hilda some Chinese lily-bulbs and showed her how to plant them in a bowl with water and pebbles. Mama said Hilda could have them in their bowl in the old dining-room on the window-ledge. There was that window that looked out on the alley, which was really not an alley but a lane, but Uncle Hartley said *allée* was French really, and maybe their alley was named *allée* by the Marquis de Chastellux when he came to visit the town. Uncle Hartley made fun of all the old things and all the same they were true, Aunt Aggie said.

There were two other windows in the old dining-room and a door through a hall like this, to the kitchen and another door leading up a few steps to the back stairs and through to the kitchen that way. There were two other windows in the old dining-room but rather dark as they opened on the porch that was roofed over and anyhow, had the vines growing.

This room has four windows, set even, like windows in a doll-house. The table is in the middle. There are three doors, one leads out to the hall, one to the sitting-room, one to the kitchen. Hilda seemed to be running this over ritualistically in her head, as if it were necessary to remember the shape of the house, each room, the hen on the dresser, the dishes shut away in the sideboard, before she dared turn her eyes actually to the table, to the tangled heap of tarnished tinsel, to the empty box that had held the glass-balls, to the miscellaneous collection of gilt stars, red, blue and pink cornucopias and paper-chains that were torn, that Mama called the paper things; there were dolls too in that lot, several babies in paper-gilt high-chairs, some dancers in fluffed-out short white petticoats standing on one toe, and angels sprinkled with glistening snow that was beginning to peel off.

Ida said could she go upstairs, was there anything but she stood at the door. She had on her blue kitchen-apron. She came in and the door swung-to behind her. She looked at the things on the table. She said, "could I take the baby in my room?" She wanted the baby in her room. I should have liked the baby in my room but he did not like me very much. Mama said, "leave him in the crib if he is asleep." Ida might wake him up, she could, why couldn't she take him to her room? What did the Philadelphia ladies whisper about? The house was very quiet. The clock in the hall ticked, you could hear it tick even if you did not stop to listen. There was scraping on the front door-steps, that might be Papa coming in—or it might be—what did the Philadelphia ladies think could happen?

We were not all alone, there was Mama, there was Ida, there was Annie with the baby upstairs. Upstairs, seemed rather far away. In the old house, the clock was at the top of the stairs, and the stairs went straight up, here they turned on a landing and you could not slide down the banisters. On the stair-wall, were some of the photographs of Venice, there was a lady too, lying on the ground with a big book open, and a skull (like Papa's Indian skull on his book-case), she was someone in the Bible, Mary-someone in a cave with long hair.

We would get some small rocks from the stream that ran in the little valley, several fields below the house, for the cave on the *putz*. Ida had found another box on the floor, she said, "you've forgotten a box on the floor." Gilbert said, "no, I put it there." Ida lifted the box from the floor, none of us had forgotten it, it was a heavy card-board box tied with string. It was the most important. It was the box with the animals and the little hut and the wooden fence that folded up that would run round the edge of the moss and make a sheep-field for the sheep to graze in. Ida said, "where are the scissors?," she cut the string of the box.

There was a picture of Pandora and her box in the *Tanglewood Tales* that Miss Helen read us, Friday afternoons if we were good, instead of lessons. Pandora let all evil things out of the box but there was one good thing left; Miss Helen explained it was a myth. The good thing left was Hope.

Everything would turn evil in the box but there was Hope left, after everything evil had flown out.

We knew what was in this box, it was an ordinary cardboard box, a large one of very tough brown paper. Ida started to roll up the string, the way she did, then came to the knots and looked at the string. Then she dropped it on the spread-out brown paper that was for the scraps. It was not time to take out the animals, we did the Christmas-tree things first, but now Gilbert jerked at the top of the box that did not fit like a lid but was like a box over another box. It stuck and Gilbert jerked at it.

Ida said to Gilbert, "hold the box," she got her fingers under the edges and worked the top of the box up; it stood like a box on a box, and Gilbert's head above it was like the jack-in-the-box when the little wire-catch is pushed off the fastener of a jack-in-the-box box.

Jack and Jill went up the hill. *Gil Blas* was the name of a book Uncle Hartley had, but Gil was a man and not Jack. "I mean, if I am Jill in the picture, the way we played when we were children," thought Hilda, "then I would be Gil who is short for Gilbert, but we never call him Gil but Gib sometimes. He did everything first, he made up names for things when we were children, he called me Deetie, people call me Deetie sometimes, that was Gilbert's name for Sister, Mama would explain and people would laugh. Sister or Deetie or other names but if I were Jill, I would be Gil, we would be twins." There were the two alligators at Papalie's who were twins, they were called Castor and Pollux.

Castor and Pollux, Eric had told us, were really stars in the sky. Ida said, "take care, don't jerk at it" and pushed Gilbert's hands away, Harold slid down from his chair and stood looking. Mama called, "is that you Charles?" as the front door opened and then shut and Papa came across the hall in his boots; he said "*Töchterlein,*" not looking at Mama. Papa is not a Moravian, he does not go to church, he met Mama at a German class at the old Seminary when Papalie was principal there. I got up and took Papa's hand. It is me he calls *Töchterlein* though that is a German word and Papa is not German. They were not all German really, Mama would explain to the University ladies, they came from Moravia and Bohemia and England though they had Germans and Danes in the brotherhood that came to America, from *Herrnhut,* where they went from Moravia when Count Zinzendorf helped them to get to America.

Some of the very old ladies in the old town could not talk English very well, and Papalie had some German books but Papa had German books too, about the stars. Gilbert interrupted, jerking at the box lid and now maybe Mama won't cut out the gilt-paper for new stars. We paste the gilt-paper on cut-out card-board, both sides, and hang the stars on the tree with a bent bit of wire or with gilt thread, threaded through a darning-needle.

The needles are on the table, the whole of Mama's work-basket is on the table. There is a strawberry of wax for thread and a strawberry with emery-powder for sharpening needles and getting the rust off. There are all these things on the table and Ida is still here and it will get late. The clock will strike. Papa will want his late-evening supper, maybe he wants it now. "I'm going out again," said Papa, as if he knew what I was thinking, but he looked round the table, as if he came from another world, another country, he was a Russian, his fur cap was in his other hand, he was a pathfinder, he had worked on the northern boundary before he came to Lehigh University at Bethlehem.

What it was, was, Mama had Uncle Fred and Uncle Hartley and Aunt Laura and Aunt Aggie and Mamalie and the old school and Cousin Edd and everybody in the old-town really. She had Gilbert and the new baby upstairs. She had Harold.

Ida and Annie belonged to the house and the kitchen and the baby.

What Papa had, was the Transit House now and his classes at the University and people who came to see him about the new instruments and reporters from the papers. What Papa had was outside, the old Observatory on the hill, the walk across the bridge at night, "like a thief or an astronomer," as he would say. What he had was the high walled-in book-shelves here and in the old study, the same but with strips of trimmed leather with brass-headed tacks along each shelf. There was the smell of leather, his old gloves had the fingers cut off so that he could manage all those little screws that were so important on his instruments.

He had a broom in the corner of his Transit House which was really a little house with windows and shutters that opened the whole roof. Snow blew in and he kept a broom to sweep out the snow from inside his house. What he was, was a pathfinder, an explorer. It was cold outside. He went out in the middle of the night again, he would lie down on his sofa in his study or he would sleep in the afternoon. He was outside this, he was outside everything, where was he? If he came in, everything was different, he was cold, his hand was cold. His fingers were long. My hand was small in his hand. "You have hands like your father," they said. He said, his one girl was worth all his five boys put together. He should not say that. It made a terrible responsibility, it made one five times as much as one should be.

They said, "she is quiet like her father." They said, "it's funny the children aren't gifted with such a brilliant father."

What was this gift? It took him out of doors, sometimes several different times at night after we were all in bed. He had a lantern like a captain on a ship. He had thermometers, he had glass-prisms in his new Transit House that Mr. Evans was coming to work with; they made different rainbows of different stars. Mr. Evans told us that, the one time he came. He said he wanted to work with the new instrument because stars were suns, didn't we know that?

What would happen now? He was not this, he was kind about it, was he really interested?

He had never had a Christmas-tree when he was a child.

There was Alvin who was killed or who died of typhoid fever in the Civil War, there was Papa, there was Aunt Rosa, there was Mercy. Mercy had died when she was a very little girl. I held on to Papa's hand. What it was, was, there was Mercy, he told me Mercy had done a sampler, Mercy had read the Bible through before she was five—was that possible? Mercy had asked to give the kitten, that was going to be drowned, a saucer of milk, before it was drowned. That was all, absolutely all, that I ever knew about Mercy.

He said, "Mercy," and gave a little neighing laugh like a horse, "fed the kitten a saucer of milk before it was drowned."

Where was the sampler? Had Aunt Rosa the sampler? Aunt Rosa was very quiet, she and Uncle John had been missionaries. She watched us trim the tree on Christmas, and did not seem to understand; that is, she did not help us, as if she did not know how to trim a Christmas-tree.

No one seemed to belong to Papa when he came in out of the cold, though Mama looked up and Ida said, "will the Professor want his evening-supper now or later?" Everything revolved around him, Mama was sweeping up the bits of gilt paper, she seemed to be thinking of something else. Harold stood looking, Gilbert did not shout now. As if he brought into the house, the night and the cold and when he laughed, it was not like Uncle Fred or Uncle Hartley, it was a sort of snort like a horse makes. "Does the Professor's beard really freeze in his instrument?" the University ladies would ask. Sometimes, they seemed to think it very funny, sometimes they were serious and said, "such devotion" or something of that sort.

Yes it was true, he must be cold out there alone with the snow drifting into the Transit House. Who understood this? Who understood what he was doing? Mama didn't. "I can't follow my husband's work," she would say to the ladies, "I don't pretend to."

Papa did not tell us what he was doing. Mr. Evans seemed very surprised that we did not know all about it. "Your father is doing very important work," he said, "I suppose he's explained it to you, on variation of latitude." We did not dare ask Mr. Evans what that was. Some day, I would ask Papa. I did not want to know really. What it was, was that he was separate, he was not really part of this table with the glass-balls, with the tinsel paper, with the work-basket, with the paste-pot, with the old gilt fir-cones that Mama said we could paint over with some new gilt that she would get when she went in to shop in Philadelphia.

But once at Christmas-time, he had taken us out, as if what he did must be different.

He said, "I want to take the children out."

Mama said, "but now? It's late, it's snowing."

He said, yes he wanted to take the children, we were surprised. Mama and Ida got our coats and mittens, there was snow on the ground and the lamps were lit along Church Street; we walked along with Papa in the snow, in the dark, after dinner along Church street.

The snow swirled around the lamp-posts and ahead, you could see the circle like an island where the next lamp was. We got past the grocer's and on down the empty street; we turned at the end by the Seminary, up Main Street where the stores were. We stopped in front of the big toy-store or the big store that had all the toys in the window for Christmas and he told us to stand there and look at the toys and find out what we wanted.

We did not know what to ask for, for day after to-morrow or to-morrow was Christmas. We went in and he said, could we find something that we would all like, something that we could all have together. That seemed hard at first but it was very easy really for we found a box of animals, then the lady in the store found a bigger box; there were animals set in the card-board, there were about twelve large animals.

The lady said, they were from abroad.

There was a polar-bear, a camel, an elephant, each an animal in itself not like the Noah's Ark animals.

We brought the box home, Mama said, "but it's not Christmas." Papa said, he got us our present now, "but they better keep it," said Mama. But we said we knew what was inside. Gilbert held the box, he would not let Ida take it, we took it upstairs, we could have it upstairs if we would go to bed, "it is very late," said Mama.

Papa shook out the snow from his hat and put his cane in the hat-rack. Ida said, "that was quite a treat going out after dark, wasn't it?" We said, "yes."

Those animals were still in the box and they had lasted, they had not broken, they were very good animals, a little larger than the usual animals but not too large for the *putz*. How often had they stood on the *putz* under the branches, was it two times or was it three times?

We had divided them up, each taking one, then coming round again and each choosing one. Gilbert had first choice and took the elephant but I did not care; for first, I wanted the deer with antlers, and Harold afterwards said, for first, he wanted the polar-bear so we each got our first animal; this was the way we divided things.

We had done this with the Punch and Judy show, of course naturally Gilbert had Punch and I had Judy and then Harold chose Joey, the clown, and he said he liked Joey better. In a way, I liked Joey better too, but it was natural for Gilbert to have Punch, me Judy, like Jack and Jill went up the hill.

Now there were these other animals, one had almost forgotten them, not quite; that was part of it; it was necessary almost-to-forget between the seasons, then the things came almost-as-a-surprise. There were those animals, Mama had given away the Punch and Judy show when we moved and some of our books. She had not given away the Christmas-tree things, they were still here, or weren't they? Suppose we opened the box and found that the polar-bear was gone or the deer with antlers? Must Papa wait? Yet it was Papa took us out, everything was different, we had never been out in the snow at night. The snow whirled round the lamp-posts and each lamp-post was an island with its circle of light on the snow.

Even the snow was different, it looked different, it smelt different.

It swirled round the lamps and the circle under the lamps. We had crossed the road that runs across Church Street to the bridge and the way along the river to the boats, but we never went there in the winter, nor to the island where he took us on Sundays in the summer because he was very unhappy when he was a little boy on Sunday. That is what I knew about him, he was not happy on Sunday and he had not had a Christmas-tree.

He went out in the dark but that night it was snowing so he did not go to his Observatory across the river but took us out. The snow blew round the lamps and we had passed Papalie's house which was really next door to us. Uncle Hartley and Aunt Belle lived there too, and we were going down Church Street, past the Bell House and the Sisters' House and the Widows' House and the old seminary and the Church where we had our Christmas-eve candles.

This must have been on the day before Christmas-eve or was it Christmas-eve?

It was a day set apart; for the first time, we went out in the dark in the snow. Harold was small and had to be pulled a little, but Papa did not carry him. Gilbert ran ahead to the lamp-post ahead and then turned round and waited for us. He scraped up some snow for a snow-ball and looked round but there were none of the school-boys to throw it at.

There was no one on the street, there were no marks of wheels or footsteps across the street.

There were lights in the Sisters' House windows. The clock struck but I forgot to count it. It was the church-clock. We turned round below the walls of the church that was built up, with steps going up. Then we were on Main Street and there were people in the snow, even with umbrellas and carrying packages. He stopped in front of the window where the toys were.

Papalie was dead. There would be some of the clay sheep he made for us, new each year or maybe there wouldn't be. The wool pulled off and got dirty but maybe Mama saved the last clay sheep, they would be the last, with the ram with the wire-horns and the lambs with match-stick legs and one or two lambs lying down without legs.

That was the thing.

That was why I waited and why I wondered if maybe Mama had given away the animals, it would be terrible; it had been so terrible that I forgot to care, I did not really care after the first minute, when we came to the new house and everything was empty, with no curtains and we slept on mattresses on the floor.

In the empty room, the next day, I said, when Ida and Mama were un-packing the wooden boxes, "can I have my Grimm?"

Mama looked at Ida and Ida looked in the box where the books were, "I can't find it," said Ida, "there is so much to do, run along, run along, ask the packing-man where he put the hammer."

Mama looked at Ida, there was something wrong.

"But I'll look," I said, then Mama said, "O, I remember now—" and Ida went out herself to find the hammer.

"I thought at the last, as the fairy-book was all coming to pieces—" I knew the worst.

In the new house with everything empty and no clock ticking in the hall, I knew that something dreadful was going to be told. It was so dreadful that I really didn't care. Didn't Mama say we were getting so old now—didn't she add—"some poor child who could not have a book—" didn't she say—what did she say? It was the first thing I asked for, when they began unpacking the boxes but it did not matter. How could it? It was only an old book, it was falling to pieces, she had given it away, some other child—I forgot it then, or rather . . . the pictures came true in my head.

I could see the first picture, the bright princess with the ball and the frog in the corner to the left and then the large dancing-bear and the girl going up the glass-mountain with spikes she stuck in the ice-sides of the mountain.

I was part of the ice of the mountain, it had happened long ago.

I did not care. Why should I? There was the princess with the brothers, she had long hair and lilies in her arms, there were ravens and the little hut in the forest. All that had been given away—it was not possible—you can not give away yourself with a star on your forehead and your brothers flying over a tower above a forest and a hut in the woods.

That was the book, it had gone anyway now; Grimm was the children's Bible Mama used to say. It was fairy-tales, but so was the Greek myth *Tanglewood Tales* that Miss Helen read in school, it was the same kind of thing, it was real. It went on happening, it did not stop.

It was like the Old Man on Church Street. He was on the other side of Church Street across the alley; the alley was really a lane with bushes; the bushes ran up one side to the street where Miss Macmullen lived who had the kindergarten, past the Williams' house. It was the Williamses who said that Papalie was our grandfather.

I was running along the other side of the street with Gilbert and some of the cousins and some of the boys that Gilbert played with. We all stood outside the iron-rails where the Old Man lived. He was with his gardener, the Young Man who had a knife or a pair of garden scissors in his belt. The Old

Man looked at us. The garden was narrow with a path between the wall of the next house and his own house.

He was a tall old man with a white beard. He said, "let the girl come in." I was the only girl in the crowd of Gilbert and the cousins and the other boys. So I stood at the gate and looked at the path and felt strange but I was the only girl so I stepped across the gate-stone to the path in the garden.

The Old Man said, "what do you want, you can have whatever you want from my garden." I looked around and I saw a tall lily plant, I said, "I want a lily," so the gardener or whoever he was, the Young Man took his knife from his belt or his pocket and cut off a white-lily.

Then I went back but the boys had all gone, Church Street was empty, I went in our front-door and Mamalie and Mama were sitting in our sitting-room like they did, talking and sewing. I showed them the lily, it was just the lily with hardly any stem; they said, "but it would be lovely on Papalie's grave," so I stuck it in the earth that was not yet grown over with grass, on Papalie's grave.

Then the Old Man said he would send his sleigh whenever the girl wanted it, so the Gardener who was the Coachman, came with the sleigh. The streets were all empty but we drove round the town. I sat with my back to the driver and Mama sat with one boy on either side, under the fur-rugs. "Whenever you want the sleigh, just ask me," said the Old Man, "it is because the girl asks; if she asks, I will send the sleigh."

One day I said to Mama, "what has become of the Old Man on Church Street who sent me a sleigh?" Mama said there was no old man on Church Street who sent us a sleigh. I said, "but don't you remember, I sat with my back to the driver who was the Young Man who cut off the lily for me that you and Mamalie told me to put on Papalie's grave, that I did put on Papalie's grave." Mama said no, she didn't tell me anything like that. Anyhow . . . when I came to think about it, this was the odd thing; the lily was flowering and the streets were full of snow. It could not be worked out. But it happened. I had the lily, in my hand.

Now Papa's hand was in my hand.

He called me *Töchterlein* and I couldn't help it. It made a deep cave, it made a long tunnel inside me with things rushing through.

There was another book with a picture; Mama cut it out. Because Mama cut it out, it was there always. People do not cut out pictures from their books, sometimes the pictures work loose but they can be pasted back with that sort of paper that Uncle Hartley showed us that Papalie had for his special plates that had to be put in the book when he was making up the book he wrote about water-things that grow in water, that he showed us under the microscope.

You could see what Papalie showed you. You could not see what it was that Papa went out to look at . . . the picture was a girl lying on her back, she was asleep, she might be dead but no, Ida said she was asleep. She had a white dress on like the dress the baby wore in the photograph, Aunt Rosa sent Mama that Mama tried to hide from us, of Aunt Rosa's baby in a long white dress in a box, lying on a pillow. The baby looked as if it were asleep, the girl in the picture looked as if she were dead but the baby was dead and the girl was asleep and the picture was called Nightmare.

The book was about *Simple Science,* someone gave it to us when we could not read, but Ida told us what the pictures were about. We knew about the snow anyway, we knew the snow was stars, that each snow-flake had a different shape, we knew that and we knew about the kettle, at least we had seen the kettle in the kitchen with steam coming out, it seemed a funny thing to put in the book, but it was, Ida said, to explain how the steam happened but I did not care about that. What I wanted to know was, what was a Nightmare, was the Nightmare real?

It was like an old-witch on a broom-stick, it was a horrible old woman with her hair streaming out and she was riding on a stick, it was a witch on a broom-stick, but the book was science, they said it was to explain real things. Then a witch was real, in Grimm it was a fairy-tale but a witch in a book called *Simple Science* that someone gave us, must be real because Ida said that was what science was. Papa and Papalie were working at real things, called science; the Old-Witch was riding straight at the girl who was asleep. It was a dream; Ida said, Nightmare is a dream. That picture is to explain what a Nightmare is.

We did not like that book, we did not notice when it was lost or given away. It was only the one picture. Mama said one of the children had screamed in the night that a Nightmare was coming. It must have been Harold, for I do not remember that I screamed. But somebody screamed, it could not have been Gilbert, Harold said it was not him.

"It was only a picture, I cut it out," she said; you could see how she had cut it, the picture was gone.

"What is a Nightmare?"

"It's a name for a bad dream."

"Why is it a mare? Uncle Hartley said a mare is a mother-horse."

"I don't know."

"Is it a night-horse?"

"Well, no, I don't know, it's only a dream anyhow."

A nightmare is a Mare in the night, it is a dream, it is something terrible with hooves rushing out to trample you to death. It is Death. It is the child with the ruffles on her night-gown who they say is asleep but she is dead. Or is it Aunt Rosa's baby who they say is dead but maybe it is asleep?

He goes out in the Night.

"What does he do there? Why does he go across the bridge to his observatory?"

"I've told you and told you and *told* you, he goes out to look at the stars."

"Why?"

"Because that is his work, it is his—work—well he is a Professor, isn't he? They give him money for teaching students, if he did not make money, where would you be, you wouldn't have a house, you would have no clothes to wear."

That is what he does. He goes out to look at the stars. Of course, now we are so much older, it is very simple, anyhow his Transit House is here just across the field that will be a lawn next spring and they will put up the sundial that says *Tempus Fugit* which Mama says is Time Flies. Time flies. He goes out to look at stars that have something to do with time flying, Mr. Evans said, that has something to do with winter and summer and the way the earth goes round the sun. "The earth goes round the sun," said Mr. Evans. As if we didn't know that. If people tell you things like that, they talk to you as if you were in sunday-school.

We would have asked him more but it's better not to have things like that explained; Papa does not explain them. Mr. Evans made it seem clear and simple like that *Simple Science* that said everything in the wrong way. We do not have to have a book with a picture of a kettle on a kitchen-fire to tell us what steam is.

But there are things that we must know. We must know why a Nightmare is called a Nightmare, but no one has yet explained it. He neighs like a horse when he laughs, he had a horse to ride when he was on the northern-boundary which is that straight line on the map that separates us from Canada that he helped draw, that he had a dog-team and Indian guides to help with him.

There was a dog with a barrel on his collar and a person asleep in the snow, in our animal book; that was a Saint Bernard dog; the person was not dead, it looked like a girl with hair blown on the snow but they said it was a boy who was asleep, not dead. You must not let yourself get warm in the snow, if you are terribly cold and then want to lie down and sleep because you feel happy and warm, you will freeze to death. The barrel had wine for the man in the snow. When he took us out to get that present, it was snowing. We walked down Church Street, then we turned down Main Street. Ida had put the top of the box down on the table and Gilbert was reaching in the box.

If the animals are there, then it did happen, then we did walk down Church Street, we three together and we chose the animals.

Gilbert unwrapped the top animals, they were the Swiss wooden goat and the Swiss wooden bear that really were not for the *putz* but Mama kept them; then he said, "here's your bear, Harold," and there it was.

It was the polar-bear and Gilbert of course remembered that it was Harold's. How could you forget how we had laid them all out on the floor, then had put them back in the box so as to see them all together, then had begun to choose?

Gilbert unwrapped the lion, he unwrapped the striped lynx that looked like a cat. He said, "I don't remember if this leopard is yours or Harold's." I said, "it's a lynx, it's mine."

I wondered if Papa remembered how he had bought the box of animals. Papa said, "well, I must be off, *tempus fugit,*" which was the letters written on the sun-dial that was still partly wrapped in its old sacking in the empty library. He let go my hand. I looked at him and saw that he was going.

[IV.]

Because One Is Happy

Then, when the storm of death
Roars, sweeping by,
Whisper, Thou Truth of Truth;
"Peace! It is I!"

Because One Is Happy

There was a time-bomb that had neatly nosed its way under the pavement edge, less than two minutes' walk from my door. At night, with carefully hooded flares, a party of the London demolition squad, prodded and poked; delicately, they inserted little wires or tubes or blades of steel and disemboweled the monster.

We did not know the monster was there, until it appeared on show, in the hotel-lobby before whose door it had landed. There it was, neat, polished, with fins like a little submarine, like a large shark. A strip of cardboard drew attention to the immediacy of the danger under which this unspecified, unnamed handful of men had worked. If we of the neighbourhood wished to show our personal appreciation of what they had done, we could do so. There was a collection plate, piled with silver, mostly half-crowns. I dropped in a half-crown and went away.

The silt of time is dynamited to powder, along with the walls of the house on the corner; while one's own walls still shake with the reverberation, there is that solemn pause; time is wiped away. In three minutes or in three seconds, we gain what no amount of critical research or analytical probing could give us, knowledge of the reactions of man in danger, of men in danger, of all men and all women; we shrink, we become time-less and are impersonalized because we are really one of thousands and thousands who are equally facing a fact, the possibility, at any given second, of complete physical annihilation.

There are no national boundaries, I do not think, "that is a German who dropped that bomb." It is something rather out of our Doré Bible, the burning of this or that city, the locusts and plagues of Egypt, the End of the World, the Day (in fact) of Judgment. Though I know that this host flies to incarcerate us or incinerate us, from Germany, I do not think in journalistic truisms, in terms of nation against nation. Light and Darkness have unfurled their banners, and though we take our place beside the legions of Light, we must never forget how each one of us (through inertia, through indifference, through ignorance) is, in part, responsible for the world-calamity. For it seems, we are not able to stabilize our purpose, to affirm in positive and concrete terms, our debt to the past and our responsibility to the future, until we are forced to face up to the final realities in a shipwreck or an earthquake or a tornado or a mass air-attack, in the small hours of the morning.

The noise is not loud enough, the planes follow one another singly, so the mind is still held in the grip of vital terror. Tonight there may be fire, how will we get out? Is it better to stay in bed or crawl out to the hall in the dark, open the flat-door and wait in the entrance, even run down the four flights of stairs and crouch in the air-raid shelter? These are purely mechanical questions, mechanical intellectual reactions, for I know what I am going to do. I listen to hurried footsteps on the pavement outside my window, the clang of fire-engines making off from a near-by station. There will be interminable silence, then that whizz and the wait for the crash, but that will be the world outside.

When the noise becomes intolerable, when the planes swoop low, there is a moment when indecision passes, I can not move now, anyway. I am paralysed, "frozen" rather, like the rabbit in the woods when it senses the leaves moving with that special uncanny rustling, that means the final, the almost abstract enemy is near.

My body is "frozen"; nerves, tendons, flesh are curiously endowed, they re-gain the primitive instincts of the forest animal. I can not move now. Like the rabbit, like the wild-deer, a sort of protective "invisibility" seems to surround me. My body is paralysed, "frozen." But the mind, has its wings. The trick works again. It works every time now. Fate out of an old Myth is beside me, Life is a very real thing, Death a personified Entity. I am on my own, as at the beginning. I am safe. Now exaltation rises like sap in a tree. I am happy. I am happier than I have ever been, it seems to me, in my whole life.

If the "heart of another is a dark forest," how much more so, one's own. Yet when actually we reach the edge of the forest, the way through it, is very clear. Few reach that edge and come back safely, or reaching it once, they block out memory of it; the drowning-man, whose whole life they say, is revealed to him, in a second or a split-second of clock-time, does not, as a rule, repeat the experience.

Our peculiar situation afforded us, not one glimpse of the unrolling film or the tapestry which Fate or our unconscious impulses had woven for us, but we were able, night after night, to pass out of the unrealities and the chaos of night-battle, and see clear. If my mind at those moments had one regret, it was that I might not be able to bear witness to this truth, I might be annihilated before I had time to bear witness. I wanted to say, "when things become unbearable, a door swings open or a window." Dying men see through that window smiling with their sphinx-secret unrevealed. Indeed, there is no personal secret; terror or danger shared opens the door wide. I was not alone, I could share terror but it seems I could not share joy with everyone. It was a universal joy, it was God or Saint Nicholas or the Little Mermaid after she had turned into a Spirit of the Air, or the Holy Ghost if it comes to that, or a wooden Doll with a blue painted-robe, called Mary, under the Christmas-tree. Indoors, it was the Christmas-tree certainly; outdoors, the whole forest of trees. It was a forest with the wind swaying giant branches and the branches brushed across the roof of a low hut.

The swaying of planes, the swaying of branches, the shattering barking of the guns, the gentle soughing of the wind—the mind, the nerves can endure just so much. Then there is the pause, then there is the "thing" which takes different forms, relates itself to some well-remembered scene of childhood or bridge or courtyard of a foreign city, first seen in a photograph, maybe at home, later flashing across the window of a train as something seen before, from a well-known world. So these scenes relate to time, to memory, yet sometimes they become so general, that they are impersonalized, they might be anywhere. So the hut in the woods (when the roar of guns and the sweep of planes over the roof, reaches its peak of the physically endurable and then passes it) may be a forester's hut, built up from a screen-story, or a hut constructed by that facile scene-designer, the unconscious mind.

The hut in the forest might be in the Hartz mountains, on the slopes of Olympus, along the beech-forests of Buckinghamshire, above a cleft in a rock in Norway, on the edge of a lake in Sweden, or in the Berkshires or the forests of Maine. I am lying on a low couch in a corner of this hut. I am alone. The room is dark, I can see what is in it, can construct each stick of the furniture, if I so will. I am however, here (in the hut in the woods) too absorbed with my abstract state of being, to particularize the details of my constructive phantasy, except to register (actually, yet in phantasy) that rain must now be sweeping across the windows.

The window-panes are of solid glass and the curtains are parted wide against another kind of darkness, the soft darkness of the massed array of pine-trees.

Miss Helen let us draw on our slates, provided she said, the drawings were not too silly.

Was a Christmas-tree drawn on a slate, in and out of season, silly? It appeared not. Straight up, like the mast of a ship, then the branches in stark silhouette, a skeleton of a tree, that looks bare; it looks really like a tent set up, with the down-sweeping branches for the tent-folds or the criss-cross of the twigs like the pattern on the tent, like Indians paint patterns on their tents. The tree indeed has come from the forest in which long ago, there were Indians. There was an Indian who said the music coming from our Church was the voice of the Great Spirit. That was when the Indians were coming down from the mountains, one Christmas-eve, to murder the Moravians. Or it must have been Christmas-eve. Everything happened—or should happen in our town—on Christmas-eve. Anyhow, this is all in a book, there were books with old pictures and drawings and photographs of our town. The Indians said, "it is the Voice of the Great Spirit," so the Great Spirit who was the Indians' God, was part of our God too, at least, they went away. You draw the down-sweeping branches carefully, for if you make just silly scratches, Miss Helen says the drawing is not serious enough.

The thing is, that you draw this tree, you rub it out with your damp sponge and polish off your slate with your bit of old towel that Ida has given you to keep in your school-desk for your slate. Once in a while, Miss Helen tells whose slate-rags are too shabby. You get the sponge at John's, where you get slate-pencils and valentines and false-faces for Hallowe'en. You keep the sponge in a little saucer and make excuses to go to the wash-room to wet the sponge, till Miss Helen says you must all do your sponges, first thing in the morning or at recess. There may be a branch of chestnut in water on the school-room window-sill, that has burst into heavy furry leaves. We do not draw the branch of the chestnut, but with the slightest lift of branches, this pine-tree on a slate may be or could be, a chestnut-tree with its candle-sticks of blossom.

This is magic against the evil that stings in the night. Its voice wails at two, at three (it is called the "siren" or the "alert") but safe, "frozen" in bed, there is magic. It is simple, innocuous magic. But sometimes through sheer nervous exhaustion, we drop off to sleep. We are not so safe then.

The serpent has great teeth, he crawled on Papa-and-Mama's bed and he was drinking water out of a kitchen-tumbler, the sort of tumbler that we put our paint-brushes in. Then, I wonder why he is drinking water out of a common glass-tumbler on Mama-and-Papa's bed. He does not spill the water. His great head is as wide as the tumbler but he drinks carefully and does not spill the water. Now I know there are three of us, I do not see their faces, but of course it is Harold and Gilbert.

The thing is, there is another snake on the floor, he may want water out of a glass, too; there is nothing very horrible about this, until the snake on the floor rears up like a thick terrible length of fire-hose around the legs of the bed. Then he strikes at me. I am not as tall as the footpiece of the bed, I could rest my elbows on the bed, like on a table. We spread out the *Arabian Nights* on Mama-and-Papa's bed and I said, "this is a girl," but Gilbert said, Aladdin was a boy. Was he? He wears a dress, he has long hair in a braid and a sort of girl-doll cap on his head. "Yes, yes," Ida says, "Aladdin is not a girl." Is it only a boy who may rub the wishing-lamp? I try it on the lamp on the stand in the parlour, but my wish does not happen, so maybe it is only a boy who may have the wish.

The snake has sprung at me and (though I know that Gilbert has been resting for a very long time, in a place called Thiaucourt in France, and that Mama went to sleep too, in the early hours of the first day of spring long passed, and did not wake up again) I shout through the snake-face, that is fastened at the side of my mouth, "Gilbert; Mama, Mama, Mama."

The snake falls off. His great head, as he falls away, is close to my eyes and his teeth are long, like the teeth of a horse. He has bitten the side of my mouth. I will never get well, I will die soon of the poison of this horrible snake. I pull at Ida's apron but it is not Ida, it is our much-beloved, later, dark Mary. She looks at the scar on my mouth. How ugly my mouth is with a scar, and the side of my face seems stung to death. But no, "you are not stung to death," says dark Mary, who is enormous and very kind. "You must drink milk," she says. I do not like milk. "You must eat things you do not like," says Mary.

Mary, Maia, Miriam, Mut, Madre, Mère, Mother, pray for us. Pray for us, dark Mary, Mary, mère, mer; this is the nightmare, this is the dark horse, this is Mary, Maia, Mut, Mutter. This is Gaia, this is the beginning. This is the end. Under every shrine to Zeus, to Jupiter, to Zeu-pater or Theus-pater or God-the-father, along the western coast of the Peloponnesus, there is an earlier altar. There is, beneath the carved super-structure of every temple to God-the-father, the dark cave or grotto or inner hall or cella to Mary, mère, Mut, Mutter, pray for us.

There is coal in our cellar and we have a wash-room and Ida puts the wash-tubs on the bricks in the little outer-room that opens on to the garden. There is a great pear-tree that has two kinds of pears because it has been grafted and it has different kinds of pear-blossoms. There is wisteria that grows up the side of the wash-kitchen.

"Can I help you wash clothes, Ida?" This is Ida, this is that mountain, this is Greece, this is Greek, this is Ida; Helen? Helen, Hellas, Helle, Helios, you are too bright, too far, you are sitting in the darkened parlour, because you "feel the heat," you who are rival to Helios, to Helle, to Phoebus, the sun. You are the sun and the sun is too hot for Mama, she is sitting in the sitting-room with Aunt Jennie and they are whispering like they do, and they hide their sewing when I come in. I do not care what they talk about. They leave me out of everything. Ida does not leave me out, "here take this," says Ida, "now squeeze it harder, you can get it drier than that." I am helping Ida wring out the clothes. Annie is wiping the soap from her arms from the other wash-tub.

Mary came later, in the new house, with her little boy, James.

But house is accordion-pleated on house and the dream follows simple yet very subtle devices. We put Mary in the old house and we can not reach beyond the band of her apron where it is fastened round her waist. Mary, help us. We must go further than Helen, than Helle, than Helios, than light, we must go to the darkness, out of which the monster has been born.

The monster has a face like a sick horrible woman, no, it is not a woman. It is a snake-face and the teeth are pointed and foul with slime. The face has touched my face, the teeth have bitten into my mouth. Mary, pray for us. It is so real, that I would almost say an elemental had been conjured up, that by some unconscious process, my dream had left open a door, not to my own memories alone, but to memories of the race. This is the vilest Python whom Apollo, the light, slew with his burning arrows.

This is the Python. Can one look into the jaws of the Python and live? Can one be stung on the mouth by the Python and utter words other than poisonous? Long ago, a girl was called the Pythoness, she was a virgin.

"What is a virgin, Mama?"

"A virgin is—is a—is a girl who isn't married."

"Am I a virgin, Mama?"

"Yes, all little girls are virgins."

All little girls are not virgins. The Python took shape, his wings whirred overhead, he dropped his sulphur and his fire on us.

"Why did you cut out the picture from this book, Mama?"

"I—I—is it cut out?"

"Mama, someone cut out the picture from this book."

"What book, Sister?" She calls me Sister, but I am not her sister. She calls Aunt Aggie sister, but Aunt Aggie and Aunt Laura are really her sisters. There are sisters in the Sisters' House and if I sing in the choir when I grow up, I will wear a cap and be one of the real Sisters. The Sisters open the big doors at the end of the church, when the church is dark on Christmas-eve and Papalie says *I am the light of the world* and the Sisters come through the two open doors with candles on trays. Then each of us has a candle with a different coloured paper cut-out ruffle around the candle so that we do not spill the wax, which is beeswax and is made from the wax the bees get when they are getting honey from flowers.

I have not forgotten that she has cut out the picture for no one else would dare cut out a picture from our book, from any book, with a pair of scissors.

"Why did you cut it out, Mama?"

"O—I—I thought you would forget."

Listen—it was a picture of—it was a picture of a Nightmare. It was a picture of a little girl who was not married, lying on a bed and a horrible creature that was like an old-witch with snarling face, was riding on a stick, like a witch rides on a broom-stick. She was going to stick the little girl right through, with her long pointed stick and that was what would happen in the night if you went to sleep and had a bad dream which the *Simple Science* (which explains things like why does a kettle boil, which we do not have to have explained) calls a Nightmare.

Look at its face if you dare, it is meant to drive you crazy. It is meant to drive you mad so that you fall down in a fit like someone in the Bible and see a light from heaven. It is terrible to be a virgin because a Virgin has a baby with God.

The snow was not whirling round the lamp-post when the Old Man sent his sleigh. The Young Man drove the horses; he was perched up on the seat, I sat with my back to him, Mama sat opposite with Gilbert on one side under the fur-rug, and Harold on the other. The snow lay very quiet, it did not whirl round the lamp-posts; it's made like stars, you can see them if you get them separate, if you get one stuck to the other side of the window; they have different shapes although there are so many that if you wrote 1 and then ooo forever, you would never write out a number, that would be the number of the snow-flakes.

One snow-flake shall not fall to the ground without your Father.

But that was not a snow-flake, that was a sparrow, but it means the same thing. Your Father walks ahead a little way; we wait under the light of the lamp that falls in a circle on the snow. I hold Harold's hand. He tugs at my hand, he does not say, "why are you waiting?" but that is what he means when he pulls at my hand in my mitten, with his hand in his mitten. He does not speak very often. Mama says she is worried because Harold is so quiet. But Harold can talk. He is not dumb, he is a small child, he is a year younger than me. I hold his hand. He has on his new blue reefer. He wore a white coat only a little while ago, but now he wears a blue reefer.

Gilbert has gone ahead. That is our-father. No, I do not say that to Harold. I do not think it. I am so happy that I am not saying anything, I am not thinking anything. I am alone by a lamp-post, Harold has hold of my hand.

Our-father is half way between this lamp and the next lamp-post and Gilbert has run out in the road and is making a snow-ball.

If this was Mama or Aunt Jennie, taking us down Church Street, they would turn round, they would say, "come along, children." He does not turn around. I will stand here by the lamp-post because I am so happy. When you are too happy in the snow, Uncle Hartley told us, you might feel warm, you might think you were warm, then you might lie down and go to sleep, "so you children must race around in the snow." As if he had to tell us. We race around in the snow. But I am not warm, not warm enough to lie down on the snow, like on a bed, yet I am warm. The light makes me warm but not warm enough to lie down on the snow, which is dangerous, if you are too happy, like that man in the snow where the Dog brings him a barrel on his collar. Papa will maybe turn round now but he does not, but Gilbert shouts, "hi, you better catch up, you'll be late." He throws his snow-ball at the next lamp-post but it does not hit the next lamp-post. Papa does not say, "hurry, come along," but on the Lehigh mountains, he walks fast, so you have to run sometimes to catch-up, but he does not say, "don't get lost." He lets us get lost under the bushes and by the little stream, when we go for pansy-violets and may-apples which have a white flower and two big leaves. The may-apple leaves are like an umbrella for the bunch of pansy-violets or the real violets we get.

It is not certain if he sees us. It is not certain if he knows that we are here.

Uncle Fred makes a doll out of the three corners of his handkerchief and it dances shadow-dances on the wall when he put the lamp on the floor. Aunt Jennie threaded the smaller needle because the big needle was too thick to string the beads on. Indians have bead-belts and moccasins, he walks ahead like an Indian who walks so quietly in the forest, you do not hear him. Some boys (not the cousins) tied me to a post and played a game I do not remember. I know about it because Aunt Aggie told me how Gilbert rescued me from the strange boys in Aunt Aggie's street, before they moved to Washington; Aunt Aggie said, "he brought you in the house, and said, 'Aunt Aggie, will you take care of Sister, we are playing rough in the garden!'"

I can seem to remember being tied to a stake and wild Indians howling and I do not know how soon they will strike at me with their tomahawks, but never in the snow.

Surely, I have not remembered this, only the lamp-post stands there and Harold and I stand there and Gilbert is about to run back and say, "come on, come on," he will rescue us, though we do not need to be rescued, we were never so happy, could never be happier. The light from the lamp is a round circle.

We wait in the snow, with the lamp, with Papa there, going on to the next lamp-post, with Gilbert waiting to shout, though he pretends he is not thinking of us and stoops down to make another snow-ball.

It goes on in what we later called slow-motion, at the moving-picture shows.

Or we stop here.

If we do not remember, it is nevertheless there. It crept up and its edge was white like the lamp and the way it came up the flat sand, was the way the snow drifts round the lamp-post.

I was high up; his bathing-suit was blue and stuck to his shoulders as we went together across the sand; he said, "no, it isn't cold, I'll take her in." He will take me in and that will be the end of me, but I am high up and the waves come close.

It is terrible to be taken in, when the waves come up, but he does not drop me in.

He puts me down in the ocean. When the waves come up, I run back, and watch the waves come up after me, but it is a long way, the water goes on and on.

Mama does not like it. She does not like the hot sun; she sits under a parasol with Ida who is taking off Harold's white dress and putting bathing-drawers on him. Gilbert is far away with some big boys and a boat.

"It is too far for you to walk," he told me.

There are pebbles, they are wet and shiny. There are shells.

Mama put the sea-shell to my ear and said, "listen, you will hear the sea," but when we got to the sea, it was too hot, she said, and she lay down in her room.

Professor Harding came with us. We ride down to the ocean in a big coach. Ida has a bag with towels and our bathing-things.

"Come, come, don't be afraid." This is a boat and the boys are catching crabs; a crab is on the floor of the boat, he makes a horrible scratching on the wooden floor of the boat. There is a little square of water in the bottom of the boat but the boat won't sink, "don't be afraid, girls are always afraid." Yes, I am afraid.

The crab comes along; you do not know which way he is walking. He walks fast, fast. Girls are afraid. Don't scream. This is the worst thing that has ever happened. The crab gets bigger and bigger and the boys laugh more and more. "He won't eat you."

How do I know he won't eat me? The boat goes up and down with the waves and the crab opens his pincer-claws and one of the boys pushes him, even nearer. Then the crab comes nearer—girls scream sometimes.

"Here," says Papa and he picks up the crab with his big hand and its claws grab round in the air and he is going to throw it back in the water.

"My crab," says Professor Harding who has on a big straw-hat like a farmer. "Taking privileges with my property."

"Take your critter then," says Papa. He calls things a "critter," a crab or the alligator.

Professor Harding pushes a tub of water toward him, Papa drops the crab in the tub, the water splashes and the other critters claw round the edges of the tub.

When the alligator fell out of the attic-window, the gardener screamed that it was the Devil.

The gardener's name was Mr. Cherry.

"It can't be," said the Williamses, "you made it up."

"Mr. Cherry, Mr. Cherry," we called and he looked up, where he was tacking up a vine that has a purple flower that fell down. There was the bleeding-heart bush under the kitchen-window and above that, was the window of Uncle Hartley's room where he slept, in the afternoon when he was at the steel-mills the other side of the river, at night. Then there was the little window above, just as you draw just the shape of such a house on a slate, when you do not draw the Christmas-tree.

The alligator fell right into the bleeding-heart bush and the bush shook and waved, like blowing in the wind and we knew what was there but Mr. Cherry did not know and was surprised.

He ran away but we did not.

We stood and watched the bush for the alligator to come out but Uncle Hartley said, "you children better run off," but we did not because Papa was coming from the wash-kitchen door; he had on his big leather furnace-glove. He must have heard Mr. Cherry shriek or saw what happened for he had on his big glove, before Uncle Hartley could go back to the house and get whatever it was he was getting. I was glad it was not Papa's pistol. Then I thought, "I am glad he is not going to shoot the alligator."

He put his hand in the top of the bush and he had the alligator by the neck and he carried him into the house and up Papalie's front stairs past the clock, round the corner and up the next steps to the attic. Uncle Hartley tugged at the little attic-window that was left open, and fastened it tight shut, "but you children better keep away from the attic," he said, "till we get some fresh wire nailed up here. Cherry will do it." Papa laughed like he does with a snort and said, "better let me do it, Cherry doesn't like alligators."

Papa has a work-bench in the little room beyond the kitchen over the wash-kitchen where we keep our shoe-blacking and shoe-brushes. He can make willow-whistles.

Mamalie said, "st-st-st-st, that alligator better go."

We said and Tootie said and Dick stood watching, "go where?"

"Well," said Mamalie, "after all—"

We said, "after all, what? Didn't someone send it to Papalie in a cigar-box, wrapped in that Florida moss?"

Mamalie said, "of course."

It is moss that we put under the tree for the animals to stand on and for the sheep to lie down in, and eat.

We made cherries out of cotton (like Papalie stuck on the clay-sheep) for May-day and Mrs. Williams trimmed Olive and Mea's Leghorn hats with real tulips and leaves. Bessie had a crown of cherry-blossom on her hat and when we had the May-day party in their garden under the cherry-tree, Bessie was the queen because it was her birthday.

When we got home, Ida said, "don't worry your mother, you can sleep in my bed to-night," and she woke me the next morning and her face was happy and she said, "guess."

I said, "guess what?"

She said, "you have a new brother."

I must have known all that, because we had talked about Mrs. Williams and the way she wore her rain-coat all the time out of doors, even when it wasn't raining and Olive told me what it was, and her wrapper indoors and then Amery came but I did not seem to know. I seemed to be surprised. The baby was born on the second day of May.

Now at this minute, while we stand under the lamp-post, he is not born yet, because he was born in May and this is Christmas and Harold is the baby.

Slow-motion. Slower and slower.

The time-clock and out-of-time whirls round the lamp-post. The snow whirls, it is white sand from the desert. Ahead, is Papa, stopped in slow-motion and then going back and back in time, back through the ages, the middle-ages, though I do not know that, Rome, Greece, but he does not stop at Greece. The snow that has stopped in slow-motion and folds us in a cloud, is a pillar-of-cloud-by-day. The lamp shining over our heads is the pillar-of-fire and the snow is the pillar-of-cloud and never in-time or out-of-time, can such children be lost, for their inheritance is so great.

Gilbert must go to France for Gilbert must inherit the pistol from Papa who was in our Civil War. Harold will inherit the mills and the steel and numbers too and become a successful business-man like Uncle Hartley. Gilbert has been asleep for a long time, in a place called Thiaucourt, in France. Harold is a grown man, a grandfather with three children of his own; he inherited the three children, too, a girl and two boys. Hilda has inherited too much but she can not let it go. There is the lamp-post and the pillar-of-fire and there is the cloud-by-day, the Mystery, and Papa far ahead, a dark shape in the snow.

The keepers-of-the-Mysteries are Wise Men and Children. The children grow into Wise Men, the Wise Men become Children.
There were three Wise men, they were Papalie, they were Papa and someone else, maybe the Old Man who was not there, they said, who never had been there, they said.
Or maybe the other Wise Man was the grandfather whom they had never seen or Uncle Will who had moved to Washington.
Or maybe the Three Wise Men were incorporated in these three children, who (microcosm in macrocosm) were symbol of all mystery, of the civilisation that their forebears had left mid-Europe, had left England to establish, to protect in this new land.
The land was new, the land was very old. The forces of the land were inchoate, the land itself was many lands, many countries, strung together loosely enough, yet strung together like those glass-beads on a string.
There was a time when the string almost broke and Papa was one of the children who went to keep the land together.
There was Alvin who died of typhoid in that war, only a year or two older than Papa and there was Gilbert who had flung his second snow-ball at the next lamp-post, who was to give his life for his land, for all lands, strung together as they were on different strings; these countries must eventually be strung together as one whole, so that the whole world shall be complete, a round ball, complete and reflecting the light of the sun, one of many round balls, strung on the great central force or pole or polar-energy of the entire heavenly universe.
But enough—this is one small earth, our earth not yet in itself, psychically projected; here the forces of evil and the forces of good are struggling; the

whole structure of civilisation may go down at any moment like the Christmas-tree in the Seminary that caught fire when the girl in the crinoline was burnt to death.

There was a hut in the woods but the sun was shining, rain did not beat on the windows. He took us there to get water-lilies.

A man with a horse and trap met us at the station. We were drawn toward a new scent, a new feel of trees, of light. It was evening.

As the day-light faded, there was new definition or exact understanding of twilight.

We had never been out in the woods in the evening.

Papa talked to the man who drove the horse, Papa had been here before; with whom? Not Mama. Had he brought those other children, Alfred and Eric and Alice (who was dead) here, before he married Mama? There was a world, a life of mystery beyond him; we could ask him about Indiana and how his father had gone out in a covered-wagon and how frightened his mother was, and how disappointed his father was to stay in Indiana because he wanted to go to California, and how he himself had run away to go off with Alvin to the Civil War and where did he find the Indian skull?

But we did not ask him what lay nearest, "did you come here with Alfred and Eric and Alice who is dead. Did you come with their Mama?"

There was another mother, she was a mystery, she was dead, her name was Martha, we must not ask about her.

Here, the cart-wheels went along a track just as wide as the wheels for there was no road in the woods, only this opening in the trees that brushed Papa's head, so that he had to duck his head, like going under a bridge in the canal-boat when we took the canal-boat and a picnic-basket and a water-melon that Uncle Fred stopped to buy, on the way there.

Here, there was no picnic-basket for we were going to spend the night in a place where we had never been, whose name was Sailor's Lake; "is it a big lake?" asked Gilbert.

Papa snorted the way he did, like a horse when he laughed, he said, "it's a pond really."

A pond is a flat muddy water-hole where there are mosquitoes, back of the shanty-hill houses behind the mill where the goat once was, that Gilbert said looked like Papalie. But were we going to a shanty-hill? We were going through a tunnel in the woods and the leaves brushed Papa's hat off and now he was holding his hat on his knees and looking up at the trees. Papa liked trees. He knew all about trees. We had a little chest-of-drawers he made, with little drawers that was too nice, Mama said, for me to use for my doll, but could I have it? Mama did not give it to me but Mamalie gave me a little old chest that was hers, for my doll-clothes.

The trees were deeper and maybe we were lost but the man let the horse go along, he did not hold the reins, he was stuffing tobacco into his pipe. He offered Papa the tobacco and Papa laughed and said he had left his pipe in the pocket of his other coat, in the back of the cart; he said he liked a corn-cob pipe, too, best.

The horse was going to step on the little frogs.

"Stop the horse," I told Papa, "tell the man to stop the horse."

"Why?" said Papa.

"There is a little frog," and the man laughed and Papa laughed. He stopped the horse and told us to get out and there were a thousand-thousand little frogs on the track, they looked like small leaves fallen on the track until they began to hop.

"We can't help it," said the man, "if they get in the way, can we?"

We saw that the thousand-thousand little frogs lay like leaves on the track in the woods, that had two marks in it, just as wide as the wheels on the man's cart.

"Where is it?" we said. But then we saw from the porch, the way the field ran down along the side of the woods. There were no flowers along the edge of the porch, there was no wisteria, no climbing-rose, no honeysuckle.

It was a hut in the woods.

There was the track from the wood-edge and marks where the cart stopped in front of the door. We came here last night. They said it was too late to run down to the lake.

"Then it is a lake?" said Gilbert.

"Of course," said the man.

"With boats on it?" said Gilbert.

"Of course," said the man.

It was a lake.

Here it was, we could not see how far it stretched because of the bull-rushes, but there were boats tied to a wooden-landing, so it must be a big lake. We ran back, up the slope of the field to the porch; there were no porch-steps; the porch floor lay flat on the grass; the grass ran up to the floor of the porch, it was a house without a garden, the field was the lawn, the grass was long and short and you could see where the wheels of the cart stopped and went away again.

No one said, "come along, come in to breakfast," but we went along and saw through the window that they were eating in the dining-room, Papa was there at the table and the man who had the horse and an old lady and one or two others. They sat at a long table; there was a glass-dish of pickled-beets on the table and a pie and Papa was drinking coffee.

We saw Papa at a table without us, drinking coffee from a thick white cup.

We went in the hall and in the door to the dining-room. Nobody said, "where have you been?" The man-with-the-horse said, "mother" to the door and the voice said, "coming" and it was his mother, we guessed or did he call his wife mother, like Papa called Mama sometimes? We could not tell if she was the cook or the man-with-the horse's mother or his wife.

There were no children.

We sat along the table where there were places, not in a row.

The man-with-the-horse said, "beets, pie, pickles?"

We said, "yes."

Papa did not say, "you can not have pie for breakfast."

We had pie for breakfast. It was huckleberry-pie and we had napkins with red squares.

The coffee in Ida's house when she took us to see her father-and-mother, smelt like this. But this was bigger than Ida's mother's-and-father's house and the windows were all open.

He did not come, he said yes, he would have more coffee.

We sat on the porch; I looked in the window and he was talking and laughing and everyone had gone but the man-with-the-horse, and they were smoking their pipes. The lady came in and put the cups on the tray; "now he will come out," we thought, and he came out with his pipe and the man said, "well, I better be off," and he knocked out the tobacco from his pipe on the railing of the porch, and he went off.

"O," he said and he came back, "Mamie leaks," and he laughed.

"Who is Mamie?" we said.

Papa said, "come and see," and we ran down the grass, looking for Mamie. It was a boat, there was Lucy and Polly and Mamie; Papa read out the names and said, "which do you want?" and we said, "Polly."

Polly is the name of a parrot. Aunt Jennie had a Polly that ate crackers, or you said, "Polly have a cracker," and if it said, "Polly have a cracker," back at you, we gave it some sun-flower seeds. The sun-flower seeds are like little nuts, if you bite into them.

Papa took the two oars. The oars caught in the bull-rushes, everywhere there were bull-rushes, we were caught here and the sun was shining.

We waited for Papa to put back the oars in the boat and he pulled the boat along by the bull-rushes, then I saw what it was we had come to see. It spread back and it was bigger than a white-rose.

"Stop, stop," I said, though the boat was going slowly.

"What is it?" said Papa.

"Look," I said, and Harold looked and Gilbert looked.

"The boat will run over it," I said. I was in the front of the boat and Gilbert was in the back with the two ropes for the rudder. Harold crawled along.

"Is it a naligator?" he said.

I said, "no, you know they come from Florida, it's gone, Papa you have run over it."

Papa said, "what?"

He went on pulling the boat along by the bull-rushes.

It was gone. I would never see it again, it would be squashed and dead, it would be torn up by the boat. I wanted the boat to go back.

Papa said, "what was it?"

I said—I said—but I could not speak because now he had pulled the boat out and given it a push with the oars and I saw what it was that we had come to see.

There was not just one water-lily there on the water, like the one we had run over. They were crowded together so that sometimes one was pushed sideways, like our pears when there are too many on a branch. They were under my hands when I reached out.

"Don't fall in," said Papa.

I saw the picture in our Hans Andersen about Peter the child, or was it Peter, the stork?

There is a story in our Hans Andersen about a stork and children. The babies like the Innocents in our Doré Bible, wait there on the water-lilies.

It was not that I thought of the picture; it was that something was remembered. There was a water-lily, painted on blue velvet, in Mrs. Kent's house, but she said it was not stylish any more to have painting on velvet. But it was very pretty. There were bull-rushes, painted on a blue umbrella-stand. It seemed that the water-lilies, painted on the velvet and the blue umbrella-stand with bull-rushes painted on it, were not in my mind, any more than the picture of the water-lilies, lying large and flat-open on the pond or lake in the Hans Andersen story.

They were not at first, there, but as the boat turned round and shoved against the bull-rushes and then the bull-rushes got thinner and you could see through them (like looking through the slats in a fence) you saw what was there, you knew that something was reminded of something. That something remembered something. That something came true in a perspective and a dimension (though those words, of course, had no part in my mind) that was final, that nothing could happen after this, as nothing had happened before it, to change the way things were and what people said and "what will you do when you grow up" and "it must be exciting to have so many brothers" or "you've torn a great triangle in your new summer-dress and the first time you wore it, too" (as if I did not know that) or "that branch of the pear-tree is dead, be careful when you children climb that tree," but it was not us but Teddie Kent who fell out of it, because he said, "the old thing is no deader than the rest of the old tree," and climbed out, just because we said, "don't," and fell down and broke his arm.

And Jack Kent ran away and was gone a whole night, and when he came back Mrs. Kent cried, and that seemed a funny thing to do, "why did she cry, Mama?"

"Well, she cried with relief, because she was so happy."

"Can one cry because one is happy, Mama?"

H.D.'s Heritage

"Mamalie," H.D.'s grandmother,
Elizabeth Weiss Seidel Wolle
(1824–1906).

"Mama," H.D.'s mother,
Helen Eugenia Wolle Doolittle
(1853–1927).

H.D., "the child." Hilda Doolittle,
1886–1961.
*Photos courtesy of Moravian Archives,
Bethlehem, Pennsylvania (MAB).*

ᥱᴑ

"But one must, of necessity, begin with one's own private inheritance. . . .
there is a Gift waiting, someone must inherit the Gift" (ch. 1, 50).

Church Street, Bethlehem, Pennsylvania. View of the church with its trombone cupola, from the approximate site of H.D.'s birthplace, 112 Church Street, now torn down. *Courtesy of the artist, Fred Bees.*

⁊

"I have felt all along a deep gratitude for the place of my birth" ("Notes" III, 254).

The Brothers' House, or Brethren's House (center), built of stone, and Central Moravian Church (foreground left) on the corners of Church and Main streets, just west of the Doolittle home. *Courtesy of the artist, Fred Bees.*

⁊

"The Brothers' House . . . the Sisters' House" were still commonly so-called when I was a child" ("Notes" II, 232).

Mrs. William Henry
(née Mary Ann Wood, 1734–1799),
H.D.'s great-great-great-
grandmother, painted in 1755
by Benjamin West, of whom the
Henrys were early friends
and patrons.
*Courtesy of the Historical Society
of Pennyslvania.*

"This Mary Ann was born
1734. She was married to
William Henry . . ."
("Notes" V, 258).

"Judge and Armorer," in H.D.'s
words, William Henry (1729–1786)
held important civil and military
positions in colonial America.
Painted by Benjamin West, 1754,
when the artist was only sixteen.
*Courtesy of the Historical Society
of Pennsylvania.*

"This was the first William
Henry; his son William Henry
married Sabina Schropp. It was
their daughter Sabina Henry who
married John Frederick Wolle,
our grandfather's father"
("Notes" V, 258).

Sabina Henry (1792–1859) and John Frederick Wolle were married in 1809. They had ten children. H.D.'s first cousin, Francis Wolle, named for their grandfather, preserved these and many family photographs in an album accompanying his memoir, "A Moravian Heritage." *Courtesy of MAB.*

John Frederick Wolle (1785–1869) was excommunicated for marrying a non-Moravian. The couple went to live in Jacobsburg, north of Nazareth, Pennsylvania, where he ran the Jacobsburg Inn and where Francis was born. Later the family was restored to the church and moved to Bethlehem. *Courtesy of MAB.*

∽

"John Frederick Wolle was born at Bethany–St. John, West Indies; his grandfather Peter Wolle was born in Schwerzens near Posen, Poland" ("Notes" I, 228).

"Five generations of Weisses," wrote H.D.'s cousin, Francis Wolle, "if the portrait at the feet of Mary Stables Weiss is included. It could be a likeness of her mother, Margaretha Stables, or of her husband's mother, Mrs. John George (Elizabeth Schneider) Weiss. Jedediah Weiss and his wife, Mary Stables, are center and left in upper row. Their daughter, Elizabeth Weiss Wolle, is at right. Agnes Seidel Howard is seated on the floor. Of her children, Bessie is held by Jedediah and Clifford by Elizabeth" (Wolle).
Photograph taken circa 1869. Courtesy of MAB.

H.D.'s great-grandfather Jedediah Weiss (1796–1873), watchmaker and
silversmith, in 1873, as shown by the photographer's signature, Stuber,
and the date on the curtain at left.
Courtesy of MAB.

ભ

"... father of Mamalie ... .he was a gifted musician ... possessed
of a magnificent bass voice. . . . He was a member of the Moravian
trombone choir for fifty years, and not once in all that time did he
miss playing on Easter morning" ("Notes" I, 230).

Mary Stables Weiss (1796–1872),
married to Jedediah Weiss.
Courtesy of MAB.

&

"Mamalie's mother's name was
Mary. . . . Her father and mother
had come from Scotland, so . . .
she was the nearest biological link
with the old world that we had"
("Notes" V, 231).

George Augustus Weiss (1821–1853),
son of Mary and Jedediah Weiss,
died a missionary in the West Indies.
Courtesy of MAB.

&

"There is a story in the family, that
at the hour of his death Great-
grandmother Weiss was in her
garden at Bethlehem and heard
him distinctly call to her . . ."
("Notes" V, 269).

The Reverend Francis Wolle
(1817–1893) and Elizabeth Weiss Seidel
married in 1849, when she was a young
widow with a daughter, Agnes. They
lived at 110 Church Street, where
H.D.'s Uncle Hartley, Aunt Belle,
and cousin Francis also lived.
Courtesy of MAB.

❦

"Papalie's name was Francis. . . . Our
grandfather succeeded the Reverend
Sylvester Wolle as principal of the
Seminary" ("Notes" 1, 228).

"Papa," Charles Leander Doolittle
(1843–1919), in his Civil War uniform,
circa 1862, age 17. He and Helen
Wolle were married on May 11, 1882.
*Courtesy of Yale Collection of American
Literature, Beinecke Rare Book and
Manuscript Library.*

❦

H.D. said of this photograph:
"There was the less extravagant flow
of hair but still the slight suggestion
of nordic poet or musician"
("Notes" III, 253).

"The six children of Francis and Elizabeth Weiss Wolle," wrote Francis Wolle,
"almost certainly taken as a present for their parents on their 25th wedding
anniversary (1873) or for the mother on her fiftieth birthday, May 27, 1874."
Front row: John Frederick, Agnes Angelica, Laura Rebecca, Robert Henry.
Back row: "Mama," Helen Eugenia, at about age 20, and Hartley Cornelius.
Courtesy of MAB.

☙

"The older girls who had seemed to Mama like formidable young ladies,
not so long ago, were only tall children now; they were her own pupils.
She taught drawing and gave piano-lessons, and Miss Helen was
the one always to be consulted" (ch.2, p. 59).

"The same six children with their mother on her seventieth birthday, May 27, 1894," wrote Francis Wolle. Helen Doolittle in white sits at her mother's right, Agnes at her mother's left, and J. Fred at their feet. Behind, left to right, Hartley, Laura, and Robert. Elizabeth Wolle wears the 19th-century style Moravian cap with the widow's white bow, as described in "Notes" IV. *Courtesy of MAB.*

ↄ

"The Gift actually was Mamalie's . . . bequeathed to her through her own mother. . . . The child could grasp the implications of the Secret through intuitive sympathy with her grandmother . . ." (ch. 5, 166–67; "Notes" V, 267).

A rare photograph of the three generations of H.D.'s Moravian female lineage together, circa 1897, at the "new house," Upper Darby, Pennsylvania. *Front row, left to right:* Hilda Doolittle; her cousin, Birdie Jenkins (1873–1959); her mother, Helen, with H.D.'s brothers, Melvin (1894–1963) and Gilbert (1884–1918). *Back row:* H.D.'s grandmother Elizabeth and her aunt, Laura W. Jenkins (1851–1935).
Courtesy of MAB.

✑

"It is summer and they come to see us; . . . Mamalie is here too but she is not a visitor. . . . I want her to go on talking. . . . Mamalie found all this out. . . . Mutter wasn't just the Holy Ghost. It was a special Spirit"
(ch. 5, 147, 154, 155, 163).

A picnic, circa 1902, with relatives and friends under the big maples in front of the Doolittle home in Upper Darby. *Front row, left to right:* Charles Doolittle; Helen W. Doolittle; Carrie Wunderling. *Back row, left to right:* H.D.; unidentified person; Sara Halliwell Doolittle, married in 1902 to H.D.'s older half-brother, Eric (1869–1920); Melvin Doolittle; boy and woman, unidentified; the Rev. Edward S. Wolle (1852–1933), "Cousin Edd" of chapter 2; unidentified figure next to tree.
Courtesy of MAB.

ↄ⊃

"'If that branch catches in the island of sand, not in the submerged sand,'" she thought, "'then I will marry Edd.' She did not want to marry Edd" (ch. 2, 63).

This trolley station across the road from Flower Observatory and near the
Doolittle home was the scene of Charles Doolittle's accident, which shocked the
child Hilda in chapter six. *Left to right:* H.D.; Melvin Doolittle; Charles Doolittle;
Miss Kast; Eric Doolittle; Sara Halliwell Doolittle (with dog); Agnes S. Howard,
"Aunt Aggie"; Gilbert Doolittle; Belle R. Wolle, wife of Hartley Wolle and mother
of Francis; Alfred Doolittle, H.D.'s older half-brother (1867–1921).
Courtesy of MAB.

ಲ

"The old street-car or steam-car went past the house once an hour; it was
going past soon. . . . It went past the house. . . . He hadn't come in but he
had been somewhere near and something had happened"
(ch. 6, 187, 190).

In the garden of the Doolittles' Flower Observatory house, Upper Darby, Pennsylvania, circa 1899. *Front row:* Melvin Doolittle, Francis Wolle ("Tootie," 1889–1979) H.D.'s cousin. *Back row:* Mr. Goheen, Florence Prince, H.D. *Courtesy of MAB.*

&

"In assembling these chapters of *The Gift* during, before and after the worst days of the 1941 blitz, I let the story tell itself or the child tell it for me. Things that I thought I had forgotten came to light in the course of the narrative . . ." ("Notes" IV, 257).

Left to right: H.D. with her brothers and half-brother, Melvin, Gilbert, and Alfred, circa 1904, in Upper Darby. H.D. felt the weight of being the only daughter among sons. Her first draft of *The Gift* shows that she once titled it *The Middle Child.*
Courtesy of MAB.

൧

"I seemed to have inherited that. I was the inheritor. The boys, of whom there were so many, the two brothers and later, the baby brother, the two half brothers, the five grown Howard cousins, not to mention the small-fry, Tootie, Dick, and Laddie . . . " (ch. 1, 37).

Moravian baptism of Native Americans in the Old Chapel (1751), as performed in the eighteenth century. Letters over participants' heads identify them. *A* = officiating minister; *B* = candidate for baptism; *C* = native worker; *D* = Native American congregations, men to the left and women to the right in the sex-segregated style of early Moravianism.
Courtesy of MAB.

დ

"Paxnous, the Shawanese chief . . . in 1755, in those most troubled days . . . brought his wife to the mission at Bethlehem to be baptized" ("Notes" V, 267).

The "gifted and pious Livonian baroness" Anna Maria von Cammerhof
(1717?–1786), née von Pahlen or von de Pahle, painted almost certainly
by the prolific Moravian painter-preacher John Valentine Haidt
circa 1745 in Germany.
Courtesy of Archiv der Brüder-Unität,
Herrnhut, Germany.

❧

"I had never heard of Anna von Pahlen before, but I could think of
her like some of the pictures Mamalie had of the early Sisters . . ."
(ch. 5, 162).

The Doolittles owned a steel-engraved reproduction of the 1862 painting by
Christian Schussele titled *The Power of the Gospel*, which H.D. refers to as
"Zeisberger Preaching to the Indians." This scene's dramatic ambiance pervades
her story of Tschoop's conversion in "Notes" II and her account of Zeisberger's
rapport with Native Americans, achieved by his speaking their language.
Courtesy of MAB.

☙

Zeisberger had won the allegiance of the whole Delaware nation and he now
proposed to the King and the Council that they take steps to have their
territory clearly defined; "let their land, by Act of Parliament, be secured to
them for ever" ("Notes" VI, 271).

V

The Secret

*. . . water to drink of the well of Bethlehem
which is by the gate.*

*Such harmony is in immortal souls;
But, whilst this muddy vesture of decay
Doth grossly close it in, we cannot hear it.*

The Secret

The stars?

"Well—here's a—" and the voice stops and they all stop talking. This is later in the new house. They are sitting under my window. I am in bed, they are under the window. *My garden is under the window* was in our first entertainment at the old School; I mean, it was my words to speak. They had made a window at the back of the platform, and we stood together in a row; we were from Kate Greenaway. I was in the middle with two boys but the boys were in my first class at school and we were all six years old and they were not my brothers.

But this is the new house. They are sitting on the grass. They pulled their chairs out from under the big maple-tree. It is summer and they come to see us; Uncle Fred and Aunt Jennie are staying with us. Mamalie is here too, but she is not a visitor. "*My*—" Someone else is there but it does not matter who it is; I think Mamalie has gone to bed, too. I wonder if she hears them say, "*my*—" then I seem to know what they are looking at, why they have stopped talking.

They always have so much to say; Uncle Hartley and Aunt Belle come too, but Aunt Jennie and Mama laugh most. Maybe that is Cousin Edd saying "it reminds me of—." They always say it reminds them of. Papa is at the Transit House, Eric is at the Observatory, looking for his double-stars. The double-stars stay together but they go round one another like big suns; we know this for he tells the visitors at the Observatory, Thursday evenings, and we tell them to sign their names in the visitor's book. This is not Thursday. You can almost tell what day of the week it is by the feel of something in the air, but it was easier to tell in the old-town because of the church-bells and the factory-whistles, the other side of the river. Uncle Hartley is going to get a promotion and go to another place than Bethlehem Steel. They will have a new house like our new house when we came here and Papa left his little Observatory for this new Transit House, which has the only instrument (except in Greenwich, England) like he has. Mr. Evans lives in the wing of the house and Eric has his room in the wing of the house over the empty library, but they are bringing out maps and books now for the Observatory library from the University library.

"The first this year—first real one, I mean—"

Mamalie is not in bed. She is coming up the stairs. The clock is ticking. It has a loud tick. Maybe she has forgotten her knitting, maybe I will run downstairs and get her knitting for her in the dark. The house is dark because the mosquitoes come in, even though we have new screens on all the windows. "Mamalie—" she is at the top of the stairs now.

"Mamalie—"

"What—what—is that you, Helen?" She calls me "Helen" sometimes and she calls Harold, "Hartley," but we do not say, "my name is not Helen" or "my name is not Hartley"—we just answer.

"Mamalie—"

"Yes—yes, Helen—what is it?"

"It's me, Mamalie—"

"O—it's you."

"Mamalie—"

"Yes—yes—Laura, I mean Helen—O, Hilda, of course, what is it?"

"Did you forget your knitting?"

"Why—yes—yes, I think I left my knitting on the window-bench in the sitting-room."

"Shall I run down for it?" I am out of bed now. I stand by her in the dark in the hall, at the top of the stairs. Their voices go on outside. "—when we hired the old post-coach, for fun—do you remember? we clubbed together for Uncle Sylvester's birthday-treat and drove to the water-gap and—" They are all there and what they said *ah* about, is a shooting-star and Aunt Jennie says you can make a wish on your first shooting-star.

I did ask Eric why it was called a shooting-star and he said because it streaks or shoots across the sky—"but would it fall on us?" He said no, there was something about gravity that would keep it from falling, but how do they know that? I do not ask silly questions like the visitors, Thursday evenings at the Observatory, who say, "are there people on Mars?" but sometimes I wonder if they are able to tell if really a shooting-star will not fall down and fall on us and fall on the house and burn us all to death. It is quiet now.

"Mamalie—"
"Why aren't you asleep, Laura?"

"O, I don't know—they're talking outside."
"That's no reason not to go to sleep, they always sit on the porch or on the lawn and talk when it's so hot—"
"Yes—because if they light the lamp the June-bugs bump in—"
"—but you're shivering—"
"It's only goose-flesh, Mamalie," I say. I don't quite know what I mean by goose-flesh, but I just say something to keep her standing in the dark.
"And why do they call it goose-flesh, Mamalie?" though I know that, too; it's because sometimes if you're cold, you get little rough pimples like a goose has, when it is in its dish waiting for the oven, but the roughness doesn't really look much like goose-flesh; it's like that thing they call your-hair-standing-on-end, but it doesn't really. But I have asked her one quick question which she hasn't answered, so if I am able, I will ask her another. I reach out and the wall is there and it is a hot night and I am cold. "Why do they call a shooting-star, a shooting star, Mamalie?"
"Well—I—I suppose because—"
"It might hit the house, mightn't it? I mean, it might shoot down and hit us?"
"Why should it?" She is brushing past me as if I were not there. She must not do that.
"Mamalie—" I feel along the wall, "where are you going, Mamalie?" She does not answer. She is like that. Sometimes she does not answer, she does not look up when she is knitting, she even sits without her knitting and is not asleep but "don't disturb your grandmother," Mama will say. It is not just because she is getting a little deaf in one ear, but we know which ear that is and stand on the side of her "good ear," as she calls it. But she is hearing something all the same; you can see that she is hearing something. Maybe, she is hearing something now in the dark. I have forgotten about the shooting-star. Maybe she will let me stay in her room. If I stay in her room with her, I might hear something.
She is feeling for the matches in her top bureau-drawer. She has her lace-caps there and handkerchiefs in sachet and there is cologne on the top of her bureau.

"They're in the left corner, at the back," I prompt her, "you told me to remind you, if you forgot." She hides the matches in different corners, as if she were afraid of them. But she has found the matches. She strikes a match and there is a little flame from the candle in a saucer; she keeps a saucer and the candle standing on the top of her bureau. She will put the saucer on a chair by her bed. It is a night-light, and she will even ask me sometimes to pour water in the saucer from her pitcher on the washstand, and then we have to pour some out again, because it is too much for the candle and then we get it just right, so that the candle will go out and not set anything on fire if it starts to sputter. She even carries a candle in the train, in her hand-bag, in case, she says, "the lights should all go out in a tunnel."

"But do they?"

"Do they what, Aggie?" Now she is calling me "Aggie." I wonder if she will notice, she never calls me "Aggie" but why shouldn't she call me "Aggie," if she calls me "Helen" or "Laura" even? Now I am Aggie; this is the first time I have been Aggie. I stand in my night-dress, and see the room and it is a different room and I am Aggie. It is summer I know, but I do not hear their voices because Mamalie's room is this side of the house, away from the front-steps and the grass, where we have the new little magnolia-tree planted.

She will never unpin her cap because she has a little bald spot on the top of her head, she says, but now she unpins her cap. I see Mamalie without her cap and she looks just the same, only maybe not so old because the light is not very bright and her hair is not all-over white but partly white, and where it is not white, you can see that it is black, but very black, not like Mama's, or mousy as they call mine.

Her eyes slant up at the sides, yes, you can see now that she looks like Aunt Aggie, only Aunt Aggie is a taller lady, taller than Mama even. It seems that it is cold, though it is a hot summer-night but there is wind this side of the house, because the curtains blow a little in the wind, and I can see that Mamalie is afraid they'll brush against the candle in the saucer, even before she says, "the curtains, Aggie."

I go over and jerk the summer-curtains; they are made of flowered stuff, like the curtains they pinned up for the window they cut out of an old screen, that they stood up for a house in a garden when I was *My garden is under the window.* It was that kind of window-curtain and this had little daisies and wild-roses running along and little yellow flowers in the corner that Mama said were English primroses and grow wild in England, but we had not seen them, only the ones that grow bunched on a stem that the Williamses had in their garden, that Mrs. Williams called "primulas" and that Mamalie called "keys-of-heaven."

It is better to get in her bed. It is not cold, but the quilt she always brings with her in her trunk, is pretty; it is made of patches of everybody's best dresses and some French stuff that was sent by one of the old-girls from New Orleans. Mamalie can tell me about the dresses; I will wait and ask her again about this black one with the tiny pink rose-buds, that was one of Aunt Aggie's to go to Philadelphia in, when she married Uncle Will. I can pull up the quilt and I can sit here and I am not afraid now to think about the shoot-ing-star, because I think she is going to talk about the shooting-star in a dif-ferent way, that isn't gravitation.

She said, "I forgot all about it."

I don't know if that is the shooting-star or the question I am thinking of asking her (because sometimes she seems to know what I am going to ask her and answers me beforehand) about Aunt Aggie's black silk dress with rose-buds, but she has not forgotten about that because she was telling me about it, only the other day when I helped her unpack. She will stay as long as she can but then she must get back to Bethlehem; it will be for one of those things, like putting flowers on Papalie's grave for his birthday or the day he died on, but she seems to like to be with us here and goes in the kitchen and makes Papa apple-pies. Now she has pulled out the bone hair-pins that she wears at the top, to keep up her braids. She has two braids and they hang down now, either side of her face, and she might almost be a big girl or a little girl, sitting in the low chair with the candle on the window-sill.

"I would have told you before but I forgot, Agnes."

I say, "yes, Mimmie," because Mama and Aunt Aggie call her Mimmie. I am afraid she will remember that I am only Hilda, so I crouch down under the cover so she will only half see me, so that she won't remember that I am only Hilda.

"It wasn't that I was afraid," she said, "though I was afraid. It wasn't only, that they might burn us all up, but there were the papers. Christian had left the Secret with me. I was afraid the Secret would be lost."

I do not know who Christian is and I am afraid to ask. Or does she mean a Christian? It is the same name as Hans Christian Andersen. I get tired of hearing them talk about the picture, someone called Benjamin West painted of a lady called Mary Ann Wood (I think her name was) and the spinet that the fan-maker in London gave to someone, anyhow their grandfather had a spinet in his house even if it wasn't that one, and that would be Mamalie's papa, why yes, that would be Mamalie's own papa and perhaps Mamalie played the spinet, though she never plays the piano.

Now it seems that I can understand why they are so interested in Mary Ann Wood and what she had, because all at once I understand about the spinet and I even wonder about the fan-maker in London and who he was and who he made fans for, and what the fans were like and why did he give the spinet away and did they bring it with them on the same boat or did they send it on another boat, and what was the name of the ship they came on, anyway?

For the first time in my life, I wonder who we all are? Why, Mamalie's own Mama was called Mary and she was from Virginia and her father and mother had come straight from Scotland, and I did not even know their names nor the name of the ship they came on. Mamalie's own mama's name was Mary, and is that why (I wonder for the first time) Mamalie always gets Uncle Fred to sing *The Four Marys,* the last thing after Thanksgiving or Christmas parties?

I never thought about who they were, very much, and anyhow I could always find out by asking them, but now for the first time I really want to know; I want to know who Christian is, because somehow Christian is not one of the ones Mama and Uncle Hartley and Cousin Edd talk about, but Christian is someone I just hear about, alone with Mamalie, as if Christian belonged alone to me and Mamalie, and didn't she say anyhow, there was a Secret?

"Christian," I say half to myself, because I can not help it though I have not meant to ask her about Christian, because Aunt Aggie perhaps knew all about him, then Mamalie might come back and remember that I am Hilda and that I am not Agnes. But I did not say "Christian" very loud, perhaps she did not hear me.

Mamalie came back, she looked round the room, she said, "what was I saying, Hilda?"

I said, "I was thinking of asking you about this scrap, it's black with pink rose-buds; Aunt Aggie said it was a silver-grey dress that she had for Philadelphia when she married Uncle Will."

Mamalie said, "you said something or somebody said something, who said something?"

I said, "it's you and me, Mamalie, I was asking about Aunt Aggie, I was thinking about—about—church—I mean, I was thinking about something—" Mamalie puts her hand up to her hair, she presses her hands against the sides of her face as if to hide the two long braids that have white threads in them but look darker when they are down, than when they are looped up, either side of her face, under her lace-cap.

"What were you talking about before I went to sleep?" said Mamalie. I do not tell her that she has not been asleep.

"We were talking—because I heard them talking—I was cold—" What will I say now? "It's too dark to read to me, Mamalie," I say, "but I was thinking I'd ask you to read. I was thinking, I'd get my new fairy-tales, I don't know, I may have said out aloud—you know how it is—'I'll get my new fairy-tales, I'll get Hans Christian Andersen'."

I said again, "I'll get Hans Christian Andersen."

"They were talking outside the window," I said, "I was listening to them and they said *ah*. They were saying *ah* because it was a shooting-star. Aunt Jennie says, you can have a wish on your first summer shooting-star. I did not think of any wish, anyhow I did not see it, I only heard them talking. I wished, if I wished anything, that I would not think it might fall on the house. I know it could not, because of gravity or something like that, that keeps the stars from falling on us and keeps the world going round. Gravity keeps the earth on its track and Mr. Evans explained about Papa in the Transit House. Eric is in the Observatory, looking at his double-stars—"

"Double-stars," said Mamalie.

"I heard you coming up the stairs and I said, could I get your knitting and you said no, I think, or maybe you didn't answer at all, and then we lit the candle."

"Yes," said Mamalie, "we lit the candle."

"Then you took off your cap—" she puts up her hand, she is feeling for her cap. I wonder why she thinks she must always wear a lace-cap?

"I wanted one of the little tight caps," she said, "like the early Sisters wore and I wanted to be one of the Single Sisters but Christian said it was best not, because already the German reformed people were accusing us of Popish practices."

I said, "what are Popish practices, Mamalie, and who is Christian?"

She said, "I thought you knew, Agnes, that I called your father Christian. It was confusing with all the Henrys."

"Which Henrys," I say, "Mimmie?" remembering to call her Mimmie.

"You know," she said, "Sabina Henry married Francis' father." (But Francis is our own Papalie who is dead). "There was William Henry," she said, "who was the son of William Henry and Christian's name was Henry. I was glad I had called him Christian, but only to myself (I suppose I never told you) because of Christian Heinrich Johann Seidel. He was Henry's uncle and he knew there was the Secret. The first Christian Seidel was with Zeisberger at *Gnadenhuetten*."

She said *Gnadenhuetten* and it does not matter what it is or where it is or what it means or anything about it. It is the same when Papa calls me *Töchterlein,* it simply makes everything quite different, so that sometimes, I am sure that I am really in the woods, like when Mama plays *Träumerei* which isn't very good music, she says, but I ask her to play it because it's called *Träumerei.*

It would be no good my trying to learn German because when I look at one of the German grammar-books in the bookshelves, it stops working. A row of words called *der-die-das* doesn't belong to it. I would rather talk German, real German than anything. I do not want to learn German, I do not even want them to know how much I feel when they say *Gnadenhuetten* like that. I am in the word, I am *Gnadenhuetten* the way Mamalie says it, though I do not know what it means.

"And *Wunden Eiland,*" she says.

It seems as if something had come over me like the branches of a tree or the folds of a tent when she says *Wunden Eiland.* She says *Eiland* which must be island and the *Wunden,* I suppose, is wonder or wonderful. I do not even want her to tell me, but I want her to go on talking because if she stops, the word will stop. The word is like a bee-hive, but there are no bees in it now. I am the last bee in the bee-hive, this is the game I play. The other bees have gone, that is why it is so quiet. Can one bee keep a bee-hive alive, I mean, can one person who knows that *Wunden Eiland* is a bee-hive, keep *Wunden Eiland* for the other bees, when they come back?

But it won't be any use just thinking like this, because if I don't say something, she might really go to sleep, or she will talk the whole thing out in German and I don't want to listen to her talking nothing but German, because then I start to think about it and if I start to think about it, it gets *der-die-das*-ish and I am angry that I can not understand or that I can not learn it quickly, but *Wunden Eiland* is not a thing you learn, it's not a thing that anyone can teach you, it just happens.

"Tell me more about the island," I say, though maybe *Eiland* isn't an island, though I think it must be.

"It was washed away," said Mamalie. "The Monocacy was then, a real river; even in Christian's father's time, there was part of the old bridge still standing, that led from what is now the Seminary grounds, across the river to the Sanctuary. Christian said it was symbolic. He felt that the Church had lost the thing that the meetings in the Sanctuary had held together. It began with the young Count (though maybe Zinzendorf himself started it or was part of it) with his 'I have a passion, and it is He—He only'. Cammerhof, whom they criticised for what they called antinomianism, was holding the thing together. The thing was symbolized by the star that Cammerhof had had designed and cut into one of the lintel-stones of the new Brothers' House that they were building. The carved words

> *Father, Mother, Dearest Man*
> *Be honoured with the Young-men's Plan,*

or

> *Vater, Mutter, Lieber Mann*
> *Habt Ehr vom Jünglings Plan*

meant more than just the words, *Mutter* wasn't just the Holy Ghost. It was a special Spirit that some of the Crusaders had worshipped. That was the Society, and *Plan* didn't mean, Christian said, just *plan* or even company, but referred to some secret-society or organization. Cammerhof was much criticised for his wild extravagance, as they called it, of imagery and diction. But he was sent to the Brotherhood direct by Count Zinzendorf. Pyrlaeus was one of them. It was Pyrlaeus who came upon the Secret, though it was the young

Count, Christian Renatus who had traced the Secret through its European origins. The emblem of the United Brethren is the Lamb with the Banner, the same emblem that the Templars in Europe had used."

Mamalie is talking like something in a book and I do not very much understand what she is saying. I have heard of Count Zinzendorf of course, who founded the *Unitas Fratrum,* the United Brethren which is our Church or which was our Church, before we moved from Bethlehem.

Unitas Fratrum is united brethren, like United States is united states, and they have a sign which is a lamb, like the United States has an Eagle, and they have a flag with a cross. Mamalie says it is a flag the crusaders used or a banner, but that was long ago, only it is all long ago.

If I think 400 years back, it is because we all had a holiday when it was 1892, which was 400 years since Columbus discovered America. But the *Unitas Fratrum* seemed to have discovered something which was very important, that was in Europe. They came to America to bring the Secret from Europe or to keep the Secret to themselves. But something happened like it always does, it seems, so that the United Brethren weren't really united. "Who was Pyrlaeus?" I said.

"John Christopher Pyrlaeus was a musician like the rest of them," Mamalie said, "but chiefly he collected Indian words and sayings and made a dictionary of them. He said it would be impossible to follow the language without the music—they were all musicians. He made notes of tones and rhythms of their voices. It was while he was talking with Zeisberger about his visit to Paxnous or Paxinosa, that Pyrlaeus realised that there might be a way of communicating or even communing—as he put it—with the Indians through their music."

"Who was Paxnous?" I said.

"Paxnous," Mamalie said, "was the famous Shawanese chief. It was Christian Seidel who fell on the idea of actually bringing them together on *Wunden Eiland;* though the Indians and settlers had met there before on various occasions, they had never met formally for a discussion of their various religious doctrines and beliefs. It was the young Count, Christian Renatus in *Herrnhut,* who had first outlined the *Plan*—that is, the Society, as he had traced it back to the Templars in Europe.

"There was the Hidden Church—the Moravians themselves had been a hidden church for centuries but the actual Hidden Church that had been destroyed and obliterated by the Inquisition, Christian Renatus maintained, wasn't really destroyed. It ran underground. That is what Christian Renatus said, their ideas, the ideas of these few, were the same as the ideas of the Hidden Church—almost it seemed that they had been part of the Hidden Church. Things people said about us here, and misrepresentations and scandals invented about Count Zinzendorf and the other disciples were the same scandals, all through the ages. The Templars, it is true—and probably always, certain members of any secret body—had their backsliders and traitors. But there was no traitor ever found among the inner circle of the Hidden Church, or the Invisible Church, as some called it.

"The Secret that my Christian explained to me seemed very simple. It was simply belief in what was said—*and, lo, I am with you alway, even unto the end of the world.* You see, those words were taken literally. I mean," said Mamalie, "Christian Renatus said the carpenter from Moravia who had first spoken to his father about the doctrine that led to the re-establishment of the Brotherhood and our coming to America, wasn't a carpenter at all. At least, he was a carpenter but Christian Renatus said he was—"

I did not know why Mamalie stopped talking. It was easy to see what she was going to say.

"But what about Paxnous?" I said, because I did not know that we had a real Indian king or chief in the family—or that is how I thought about it, although Christian Seidel who was with Zeisberger at *Gnadenhuetten* and the old uncle who was named Christian (who would be my great-great uncle, if he was my uncle) and Mamalie's first husband, Henry Christian, weren't related to me at all, I suppose. Only if we were *United Brethren* and I was one of them, then it was really in the family. Anyhow, I had thought about that other Lady who was Papa's first wife and it seemed she was a sort of mother, then Aunt Aggie's father who was Mamalie's first husband, would be a sort of grandfather. Well, I did not really think this all out but that is the feeling I had. Anyhow, hadn't Mamalie called me Aggie?

There were all these questions in a row, each with its particular question-mark. I did not think them out nor see them in writing but they were:

What was the name of the carpenter (if he had a name)?

What does Paxnous mean (if it means anything)?

Where is the dictionary that John Christopher Pyrlaeus made?

Did you play the spinet, Mamalie? Did you play *Four Marys*?

Who were the four Marys, and why were there four?

Who has our Grimm, and did they lose the picture of the Princess and the Frog, that was loose and partly torn across?

Why are they all called Christian or does it just mean that they are Christians?

Why do they make it a Secret because anybody can read what it says in the Bible, *lo, I am with you alway*?

Did great-grandfather Weiss like Christian Henry more than he liked Francis, who is Mama's own father?

Or wouldn't he say?

Why do you always think there might be a fire or didn't you, was it me or Mama thought it?

Why are you frightened and put your hand to your hair? (I want long hair but if an Indian came to scalp you, perhaps it would be worse.)

Why did Mamalie say, they might burn us all up? (She was afraid of being burnt up but she was more afraid that she might lose the papers.)

What were the papers?

"What were the papers, Mamalie?" I said.

"Christian had found the documents that had been hidden away. He did not know if they were actually hidden or got misplaced or lost. Anyhow, Bishop Benade asked Christian to go over the papers and make a rough catalogue of the books before they moved them from the old Brothers' House to their new church library. There were old maps and drawings and lists of the Economy and tattered note-books and unbound folios of receipts for medicines of herbs and simples that some of the Sisters were famous for, and church-music, of course, and all the old documents from the War of Independence when they made the whole town into a hospital, and the comings and goings of George Washington and Lafayette and so on and so on, but Christian wasn't so interested in all that after he found the old birch-bark case.

"He thought at first it was an old music-scroll, he pulled out. But it was a document written in curious characters, Greek, Hebrew and Indian dialects and writing and marginal notes of music. The paper scroll bore the names of

Cammerhof, Pyrlaeus, Zeisberger and Christian Seidel with (my Christian supposed) the list of medicine-men or priests of the Indian tribes, done in their picture-writing. I do not know exactly what relation the first Christian Seidel would be to my Christian. But Christian saw his own name written and the cup with the S that his uncle (for whom he was named) used as a seal for his letters and private papers.

"There was the same motto in French, but Christian had thought the seal of the cup with the letter S was a personal signature or design of his uncle; he had not known that the early Christian Seidel had used it. Christian thought the cup was because *seidel* in German, means a mug or jug or cup, but he found, when he began deciphering the papers that the Cup linked up with the early branch of the church that went back to the 9th century in Europe, that was called the *Calixtines* which is a Greek word that has something to do with a cup, like calix is the part of a flower that is shaped like a cup.

"The papers were headed by the motto and that is what had caught Christian's eye, as he turned over the old sermons and the notes on the Choirs and the Economy (as they called the early system of sharing all things together, when they first founded the town). The motto was *l'amitié passe même le tombeau.*"

I suppose that is French, it must be because Mamalie said it was, but it doesn't make any difference to me, I mean, it sounds all right and even I could understand it because *tombeau* sounds the same as tomb and *passe* is pass, something passes the tomb, like Jesus at Easter, but nothing happens to me, like when she says *Gnadenhuetten* or when she says *Wunden Eiland.*

"Christian thought it was the same seal," said Mamalie, "but it was a little different because either old Christian Heinrich wanted to change it, because he didn't know what it was about, or he did know what it was about and didn't want to use the mystic sign of the Lord's Chalice on his ordinary letters. Anyhow, he made the cup now look like an urn and set the S on a shield in the front. Maybe it might have been just by chance that it happened, only Christian was concerned because the motto was the same. It was as if Christian, my Christian felt the burden of the discovery personally, as if seeing the motto from the seal his family used and the conventionalized urn, without its top, simplified into an unmistakable Mystic Chalice, made him feel that the thing belonged to him. The thing belonged to him."

"What was the thing, Mamalie?" I ask, though I can see it is going to be one of those "things" that happen sometimes, that there are no words for, that you find words for and the words disenchant it, like the other way round of an enchantment, when people say words in an Arabian Night's Tale and a person turns to stone or a locked door opens. A locked door opens.

"The trouble was, the notes were written in Greek and Hebrew and they had added in one of the Shawanese dialects, *what I have written I have written* which you remember Pilate said, when they asked him to take down the words, *Jesus of Nazareth, King of the Jews.*

"Christian did not want to take the papers to the Elders because he had heard his uncle talk of the scandal, as it was called, of *Wunden Eiland.*

"The old uncle, Christian Heinrich, had come from Europe; he was the brother of the one in Russia who sent his portrait to Christian's father, Pastor Charles Frederick Seidel, and the brother was Heinrich too, or Henry, but he was called Henri Chevalier de Seidel. Christian Heinrich wanted to know all about the old times and the old people and he learned something of the very early days apparently, from old Bishop Nathanael Seidel, who was a very old man and anyhow, didn't want to talk about the Secret and the first Christian Seidel or perhaps he had forgotten. But Christian gathered from these talks with his uncle that there was some mystery or some scandal.

"We could not make out what the scandal could be and Christian was always curious and here it was, all written, but written in almost undecipherable characters. Christian was enough of a scholar to see that Cammerhof was now and again having his little joke. The papers were a copy of an original that had been burnt after the scandal."

"Burnt after the scandal," she says again, "burnt," she says. Then she looks at the candle, then she looks over at her bureau as if someone were there, but there is no one there, then she says in quite a different voice—"*until the Promise is redeemed and the Gift restored.*"

"What, Mamalie, what are you saying?" O, I have called her Mamalie, maybe now she will remember that I am not Agnes.

"Mimmie, Mimmie," I say, "what did you say, Mimmie?"

The light might go out in a tunnel, she had said; all the lights might go out in a tunnel and we have only this little night-light and it's been burning now for quite a long time or maybe it hasn't, because I don't know how long I have been here listening and the curtain is blowing against the saucer, the curtain-rings at the top of the curtains rattle, as if it were really a strong wind blowing. But this is summer—maybe it's a thunder-storm, they come on, after very hot days; Mama will say, "it's sultry, it feels thunder-y"; I don't know if this is going to be a thunder-storm.

"It's all right, Mimmie," I say, "it's all right."

I don't know why I say that because Mamalie isn't frightened of thunder-storms, but she is afraid in a tunnel and she has a night-light by her bed always and the curtains are brushing the saucer and she is holding her hands up in a funny way as if she were going to keep the saucer from falling off the window-sill, but she doesn't touch the saucer. She holds her hands flat up, not together, not like praying.

"Mimmie, listen, listen—it's all right. Even if the candle goes out, I can find your matches, I can find your candle-box in the dark, I can see in the dark—they say, I can see like a cat in the dark. Mimmie, I am not afraid of the dark."

"Nor was Christian Seidel," she said, "nor was Cammerhof, nor was Zeisberger nor was Pyrlaeus. They went into the dark alone, but it was a greater darkness than we can imagine with our outer senses. It was the darkness of the inner senses. It was a test. Zeisberger drew back before it, it was tempting the Lord thy God, he said. Christian deciphered all that and these very words were written but they were written in different parts of the document, so that if you did not have the clue, you would never find them and sometimes you could see where Pyrlaeus had had a hand in keeping the matter secret. There is where I helped.

"I would find the lines of music that Christopher Pyrlaeus indicated, mostly from Gregor's metres—he wrote them as if they were just tones and notes of the Indian voices, like annotations on the side of the page. There were marginal notes in music but Christian was not trained in reading music, that is why he brought the papers to me. They were not papers exactly, it was a long scroll, it might have been parchment or very thin deer-skin, treated with some sort of oil or varnish. Even then, Christian could not be sure if or if not, the writing and the picture-writing might not vanish under his very eyes, as the scroll had been wound tight ever since it had been flung aside with some of the old manuscript rolls, the Brothers had discarded and not burnt yet.

"John Christopher Cammerhof who was the ruling spirit, really asked what did St. Paul mean then by test or try the Spirits? Pyrlaeus said there was their old precedent in Europe for choosing the bishops by lot, as the disciples were chosen when Judas left the circle. There could be no harm trying the choice by lots. They selected texts and wrote them on narrow strips of paper and put them in a bowl or basket; it was all written out; they asked Anna von Pahlen (who was the noble Livonian lady who had left her country and estates, to come with Cammerhof to the settlement) to draw the lots for them. I don't know what was written on the other strips of paper, I only know that Anna von Pahlen drew out *I will give him the Morning Star.* So they accepted the challenge of Paxnous's medicine-man, as the head-magician or priest of the tribes was called. The meeting was at *Wunden Eiland.*"

Mamalie had said that Zeisberger had started it or Zeisberger had come across the Secret first, but I did not like to ask her why now, he did not want to go on with finding out the Secret.

I could see Zeisberger because we have a picture of him; he is preaching to the Indians; it is a dark picture, they call it a steel-engraving, like the *Washington at Mount Vernon* that we have, hanging in the sitting-room.

I had no picture of the others but I could think that John Christopher Cammerhof was a little thin man and that Christopher Pyrlaeus had a white wig, like George Washington in the other picture. Cammerhof would have dark hair and his hair would fall forward and he would brush it out of his eyes and he would laugh—he would laugh because Mamalie had said that her Christian was enough of a scholar to see that Cammerhof was having his little joke.

I had never heard of Anna von Pahlen before, but I could think of her like some of the pictures Mamalie had of the early Sisters, but she would not wear a tight cap, but maybe she would, maybe she would be a Moravian Sister, if she had come to the Settlement with Cammerhof.

I could think of Anna von Pahlen almost as a Princess. I do not think Anna von Pahlen had any children.

I think Pyrlaeus had children and that he taught them to play the spinet and I think Pyrlaeus had candles in tall candle-sticks and that Cammerhof had an ink-stand and that he had quills sticking up in it, like a porcupine. I think John Christopher Cammerhof had a lot of quill-pens.

I could see what it was about.

They were exchanging hostages, like in war but it was a different kind of war. It was a war of the Spirit or for the Spirit, the Spirit was the Indian's Great Spirit and the Spirit was (for this inner band of United Brethren) a Spirit like the Holy Ghost, which nobody seemed really to understand but which they understood.

The Holy Spirit would come upon them (like it did, when everyone talked different languages in the Bible) with tongues of flame, or the Holy Spirit would not answer their prayers.

They were together, these few and Anna von Pahlen and others whose names were written in the list, and there was a list of Indian names. There was something very important about exchanging names because the inner band of Indians believed the name a person had, was somehow another part of him, like a ghost or shadow and Anna von Pahlen was to have the name of Paxnous' wife, who was Morning Star in English but she had the Indian words for it, written with notes of music to show exactly how it sounded.

Mamalie found all this out.

Morning Star was not really the ordinary name of Paxnous' wife but her special inner-name, and Paxnous' wife was to be called by another name, too. Anna said one of her many names in Europe was Angelica; she had a long name, Anna Angelica and a lot more, and as they called her, ordinarily, Anna, she would give Paxnous' wife the name Angelica, in exchange for Morning Star. They explained this to the Indian magician or medicine-man; Pyrlaeus was the great authority on Indian languages but he asked Zeisberger to talk to them because it was Zeisberger who had started the whole thing, though now, at the last he had said *thou shalt not tempt the Lord thy God.* But Zeisberger was with them at *Wunden Eiland.*

"How was it Zeisberger started it, Mimmie?" I said, for now I understood I had another name; now I was Agnes, now I would really be Agnes and Aunt Aggie's name was Agnes Angelica, so perhaps they had named her Angelica because of Anna von Pahlen, then I would be part of Anna von Pahlen, too, and I would be part of the ceremony at *Wunden Eiland* and I would be Morning Star along with Anna.

"How was it Zeisberger started it, Mimmie?" I said and I said, "what was his name, Mimmie?" for it occurred to me now that I did not know his name and I had wanted to ask the name of the carpenter at the beginning, too.

"David," she said. "David Zeisberger had come far up the valley," she said. "It was beyond *Gnadenhuetten* which was then a day's journey from the town, but I don't know just where he went. Anyhow, an Indian who must have been a friend of one of the *Gnadenhuetten* Indians, stepped out from the circle round the fire and said, 'for you, we will answer the question'. I do not know just what the question was.

"The Moravians had not asked for furs, they had not traded with the Indians, this in itself seemed strange; they had not taken land—and had explained carefully how they had acquired land from John Penn, which had already been paid for. Some of the Indian tribes argued the matter and said that Zinzendorf had no right to land that had been taken from them by a trick of the white-men (it was something to do with the famous walking-treaty) so Zinzendorf paid again for land which was disputed.

"It was Pyrlaeus who worked most of this out, though it was Zeisberger who started it. David Zeisberger asked a question which had never been asked before, not at any rate, by white-men whom the tribes respected. Zeisberger was caught up by their Great Spirit, the tribesmen had concluded, and the tribes up the valley had sent further to report and it was one of Paxnous' most famous medicine-men or magicians who stepped out when Zeisberger asked the question, for though these medicine-men had gathered on the edge of his circles, they had not made themselves known before.

"Paxnous' priest was wrapped in one of those bear-skin or buffalo-robes, but he had a small symbol, a rayed-out star or maybe it was the sun, worked in tiny shells on the breast of his deer-skin jacket.

"He seemed to fling the robe over his shoulder in a special way, as if he meant only David Zeisberger to see the pattern on his jacket.

"The Indian said, 'we will answer your question in the names of the inner tribes,' but David Zeisberger was a little confused as he did not know exactly what his question was. Then he realised it was a question he had asked before. Only perhaps, Christopher Pyrlaeus said afterwards, David Zeisberger had, by accident (searching in the unfamiliar dialect) this time, asked it dif-

ferently. Zeisberger only asked, after he had finished his talk over the circle in
the fire-light, politely to hear (now that he had spoken of his God) more of
their own Great Spirit.

"He had often asked this question and the Indians had sometimes taken
him to their lodges and shown him buffalo robes and carved poles and bowls
and painted masks and feather-crowns that they used in their ceremonies.
But this was a strange Indian and he held out a belt which was different from
any Zeisberger had seen, a different kind of work, I mean, and it was very
old, Zeisberger could see, and it was marked with alternate patterns of gold
or old tinted silver; it was marked with an alternating pattern of a circle or a
flower and a star, but the star was simply a cross, like in ordinary cross-stitch
sampler work and the flower was not much more than a badly drawn circle,
such as a child might make who tries to draw a daisy or a rose on a slate."

"Was this at *Wunden Eiland*?" I said and Mamalie said, "*Wunden Eiland*
came later.

"The question Zeisberger asked was perhaps accidental—I mean, maybe
the way he said the unfamiliar Indian words meant more to the Indian priest
(for it seemed he was an important priest or medicine-man) than was meant.
Pyrlaeus thought there might have been some slight misunderstanding,
though the question had been asked and the answer had been given in the
rather special way the strange Indian lifted his robe (as if revealing some special badge or emblem) to show the pattern worked on his jacket, and the
answer was given, in some way, in the words that Zeisberger spoke when he
accepted the belt with the cross-pattern and the flat roses.

"It was more than an exchange of outer civilities, it was an inner greeting
and it seemed a pact had been made (though Zeisberger, fumbling with the
dialect, did not quite know how it happened) to have a general secret-meet-
ing of the wisest of the tribes, the Indians and the Moravians, and to set
special questions to their individual Gods or Guiding Spirits.

"In fact, the answer given by the Spirits, was to decide the future of the
whole country, was to answer a question that the warriors had long been
debating at their war-councils, as to what was to be the relationship of the
Indians further up the valley, was in fact—and this was the pity of it—to give
the answer that the warriors had debated at their councils, as to what was to
be the relationship in future between the white-men and the Indians, altogether. Already tracts of land further north were depleted of their wild ani-

mals, and the tribes were moving west and there was to be a final settlement soon. It was Paxnous who had won in the argument of warriors (who wanted to dismiss all personal enmities throughout the whole land and fall on the white-men, once and for all, and exterminate them) by asking that at least, they might first consult the Great Spirit with the inner words of ritual which were only used on very rare occasions, perhaps once in the lifetime of a great chief."

Now Mamalie told this story which I did not altogether understand but pieced together afterwards—I mean, long afterwards, of course, because the "thing" that was to happen, that was in a sense to join me in emotional understanding, in intuition anyway, to the band of chosen initiates at *Wunden Eiland,* had not yet happened.

The "thing" that was to happen, happened soon afterwards, maybe that very autumn or winter, it was before Christmas, say in November, or it was after Christmas was well over, say in February, but I can not date the time of the thing that happened, that happened to me personally, because I forgot it. I mean it was walled over and I was buried with it. I, the child was incarcerated, as a nun might be, who for some sin—which I did not then understand—is walled up alive in her own cell or in some ante-room to a cathedral.

It was as if I were there all the time, in understanding anyway, of the "thing" that had happened before I was 10, the "thing" that had happened to me and the "thing" I had inherited from them. I, the child was still living but I was not free, not free to express my understanding of the Gift, until long afterwards. I was not in fact, completely free, until again there was the whistling of evil wings, the falling of poisonous arrows, the deadly signature of a sign of evil-magic in the sky.

The same fear (personal fear) could crack the wall that had originally covered me over, because to live, I had to be frozen in myself—so great was the shock to my mind, when I found my father wounded. I did not know, as Mamalie began talking, that *Wunden Eiland* was Island of the Wounds; it came clear afterwards. Bits of it came clear, as I say, in patches; the story was like the quilt that I drew up to my chin, as I propped myself up in her bed, to listen.

The Gift actually was Mamalie's. She had inherited it from her own father or her uncle or her great-uncle who was a master musician, as Zinzendorf had been a master-singer. The Gift also might have been bequeathed to her through her own mother, in whose family there was the usual Scotch legend of one of the family (maybe, far back in Scotland) being far-sighted or being second-sighted.

I did not know that Mamalie was a musician, she never told me that she played the spinet and she put aside her papers and the notes that she had worked over, after Henry (Christian) Seidel's death. He died when he was 26, and so carried out in a way, the fate and the legend of Cammerhof who died at 29, from overwork, as even the Elders agreed, from zeal in the prosecution of his duties, though there was a blot, as they called it, brought on the Church, through his extravagances, his fanaticism and his Liturgy of the Wounds, that had been practised with the chosen band of the inner devotees, at *Wunden Eiland.* That is why it was called *Wunden Eiland,* and it was there that Paxnous or Paxinosa, the famous Shawanese chief, pledged the soul of his wife Morning Star, to the Brotherhood. When they drew out the text, *I will give him the Morning Star,* the Indian medicine-men who talked mixed English and a little German with the Moravians, shouted in one voice *Heil* or *Hail* and then *Kehelle.*

I could not see this, as I sat before I was 10, in Mamalie's bed watching the flickering of the night-light, sensing rather than understanding her strange story.

It seems that she and her husband, my other grandfather, if I could put it that way, in going over the notes, had worked out some of the Indian rhythms; Mamalie herself picked them out on the little spinet. Then "it" came over Mamalie, even as "it" had flowed about them, at that first meeting at *Wunden Eiland.* The first was almost their last meeting, because the rumour came to the more conventional members of the Unity, that Cammerhof was relating their Church ritual to some Indian magic; it was witchcraft, they said, and witchcraft in those days, was still alive in Europe and had swept the New England states, at Salem, even in America.

It did not matter that Christian Renatus back in *Herrnhut,* had discovered a clue; the machinations of long dead Knights Templars in a Europe from which they had fled, was anathema to the stricter churchmen. It did not matter to them, and they could not altogether be blamed for not seeing that Anna and Christian and David Zeisberger and the Indian Paxnous and some of the devotees of the liturgies of the Worship of the Wounds, should have perhaps fallen on a secret, that properly directed, might have changed the course of history, might have lifted the dark wings of evil from the whole world.

Roughly, a hundred years had passed, since the founding of the town and the rituals practised at *Wunden Eiland,* which Mamalie had explained was actually an island in the Monocacy river which, in Mama's day, was called a creek, though it could occasionally break its boundaries in the season of floods, as that time Mama told us about, when the deer that Papalie had in the Seminary grounds, were lost.

A hundred years had passed, since the founding of the town, I mean, when the later Christian found the papers or the scroll of flexible deer-skin, which told the story of the meeting of the chief medicine-men of the friendly tribes and the devotees of the Ritual of the Wounds. The later Christian who was no mean scholar, glimpsed here a hint in Hebrew or followed a Greek text to its original, and so pieced out the story of the meeting, deciphered actually the words of strange pledges passed, strange words spoken, strange rhythms sung, which were prompted, all alike said, by the Power of the Holy Spirit; the Holy Ghost of the Christian ritualists and the Great Spirit of the Indians poured their grace alike; their gifts came in turn to Anna, to John Christopher Frederick Cammerhof, to John Christopher Pyrlaeus, who was not only a scholar and authority on the Indian languages but a musician as well.

Pyrlaeus had indicated the rhythms of some of the Indian Invocations, and it was while Mamalie was working these out with the help of one of the old hymn-books, that the Gift came to her.

Pyrlaeus, to keep the thing a secret, had occasionally indicated a run of notes or a bar of music from their own ritual to give the key or the clef or whatever it was he was trying to give—anyhow, it would only be a trained musician to begin with, who could hope to follow even these outer promptings, but Mamalie not only did this but pierced through to the inner meaning. I did not know—did any of them know—that my grandmother had not only a delicate tone-perception but actually a working knowledge of musical composition?

Well, where had Mamalie's gift gone then? I did not ask her but I sense now, that she burnt it all up in an hour or so of rapture, that she and her young husband together, recaptured the secret of *Wunden Eiland;* and not only the

secret but the actual Power that had fallen on Anna and Zeisberger and Paxnous and Morning Star, fell, a hundred years afterwards, on the younger
Christian Seidel and his wife, Elizabeth Caroline, who was our grandmother.
It seemed, Mamalie outlined it, that in trying over and putting together the
indicated rhythms, she herself became one with the *Wunden Eiland* initiates
and herself spoke with tongues, hymns of the spirits in the air, of spirits at
sun-rise and sun-setting, of the deer and the wild squirrel, the beaver, the
otter, the king-fisher and the hawk and eagle.

She laughed when she told me about it, so I know that she and Christian
(or Henry) who was Aunt Agnes' father, must have been very happy.

"It was laughing, laughing all the time," she said, "it was not just Minne-
ha-ha who laughed, we all laughed, like scales running up and down," said
Mamalie. "O," said Mamalie, "I could not tell you of that laughter, it was the
laughter of leaves, of wind, of snow swirling, it was the laughter of the water;
indeed, it was the outpouring of the Mystic Chalice that Paxnous' priest too,
had a name for; it poured from the sky or from the inner realm of the Spirit,
this laughter that ran over us.

"The laughter ran over us and the deep tones of the men's voices and the
high pure silver of Anna's voice, mingled in a sort of breathing hymn; it was
breathing, it was breath, it was the S that was carved upon the Chalice that
my Christian had recognized as the ordinary letter-seal of his own uncle.

"It was the Cup and maybe it was not just by accident that Christian was
surnamed *seidel*, as their Indians said their own names had meanings, as we
know from the more obvious ones, well, like Little-bear or White-eagle or
really most obviously from Minne-ha-ha, Laughing-waters. This was only
the beginning. It would go on, for it worked—I mean, the thing they were
waiting for, happened; God, our God, the God of David Zeisberger, the God
who had prompted the carpenter of Moravia, to tell the tale of the Hidden
Church and the Hidden Seed, to Count Zinzendorf, met the God of Paxnous. There was no special secret. It was something we had always known
but had not acted on. At least, Shooting-Star said that."

Shooting-star? We are back at the beginning. This is just a bed-room.
Why, I am sitting up in Mamalie's bed and there were voices outside my
window. *My garden is under the window* is the first line of a poem that I
recited, the first time I recited anything on a stage. It was a large audience,

they clapped and Miss Helen said I must go out and be out of the window, and make a bow. I made a bow. Now, this is something like that. They were acting something.

Mamalie has forgotten that she was not at *Wunden Eiland;* she said, "the laughter ran over us" but she was a hundred years later and she just picked out notes (that she had carefully looked up in the hymn-books and in the old folios) that John Christopher Pyrlaeus had indicated to her, down the side of a page. Mamalie must be very clever. She never told me about this. She never, I know, told anyone about this. And now she is telling me about it. It is as if she had been there at that meeting, only she couldn't have been there. How does she know they laughed? How does she know that the S on the cup meant Spirit, or now she says it differently . . . " then Christian knew that it was all meant to be from the beginning. The S on the Cup was the *Sanctus Spiritus* that the inner church had worshipped and Christian Seidel (the first one) had been an inner-member or an initiate of that church.

"The inner members of the lodges and cults of the friendly tribes—and for that matter, maybe of the unfriendly—spoke the same language. The serpent shaped like an S, carved on the pole outside their lodges or painted in their picture writing, was the same serpent—it was not the Devil; it was not a question of witchcraft or devil-worship or snake-worship. The inner band of the initiates, worshipped the same Spirit, the *Sanctus Spiritus.* Why, when you say that," said Mamalie, "you can hear the breath of their singing. It is *be ye wise as serpents*—that is another kind of serpent than the Devil," said Mamalie.

The Devil? What has Mamalie said about the Devil? Who is Shooting-star and where has he gone? Where, for the matter of all that, is Mamalie? "Where are you Mamalie?" I say.

This is the patchwork quilt, here is the moiré silk, they call it, and the watered-silk that old Aunt Sabina, who I only just remember, had for her great-niece, Anna's wedding. But that was another Anna. It is confusing, because they all seem to have the same names, Christian or Christopher, Anna and Elizabeth, but Mama's name is different. My name is quite different, but Mamalie called me Agnes. Agnes means a lamb, I know that and the Moravians have the same lamb with a flag that Mamalie said the crusaders or the Templars had, for their sign.

There was a seal that had a cup and an S on it. The S was for *Sanctus*

Spiritus that means the Holy Ghost that nobody seems to understand but that Mamalie said, that Anna von Pahlen and John Christopher Frederick Cammerhof found at a meeting at *Wunden Eiland,* that was a scandal. What is a scandal?

It was a blot on the church, they said and they didn't have any meetings like that any more and Mamalie says that Christian—her Christian—found that they had made a pact or a pledge, but it was in the Spirit, in the *Sanctus Spiritus* and it seems they didn't keep it. They couldn't keep it because the stricter Brethren of the church said it was witchcraft. What exactly is witchcraft? You can be burnt for a witch. Is Mamalie a witch? She is crouching over the candle, she is holding the saucer with the candle in it, in her hand. What is Mamalie saying to the candle?

"—until the Promise is redeemed and the Gift restored."

But she said that before. She said that when she was telling me about the copy of the Promise that they made to one another, that was written on deer-skin, or maybe it was parchment. They made a Promise but it was not Mamalie's fault if they did not keep the Promise; how could it be? I suppose the Gift was their all talking and laughing that way and singing with no words or words of leaves rustling and rivers flowing and snow swirling in the wind, which is the breath of the Spirit, it seems.

Mamalie helped her husband who was named Henry, but she called him Christian or maybe his name was Henry Christian—anyhow, he was dead. I mean, he was dead, almost from the beginning, because Aunt Aggie was not a year old, I think, when he died. Morning Star was the Indian Princess who was the wife of Paxnous, who was baptized by the Moravians. She was really baptized, it seems, but Paxnous was not baptized but the Indians took Anna von Pahlen into their mysteries in exchange for Morning Star; I mean, Anna was Morning Star in their mysteries and Morning Star (who had another ordinary Indian name like White-cloud or Fragrant-grass or one of those names) was Angelica which was another name of Anna von Pahlen, who was really Mrs. John Christopher Frederick Cammerhof, but I like to think of her as Anna von Pahlen.

Mamalie is talking to the candle. Really, it is not her fault.

"It is not your fault," I say.

I am sure it is not her fault, whatever it is. Maybe she was afraid they would burn her for a witch (like they did at Salem, Massachusetts) if she told them that she could sing Indian songs, though she didn't know any Indian languages, and that she and her Christian had found out the secret of *Wunden Eiland* which the church had said was a scandal and a blot.

Mamalie used to say, "a black rose is growing in your garden" sometimes, to Mama or Aunt Laura (Mama told me) if they laughed too much and got excited, but Mamalie never said that to me, I think. Maybe, she is remembering the blot when she says a black-rose; a black rose is really a shadow of a rose and you do not have a shadow, of course, without light. There's just this candle in a saucer, in this room. It's not bright enough to make a very dark shadow. It's just that the room is all shadow without any corners of things showing, like they show when Uncle Fred put the lamp on the floor when we were children, and he made shadow-pictures on the wall. Maybe, it was all shadows and pictures in Mamalie's mind, maybe there never was such a parchment, maybe there never was such a meeting at *Wunden Eiland,* maybe there never was a *Wunden Eiland.*

"Maybe there never was a *Wunden Eiland,*" I say.

"What—what—" she says, "Lucy."

Now, who is Lucy? Is that old Aunt Lucia that we used to take sugar-cake to, at the Widows' House?

"I told you it was all written, I told you the parchment was—was—Lucy, water" says Mamalie and she seems to be choking. Now I am frightened. "Lucy," she says, "someone must find the papers, someone must work out the music, now Christian is dead. Lucy," she says, "who can do the work— who can follow the music? Music, Lucy—" she says. Now I am frightened. I put one foot out of bed. I get out of bed—I walk round the bed. I stand looking at Mamalie. I take the candle from her hand.

"Be still," I say, "be still, it's all right." I do not call her Mamalie, I do not even call her Mimmie. "It's all right," I say, "it's all right, Elizabeth."

I think this is a good idea to call her Elizabeth though it rather frightens me. If she thinks I am Lucy, then I am not Agnes any more, and if I am not Agnes, she is not Mimmie any more. I think it must be old Aunt Lucia she is talking to, at the Widows' House, who died.

Ida used to put an apple-pie or sugar-cake in a basket with a clean napkin over the top, and Gilbert would carry the basket and we would take the sugar-cake or the apple-pie to Aunt Lucia. Mamalie says "Lucy," but I think this is old Aunt Lucia who wasn't an aunt at all, but we have many aunts and

Mama has many aunts who were sisters in the church to Mamalie, so I suppose they were aunts to us, in the church.

It is all about the church. It is something the church thought was bad and Mamalie was part of it, though she wasn't really, because it was a hundred years afterwards but she said, when she played the songs, it all came back. Songs bring things back, like that, it seems. Did she sing the songs? I never heard her sing. I don't think Mama ever heard her sing. She asks me to sing *Abide with me* and Mama plays the tune for it; Mamalie always asks me to sing, I think she is the only person who always asks me to sing.

She asks me to sing *Fast falls the eventide. The darkness deepens.* She is always afraid, it seems, in the dark and she asks me to sing *The darkness deepens.* It's not really dark in this room but then I am not afraid of the dark, I am afraid more of a bright light that might be fire and a shooting-star, falling on the house and burning us all up.

It all started with the shooting-star and my asking questions, but the question that David Zeisberger asked (Mamalie said) might have changed the course of history, so it is important, after all, sometimes to ask questions. I think of questions I could ask Eric sometimes or I could ask Mamalie—but there is no use saying, "who is Lucy?" because for the moment, it seems that I am Lucy.

But I must do something, she might come back in a hurry and wonder where she is. But it might be better if she did come back because where she is, she is thirsty and she talks about the parchment being burnt and herself being burnt and the Promise and the penalty if they didn't keep the Promise and about Great Wars and the curse on the land, if we did not keep the Promise and how Morning Star was the soul, God gave the Church and the Church did not recognize Morning Star, even though the *morning stars sang together.* But they didn't. The Morning Stars didn't sing together, she said; she said, "Shooting-star, shooting-star forgive us" and something about a curse and things like that. I really did not know what to do. I was glad she was talking quietly, almost whispering, for I would not have liked it if Mama had burst in or Aunt Jennie, laughing and joking and saying, "what—what—you two not in bed yet?"

I remember that Aunt Aggie did say that Mamalie was very sick, and while Mamalie had that bad fever, she was sent to stay with old Auntie Bloom for over a year and Aunt Aggie called Auntie Bloom, Mimmie too; Aunt Aggie thought Auntie Bloom was her own mother, for a long time, she said. I suppose this is it. Aunt Aggie is now living with Auntie Bloom and she is a very tiny little girl and I am not Aggie any more but I am Aunt Lucy or Aunt Lucia, and I suppose I am nursing Mamalie because the Moravian Sisters made medicines and had patches of old gardens with mint and sage and things they made into medicines.

I am the nurse of Mamalie who is very ill and had some sort of fever, maybe brain-fever, they said, anyhow I think it is very sad that she was afraid (when she had her fever) that Shooting-star was angry with her. Though she had never herself, seen Shooting-star, she got herself so mixed up with the old notes and music, that she thought that she was Anna von Pahlen, then maybe she thought that she was Morning Star and maybe she wanted to get the old Indian songs back so that the morning-stars really could sing together. When she asks me to sing, it is ordinary things like *the darkness deepens* but maybe it is not ordinary, *Lord with me abide.*

She said she was thirsty; I wonder if it wouldn't be a good idea to get her a glass of water from the wash-stand and pretend to be Lucy and try to get her to go to bed? I go to the wash-stand. The wash-stand jug is nearly full of water and it is very heavy. It would be terrible if I dropped the pitcher; this is a jug or a pitcher, like the *seidel* that was the cup with the S, that was *Sanctus Spiritus,* that was the sign of the communion so that the old uncle turned it to an urn and put the S on a shield, Mamalie said, but Mamalie said he had the same words in French, *l'amitié passe même le tombeau. Tombeau* is tomb, of course, anyone could see that. That Shooting-star must not be angry—how could he be? I was afraid of a real shooting-star and Mamalie is afraid of an Indian priest who is called Shooting-star, at least, I think it must be that medicine-man she told me about, who gave David Zeisberger the belt that had little cross-stitch pattern for stars and flat circles, Mamalie said, for daisies or for roses.

Now it seems while I pour out water from the pitcher in the glass that I am Hilda pouring out water from a wash-stand jug that has roses and a band of dark-blue that looks like a painted ribbon round the top. The tooth-mug matches the pitcher. There is a soap-dish with a little china plate, with holes in it that is separate, so that the water from the soap will drip through. The basin has the same roses.

The pitcher is heavy but I do not spill the water.

The quilt has pulled off the bed where I got out.

The water seems cool enough. I put down the jug anyhow, and now I take the heavy glass up and feel the outside and it is not so very cool and I remember it is a hot night. Now, I am not cold and I remember it is a hot night. I could go to the pantry and get some cracked-ice but that will be a little trouble and the others will be sure to burst in and say, "why aren't you in bed" and spoil everything.

I walk round the quilt that is partly spread on the floor, and I do not step on the patch that was Aunt Sabina's moiré or old Cousin Elizabeth's watered-silk. I must remember that Mamalie is just Elizabeth, not old Cousin Elizabeth, and I get round the bed and she is sitting there and the candle is there with the saucer and the curtain is hanging straight and there is no sort of wind. I remember there was a wind that rattled the curtain-rings, but there is no wind, and if I listen, I can begin to hear footsteps and their dragging the chairs up the porch-steps from the grass like they always do, in case it rains in the night. I had thought there might be a thunder-storm because Mama says on very hot nights, "it feels thunder-y." It had been feeling thunder-y though that is perhaps not what it was; I mean, it was what you mean, when you say your hair stands on end, though it doesn't really. But that was maybe, the best part of it, like listening to a ghost-story at a party in the dark.

It was like listening in the dark, though we had the candle, and maybe it was just a story in the dark with a candle, about something that didn't happen at all, like the ghost-story about the man who nailed his coat to a coffin and then screamed because he thought a skeleton hand had got him. Only this was something different, though I couldn't tell just how, only that it made Mamalie shiver and then say that, about Shooting-star forgiving them or something. I think maybe, it was a sort of dream, maybe it did not happen. Maybe even, I made it up alone there on the bed while Mamalie was sitting at the window, maybe Mamalie didn't even say anything at all, maybe it is like that time when I saw the Old Man on Church Street and he sent his sleigh and Mama said it never happened. Maybe it is like that thing that happened, that Mama said didn't happen, when the Young Man who at first I thought was the Gardener, cut off or broke off a lily with a short stem that I held in my hand like a cup. Maybe . . .

I think if I just take the glass and hand it to Mamalie and she just says, "thank you, Helen," or "thank you, Hilda," then it will be that I was asleep or half-asleep on the bed and that I dreamed all this and that maybe, I did after all, only dream about the Old Man and the drive in the snow when all the streets were empty, when we drove past our houses on Church Street, and Mama sat opposite me with Harold and Gilbert under the fur-rug, and the Man who at first I thought was the Gardener, sat up in front and drove the horses.

Maybe, that was just a dream and maybe the lily with the short stem that I held in my hands like a cup, was something I dreamed, just as maybe I dreamed that Mamalie said that our church-beginnings went back to the 9th century (and that would be a thousand years ago) and that there was a branch of the church that was called *Calixtines* that had something to do with a Greek word, she thought, for cup, like calix is a word for part of a flower that is like a cup.

There were flowers that were like flat daisies or roses, she said, on the old belt and Ida said they called water-lilies, water-roses in German, so maybe the lily I held in my hand and afterwards put on Papalie's grave (straight up, stuck in the ground so that it looked as if it were growing there) could be a rose, too. Maybe it is the white-rose and the black-rose that Mamalie used to talk about, to Aunt Laura and Mama (when they got too excited and laughed too much about nothing at all) is the shadow of the *Calixtines* rose, that I had given me by the Man who I thought was the Gardener, who drove the sleigh. Maybe, when Mamalie looks up and says, "thank you, Hilda, isn't it time you were in bed?" I will see that it was all sort of a dream, that I made it up, that Mamalie never did say anything about an Indian who was at *Wunden Eiland,* who was named Shooting-star.

Maybe it was just that I was dreaming something, because I was afraid a shooting-star might swish out of the sky and fall on the house and burn us all up. Maybe, it was because I was afraid of being burnt up that I made Mamalie in the dream, say she wasn't just afraid of being burnt up—though she was afraid—only she was more afraid that she might lose the papers. The papers were lost.

"Here is your glass of water, Mamalie," I say.

But though I call her Mamalie, so that she can now be herself out-of-a-dream, she says, "thank you, thank you, Lucy." She says, "yes, Lucy, you're right . . . Maybe it's best not to brood and worry. It was for Christian's sake;

he thought, in some way, we had failed to keep a promise, he thought, in some way, if we could reconstruct the fragments of writing and of music, we might redeem the Promise, we might even restore the Gift. No, Lucy, I don't want the old copies of the liturgies and the folio of the *Creation* now; I think, I see that it's better to give up music altogether. What was it young Brother Francis was saying yesterday? Yesterday, he said that nothing is lost, there are things, he says (like the invisible plant-forms in the drops of water he studies, under his new microscope) in the human soul, that have not yet been discovered.

"It was cool in the room and when he finished the communion-prayer for the sick, I felt that I wasn't burning up any more. Don't mind, Lucy. It was the fever. I was burning up with fever. Yes, Lucy, tell Brother Francis when he comes for vespers—"

She says "vespers" and the word "vespers" means those meetings they have sometimes, almost like love-feasts, when they have coffee and sugar-cake around the table.

It is sitting round a table and talking about Sand Island and *Christiansbrunn* that was named for young Renatus, and the *Singstunden* and *Liturgien* and the famous water-music on the river in the old days, and the tree here or the tree there that was cut down, what a pity! And remembering the time when the steel-mills had not even been thought of, and now Brother Francis is taking her hand and saying that he will not speak again of these things that have troubled her unless she herself particularly wants it, and that he will tell no one of it; it must have happened, he said, he could not doubt her word, nor question the reality of the experience and Henry Seidel's concern about the matter, though poor Brother Henry had been overworking for a long time and had burnt himself up with zeal and devotion.

There had been strange forces at work, he said, in this great land from the beginning, and the Indian ritual in the early days, was not understood and after all, it was not so very many years since the massacre at *Gnadenhuetten.*

(*Gnadenhuetten?* So they had been killed at *Gnadenhuetten.*)

I can not follow what Elizabeth Caroline and Brother Francis are saying, I can not hear what they are saying, but I have a feeling that our own grandfather had heard stories from his grandfather even, that brought fear and the terror of burning and poisonous darts (that *arrow that flieth by day*) very near.

It was not just a thing that had happened even in the days of Papalie's grandfather, it was something that might still happen.

I seem to hear him talking it out with Mamalie, very clearly and in the most understanding and sympathetic way, recalling the early missions and the work of Zeisberger and the young Count, Christian Renatus in *Herrnhut,* yet seeing the other side, seeing the extravagances of young Christian Renatus and his group, the plays and processions and the strange gatherings, as a sort of parody on their Saviour, and the story of the Gospel, which shone clear and in simple symbols for him.

The Redeemer was not to be parodied (however sincere the feeling back of it) in robes and processions, through the streets of this very town. Our Saviour was not to be worshipped in a startling transparency, which showed the wounds, wide and red and blood dripping, when a candle was pushed forward, back of the frame, in the dark.

There were actual extravagances too, practical issues, the question of church-funds, squandered in these elaborate meetings, that were ritualistic sort of parties, really, where certain favourites of the group bore the names of the followers of our Lord.

These things, remembered, heard about, forgotten, passed through Papalie's mind; he did not want to offend dear Sister Elizabeth Caroline, who had so recently lost her husband. He would wait. But he feared that she had been carried away by some feverish phantasy; he had loved and admired his colleague, Henry Seidel, and their families had been bound up in the interests of the Moravian Brotherhood for generations. He thought of Henry's little daughter.

"I will look in, on little Agnes, on the way home," he said, "I met Sister Maria Bloom actually, coming here," he said. "Rest," he said, "I will look after your little Agnes."

I seem to hear him say "little Agnes," or is it Mamalie who says "Agnes?" Mamalie says "Agnes," so whoever I am, I am not now Lucy.

I was Lucy or old Aunt Lucia when I went over to the wash-stand, when I thought, "if she looks up and says, 'why aren't you in bed, Helen' or 'what are you doing here in my room at this hour, Hilda,'" then I will know that all that about Shooting-star was a dream or a sort of waking-dream or just thoughts, while I was sitting there in her bed, picking out the patches of the old dresses they wore, and the *pervenche* blue, she called it, that one of the old-girls from New Orleans sent Mamalie in a letter once, to show her the colour of her bridesmaid's dress, when her sister was married.

That was that other patch, very blue but not very bright blue, like some of the pansy-petals, when they are two colours of blue. We didn't talk about that patch but I can say, I was thinking of asking her about that patch—it's not a very large patch—if she asks me what I was thinking, or even what I was saying.

Really, I am Agnes now, so I suppose I ought to call her Mimmie again, "here is your water," I say, "Mimmie," and she says, "yes, water—that is what he said: he said *unless you are born of water and the spirit* and the *Sanctus Spiritus* was the Spirit but it was the Spirit, he said, undiluted; we are not ready for such a spiritual in-pouring, he said, at least very few of us are and he said it was all right about your father, Agnes, and he said we would tell you all about it, or I should tell you about it. But do you know, Agnes, I forgot all about it. I should have told you sooner, only I forgot all about it. Of course, Lucy said, I talked a lot in the fever but she said it was just the fever and anyway, whatever it was about, the burning had nothing to do with us now. Lucy said I talked about *Gnadenhuetten* and was afraid if the Promise was not kept or the Secret of the inner gatherings revealed, some curse would come on us, I don't know what curse—I don't remember—only Lucy kept telling me that *Gnadenhuetten* had already happened. It had happened long ago, Lucy said, but it seemed it was happening to me in the fever—only perhaps it was a dream in the fever—but when I said 'water, water,' it seemed, when they brought it, I would not drink it, because the springs and wells were poisoned, I said—until young Brother Francis came and said he knew all the springs and rivers and little lakes for miles and miles around.

"He went off, you see, on long trips to get those specimens of water that have invisible moss in them—so he said he knew all about the springs and he knew they were not poisoned and he asked Lucy to pour him a goblet of water—it was an old goblet that Lucy had from her mother's things and it was a beautiful shape like the communion-cup and I said it was like the communion-cup and he said, 'yes,' and he said 'yes,' and he didn't say 'a cup of cold water,' though I thought he was going to; he said, 'we know so little about even a drop of water, how could we know the inner secrets of God? And if we did know the inner secrets of God, God would not strike us down, because we had betrayed them in a fever'. 'But *God our God is a jealous God,*' I said, because some of those old texts had frightened me and '*thou shalt not suffer a witch to live,*' I said, but he did not pay any attention to me and he said, 'what wonderful crystal, Sister Lucia,' and Lucy said, 'ah, it was the last one of a set—' I had heard all about it so often that I did not listen. And while Lucy was telling the story, he began to sip the water and Lucy said, 'Brother Francis, I want to show you the silver acorns that were twisted into a brooch like a little crown, that we've had—I don't know how long—in our family,' and she moved over to the desk in the corner and Brother Francis got up to follow her and he said, as if he had forgotten or was vaguely troubled, as to where to put the goblet, 'ah—do you mind?' and I found I was holding the crystal goblet in my hand."

"It was cut in little triangles round the top and I saw them reflected in one of the tiny triangles; Lucy had opened the window and far, far away, they were standing, two tiny figures, Lucy in her white cap and tall young Brother Francis in his black coat and the bit of white, beautifully folded at his throat, and they were talking, I felt, about the garden and I did not hear what they were saying but it seemed that there was a voice saying something about *a river . . . as crystal, proceeding out of the throne* and I knew that was in Revelations and I remembered the Promise of the Kingdom and the Trees, there were twelve of them; I remembered that *the leaves were for the healing of the nations* and I drank the water in the goblet . . . what was I saying, what was I saying Hilda?"

I said, "you were saying you were thirsty, Mamalie and I got you some water from the pitcher on the wash-stand, it isn't very cold; I was thinking, would you want me to run down and get some cracked-ice? I could run down and get some cracked-ice from the refrigerator. You were saying . . ."

Mamalie, Mamalie, Mamalie, what were you saying? Wait Mamalie, there are a thousand questions that I want to ask you. You haven't told me the name of the carpenter from Moravia, who told Count Zinzendorf first, about the Brotherhood, so he came to America, nor the name of the boat or the other ships and the sea-congregation; did they sing on the sand?

Mamalie, Mamalie, you have told me nothing at all, really; did they ever find the papers that were lost? Mamalie, this is all frightful, I could cry with sorrow and grief that you won't tell me more, because now you are holding the common kitchen-tumbler in your hand and it's only a kitchen-tumbler, I remember Mama saying, before you came, "we really must look out an odd glass or a pretty cup for the wash-stand in the spare bed-room, before your grandmother comes."

Why, Mamalie, I could die of grief when I think we had just such a common kitchen-tumbler instead of a crystal goblet, and Mamalie, don't you want the cracked-ice, but you understand, I was so excited, I couldn't wait a minute, I wanted to hear more about *Wunden Eiland* and *Gnadenhuetten* and they were killed—they were killed, the little huts of the blessed, in the habitation of Grace, are burning and the leaves on the young dog-wood trees are withered and Paxnous is far away because he was trying to keep the tribes from fighting.

O, Mamalie, there is such a lot I want to know, I want to know what Paxnous' wife looked like, she was a sort of Princess and O, there is Anna von Pahlen, my dear, dear Anna who was Morning Star like the Princess with the nine brothers in the story that was lost, and she had lilies too, like I had a lily, only it was a short stem like a white cup, like a goblet, not like the branch of lilies the Madonna has on Easter cards or Jesus has on Easter cards where He came out of the tomb, *passe le tombeau.* Yes, Mamalie, that was right of that old uncle Christian Heinrich Johann to keep the little urn instead of the goblet, because the goblet belongs to the Secret we have together.

Mamalie, Mamalie, don't go away, Mamalie; I told you I'd get you some cracked-ice because you were burning with a terrible sort of fever, which was when you remembered how you were burnt—but you weren't burnt at *Gnadenhuetten* when the Indians massacred the inhabitants of Grace, but it was the other Indians who did it; O Mamalie, say it wasn't Paxnous, who gave his wife, the Princess, Morning Star, to the Moravians.

Mamalie, don't go away. Because the thing that will happen, will happen to me, this winter after Christmas or before Christmas begins, about November, but I won't remember. I will forget, like you forgot all about *Wunden Eiland* and the papers that were lost and I will be afraid too, there will be the *Storm of Death* that *roars sweeping by* that I sang to you in a hymn, and it was just words in a hymn but it will be the *Storm of Death* and it will roar, it will roar over my head and there will be children huddled in little shelters, and there will be fire like there was at *Gnadenhuetten* and I will remember the fear that you feared; it wasn't your own fear but you remembered the fear that Anna von Pahlen had and that John Christopher Cammerhof had and that even my own Papalie remembered hearing about, from his own grandfather, who maybe heard about it from people who really knew the inhabitants of Grace who were at *Gnadenhuetten* who were killed by the savages. Mamalie, there will be savages and they will have ugly symbols like some of the bad Indians, to bring ugly and horrible things back to the world and the *Storm of Death* is storming in my ears now; Mamalie, wait, there is so much I want to ask you.

Mamalie, Mamalie, you say you don't want any cracked-ice, though I could run down to the refrigerator and get you some cracked-ice, that Ida always has, in a bowl for ice-water in the refrigerator. Mamalie, you said *rivers of crystal* and that is like the ice-storms that we have, when the trees glisten like glass in a fairy-tale of a glass-mountain, and there is always the moment in the woods, when you remember a path (that you couldn't remember) that will run to an old ford across a stream or a river, that will run to a spring that is called *Christiansbrunn* because it was Christian Renatus who helped find out the Secret, though hardly anyone knows now that there even was a secret.

Mamalie, you are holding the glass of water and you are looking at the glass of water and you saw a picture in the crystal-goblet, that was Papalie and Aunt Lucia who were standing at a window and I think there was a white curtain blowing in the wind, but you didn't tell me. Mamalie, don't get lost, I must go on, I must go on into the darkness that was my own darkness and the face that was my own terrible inheritance, but it was Papa, it was my own Papa's face, it wasn't the face of the Wounded One at *Wunden Eiland* though I got them all mixed up, but I will get them separated again and I will hold the cup in my hand that is a lily, that is a rose, that is. . . .

What It Was

Why then have I delivered myself to death, to fire, to sword, to beasts? But he who is near to sword, is near God: with beasts, with God.

St. Ignatius

What It Was

What it was, was not appreciable at the moment. What happened did not take long to happen.

We were sitting round the round-table in the sitting-room, there was a painting-book and a glass for paint-water and Ida had gone upstairs and the baby was asleep and Eric and Mr. Evans were at the Observatory or the Transit House, or in their rooms in the wing of the house.

Mama and Papa had gone to Philadelphia, the way they did, if it was raining or if there were clouds, so Papa could not work. Papa would leave the party or what they called a reception, if he thought it was going to clear up and Mama would have to come home alone afterwards, if she wanted to stay on after he left.

We did not ourselves go in to Philadelphia very often; it was a long trip with a sort of street-car with an engine that ran the two miles to Cobbs creek that was the city-limit and then another half-hour in the ordinary trolley, to Wanamaker's to see the Christmas things or to go with Mama to see Cousin Laura and Cousin Emily Bell on Spruce Street. This was our house. We had moved here after Christmas, one winter.

I had come first, alone with Papa and Mama and we had stayed at Fetters' Farm, which was the nearest house except the farm-house and the cow-sheds which belonged to the Flower Farm. An old man had left his farm to the University for an Observatory and this was it; it was Flower Observatory and Papa was the astronomer and Eric and Mr. Evans helped him with his work.

We had a big thanksgiving dinner and the uncles and the aunts came, and Mama gave an Easter party, like we always had and the University ladies helped hunt the eggs with their children that they brought. Mama drew bunnies in ink, on top of the invitation, or a nest with a duck or a chick with its egg-shell, and some of the letters they wrote back to say they were coming, had ducks or bunnies drawn on, too.

Everybody liked the little baskets Mama bought, and Harold and I helped with the smaller children, but it was a long way to Philadelphia and we did not have little parties, only sometimes one big party like that, or when they all came, Thanksgiving-day. People did not run in and Mama did not run out across the garden to Mamalie or up Church Street to Aunt Jennie's, and Uncle Fred did not go past the house and wave his music at us (when we shouted at him to come in) and say, "I'm late for choir-practice."

Eric took us for walks. There was not the river and the boats and the summer-house on the island. Dr. Snively lived two miles down the road and the Snivelys came sometimes with their pony to take us out; they were DeForest and Margaret and Ethelwyn and Muriel. They lent me their books and I lent them mine. They had a *Red Fairy Book* and there were some of my old stories in it, but with different pictures. The mail-man did not pass the house but we had to go for the mail to Upper Darby which was a little town, Mama said, a village. It was just below the school where we went. We did not like the school but we never said anything about it. Maybe, Gilbert did like it, he played base-ball with the older boys. Sometimes Harold and I went off on the path in the woods, but they would not let us go beyond the first fence through the woods, because there were gypsies camping there sometimes. It was the Sellers' woods. The Sellers had a big old house that we went to sometimes. The Sellers were Quakers or Friends, they called them. The best house was the Ashursts, that was about two miles away or nearer, if you went across the fields, or maybe it wasn't much more than a mile. The Ashursts only lived there in the summer, the house was called the *Grange* because that was what they said the Marquis de Lafayette had called it or they named it for his house, anyhow he and George Washington had walked along a road through the woods that they called Lafayette's Walk. There were box hedges and a big round bed of heliotrope in the summer, in front of the house.

It was quiet in the room and Gilbert was cutting out some paper-soldiers with Papa's shears that he wasn't supposed to take from Papa's table, unless he put them back, before Papa got home. Harold was helping me with the paint-book that was almost all painted in, and the piano was there, like it was in the old house with Mama's books of music piled on top; she played *Träumerei* when I asked her, but she did not play the piano so much. She said I must have music-lessons but it was too far to go to Philadelphia but Doctor Snively said I could come to their house and have a lesson when Margaret and Ethelwyn and Muriel had their lessons, twice a week on Tuesday and

Friday. Mama said it would be too much to ask, and Doctor Snively said the children were so happy to have neighbors at last; DeForest was Gilbert's age or a little older and Margaret was a little older than I. I was between Margaret and Ethelwyn. Soon, I would begin these music-lessons, Mama said. The piano was open and there was the Venus that Mama had brought back from Europe, from Paris. The Venus was called *Venus de Milo* and there were the same pictures we had in the old house, and some more of the photographs of places they had been to in Europe, on the stairs.

The old street-car or steam-car went past the house once an hour; it was going past soon; we knew when the times were, ten minutes past the hour when it was on time. There was a switch opposite the Fetters' farm, where the two cars passed each other, the one going to the city and the other, coming back, and sometimes they were late. We would wait for the steam-car, that ran with a sort of engine but not fastened to the car but part of the car. It went past the house and we waited because perhaps they would come back but they did not come back, so we went on.

Gilbert went out in the hall, then he came back. Then he took the shears and put them on Papa's table. "But he hasn't come back," I said. Harold was painting a yellow ruffle on a dog that looked like the dog in our old Punch and Judy; the dog in the colored picture, that we were meant to copy the uncolored picture from, had a red ruffle. I did not know if Harold was making it different on purpose, you can hardly see the yellow in the lamp-light.

"The yellow will look different in the morning, yellow looks different at night," I told Harold; I did not say, "but you should have painted the ruffle red," because we did not always paint the picture the same as the colored picture on the opposite page.

I said, "yellow looks different in the morning," Harold said, "I know." The clock was ticking very loudly. Annie should come in and tell us to go to bed but when Papa and Mama were out, they did not always tell us. Now it would be another hour for the trolley to pass the house. We had a drive-way past the house, it would be better, Mama told Doctor Snively or the Ashursts when they drove up, and their wheels scrunched the pebbles, in the spring, "the University is having it properly tarred and rolled," Mama said. There were three big maple-trees and a wild cherry-tree, by the road, but they said it was not any good for fruit, and in the wrong place, anyway, and it would have to be cut down; there were little trees planted back of the kitchen, they were peach-trees but we had not had any peaches yet. The Ashursts sent things from their garden, iris-roots and different shrubs for the shrubbery.

Well, now there was only the next car to wait for, or Ida or Annie to come in and tell us to go to bed; Gilbert was waiting, his elbows were on the table, he was pretending not to look at us but he was looking at us. This was the same table that we had in the old house, in the sitting-room there. We put on a white cloth and flowers and presents on this table for birthdays, but there would be no birthday for a long time, all of our birthdays came near together, mine in September, the two boys' in October. Harold went on painting.

There was a bump on the front-porch by the steps, as if someone were coming up, "perhaps it's them," I said, but then it was quiet. Gilbert started putting his new cut-out paper-soldier in the shoe-box, where he had the other old ones. Then I thought I heard someone bump again and I ran out to the front-door. I opened the front-door. The light from the lamp in the hall showed the porch, it was empty, there were two benches built in the wall that made a little open-room of the roofed-in part of the porch, by the door.

It was dark and I could not see; the bright light from the hall went over the floor of the porch only as far as the steps, then the dark. I stood and looked at the dark, beyond the porch-steps and then Papa walked across the light.

He walked right across the floor and I said, "O, Papa," and ran out, with the door wide open. I took his hand and I said, "O, Papa," and he didn't say anything. He did not hold my hand tight in his hand, he did not take my hand the way he did, his fingers did not close tight round my hand the way they always did. It had never happened before that his fingers did not close round my hand.

His hand did not seem to belong to him, his arm seemed like the arm of a scare-crow or a rag-doll. I pulled at his sleeve and his sleeve and his arm did not seem to pull him. I pulled at the overcoat he had on, I pulled at his coat, he was swaying back and forth. Was this a drunk man? Is this how drunk people act and he had no hat on, and now I pulled him to the open door and I looked at him . . . and I looked at him.

I pulled him in the door, he stood on the rug on the hall-floor. There was the rug on the floor and I did not see anything but Papa's face but I knew what was in the hall, but it went far away, then it came clear, then everything in the hall was peculiar, I mean it had some special place and some special reason for being there, as if it were things you cut out of the back of magazines and paste in your paper-doll house. That is not just what I mean, but that is what I mean.

The clock stood there and ticked and it was a clock that belonged to a story, it was a clock that had a door that went into a tunnel, that led to a house in the woods, and the Old Man and the Old Lady on the mantelpiece in the hall (that they had brought back with the square dish with the tulip and the rose painted on it, from Dresden) were like an Old Man and an Old Lady in a fairy-story that come alive after the clock strikes midnight.

The clock would not strike for a little while, the car ran past the house at ten minutes past the hour and the car was late and then we had waited a little, so the clock would not strike the hour for perhaps half-an-hour or almost three-quarters of an hour. The hour was cut in half, it might be almost the half-hour, because Gilbert had said when he came back from putting Papa's desk-shears back on his table, "the old car's late, as usual."

He had said that, I remembered it now. Harold was sitting at the table and I said, "yellow looks different by day-light," and he said, "I know." Harold was sitting at the table and Gilbert was putting his new cut-out soldiers in the shoe-box. But really we were in the hall.

Gilbert shut the front-door. Harold was there by me and I pulled at Papa's coat. I pulled at his coat and I pulled him in to his study and Gilbert got the lamp from the hall. When he was pushed down in the chair by his table, my face was almost as tall as his head when he was sitting down, so it looked nearer.

The blood was running down from the side of his face that was by me, and there was dust on his coat and the arm that I had pulled at, on the porch, hung down over the chair.

His eyes were wide open but he did not seem to know us. He sat in his chair. There was the lamp on the table that Gilbert must have put there and Gilbert was not there. Harold and I were alone with him and he did not seem to know us and he did not shut his eyes and his eyes went on looking and looking.

I ran into the kitchen with Harold and we filled the wash-basin with water and brought back a towel and Harold stood there and now the water in the basin was almost as red as the blood on his face, and his beard was thick with blood and I went on washing his face with the towel and wringing out the towel in water, like Ida showed me how to do when I was a little girl and helped her and Annie wash clothes, but that was in the old house.

This was the new house and we thought, "what fun it will be to move and go to a new house," and now we were here and we had little peach-trees in the back-garden by the kitchen-porch and we had new plants and roots for the shrubbery that the Ashursts sent us. Where was Mama? Was Mama outside, was she dead?

Where was everybody? I went on wringing out the towel and the basin got more red and it did not really seem to matter. Nothing mattered because everything was somewhere else. Gilbert was cutting out paper-soldiers and I was watching Harold paint the dog-ruffle yellow and we were sitting at the round-table in the sitting-room and we were waiting for the car that came if it was on time, ten minutes past the hour, but it was late as usual, Gilbert said.

Where is Gilbert? I must go and empty this basin and get some more fresh water. I must get another towel. But I can not leave him alone and we are alone in his room. This is his study. There is the desk, there are his ink-bottles and his pens and the shears that Gilbert took and that Gilbert put back, and I said, "but he hasn't come in yet."

He hadn't come in but he had been somewhere near and something had happened, while the car went on past the house. Was it robbers? Something had happened, that only happens in stories, the Arabian Nights had a picture of a lady whose head might be cut off but it wasn't, because she went on telling a man in a turban, who was a Turk (or did they say he was Arabian?) a new story. This was a picture in that book or it was the Bible picture when we spread the illustrated Bible open on the floor, before we could read the writing. He was on the stairs, too. On the stairs, He was looking and looking and never shutting his eyes and the thorns made great drops of blood run down his face and Mama thought it was a beautiful Guido Reni.

Harold was there, he held the basin. I could not get the thick blood out of his beard. It tore like my doll's hair, when it gets tangled. If the water was hot, maybe we could get the thick blood out of his beard. I wanted hot water and I wanted a new towel, but if we went out for some more water, then he would be alone. You can not leave him alone, staring.

He looks at the book-case where he has his *War and Peace* and Victor

Hugo's *Les Misérables* and some German books in German. Those are his reading-books (his other books are all along the wall, the other side of the table) and his Gibbon's *Rome*. I have tried to read in these books, because they have covers striped like marbles, with dark blue on the back and triangles of dark blue on the corners, he said I could read them, but I did not read very far in Gibbon's *Rome*.

He is looking at the glass doors of the book-shelf, it is part of an old desk, there is a drawer in the desk that opens; in it, he keeps his pistol. "Did you ever shoot a man?" He said, he never did that he knew of, but now someone or something had shot him or hit him, like an Indian with a tomahawk. You could see that something had hit him. If he goes on looking at the glass-door of the shelves, above the old desk, where he keeps his pistol in the drawer, I will have to push his head round, I can't have him go on looking at one thing like that. If he would close his eyes, it would be better, it would even be better if he fell down but we would not be able to get him up; do dead men sit in chairs?

He walked across the bright light from the open door and I said, "Papa," and he didn't say anything. What he says, when I say "Papa," is "little one" or he says "*Töchterlein*" and when I take his hand, his hand shuts round my hand like it does, and he holds my hand almost too tight sometimes and he even calls me daughter.

Then Ida was there, she said, "what?" I saw her stand in the door, she said "how? Where?" She went away. She had her hair up, she pins it round her head, she takes it down in front of the little mirror in her room and makes two long plaits of it, but she hadn't taken it down; I might have thought she was in bed, but I had not really thought about her; now she was there. She went away. The door to the wing opened and Eric and Mr. Evans were there; now I saw why Gilbert had gone away, he had gone to get Eric and Mr. Evans. Ida came back, she had more towels, she pushed me away, she said, "run away, run away"; what did she mean? She had a bowl, it was one of the big china bowls, there are a lot of them and they all fit in together, she had water in the bowl but we had done all that; Harold still held the basin, she said, "put it down, I'll see to your father," as if he were coming for his evening-coffee, or something; she pushed in front, I could not see Papa. Eric and Mr. Evans stood there in the way.

Now I stood there trying to get round to Papa, but they said, "it's all right."

Mr. Evans said, "you children run along"; where were we to run to? Now Mama was standing in the doorway. There was Papa in the chair, Ida, Eric and Mr. Evans and Gilbert and Harold and me, and Mama in the doorway. She said, "Charles." That is all she said.

She had on a lace-scarf or a lace-shawl over her head, like she wears when she doesn't wear a hat, when she goes out at night. It was black-lace over her head like the lady on the inside lid of the cigar-box that Papa gave me. He saved two boxes and gave them together, mine had the lady with the shawl like Mama had and Gilbert had a man in a big hat with a bull-fight on the little pictures round the edge, on the inside of his tobacco-box.

They were cigar-boxes, there was writing in Spanish, he said it was from Cuba.

Now he saved the two boxes and gave Gilbert the one with the man and me the one with the lady. Maybe, Harold was too small for a box. I never, till now, wondered what Harold had, but maybe he was too small. This was in the old house, we cut out pictures for valentines and kept them in the boxes, then we kept fire-crackers in the boxes. He always gave us his boxes. Now I must have remembered the box because of the lady with the lace over her head and the little pictures were of red and white flowers and there was a gold edge around the whole picture on the inside lid, like a valentine. It was like that.

He smoked a cigar after dinner sometimes, or when professors came to talk, but he liked his pipe. The bowl with the tobacco was on the top of the chest of drawers that ran along the wall, this side of his table. He had them made for his study, before we came here. He let us look over the blue-prints with the architect, who came from Philadelphia with the blue-prints for the new house, and he would take his pen and make a little mark here, a door here or a cupboard under the stairs. This was that house.

We had watched him draw a square for the extra door in the hall that led out to the field that was now the orchard, since the peach-trees were planted. We had seen the blue-print for this room, the double-window that looked out on the orchard, the book-shelves, built in for his books and nautical almanacs that were on the other side of the table; there was the sofa where he lay down in the afternoons, sometimes when he had been working at night. There was the door where Mama was standing with the lace over her head, there was the wing-door that had opened a crack when Gilbert slid in first, that had opened wide when Mr. Evans and Eric walked in.

Gilbert must have run down the wing-stairs to get there first. That is what he had gone away for (perhaps even to the Observatory or the Transit House), he had not really left us alone but Harold and me were alone for a long time.

Now they did not say, "where did you find your father?" They did not ask, "who found him?" They did not say, "but this is your father, were you alone with your father? Did you wash his face? Who got the basin? Who held the basin? Who washed his face?" They did not say any of this, because now Ida had spread a towel over his coat, as if it was the barber's, and was pressing round his head with her hands.

No one said, "but who found him?" They said, "run along, run along." Mama did not look at us, she was looking at Papa. She did not say, "O, children, children, who was it found your father?"

What we did was, we sat on the sofa in the sitting-room. There was the paint-glass on the table and the paint-brush where Harold had dropped it when he ran out, and there was the shoe-box with Gilbert's soldiers. Now I heard the clock tick. I had not heard it for a long time but it must even have struck because Mama was back and the car only ran once an hour. I did not hear the clock strike. It was long after our bed-time. Gilbert sat at the top of the sofa and I was next and then Harold. We did not say anything to each other.

Eric and Mr. Evans came in, they talked about "concussion" and they wondered how soon the doctor could possibly get here. Who had gone for the doctor? You would think it would be Eric or Mr. Evans; maybe they got Annie to go for the doctor. Where would the baby sleep tonight? What was "concussion"? Had he been out there a long time, had he maybe been on the streetcar before this one? Had it happened an hour before? Or had it just happened when it did? Had he fallen off the car? Had someone tried to kill him? Was he dead? How would they get him upstairs? What was Mama doing? What is concussion? Someone must ask but I did not know if it would be me or Gilbert.

"Yes, yes, yes," said Eric, very fast, all in one word, and as if he were answering himself, "yes, yes," very quiet. He stood there and Mr. Evans said, "concussion of the brain and his collar-bone is broken."

Why did they stand here talking? Why didn't they do something? Or had Annie been sent for the doctor? What was Mama doing alone with him, had they taken him upstairs, how would they get him upstairs?

"Yes, yes, yes," said Eric over and over, and he felt for a cigarette-packet in his pocket and he pulled it out and threw it on the table. The little bent green card-board cigarette-packet lay on the table. It was lying on the picture of the dog with the red collar. Someone must say something, Gilbert got up and picked up the packet, he said, "there's a cigarette left, Eric, you threw away a cigarette." Eric said, "yes, yes," and took the cigarette and did not light it.

Gilbert had got the cigarette-packet and he had said, "Eric, you threw away a cigarette," and Harold would not be expected to say anything, so I must say, "what is concussion?"

Gilbert was sitting there again and I said, "what is concussion?"

I heard my words and the way I said the word, which I had never heard before and now we would know. It would be something that made him stare at the glass-door of the book-shelf and not say anything. It was something to do with his head, "concussion of the brain," Mr. Evans had said. Maybe, it meant that he would be crazy and never speak any more, or maybe it meant that he would die.

Mr. Evans turned round as if he had not seen us. "What are you waiting for?" Mr. Evans said.

What did he think we were waiting for?

"Isn't it time you went to bed?" Mr. Evans said. We were there in a row and Eric was twirling the cigarette round in his fingers, then he dropped the cigarette. I waited for Gilbert to pick it up but he did not.

"Ah-er-er—" said Eric, that way he talks, "it's not—it's not—" He did not say, "it isn't dangerous," he did not say, "it isn't anything" because he did not tell lies. He did not tell lies to us, he bought us *Puck* and *Judge* which are funny-papers and Mama would say, "you must not spend all your salary the first of the month, on the children, you need some new socks," but he went on buying us *Puck* and *Judge* and a bound volume of *Saint Nicholas* though it wasn't Christmas or anybody's birthday.

He bought me a big *Little Women,* that had more in it about how they grew up and he took us for long walks and we found a violet-farm near Overbrook. The people there were French and they let us pick all the violets we wanted, though we couldn't talk to them. We tried to understand and they tried to understand and they said, "père?" to Eric and Eric told us he did know that that was French for father and he said, "no, no," which we found was the same in French.

They asked us to have coffee in their little house and they had flat wooden trays for the violets. Then Mama said we must get some more violets and she was very happy and she gave us a dollar to buy them next time; it was too far for her to walk, but she kept telling the University ladies that called, "think of it, it's several miles, you can see the glass-frames from the front-porch when the sun is shining on them, and the children came on it quite by accident— it's a violet-farm, they have double parma-violets, the children bought me almost a dozen different kinds of single and double-violets, they can hardly talk any English but they got the children to understand they could come back and pick violets to take away."

Those were the sort of big bunches that are very expensive in florists' windows on Walnut and on Chestnut Street in the city and they sell them in tight bunches on the street, with silver paper round the stems and wires, but Mama said "look they're all loose, such long stems, I really never saw such lovely violets."

It was like that, and she said violets were her favorite flower but roses were hers too, because June sixth was her birthday.

I had thought of birthdays and that they were a long way off and so they were, but Mama's birthday was in June and so would come sooner than ours. The baby's birthday was the second of May but I was thinking of Gilbert and Harold and me when I thought of how we always had a white cloth on the round-table where the paint-box was, and spread the presents on it.

Mama's table was easy because we covered her presents with roses.

Eric said, "we don't know exactly, I mean concussion of the brain is—is if someone gets hit very hard or—er-er—falls down, then when the head is struck very hard—" I wanted to know exactly what it was and I could see that Gilbert's shoe was kicking at the edge of the rug that wasn't lying quite flat on the floor. If we wanted to get the rug flat, we would have to get off the sofa and lift the sofa, so the little wheel that was fastened in the sofa-leg to push it around with, would go straight on the rug. We could not get off the sofa, we could not move.

We were frozen stiff to the sofa, in a row, but Gilbert was showing that he could move, if he wanted, by scuffing with his heel at the rug, where it humped a little, where it had not been pushed quite flat when Ida or Annie had moved the sofa in the morning when she did the sweeping. It was easier anyhow for Gilbert to scuff at the floor because his legs were two-years longer. Harold's feet were straight out and he was sitting straight up, as if he were having his picture taken.

I could not scuff at the carpet though my feet reached the carpet, but I pushed myself back so that maybe Harold would feel that I wasn't really waiting so hard, and then maybe Harold would sit back.

"It's like that," said Eric, "if a man falls down—"

"Did he fall down, then?" I was the one that was doing the talking. Gilbert was too busy fastening the leather pad over the knee of his black stocking, that didn't need fastening.

"We—we—don't know—"

Then the clock sort of hammered like a hammer with nails, and Mr. Evans said, "probably your father slipped, as he was getting off the car, or the car may have backed unexpectedly—there should have been a lamp-post set up at the gate, in the beginning. It's quite obvious that your father slipped, that his foot slipped."

Papa wasn't like that. He wasn't the sort of person whose foot slipped.

Mr. Evans walked to the window, then he walked back. Gilbert slid off the sofa.

Mr. Evans said, "I'll take the lantern and go out and see if—" he stopped and Gilbert said, "I'll come with you. He lost his hat."

Mr. Evans said, "no, you wait with the—children. I'm only going out to see if I can find any traces—I mean, do you know, Eric, if his wallet and his watch were taken?"

"I didn't look," said Eric.

"His wallet is in the inside of his coat, or sometimes his overcoat," Gilbert said, "and his watch is in the little watch-pocket."

Mr. Evans said, "did you see them there?" How could Gilbert have seen them?

"No, no," said Mr. Evans, "you stay here," because Gilbert went to the door and was out in the hall, but he came back.

"They put his over-coat on the bench in the hall," Gilbert said, and Mr. Evans went out and Mr. Evans came back with Papa's black wallet and he laid it on the top of the piano and he said, "that's all right."

He was thinking and we knew he was thinking, "then well, it wasn't robbers," but did that make it any better? It would be almost better to think it was robbers, that they had hit Papa for something, that there was some kind of a reason for it, not just this waiting and wondering what concussion was. Mr. Evans went into the hall again, then he opened the front-door, then we heard his feet go down the porch-steps.

His feet went down the steps, the lantern was in the hall of the wing. He could go to the hall in the wing, by walking through Papa's study that had that door that opened into the wing.

He did not go through Papa's study. He had gone down the porch-steps. Then he would turn round the rockery, in the corner between the porch and the path to the wing that led off the drive. If we listened, we might hear when he opened the wing-door, but we did not hear.

Gilbert walked round as if nothing were happening and then he took off the lid of the shoe-box that his paper-soldiers were piled up in. He just took off the lid and shook the box, the way he does to get the paper-soldiers in flatter, and he pressed them down with his hands, like he does to make them not take up so much room and I got up and walked a little.

We were going to walk around the room and we were going to take a book out of the book-shelf, that Papa had made. The book-shelf was on the wall over the sofa. Papa had his work-bench and his saw and hammer and tools in the cellar now, "but it's a perfect work-room," the ladies from the University said, when they were being shown around the house, "and so warm with that huge furnace." There were high little windows in the cellar and it was like a big room with the windows small and high up. The floor was cement, Eric said the floor was cement. It was hard but the cellar was not dark like the cellar in the old house and there were the rakes and the hoe there, and we had the same big box with the lid, with our shoe-blacking things in it.

Papa made the shelf over the sofa, it was varnished too. It was William Morris furniture, Mrs. Schelling said, whatever that was, and he made me a bench for my room like that, and he made a wooden table for the porch.

We were going to walk around the room. Gilbert had begun it, and we were going to do things like we always did, so I said, "Harold, you dropped your paint-brush on the floor, did you know?" And Harold slid off the sofa and picked up his paint-brush and he picked up Eric's cigarette.

He stood looking at the cigarette, as if he did not know what to do next but Gilbert had picked up the shoe-box and was shaking it to get the paper-soldiers to take up less room, because the lid bulged when it was on and would fall off, if he did not tie it up with string or get a big elastic-band from Papa's table. He would go and ask Papa for a big rubber-band for his box of paper-soldiers, everything would be just like that, but Harold would have to say something or do something, because just to stand there was not doing what we were doing.

I mean, we were doing a charade or a game we called dumb-crambo, when you act words. But Harold would have to be pushed like you do Laddie and Georgine when they make us have them in our games. Only Harold is older and Harold is not a dumb child, though Mama still says she is worried because he talks so little. But why should Harold talk?

"What's that?" I said to Harold as if I did not know. "O, it's that cigarette," I said, "O Eric, it's that cigarette you lost. We found the cigarette you lost."

Now Eric would come in too and we would play this charade like we did in this room, with the audience sitting in the other room that was the parlor or people called the parlor a reception-room now. The double-doors could be shut, so when we played charades, we shut the double-doors and worked out the word, then we opened them.

Then we left them open where the Rosa Bonheur *Horse-fair* was on an easel and the picture Mama painted of *Willow Eddy,* that was a place, on the old river, where she used to go with trips with Cousin Edd and Cousin Ruth and where she once went to see a gypsy fortune-teller.

That was a long time ago and that was before Mama married Papa.

Eric took the cigarette.

Then Eric looked at the cigarette.

I often wondered what the fortune-teller told Mama, all of it I mean; Mama said the fortune-teller said, she would have a child who would have a gift but Mama always said to the University ladies when they talked about Uncle Fred and the Bach Choir at Bethlehem, "it's funny that the children are not gifted."

Now, if Eric were playing a charade, he would light his cigarette. Now I could not tell everyone what to do, but I waited and he saw I was waiting.

The fortune-teller said Cousin Ruth would not marry Sammy Martens and Cousin Ruth was cross, Mama said, and Sammy Martens went away to Pittsburgh where his uncle was in the steel works there, and Cousin Ruth never married anybody. The fortune-teller, Mama said, had told her she would marry someone; it would be someone with a gift (or there was something about a gift) or it would be a foreign person who was rich but I do not know who that was, and Mama did not tell us about any foreign people she knew who had come to Bethlehem who were rich, and who had gone away, maybe it was someone from the steel-mills there, because people were always coming to talk to Uncle Hartley from Pittsburgh.

Eric put his hand in his coat-pocket and he found his box of matches. Gilbert got up and got the flat green-saucer ash-tray from the mantelpiece.

There are the Boy and Girl there; in the hall, is the Old Man and the Old Lady; Mama brought the Boy and the Girl back, too, from her honeymoon. The Girl has her skirt tucked up and they both have bare legs and they are fisher-boy and fisher-girl. The Boy has a net on a stick, like for catching butterflies, over his shoulder and the Girl has a basket and there are two blue fish-heads poking out of the lid of the basket.

Eric dropped the match in the flat green-saucer ash-tray, and Gilbert put the ash-tray on the table and Gilbert said, "where's the new copy of *Saint Nicholas,* Hilda, where did you put the *Saint Nicholas?*"

I was watching Eric to see if his cigarette was really lighted, but it was and he was smoking, and he looked at Harold as if he had just seen him and he looked at Gilbert, then he took a pull on his cigarette and looked round the room, then he said, "thank you, Harold," then he said, "thank you, Gilbert, thank you"; he said, "yes, yes, yes," like he does, all in one word and said, "what are you doing? What are you painting, Hilda?"

I said, I wasn't painting, it was Harold and Harold came and stood by me and Eric turned over the pages of the paint-book.

"O," said Eric and he turned back the pages and he said, "maybe that painting isn't dry yet, I don't want to smudge your painting, Harold."

He pressed the middle of the book flat with his other hand and we were back at the picture of the dog with the collar and the clown with the hoop and the lady who was standing on a horse on one toe and who would jump through the hoop. This was a circus and we had been to a circus; when we first came to Philadelphia, Papa took us to a circus; there was a lady in a cage with lions, dressed like the Prince in my old Grimm and she shot off a pistol and she said hi-hi and cracked a whip and shot off the pistol again and the lions jumped around the cage but Papa said they couldn't possibly eat her, they were old lions, he guessed and he laughed because we thought the lady would be eaten.

"It's dry," Harold said.

"Yes, yes," said Eric, "O yes, I see."

I said, "he did that a long time ago, he did that before—" and then I remembered the bump on the front-porch and the way Gilbert had put back the desk-shears and the way I was thinking I was glad that Annie had not come in and told us to go to bed.

Gilbert was watching Eric turn over the pages, now Eric turned over to the boys fishing on the bridge and the mill with the boat and he said, "that's a nice boat—I—er—we must take a trip on the river sometime, I mean the Delaware river," he said, "we could take one of those steam-boats at the wharves at the end of Market Street, we could take a whole day trip, there is a steam-boat, Mr. Evans told me, that runs right down the river to Cape May."

I said, "what is Cape May?" and he said, "O, it's the name of a place, it's in New Jersey, it's the sea-shore."

Gilbert said, "like Point Pleasant where we went once," and Eric said yes, it was; he hadn't been to Point Pleasant but that is what it was like, there was lots of sand and shells and you could walk for miles along the ocean and there was always a place where you could buy balloons he thought, but he was sure we could get peanuts, he said. He said peanuts grew in New Jersey and they had farms of peach-trees and he said things grew in New Jersey like melons because it was so sandy, we would find a place and get a water-melon, he dropped the ash off into the green saucer.

"Let me see," he said, "we can't go yet, we'll go as soon as the excursion-boats start, we could even," he said, "take a boat to Baltimore."

I had a girl in Baltimore was a song we sang.

Nellie was a girl that Eric was going to marry but when we said, when he was shaving in the bathroom in the old house, "how's Nellie, how's Nellie?"

and sat on the edge of the bath-tub, he said "I wouldn't—" and he turned his face to get the light on the side from the window, where he was shaving.

We waited for him to get off the soap from his chin, and we waited for what he would say, but he didn't say anything so "*I had a girl in Baltimore, Nellie, Nellie Nellie,*" Gilbert went on with it, to the wrong tune, he was just singing anything.

Then Eric turned round with the soap off his face and he was wiping the razor on a towel and he took up another towel and dabbed at his face and we saw blood on the towel.

"You cut yourself," Gilbert said.

Eric said, "yes, yes, yes," and then he said, "confound it," which isn't real swearing but Mama said we must not say it. Gilbert kicked his heels on the bath-tub. We had the window open and we floated our soap-bubbles out of the window till someone wanted to come in, "I told you children you must not lock the door and play games in here," Mama said, so we were not to lock the door.

Eric held his handkerchief to his face now as if he had the tooth-ache, we said, "Nellie, Nellie," at him again, and he looked at the handkerchief and did not put it back and there was the cut on his chin but it was not bleeding very much now and he said in a different voice, "I would be very glad if you wouldn't make games about Nellie any more or—or say Nellie to me any-more."

Then he went and got his coat and went out to wherever it was he was going.

He was turning over the book and he came to the orchard and the cow in the orchard. It was spotted like the pony in the circus-pictures. It was like that terrible time, that we never told anybody about, when we were going to a farm in the country and it was a big farm with an old lady and a barn and pigs and about six cows and a bull tied up and hens, and the old lady said we could feed the hens.

What it was, was that Papa and Mama were going to the World's Fair, but they said we must have a happy time too, so we talked about it and talked about it and they thought Point Pleasant was too far and it would be better if Ida took us near, where her cousin had a house; there was a big farm,

Cousin Clarence wrote, he had a little church near there, Mama said, and he would look after us.

So we went and looked at the farm and the old lady said it would be nice to have children and we would all help her feed the hens.

Then we went back to the station, where Ida's cousin had a little hot brickhouse near the station rails. And Ida said, "I don't think we want to go to that farm, it's dirty, we don't want to go there. Here is this nice place and Gilbert can play with Fritzie and you and Harold will be so happy. Now this is a nice place, Mrs. Schneider says we can stay here," and it was terrible, and I do not know what happened that we were so hot and the lady was always cross and went and sat with Ida on rocking-chairs and always said, "run away, don't bother me," and Gilbert went off with Fritzie, who would not let us ride his rocking-horse, to get frogs and Harold and I were so hot and there was no one to talk to, but Cousin Clarence came and took us to see nice people who let us sit on their porch and they had apple-trees.

It was waiting and waiting and every day saying, "have they sent us a letter?" And the lady who was the mother of Fritzie said, "maybe your father and mother sent you here to get rid of you, but I don't want you, you needn't think I want you"; I saw her count green dollar-bills with Ida. And I thought, that is the money that Papa gave for us to go to the farm and Ida was counting two heaps of the money and they each had a heap and maybe it was true, maybe they had gone to the World's Fair and would never come back, but I was afraid to ask Cousin Clarence because the lady smiled so much and talked with him, and seemed kind and said she was so glad to have us and it was a pity but the farm he had chosen for us was too far away and anyhow old Mrs. Apfelholzer was not anxious to have the children, she said, "she couldn't have them," and that was a lie.

This grown lady told a lie, because the old lady said she wanted us to help her with the hens.

Ida didn't seem like she was and when we were going home at last, she said, "tell your mother you had a good time, will you," and she gave me a quarter.

I did not know what to do but when Gilbert started saying he had caught frogs with Fritzie, I didn't say anything. It is a dreadful thing if your mother and father go to the World's Fair and you can not write a letter and you can not even read a letter if it comes and even if it comes and you might be able to steal it and take it to Cousin Clarence to read, the lady who was the mother of Fritzie got the letters first and we could only just read our names on the envelope but she kept the letters.

No, I did not really think of all this, when I saw the picture of the apple-orchard and the cow, but that funny thing happened that sometimes happens, when there is a hole in the floor or a stone on a walk will open and I will step in and fall down and then I stop running and walk around the stone.

It is something that happens. I never tell anyone about it, for I really do not know what it is about, but it seemed to be there all the time that summer when we were at that hot little brick-house, with a horrid flower called a fuchsia that she said, "don't step on," all the time and none of our toys and books because we were going to a farm where there was a barn and pigs and cows and hens and where we could live like farmer's children and where they said we could get eggs.

Cousin Clarence had written Mama about it and then this lady said old Mrs. Apfelholzer didn't want us and that was a story; it was a grown person who was Ida's cousin, telling a lie.

Cousin Clarence did not know she was telling a lie and he took Harold and me to a nice place to sit on their porch and they gave us lemonade in blue glasses and they gave us apples and they said, "I wish you were staying here with us," but we had to go back to the hot little house and the lady said, "well don't eat it then," when I did not like the sausage and pickles and she just took my plate away and she said to Ida, "that will learn her."

So I didn't have any lunch and I didn't tell Cousin Clarence.

Eric turned the pages and he said, "you've almost painted all this book, haven't you?"

He turned the pages back again quickly and bits of the different edges of the pictures were there, and I saw a red slice of paint or a blue, or green of the grass before the big house that looked like the Ashursts' house, where there were bees in the round bed of heliotrope.

The pieces of colour did not fit together and seemed to go very fast, like turning that kaleidoscope, it was called, that we took apart and it was little pieces of coloured glass and we could not put it together again. It was like that old round box that was at Aunt Millie's house, that Mama had played with when she was a little girl. You put in a strip of long coloured pictures, the pictures were like the different pictures of a long funny picture in *Puck* or

Judge but they were all in one long piece and were not funny; they were a girl rolling a hoop or a boy jumping a pony over a fence or a lady like our circus-page in this book, jumping through a hoop in the same kind of clothes, or a man walking with a bear, until it stood up on its hind legs.

The colours were separate and bright like the colours in this book, so now when Eric turned over the pages so quickly, it was like lying on the floor with the round box of the gyroscope going round and round. It made you dizzy after a while; you looked through little slats that were just one large slat when the box went fast. Now that was like this.

I held onto the table-edge because the box was going so fast and I remembered only a bit of colour, the pink and ugly-red of the fuchsia-flowers that were so ugly and the blue-glasses that they gave us and the lemonade, a different colour in the glass, and then the old lady like a good old-witch with a broom, who said, "but I always wanted children to hunt my eggs, I need children on this farm," and a picture of an old witch with Hansel and Gretel, because really old Mrs. Apfelholzer (her name was) could not have been a bad old woman in a dirty house like they said, but it was Ida's cousin who was bad and divided the money up with Ida.

I saw the green of the dollar-bills as they counted them out like counting cards, for there were three of us and we were to be at that farm while they were at the World's Fair in Chicago, and this was the money for it.

I saw the soap-bubble in the tree out of the bathroom window but that was a whole soap-bubble like a balloon made of glass, like the glass-mountain the Princess climbed but it was with nails that she climbed up.

I saw the face of the Man on the stairs and the way his beard was curly like my doll's hair and Mama said if Papa cut off his beard, she would leave him and everybody laughed; I would not leave Papa if he cut off his beard.

Eric has no beard.

Even the table goes round like the gyroscope, on the floor of Aunt Millie's conservatory that isn't a conservatory any more, but she keeps her old things there and boxes on the shelves where there used to be flower-pots.

Aunt Jennie gave me a Chinese-lily that you plant in a bowl with pebbles.

The bowl Aunt Jennie gave me was blue and shiny, the same kind of shine that the green-saucer has that Eric puts his ash in.

Eric puts his ash in the saucer, he throws the end of the cigarette down and it smokes beside the match-stick.

The ash curls up and I go on looking at the smoke of the cigarette.

Eric shuts the book.

Gilbert is standing by the piano, looking at Papa's wallet.

The table is round like a big wheel.

There was that man in the milk-cart who asked me if I wanted a ride, coming up the Black-horse hill, home from school and I said, "yes" and I climbed in.

The horse was pulling at the milk-cart, going up the hill, and I was thinking it was fun to have a ride in the milk-cart. They drove the carts in, early, to the market on Market Street in Philadelphia, and they came home and slept while the horse climbed Black-horse hill. The milk-cans rattled in the back of a cart, and the horse's back came straight, when we came to the top of the hill. There was Fetters' Farm, at the top of the hill, and the switch where the cars met each other, and the cart jerked and the horse began to run.

I looked at the man and I saw he was . . . he had . . . and he said . . . but I said, "I get out here, I live here," but I did not live at the Fetters' Farm.

I thought he might not stop the horse, so I slid out and I jumped over the wheel that was going fast and I stood by the switch and I saw Mr. Fetters was driving some cows out of their front field and Mrs. Fetters was shelling peas, on the porch.

I could pretend to go in, at the Fetters' gate, if the man looked to see where I was going, but he did not stop. I saw the back of the cart and the milk-tins that rattled and I crept under the fence, so as to get out of the road and went home through the field, by the side of the road.

The wheel was as big as this table and this table was going round but maybe that was the gyroscope or the soap-bubble that I blew out of the window and once I thought if I had three wishes, like they have in fairy-tales, I would wish for a soap-bubble to stay as it was with the different rainbows in it and floating over the pear-tree, like a balloon but in my wish it would never break. That was one of my wishes.

Now I do not know what I would wish, except that the table would not go round like that wheel when I jumped, and that Eric would take us to a hut in the woods and that we would have *Saint Nicholas* every week instead of only once a month.

Gilbert had asked me where was *Saint Nicholas,* but I did not answer and maybe, he was looking for it on the piles of music and magazines on the piano.

Mr. Evans came in. He had Papa's watch in his hand, he said, "I found the Professor's watch and there's someone turning in the drive, I think it's the doctor."

Mr. Evans put down the watch by the wallet that Gilbert had put down again on the piano. Gilbert took up the watch, "it's stopped," he said, "the glass is broken and it's stopped."

Eric took Papa's watch and shook it, Mr. Evans said, "it stopped at quarter past nine, it must have been when—"

There was the crunch of wheels on the drive and Gilbert went to the door.

Mr. Evans said, "but I thought you children were in bed."

The table stopped going round.

"What is concussion, Mr. Evans?" I said.

[VII.]

Morning Star

Thou wert the Morning Star among the living,
Ere thy fair light was shed,
Now having died, thou art as Hesperus giving
New splendour to the dead.

"What is concussion, Mr. Evans?" I said. But I could not hear what he said because there was a roar and then the floor sank.

It was sinking and I was sinking with it, and this was ironical and strange after all we had been through. Now it was ironical and bitter-strange because this was January 17, 1943 and we had done all that. The papers would be burnt, that is what Mamalie had said, she had said the papers would be burnt or she would be burnt and now it all came back again, now I would be burnt and it did not matter what happened any more, only I did not want to be burnt.

I would sink down and down and all the terrors that I had so carefully held in leash during the great fires and the terrible bombing of London, would now break loose because we hadn't had any big raids for some time and we had forgotten how to act.

We had not quite forgotten because Bryher had come out of her room and switched off her light and we carefully shut all the doors. I counted the doors. "There are seven doors," I said, although of course we knew this. The hall is narrow, opening from the front-door. "I think I'll open the front-door," I said, but Bryher said, "no." She sat down on one of the hall-chairs and we switched on the small table-lamp and I said, "I think I'll open the front-door."

Now I thought, would it be better to dash out through the kitchen to the back-door to the fire-escape or would it be better to go out of the front-door and rush down the five flights of stairs? There is the black-and-fawn-striped carpet in the outer hall and blacked-out windows along the stairs and a muffled blue-shaded light burning on each floor. The lift is useless in a raid, as the electricity may be cut off at any moment, "and there you will be," said the hall-porter after one of the big fires, "madame, stuck in the lift and maybe burnt to death and no one could get at you."

The noise was so terrible now, that I could not hear what she was saying but she was saying something. She got up from her chair and took a few steps across the red and grey patterned rug and she stood by my chair. I did not move. The chair would go down too, as if we were both in a lift, an elevator, and we would keep on going down and down. But now the floor was level and I was not going down.

She was not shouting at me but she was speaking carefully. I could see from her face that she was afraid that I was afraid. I was afraid. She said it again and now I heard her words though the noise of little bricks went on; the bricks went on rolling along and knocking against one another and there was now a terrible quiet that was worse than the roar of the guns. "It's nothing," she said, "it's just practice." I knew it was not practice.

I knew the wall outside (not our wall) had fallen. "At first, I thought it was our own wall," I said, "it's because it's so very near. I thought it was our own wall." She said, "no, it's not a wall." She did not shout but her face like a mask, repeated words. I saw the shape of the words and the way she was keeping her face quiet. Then I heard the words. "It's our new gun," she said.

All this time, nothing mattered.

I said, "it's not that it matters. I have no shoes on." I felt what I had not allowed myself to feel in the days of the first danger, that it would be humiliating to rush out on the winter-street in a pair of worn bed-room slippers.

"I left my handkerchief in the other room," I said. Now it seemed that I would be all right if I could manage to open the door to my bed-room and get some outdoor shoes. Chiefly, it seemed odd to have rushed from the front-room where I had been doing needle-work under the shaded lamp, without my handkerchief. I had tucked it between the seat and the padded arm of the chair where I could get at it, and now I had lost it.

It would be an easy matter to open the bed-room door, to get a handkerchief out of my handkerchief drawer, you would think. But it's like a boat, at these times; it would be like going below from an upper-deck in a sudden storm. All one's reactions are different, it would be quite a journey to the door, not more than ten feet from my elbow.

My elbow, both my elbows rested along the straight wooden-arms of the chair opposite her closed bed-room door. We had had all the glass-partitions boarded up and the sky-lights over the doors.

None of our windows were broken although there were some thousands of panes of shattered glass over our pavements when the bomb fell at the other end of the square. But we are at the back of the building and this end did not have any windows broken. Now the little bricks went on rolling but my old protective reaction had not yet encased me inside steel, inside ice.

And yet actually, there I was sitting perfectly quiet, with two arms resting along the arms of the chair; "why, it's just as it always was," I said to myself, "I have not rushed out into the hall, I have not screamed, I am sitting here and anything may happen but the door is shut, all the doors are shut." It was this that unnerved me though actually, now I was sitting just as quiet as I had always been, only now, though I sat with my elbows along the arm of the chair, it was different. I wanted to open the door to the outer-hall. I wanted to hear voices. I wanted to talk to someone. Not just Bryher who stood now, still looking at me, who had said words out of a mask, that were words not spoken in a play, not spoken in another dimension, not uttered in a dream; they were words that were spoken here in this hall of my flat in London, as if the flat and the words went together and I was sitting there and actually it was my flat, my house, my home and actually, it was all happening outside.

The bricks were rolling along and now it was quiet but suddenly there was the same terrific roar and the terrible explosion and the walls shook but the doors did not fly open, pushed outward by the repercussion of the blast as they had done sometimes. So it was not so near or it was nearer, anyhow what she said went with it and I had lost my trick of getting out, of being out of it.

I had learned a trick, lying on my bed, through the closed door, not ten feet away from my right elbow. It had been, I had felt, like a ship; I was snug and comfortable in my bunk, my bed was like a bunk pushed against the wall, in the corner with the outer wall at my head. Then the roar of the wings and the slight trembling of the walls were like the vibration set up in a great ocean-liner, and I was on a great ocean-liner and the ship might or might not go down. And then there would come that moment when I had left myself lying secure and it did not matter what happened to the frozen image of myself lying on the bed, because there was a stronger image of myself, at least I did not see myself but I was myself, whether with attributes of pure abstraction or of days and in places that had been the surroundings of my childhood, or whether as sometimes, it seemed, in one of the vast cathedrals of Italy or in a small bee-hive, that was a tiny Byzantine church outside Athens or was actually the bee-hive tomb of the pre-historic King Agamemnon outside Mycenae, or whether it was a dome of a Mohammedan tomb on the sands of Egypt that rose familiar beyond the gigantic columns of the temples, or whether it was . . . whatever it was, now all the accumulated wealth of being and impression would go down with the ship that was rising and falling.

But it was only my own chair and I never had screamed, I never had fainted, why was Bryher still standing there? She looks at me. Her face is as carved and cold as a Chinese mask, but white, not yellow, not brown or gold. There should be bronze faces and brown and gold faces, there should be the meeting—what was it that Mamalie had tried to tell me?

Now Mamalie was speaking and there was a rattle of the curtain-rings as the curtains blew a little inward. It wasn't a thunder-storm, no, it was a star that was going to fall on the house. It was a shooting-star that was going to fall on the house and burn us all up and burn us all to death. Bryher is looking at me, she does not know why I am able to sit here, I am sitting here because there is a Star, Mamalie told me about it. There was a Promise and there was a Gift, but the Promise it seems, was broken and the Gift it seems, was lost. That is why, now at this minute, there is the roar outside that will perhaps this time, shatter my head, shatter my brain, and all the little boxes that have been all the rooms I have lived in, had gone in and out of, will fall . . . fall . . . she need not tell me again. Why does she tell me over and over, if it's true, that the sound of the bricks falling is the sound of our own guns?

"It's the sound of our own guns," she says again.

"All right," I say, "it's all right."

She sits in the other chair and we seem like two people on the deck of a ship in a storm. We are sheltered in a state-room or in one of the little upper-deck cabins or smoking-rooms, but we are not smoking. Everything around us has been smoking, ashes seep in and lie for months on the underside of bureau-drawers that are too heavy to pull out. Superficially, the place is neat and dusted. Superficially, it is all right.

I saw, I understood . . . a memory of my grandmother's or her grandmother's—a lost parchment, terror that led back finally to the savages, burning and poisonous arrows.

This, I could remember, through steadily and stealthily letting pictures flow past and through me. When the terror was at its height, in the other room, I could let images and pictures flow through me and I could understand Anna von Pahlen who had been the inspirer of the meetings at *Wunden Eiland* when the unbaptized King of the Shawanese gave his beloved and only wife to the Brotherhood; I saw it all clearly.

I saw how young Christian Renatus, an artist and a poet, had indeed perceived clearly the secret of the lost church.

All this I saw running in luminous sequence but this I could not write down, though I sketched the preliminary chapters. In the other room, my bed-room, were the chapters, but how could I see and be and live and endure these passionate and terrible hours of hovering between life and death, and at the same time, write about them? Yet now, as I sat in the chair and said again, "yes, Bryher it's all right," I passionately regretted only this. That the message that had been conveyed to me, that the message that my grandmother had received, would again be lost.

Now it was perfectly clear that I had been conditioned, as it were, to something of this sort. Men, at this moment, were perhaps being blinded and beams were falling on children shut up in underground shelters and a small cat was caught in a slide of chimney-bricks but the cat would claw its way out and the cat would be found in the morning, sitting on the charred hearth-rug before a fire-place that was all that was left out of the walls around what had once been its home.

I myself, cat-like, had clawed my way out of the avalanche of ruins and sat back again on a hearth-rug before a fire-place that was all that was left of what had once been home. Like the cat, I blinked my eyes and I saw in the dark; I could see, when the waves of planes went over the roof, a meeting of various people; Anna von Pahlen, the Santa Sophia or Holy Wisdom or the Holy Spirit of the gatherings, had given her name Angelica (which was my Aunt Agnes' name, too) to the wife of Paxnous, and this was his only wife, his beloved and they drew out the written texts from a bowl or basket. Why, I could see the writing on the slips of paper; Cammerhof would write small and delicate copper-plate script and this second Indian priest or medicine-man, Philippus as he was commonly called, made the mark of the cross and the small flat flower that was the original seal or sign of the pact or the sanctity between them.

This, I did not now see but I remembered how I had seen it. I remembered how my mind after a certain pause of tension and terror, had switched, as it were, into another dimension where everything was clear, where people moved in the costumes of their period, thought back to their old oppressions in Europe and planned a secret powerful community that would bring the ancient secrets of Europe and the ancient secrets of America into a single union of Power and Spirit, a united brotherhood, a *Unitas Fratrum* of the whole world.

This had not worked out but it might have worked out and it would work out, I had thought, if I could follow the clue through the labyrinth of associated memories. But I only remembered that I had had this power, the power had gone now, I was a middle-aged woman, shattered by fears of tension and terror and now I sat in a chair and only remembered that I had been caught up in a vision of power and of peace and I had remembered my grandmother's words exactly.

She had called me Agnes, and she had called me Lucy.

I was Lucy, I was that Lux or Light but now the light had gone out. There was not even a small candle, although the lamp on the table by my elbow was burning with a soft glow. In the old days, I had kept a bag ready, packed with a few precious possessions but now I had no shoes on, only a worn pair of bed-room slippers and I had left my handkerchief pushed down between the arm and the padded seat of the chair in the other room, and I couldn't go on this way. I must, if possible, get through this, but I could not go on with it, and I could not achieve the super-human task of bringing back what had been lost, so the Promise might be redeemed and the Gift restored. The Gift was a Gift of Vision, it was the Gift of Wisdom, the Gift of the Holy Spirit, the *Sanctus Spiritus;* actually, it was the same Spirit that Paxnous' people worshipped, with somewhat the same ritual as that of the initiates of *Wunden Eiland.*

"During the first real raid," I said, "after the fall of France, before you had come back from Switzerland, I propped the front-door open and Mrs. Williamson across the hall, sent her maid over to see if I were all right." I said, "People from upstairs came down and people below, dragged out their bedding and slept in the hall. That was the first real raid." I said this mechanically, going back, as if in some way (although I had not dwelt on these details) it was important now to remember the first raid.

The other raids were blurred over, part of the sequence of events, something to be lived through, something that had been endured. Now this raid linked up only to the first raid, because apparently, we develop our protective colouration, and having developed my own brand of protective colouration (this freezing like a wild animal in the forest, then this getting out, as it were, into a realm of abstraction or purely personal memories) I had not been shattered by any of the great raids as I was now shattered. As if the first real raid linked up with this raid, as if almost this were to be the last.

This, it occurred to me, is my last place, my last little room; this hall-way with the small mirror framed in Italian inset polished wood, with the same little sort of scenes you see painted on the walls of the Pitti Gallery or in museums at Pompeii is my last habitation. This truly occurred to me and I was angry and I could not walk even if I wanted to, for although I felt cold, I was not frozen, not frozen into a state of acute perception, actually covered, as Wisdom is, with armour. No, I was unprotected. I had no steel-helmet and I had no mother-of-pearl shell around me. I was broken open, the mollusc or oyster or clam that was my perceptive abstract self or soul, had neither the super-human reasoning nor the human habitation; I was not clothed in the spiritual armour of light, nor was I clothed in intellectual armour of abstraction.

I could visualize the very worst terrors, I could see myself caught in the fall of bricks and I would be pinned down under a great beam, helpless. Many had been. I would be burned to death.

I could think in terms of one girl in a crinoline, I could not visualise civilisation other than a Christmas-tree that had caught fire.

There had been a little Christmas-tree here on the table, where the lamp now was. That was the first tree we had had since the "real" war and the fragile glass-balls, I had boasted, had withstood the shock and reverberation of steel and bursting shell; "these little balls," I had said, when I unpicked them from the tangle of tinsel and odds and ends of tissue-paper packing, "are symbolic"; unpicking shredded green tissue-paper from a tinsel star, I said, "look at this, it's as bright as ever and this glass-apple isn't broken."

"It's the second wave," she said. So she had given over the myth about its being only an unexpected late-evening practice; the noise of the guns was now deafening but it did not drown out the familiar, rhythmic roar of the giant-propellers over our heads.

"Yes," I said.

She had said the sound of bricks falling was only the guns and now that she had conceded that we were again in the whirlwind, the tornado of enemy night-fighters, I would meet her half-way. I did not have to shout. A voice speaks under the roar if you keep your head and don't let the shriek that is caught in your throat, get the better of you. Now that I saw that Bryher was accepting the fury, we could accept the thing together. We had accepted many things together but this last trial, this last acceptance, might still be the last.

I said speaking carefully, "it's that new gun upset me."

She said, "it was like that in Cornwall, last summer when they got the fishing-village. It was like the sound of the shingle, it was like pebbles and stones rolling under a wave as the wave draws out."

"That's more poetical," I said, "I felt it was like bricks falling and rolling over and over on the pavement."

She said, "it's the same gun. The sound of stones scraping one another, your bricks as you call them, is the empty cartridge-cases falling on the pavement."

"It must be very dangerous if you're caught out," I said.

She said, "no, you have three minutes from the blast of the gun to the falling of the shrapnel or the shell-cases. They explained it to us down there, before it happened."

So much was explained to us before it happened, but no one had explained this. This had happened. This must not happen again.

As if following my thoughts, Bryher said, "I felt like you, in Cornwall last summer—it's the first raid after the long interval—I had my first raid after the interval, last summer. It was worse, I felt, than anything that had happened here. It was because it was my first raid after the interval."

After the interval?

Would these memories go with us? I did not want specifically to live with actual memories. Chiefly, there was Bryher sitting there with her face collected, ears set close to her head, the short-cropped head. What she said was oracular and always had been.

But I didn't care about oracles any more. I didn't care about memories. I was sick to death of tension and tiredness and distress and distorted values and the high-pitched level and the fortitude which we had proved beyond doubt, that we possessed. I had passed the flame, I had had my initiation. I was tired of all that. It had all happened before. Words beating in my brain could get out, not beat there like birds under wire cage-roofs or caught in nets. What was that? The soul? Something being caught or not-caught in the net of the fowler. We were caught. We were trapped. I was sick to death of being on the *qui vive* all the time.

I was tired of trying to understand things, I was tired of trying to explain things. I had done my part. Bryher and my child could go on. I was tired of being the older, the stronger, the more perceptive. I was sick of fanatic courage, my own and that of those about me. We had had too much. The mind, the body is not built to endure so much. We had endured too much. I was tired of it. I could not be brave, I would not be philosophical, it was all a trap, a trick, there could be nothing worse.

I was tired of being grateful just for a quiet night—I was sick of being grateful for things that we had always taken for granted. I was sick of my own high exalted level, this climbing up onto a cloud, a dimension out of time. I hated the thought of *Abide with me.* Though indeed, indeed—the trite old words of the familiar, long forgotten hymn-tunes had come true. What had I known of the *darkness deepens* when I sang to my grandmother? I had sung those words as an inquisitive, sensitive, over-strung, possibly under-nourished child and now that I was over-strung, under-nourished, it all came back.

I had gone round and round and now I had made the full circle, now I had come back to the beginning. But the words of the hymns were trite, were trivial and the net of the fowler was no longer a neat Asiatic metaphor but an actuality. *But it shall not come nigh thee,* at this moment was almost a displeasing thought, for sometimes when the mind reaches its high peak of endurance, there is almost the hope—God forgive us—that the bomb that must fall on someone, would fall on me—but it could not—it must not. Because if the bomb fell on me, it would fall on Bryher and Bryher must go on. That is the way we are trapped, that is the way I was trapped.

Bryher was my special heritage as I had been hers, but she would go on. She did not need me as she had, at the end of the last war, and the child was grown up. The child? "What was the name of the carpenter (if he had a name)? What does Paxnous mean (if it means anything)?" The child is asking questions. It will go on asking questions. If it does not get an immediate answer, it will go on asking more questions.

The question marks link tails or heads, they make a long chain or necklace. Is this the necklace of double Esses of the Guilds and Societies of the middle-ages? The SS is *the Sanctus Spiritus* anyway, and my grandmother had answered some of the questions; no one at any rate, had ever answered more faithfully, more astutely and more intelligently.

Bryher said again, "it's the second wave."

Yes, we were drowning again. We had had almost a hundred air-raids in succession in the worst days; that was after the Battle of Britain and we had recovered and now the tide-wave of terror swept over us again. We were drowning again.

But we were sitting there in the little hall with the seven doors and the doors were all shut, none of them had swung open as they had sometimes in the worst days and none of our windows were broken and we were alive and my child was safe for the moment anyhow. The noise from the heavy guns in the park was terrific and shook the walls but it was an even tremor, like the steady shaking of a great ship, vibrating to the throb of the massive hidden engines. The guns were the engines that would (or would not) take us through the storm.

The second wave! We would go down, we had gone down, the wave was breaking over us and if we came up to the surface again, there was only one certainty; there would be the third wave. Would the third wave be the last wave? It is true that the psyche, the soul can endure anything. But one did not want the body broken—we must not think about that. I am sitting in the hall in one of the little chairs. Actually, we can breathe, we can talk.

"It's not just this raid," I said, "it's remembering all the others."

The terrific shattering reverberations of the great guns slackened for a moment. There seemed to be less shaking and rumbling and an echo as of thunder-storm, further off, was probably distant guns following the flight of the bombers that had already passed over our heads. The surprising thing was that we hadn't all gone raving mad; I do not believe actually one of our friends had left town, driven out by fear. We had had a few week-ends and the short summer breaks but actually had scarcely missed less than a half-dozen of the near-hundred continuous days and nights of bombing, not to mention the later still terrific but less sustained attacks.

Bells clanged, an air-raid warden shouted "are you all right in there," some-one in a pause called in the hush, "puss-puss-puss-puss." Somebody's cat would or would not respond from behind a familiar ash-bin or an unfamiliar heap of smouldering bricks and mortar. It had been worth while. It had been worth while to prove to oneself that one's mind and body could endure the very worst that life had to offer—to endure—to be able to face this worst of all trials, to be driven down and down to the uttermost depth of subconscious terror and to be able to rise again.

"Well, then it's nearly over," I said.

My hands were cold with that freezing uncanny coldness that one associates with ghosts and ghost-stories and sitting in a circle in the dark when they told the story of the man who died of fright because he had nailed his coat to a coffin and thought a skeleton-hand had got him. That was a delicious tremor of expectancy, at a party sitting in a circle in the dark. Well, hadn't this been a sort of party on a grand scale, on, you might say, almost a cosmic scale?

Being shut up in a cupboard in the dark was really associated with games of hide-and-seek and the skeleton-hand of death was something to be scared of at a party and to watch other people being scared of, afterwards at the next party. Going down and down in the dark was a sensation to be watched, to be enjoyed even. I had touched rock-bottom. I had gone down under the wave and I was still alive, I was breathing. I was not drowning though in a sense, I had drowned; I had gone down, been submerged by the wave of memories and terrors, repressed since the age of ten and long before, but with the terrors, I had found the joys, too.

The gate that opens to let out the Old Witch serves, this is the odd thing, to release Saint Nicholas and the Princess with the Star on her forehead who was Mamalie's Morning Star whose name was Angelica and Aunt Agnes' name was Angelica, so when Mamalie called me Agnes, I was Morning Star or I was Anna von Pahlen who had been a sort of Princess in Europe. So Europe and America had at last been reconciled in the very depth of my subconscious being.

On the opposite wall, the mirror was still set at its correct angle. It was a smallish square of glass set in a wide frame of Neapolitan or Pompeii inlaid-wood of different colours. It was set square and solid against the wall and we had not thought it necessary to take it down when we put away the china and had the glass over the doors blocked in. The mirror-frame did not budge, although there was a slightly different pitch or tone to the new reverberations.

"I don't know whether they're flying higher or lower or whether it's them or whether it's us," I said.

"It's not us," Bryher said though my remark had not required an answer. But even if she had not answered it, it would have been immediately answered by the short, staccato perfectly measured beat of a new utterance.

"I don't know where that comes from," I said, "I thought we knew all the gun-positions."

"It must be a mobile-gun," she said.

"Yes," I said.

"Anyway, it's the third wave," she said.

And now theoretically, although one should have been beaten down deeper into the depth of fear and apprehension by the yet wider, sharper and at the same time, deeper unmuffled roar and snarling of all the guns, it would seem, in all the world, barking and spitting at the tail of the dragon (the third wave) as it took its predicted course over our roof-tops, one was not beaten down but caught, static and possibly again frozen with the old protective layer of icy armour, just where one was sitting, in just that one particular chair of the set of six, in just this entrance hall to this particular flat in a once pleasant part of London.

Chair, table, the table opposite snapped out into high-relief like furniture on a stage under a new flood of light. The light was the same, burning under its rose-paper shade at my left elbow. But there was the table opposite, there was the high-light on the cloth of Bryher's skirt where it was pulled tight by her knees having caught the hem of the skirt as she sat down. She remained sitting like a statue with the folds of her skirt unchanged.

She had sat down and she had not moved but soon we would snap out of this; this high-powered tension could not go on forever. It must stop sometime. The yap-yap of the mobile-gun had moved on, anyhow there was the prolonged rumbling again from the great park-guns and the yap-yap of the mobile-gun would have been drowned, if it had not already ceased, in that more powerful thunder. It was not inside one's head. It was outside. It was terrific and searing and terrible but it was outside.

Everything was outside; there was the chair with Bryher sitting on it and the folded cloth of the skirt, pulled too tight across her knees. The reverberations and the still sinister whirr of the enemy propellers overhead, would become one with all the past, and this moment was already past and Bryher sitting there was long familiar, with her head slightly too heavy, it seemed, on her throat, and whatever she said would be prophetic though she would say it to me slowly, afraid that I was afraid, in words spoken in an over-natural naturalness, so that I would not know that she knew I was afraid.

But I was not afraid. The noise was outside. Death was outside. The terror had a name. It was not inchoate, unformed. Wunden Eiland? Was that this island, England, pock-marked with formidable craters, with Death stalking one at every corner?

It is very quiet. My knees are trembling and I am so cold. I am terribly cold but though my knees are trembling, I seem to be sitting here motionless, not frozen into another dimension but here in-time, in clock-time, "I wonder what time it is," I say to Bryher. "It wasn't a very long raid," I say to Bryher, "I wish we could talk to someone."

Now I remember my own personal friends, in the immediate neighbourhood and scattered over different parts of this huge and battle-scarred town of London.

"I hope Arthur didn't get it," I say, "or May or Cole or Gerald. It's too early to ring anyone, but perhaps you'd try—I hope everyone's all right." Bryher is talking on the telephone in the other room. Now there is that new sort of pain, of a half-frozen person drawn indoors near a fire. Slowly, the blood resumes its accustomed channels, the frozen image slumps forward in the chair, the arms relax along the arm of the chair. He has gone again. This time He was very near but He has gone again.

They told us that gravity or something of that sort would keep the stars from falling. But their wisdom and their detachment, hadn't kept the stars from falling. The bombers had gone now but the reaction after the prolonged battles is sometimes more shattering than the raids themselves. But the terror and the tension and the disassociation must come to an end sometimes.

Bryher is standing in the door. We will open all the doors now and I will with an effort, get out of this chair and stagger into the kitchen and fill a kettle and strike a match and arrange a tea-tray.

"I'll get tea now," I say, "who did you get and were they all right?" I do not wait for an answer, although I hear her say, it was all right, everyone was all right. Everything is all right. She opens her own door and pushes open my bed-room door and she goes on talking.

"Yes. She was alone but she was all right. She thanked you for suggesting that we ring her."

"But you rang them," I said.

"But you suggested it," she said.

I push open the kitchen-door and turn round. I stand by the kitchen-door opposite the mirror, *in a glass darkly*. But now face to face. We have been face to face with the final realities. We have been shaken out of our ordinary dimension in time and we have crossed the chasm that divides time from time-out-of-time or from what they call eternity.

I heard Christian Renatus saying:

> *Wound of Christ,*
> *Wound of God,*
> *Wound of Beauty,*
> *Wound of Blessing,*
> *Wound of Poverty,*
> *Wound of Peace,*

and it went on and on, while underneath it, there was the deep bee-like humming of the choir of Single Brothers and then the deeper sustained bass-note that must have been Christian David who had a voice like my great-grandfather who made clocks and kept bees and was called *princeps facile* of musicians. *Princeps facile* they called him in Latin and then there was another language about passing the tomb. *L'amitié passe même le tombeau,* that was; that was French and it was the motto on the seal that the old great-great uncle had and it was the writing at the head of the parchment that my other grandfather, Christian Henry Seidel found.

L'amitié passe même le tombeau.

Now Golden Eagle with his arrows, has driven off the enemy; it is a cry and it is a liturgy, the litany of the wounds; pity us, sings Christian David deep down so that the even flow of the subdued bee-like humming of the choir of Single Brothers seems like a swarm of bees around the deep bell ringing, ringing in Christian David's throat, pity us, he says every time that the young Count Christian Renatus pronounces another one of his single strophes of his liturgy of the wounds. Our earth is a wounded island as we swing round the sun.

Harken to us, sings the great choir of the strange voices that speak in a strange bird-like staccato rhythm but I know what they are saying though they are speaking Indian dialects. The two voices answer one another and the sound of Anna von Pahlen's voice as she reads the writing on the strip of paper from the woven basket that Cammerhof has just handed her, is pure and silver and clear like a silver-trumpet.

I will give him the Morning Star, reads Anna and the head of the Indian priests, who is Shooting Star, later to be baptized Philippus, answers in his own language, *Kehelle* and then Hail, and they call together to the Great Spirit and the Good Spirit who is the God of the Brotherhood and the God of the Initiates . . .

. . . it comes nearer, it is the shouting of many horsemen, it is Philippus, Lover-of-horses, it is Anna, Hannah or Grace who is answering. Now they call together in one voice . . . the sound accumulates, gathers sound . . . "It's the all-clear," says Bryher. "Yes," I say.

London
1941
1943

H.D.
The Gift

&

NOTES

Bethlehem, Pennsylvania[1]

After this, a respectable merchant offered to sell them a piece of land about ten miles south of Nazareth in the forks of the Delaware, on the Lecha, an arm of the river Delaware, and Bishop David Nitschman arriving in 1740 with a company of Brethren and Sisters from Europe, they resolved unanimously to buy this land and make a settlement upon it. It was wild and woody, at a distance of eighty miles from the nearest town, and only two European houses stood in the neighbourhood, about two miles up the river. No other dwellings were to be seen in the whole country, except the scattered huts or cottages of the Indians. In this place the Brethren built a settlement, called *Bethlehem,* which by their perseverance, industry, and the accession of several colonists from Europe, increased considerably from time to time.

From the German of *George Henry Loskiel*
Translated by *Christian Ignatius La Trobe.*[2]

Loskiel's introduction to his *Geschichte* is dated 1788, Strickenhof in Livonia; La Trobe's preface to the translation is 1794, London. From the University of North Carolina Press, 1944, Adelaide L. Fries in *The Road to Salem* gives the most concise paragraph on the history of the "Brethren" that I have yet seen. Miss Fries writes in her preface:

The Unitas Fratrum or Unity of Brethren commonly called the Moravian Church, was founded in 1457 by followers of the Bohemian reformer and martyr John Huss. During the first dramatic period of its existence it endured many persecutions, spread through Bohemia and into Moravia and Poland, grew vigorously, preached the Gospel, established schools, printed books, and attained prominence and wide influence. In the anti-reformation of the seventeenth century, it was almost annihilated, but the third decade of the seventeenth century, descendants of the Ancient Unity emigrated from Moravia into Saxony, where the Unity was resuscitated on the estate of a young nobleman, Nicholas Louis, Count Zinzendorf.[3]

I.

[Dark Room][4]

The Seminary as they called the old school began with a nucleus of twenty-five girls transferred from the Ashmead house in Germantown in 1742.[5] Its chief patroness or foundress was the young Countess, Henrietta Benigna Justina, who as a girl of sixteen came with her father Count Zinzendorf from London to Bethlehem. She went back with her father to London (to Lindsey House on the Thames, Chelsea) but later as the wife of Baron John de Watteville, "Sister Benigna" made the dangerous crossing in 1748, and again in 1784.[6]

In the early and later eighteenth century records of visitors to the town, there is a singular flowering of gracious names and titles. There is the Chevalier de la Neuville, Chevalier Conrad Alexandre Gerard, Don Juan de Miralles, Marquis Francais Jean de Chastellux, the Swedish Baron von Hermelin, the Polish Count Casimir Pulaski and so on.[7] But a century later we enter the world of industries, our original "Lecha, an arm of the river Delaware" is now known as the Lehigh, and anthracite coal has already made the valley famous. Yet the old town and the old school have not yet succumbed to early nineteenth century industrialism.

The school had possibly reached the peak of its popularity and prestige in our grandfather's time. He was vice-principal for five years, principal for twenty years, in the period that preceded, included and followed the Civil War. Southern families of pre–civil war days sent their daughters to Bethlehem to learn French and German, to play the piano, to construct bouquets of wax-flowers and to embroider and work flower-patterns—with not a little piety-without-tears thrown in for good measure.[8]

Our grandfather's stay at the Seminary marked the change-over of the American scene; the old European tradition is about to be swamped out by the progressive American and the name of the birth-place of our Lord now begins to appear incongruously stamped on steel-rails and girders.

Papalie's name was Francis. Our grandfather's name was Francis Wolle. He was born in Bethlehem, Pennsylvania. His father, John Frederick Wolle was born at Bethany–St. John, West Indies; his grandfather, Peter Wolle was born in Schwerzens, near Posen, Poland.[9] I have referred to Francis Wolle as Francis Sylvester in the later pages; our grandfather succeeded the Reverend Sylvester Wolle as principal of the Seminary, so I have simply doubled on a family-name.

Sylvester or Silvester is "from the Latin *silvestris,* belonging to wood or forest." Sylvester too is akin to Sylvanus and hence in association with Pennssylvania,[10] whose wooded rivers, our grandfather explored so thoroughly in his expeditions for his moss or *algae.* Francis Wolle's books are: *Desmids of the United States,*[11] *Fresh Water Algae of the United States,* two volumes, text and plates[12] and *Diatomaceae of North America.*[13]

Old Father Weiss,[14] our grandmother's father, "although a master of this trade (watchmaking and general silversmith's work) is better remembered in connection with the music of Bethlehem and . . . bought the stone 'oatshouse' . . . built there a house in which he carried on this industry for more than four decades."[15]

The name Weiss is common enough in connection with the Brotherhood and its activities; there are Matthias and Margaret Catherine listed among the passengers of Captain Garrison's *Little Strength.* They are from the company assembled from Herrnhaag and Marienborn. These meet the Herrnhut group at Rotterdam, September 1743, and Captain Garrison carried them to Cowes where they picked up the members of the English colony. The ship bore the ensign "a lamb *passant* with a flag on a blood-covered field."[16] This was the second Sea Congregation.[17]

We hear of Jonas Paulus Weiss[18] with the alternate spelling, Jonah Paul Weite[19] who, back in Herrnhut, has words with a certain Andrew Frey, who sailed from Pennsylvania with the returning members of the first Sea Congregation. We are grateful to Andrew Frey, "later an enemy and traducer of the Brethren"[20] for his colourful "Account" of the Herrnhuters or Moravians, their "Festivals, Merriments, Celebrations of Birthdays, Impious Doctrines and Fantastical Practices."[21]

Brother Andrew looks askance on the debonair deportment of the young Count, Christian Renatus or Christel as he calls him, on the occasion of a celebration, "the Count and his Retinue being arrived from *England.*"

Says Brother Andrew, (the italics and capitals are his): "I went to *Jonah Paul Weite,* he having daily business with the Count; I promised myself that he would speak a Word for me, and related to him all *Christel* had said; But after I had gone through all which I proposed to have presented to the Count, *Paul* said to me, That he had attended to all my Complaints of the

Brethren, and he would now declare what he thought of me, namely, That I was a very serious, regular and pious Man, but likewise an Enemy to the Saviour; adding that *Christel,* and all the Brethren of whom I made such loud Complaints, were better than me, and that all the Blame lay upon myself."[22]

There is the astute Lewis William Weiss, later counsellor-at-law and Justice at Philadelphia whose name figures in legal documents relating to matters concerning the early welfare and interests of our Brotherhood, on both sides of the Atlantic.[23]

There is the later Anna Maria Weiss whose name is listed with that of Rebecca Langly, "a young English woman of genteel breeding and formerly opulent family . . . who had brought fine needlework at Bethlehem to its highest point of excellence." Rebecca designed the banner, "attached to a lance when borne to the field," which was offered by the "single women of Bethlehem" to Count Pulaski, "with designs beautifully wrought with the needle by their own hands."[24]

This banner was rescued by his First Lieutenant when Pulaski fell in battle at Savannah, 1779. The poet Longfellow's "Hymn of the Moravian nuns of Bethlehem at the consecration of Pulaski's banner" was written, it is recorded, "before he knew that the Moravian sisters were not nuns."[25]

Our grandmother's father, Jedediah Weiss is representative of the constructive or creative period following the American Revolution and preceding the Civil War. "The acme of the period was a complete rendition, in the church, on Whitmonday, in 1839, of 'The Creation' . . . by a hundred and twenty-five participants."[26]

My cousin, Clifford Howard, remembered our great-grandfather. "Although I was not seven years old," he wrote me shortly before his own death, "when he died, I remember him very distinctly . . . a handsome old man. He had a lovely garden and kept bees, and I can still see him, wearing a broadbrimmed hat and carrying a sprinkling-pot . . . as he moved about among his flowers, wholly unmindful of the bees that buzzed about him.[27] . . . he was a gifted musician, not only possessed of a magnificent bass voice, but a skilled instrumentalist as well. He was a member of the Moravian trombone choir for fifty years, and not once in all that time did he miss playing on Easter morning."[28]

. . . *the gift that Uncle Fred had.* J. Fred Wolle's name is associated with "that superb achievement, the three days Bach Festival of May 23–25, 1901, which attracted the attention of musicians throughout the country and even in Europe, and elicited almost unqualified praise from eminent musical critics who were present; when as the reward of Mr. Wolle's ability and perseverance, the Christmas Oratorio, the St. Matthew Passion and the Mass in B Minor were all rendered complete by his well-trained choir."[29]

This was our mamalie's youngest child, old Jedediah's grandson. I myself never attended this nor the festivals that followed. For me, personally, Uncle Fred's musical contribution is a simple ballad.

The Four Marys[30] was my grandmother's personal preference. Jedediah's mighty bass and the "surge and thunder" of his trombone had not stilled in her a delicate Celtic lyric that ran alongside the mighty torrent of German classic tradition.

It had threaded its way into her heart and into mine; it was an unspoken tradition, breathless, almost voiceless; this was something we understood together and perhaps we two only. If Jedediah gave Uncle Fred the whole ocean of musical-consciousness called Haydn or called Bach, well, it was something over which we had no control, we could not argue about it.

We hadn't any gift, Mamalie hadn't any gift either, it appeared, yet she was firm and adamant on one point, now Fred . . . to finish, Four Marys. Who were these four Marys?

They were, it appeared, *Mary Seaton, Mary Beaton, Mary Carmichael and me.*

Mamalie's mother's name was Mary,[31] and she was from Virginia; in fact, only just, as she might, it had been whispered, have been born at sea. Her father and mother had come from Scotland, so Mary, Mamalie's mother, had "started" in Scotland; she was the nearest biological link with the old world that we had, as Papalie's father, born in the West Indies, was already a stepping-stone away from the continent of Europe and what was then, as it happened, Poland.

Perhaps the song contained a mystery and symbolism of which I was only vaguely conscious. There were four Marys, four mothers, four points of the compass, four sides to a square, four seasons to the year. The four Marys were the world, four-square and another world . . . the fourth dimensional was not a state that I was then likely to have heard discussed. But this Mary and this song did make a furrow or runnel in my emotional or spiritual being that later let through a stream-of-consciousness that, in retrospect, is more precious to me than the St. Matthew Passion and the Mass in B Minor. For it was my own interpretation of the *Gift*, as Mamalie later in this story, reveals it to me.

II.

[Fortune Teller][32]

The Brothers' House . . . the Sisters' House[33] were still commonly so-called when I was a child. Actually, the official terms were choir-house of the single men and choir-house of the single women. In the early days of the renewed Brotherhood, "a division of the membership on the basis of differing age, sex and station in life, for the purpose of specialising religious culture, had been gradually developed. The word *chor* was applied in German to each such division, and this was then rendered into English by the word choir."[34]

The first established choir, was that of Anna Charity, the daughter of Father Nitschmann. "Under the system of that time, she was raised to the position of a kind of sister superior of all the single women of the Moravian congregations and settlements."[35] Anna established the choirs at Bethlehem along the lines of her original group, of May 4, 1730, which was "a special covenant of consecrated service among seventeen young women and girls." Anna returned to England and later to Herrnhut. She became Count Zinzendorf's second wife.[36]

Although the character of the choirs had changed before the close of the eighteenth century and the choir-principles, choir-liturgies, choir-festivals for the most part, became obsolete during the next fifty years, yet certain hymns remained dedicated or associated with certain groups, the single men or the single women or the widows or the children. These hymns played from the steeple or cupola of the church, announced the death of one of the members of the congregation.

In this reconstructed reverie, the little Helen Eugenia Wolle, child of a long line of musicians, could easily distinguish to which "choir" each particular hymn belonged; she could tell for *what sort of person* the hymn was being played, *if it was one of the old Brothers from the Brothers' House* for instance. *She could tell whether someone was born or someone had died.*

Actually these particular hymns or chorals, rendered by the trombonists from the church cupola, were played only at the hour of the death of Single

Sisters or Married Sisters or Widows or Widowers and so on—or for children. I distinctly remember being told however, when enquiring about the solemn, slow but somehow comforting music that floated down from the church-roof, that there was music at that odd hour because "someone has just been born."

My own mother must have been told this, too, as a child, for it was her mother, our grandmother who explained this to me.

The river was wide. This is of course, our original Lecha, now Lehigh, a branch of the river Delaware. We must remember that this, like all the rivers of the United States of America, are Indian rivers. If we restore its name, perhaps we re-invoke faintly the original unblemished character, before "the pitiless ravages of industry upon the picturesque, which have never ceased along the course of the Lehigh River, had fairly set in."[37]

The Lehigh or Lecha took its name because it was a *branch* or *fork* of the parent stream; this was the mighty Delaware river, first called by the Dutch the *Zuydt* or the South river until the Swedes took over and named it the *Swenska* or Swedes' river. But as we must have a "foreign" name, let us be thankful that it fell to Lord de la Ware to force "his claim and name."[38]

We now have the Delaware river and the Indians roaming, fishing, hunting along its wide course, are called the Delaware Indians. The Indians of Lord de la Ware? No! These are the *Lenape* which means simply Indian or Indian men and the river is the river of the *Lenape* or the *Lenape-wihittuck.* The west branch, *where there are forks* was *Lechauweeki, Lechawiechink* or *Lechauwekink;* this, shortened into *Lecha,* becomes *Lehigh.*[39]

The canal had long merged into the landscape with its amenable tow-path, its old lock-houses and water-gates and saw-mills. Not so in my mother's grandfather's day.

Jedediah and his contemporaries were shocked when a "large force of diggers"[40] invaded the locality of the quiet town in the summer of 1829 and felling a number of their beloved trees, dug or cut the ditches that were part of an elaborate water-way from Lake Erie to the Delaware and hence to the sea.

We are told that "havoc was also wrought with the fertile acres between the

Monocacy and the Lehigh"[41] and the famous old grist-mill up the Monocacy was rendered useless. The Monocacy loses its character but not its name. The stream flowing into the Lehigh above "the old Indian ford" was called *Menagassi* or *Menakessi* (*Monakasy, Monocasy* or *Monocacy*) that is *creek with bends*. The site *at the bending creek* was named *Menagachsink* and the name was later applied by the Indians to the town.[42]

Count Zinzendorf . . . from his orchards at Berthelsdorf had had these same Indians in mind long before he actually established his "Church within the Church"[43] among the people of his own estates and villages.

Berthelsdorf in Upper Lusatia, Saxony was then ten miles from the Bohemian frontier. The grandfather of "our Count Zinzendorf" had taken his stand with the Protestants during the Reformation and had settled in Saxony; the original estate in South Austria passed over to another branch of the family. But "our Count Zinzendorf," among other notable titles, still remained heir to that most picturesque one, "Hereditary Warden of the Chase to his Imperial Roman Majesty, in the Duchy of Austria, below the Ens."[44] He was as well "Nicholas Louis, Count and Lord of Zinzendorf and Pottendorf; Lord of the Baronies of Freydeck, Schoeneck, Thürnstein and the Vale of Wachovia; Lord of the Manor of Upper, Middle and Lower Berthelsdorf."[45] It was here at Berthelsdorf that he threw in his lot with that small band of persecuted Protestants from Moravia that led to the renewal of the *Unitas Fratrum* or Unity of Brethren.

It was in the late spring of 1722; the exiles or refugees had first approached the mansion of Hennersdorf, the property of the Countess Gersdorf,[46] the grandmother of the youthful Count Zinzendorf. The Countess did not herself take them in but recommended them to Rothe, the pastor at the neighbouring village of Berthelsdorf. The young Count being in Dresden at the time, his steward gave reluctant permission to the group of pilgrims to remain on the estate. There were two brothers with their households, ten persons in all under the leadership of the redoubtable Christian David, the Moravian carpenter (a convert from Romanism), the most conspicuous leader or agent of this subterranean or "underground" religious movement.[47]

It is said that one of the weary home-sick women of the party set up a wail on perceiving the desolate tract that the reluctant steward had assigned to them. "Where shall we find bread in this wilderness?" she said. But Christian

David seized his axe, struck the nearest tree and retorted, "Here the sparrow hath found a house, and the swallow her nest; even thine altars, O Lord of Hosts." [48] These first shelters form the nucleus of The Guard or Protection of the Lord, the *Huth des Herrn,* hence *Herrnhuth* or *Herrnhut,* whose inhabitants, in less than ten years, numbered some 600 refugees and pilgrims.

 . . . that first Christmas-eve.

"The place having as yet no name, it so happened that on Christmas Eve we called to mind the birth of our Saviour, and as there was a thin partition-wall between our dwelling-room and the cow-and-horse-stable, Count Zinzendorf in the tenth hour of the night went over to the stable and commenced to sing with great fervency of spirit:

> Nicht Jerusalem: Sondern Bethlehem,
> Aus dir kommet was mir frommet.

And thus on Christmas Eve, 1741, this new settlement received the name of Bethlehem." (From the diary of John Martin Mack.) [49]

 The Bethlehem Christmas Hymn is set to Gregor's 46th metre. There have been a number of metrical translations of Adam Drese's *Jesu rufe mich.* A simple rendering would be:

> Call me, Jesu, from the world: I want to hurry
> to you now, without waiting.
> It was not Jerusalem, but Bethlehem that saved
> us from starvation: no, not Jerusalem.
> O noble Bethlehem, so rich; all our joy comes
> from you, dearest Bethlehem.
> You can not be a little town as they have said,
> because to everyone, everywhere (even to the
> outcast) you bring help and light.
> Show me (I am so far away) the star that will
> guide me, that will lure me, too from my evil
> ways; O show me your star. [50]

But here are the actual words as Nicholas Louis, Brother Louis or *Bruder Ludwig* chanted them "with great fervency of spirit."

Jesu rufe mich
Von der Welt, dass ich
  Zu dir eile.
    Nicht verweile;
Jesu rufe mich.

Nicht Jerusalem,
Sondern Bethlehem
  Hat bescheret
    Was uns naehret;
Nicht Jerusalem.

Werthes Bethlehem,
Du bist angenehm;
  Aus dir kommet
    Was mir frommet,
Werthes Bethlehem.

Du bist, wie man spricht,
Nun die kleinste nicht;
  Allen Leuten,
    Auch den Heiden
Bringst du Heil und Licht.

Zeige mir den Stern
Der mich, aus der Fern,
  Von den Heiden
    Lehr abscheiden;
Zeige mir den Stern.

. . . The Indians had long since left this valley.

We are told that the last visit of the Indians to Bethlehem, in any considerable number was in 1792 when fifty-one chiefs and other representative men of the Six Nations arrived at Bethlehem, on their way to Philadelphia. Bishop Ettwein one of "the Moravian Brethren in whom they had confidence"[51] had been nominated by them, as their representative, the year before.

Three Seneca chiefs, Corn-planter, Half-town and Big-tree[52] with Bishop Ettwein met in preliminary conference with the congress and President Washington in Philadelphia, to consider the redistribution of land and the land-grants after the War of Independence. Now in March 1792, the Indians make their way down the Lehigh river on to the Delaware, to conclude the final treaties. We are told that the canoes put in, in large numbers along the shallow reaches of the Lehigh river. Two of the original three Seneca chiefs were present and the names of a few others are given. "The principal one was the famous Red Jacket. Corn-planter and Big-tree were again of the number. Others were Farmer's Brother, Little Billy, Captain Shanks and La Fayette's young Oneida, Pierre Jaquette, who died in Philadelphia." We are told that "Red Jacket responded in dignified language to the Bishop and the old man, Good Peter, to the young ladies."[53]

It might well be recalled here that contrary to the usual precedent of colonists, traders and preachers, Count Zinzendorf had succeeded in making a formal treaty or pact with the kings or chiefs of the Iroquois or Six Nations. The Six Nations were the Mohawks, Oneidas, Onondagas, Cayugas, Senecas and Tuscaroras.[54] It was July 1742, the summer following that first Christmas-eve that Count Zinzendorf or Brother Louis made off with scant retinue much to the surprise and chagrin of the Pennsylvania settlers, ("who realized the dangers better than he") into the wilderness. He took his seventeen year old daughter with him, "going into the forests to visit the Red Men, of whom neither she nor her father seemed to have any fear, though we Pennsylvanians knew only too well how dangerous and uncertain they were."[55]

Perhaps Brother Louis and the child Benigna had some curious related power or magnetism that protected them, at any rate princely indifference to danger and superb dignity of bearing met with princely indifference and equally superb dignity. It is an astonishing fact that the Six Kings of the Six Nations presented Zinzendorf with the famous wampum or "fathom of one hundred and eighty-six white beads."[56] As white is the almost universal symbol of peace and good-will, this fathom was a peace-treaty, a safe-conduct and even more, a pledge or pact, *thy people shall be my people.*[57]

The Count in return, presented the Six Nations with a "seal inscribed with the words Jesus Jehovah, to be stamped in wax" by which "the chiefs might identify any of the brethren."[58]

The Last of the Mohicans. We are given in the last chapter of the classic school-boy romance, a picture of Chingachgook,[59] "the stern and self-restrained warrior"[60] addressing the people on the occasion of the funeral ceremonies, held over the slain body of his son Uncas. The book ends with the words of the half-mythical chief and patriarch of the Delawares. "It is enough," he said. "Go, children of the Lenape, the anger of the Manitou is not done. Why should Tamenund stay? The pale-faces are masters of the earth, and the time of the red-men has not yet come again. My day has been too long. In the morning I saw the sons of Unamis happy and strong; and yet, before the night has come, have I lived to see the last warrior of the wise race of the Mohicans."[61]

Actually our poor friends had got into very bad ways. They were settled along the upper reaches of North river or the Hudson, in the state of New York. Christian Henry Rauch had arrived in New York in 1740 before the actual establishment of the centre at Bethlehem. In a note on the Moravians in the Appendix of *The Last of the Mohicans,* it is said that "very soon after landing he fell in with the Mohicans from Shekomeko or Pine Plains."[62] He accompanied them back to the Indian village. But here unhappily, we witness a scene of degradation with little or nothing of the picturesque, ritualistic trimmings so dear to the early nineteenth century romantic.

This was a trader's station.

The Mohicans were traditional enemies of the Mohawks, whom we have just listed with the other five tribes of the Six Nations. So our wampum or fathom has no place here.

Our Indians in Pennsylvania at this time, did not see their "chief's sons lie drunken in the street."[63] But the fur-traders had made a good business on the upper reaches of the Hudson.

It is said that Christian Henry caused not a little amusement among the degraded warriors.[64] He was a pale-face with no connection with the white community and he carried no weapons.

He did not want to bargain, as they had imagined he would do, in an under-hand way, against their usual patrons. What did he want? They asked him. He told them frankly that he wanted their allegiance to his King. But who was his King? There was the big-white King of the English and there were other chiefs or Kings; there were the Dutch, there were the French. But he wasn't English or Dutch or French though he could understand words of these tongues and could make himself understood in one language if another failed.

Anyhow, they managed to converse together. Christian Henry told them about the death of his King, how he had died impaled on a stake, tortured by his enemies. They understood that. But Christian Henry wasn't asking them to *do* anything. The last white God-talker had said, "you must not steal, nor lie, nor get drunk." But they had the answer to that. "Thou fool, dost thou think we don't know that? Learn first thyself, and then teach the people to whom thou belongest to leave off these things; for who steals, or lies, or who is more drunken than thine own people?" [65]

Chingachgook or Tschoop, the leader of the gang, suggested that they should not kill him after all, as they might get some fun out of him, and it was apparent anyway, that he was not all there in his head. And he might talk again. He did talk again.

He was quite alone with them. His original companion a young man of Rhinebeck, New York [66] had been dismissed before the journey's end. They were all very merry and drunk but no one was as drunk as Tschoop. It was astonishing how that pale-face could talk. You could understand almost everything he said until the fire-water got into your head and then you could understand things he wasn't saying and you could make your own pictures and your own words and dreams took shape and—what had he said?

There shall be no time. What did he mean by that and something about *no moon* and *no sun* because the Sun—because the Sun—but that was the great totem, that was the great symbol and he had sworn—what had he sworn? All that was so long ago and *there shall be no time* [67] and what happened long ago, was happening now, so the pale-face said, and what had happened would happen again because there was no time—and sometimes he said it in French and sometimes in Dutch and if he could talk the Mohican speech, then Tschoop would have the answer, but the answer was something that he had never had to put into words for the traders, so there were no words now.

There were no words. There were pictures that wrote themselves like the old hunting-scenes and the battle-scenes painted on birch-bark and he could see his thoughts going round like the tattoo-brush or the tattoo-quill or knife across his features. His features were tattooed with his thoughts and everything was bright with the sumach-berry. But there was a still brighter colour. He must not say it again. He must not say it again. "Say it again," shouted Tschoop.

"Made of one blood," said Christian Henry, *"purchased with his blood . . ."*

"Stop," said Tschoop, "go on—go on," said Tschoop. It was that word, he waited for it to come round in inevitable sequence, he waited and dreaded, he ordered Christian Henry to go on. He ordered him to stop. He sent out the band of revellers because they shouted in the wrong place. He must be alone with this. It was the word "blood."[68]

It set up a rhythm in his brain and he seemed to hear the wild high wind in the great forest trees outside the lodge or wigwam, echoing "blood," though there was no wind that night (it was a summer night) but outside the triangular pegged-back opening to the lodge, he seemed to see a flurry as of white feathers drifting or of snow—but it was summer, there was no snow.

Then he heard the word "blood" again and looked around the circle for corroboration, for sympathy, but his companions had gone as he had told them to.

"Blood, blood, blood," thought Tschoop, "what is this cry to battle? And who proclaims the battle?" Blood? Was he hot? Was he cold? Ha—there it is—the thing that is hot, that is cold.

Tschoop had seen many pale-faces in his day and he knew the way eyes narrowed or widened, fingers fumbled or clasped themselves in curious un-trained unfamiliar and weak gestures that gave away secrets of the inner man—and such secrets! The white men, the pale-faces had no secrets. What they wanted was gain, their peculiar "wampum" that was dull metal, no bright bead or shell. But here was a pale-face that was indeed pale, but not with fear, not with greed, here was a face that was as cold as ice and as white, but not with death. Or should it be with death? With a gesture, Tschoop could yet reach forward and throttle this throat or flick a finger from his belt that would land the dagger in the half-wit's temple. Was it worth the effort? He was funny, this fellow, with nothing to protect him, with nothing to hold him, finding words that the traders had never mastered, making words speak as the traders had never made them, making words sing and sting.

For the sake of hearing a few more of those curious words that worked strange havoc in his brain—was it fire? Was it snow?—Tschoop challenged Christian Henry. "Blood, blood, blood," said Tschoop, "a fine fellow, a fine warrior to set a war-cry ringing in a strange encampment. Where are your fellow-warriors," challenged Tschoop, "they are not outside in the forest for if a deer broke a dried twig or a single winter-green berry should fall from its stem, I or one of mine would hear it. Blood, blood," cried Tschoop, "of whom do you speak and of what?"

Christian Henry was very tired. "I have been telling you," he answered.

Tschoop said, "I heard the word *blood,* I did not hear what you said."

Christian Henry said, "I am very tired; may I sleep now?"

Tschoop said, "I did not hear what you said. I heard the word *blood.* But I know what you said. I know what you said was not what the others said, for what you said did not bring the same lines to the face"—he was more than bi-lingual now, he used a word from their ancient language that would have meant paths through the forest—"that the others made. There were new lines"—he said new paths, really—"on the face."

Tschoop said, "you do not ask on what face or on whose faces? You are too tired to ask, or you have lost the gift of the words"—he used a word for gift that translated would mean ghost or spirit—"but I will tell you, I mean the faces of these Mohicans and the map was different." (By map, he meant of course, the pattern of the lines, the face being a mountain or a landscape in his phantasy.)

"Another, not-trader, who came to talk to us, told us there was God, told *us,* there was God! We sent him away. The next told us, not-steal, not-lie, not-drink. We said, but your own people steal more, lie more, drink more than we do. Go to them. We sent him away." Tschoop waited a moment, then he repeated, "we sent him away. We sent them both away. But you, we will not send away." He waited to see if Christian Henry would drop on the floor with fatigue, but Christian Henry, though he seemed a moment since, to have been swaying slightly, was still standing. "Shall I tell you why we sent the others away?" asked Tschoop, rhetorically. "It was because," said Tschoop, "there had been a little trouble over a small matter of deer-land with the Mohawks; it had nothing to do with the traders, but several pale-faces drifted down the river, I mean," said Tschoop, "the Mohawks and the Mohicans were not on the war-path and we decided to send any more interfering pale-faces back with our own guides and canoes after that, until the hunting-season began again anyway. Anyhow these two pale-face god-talkers were of this country and under the great chief pale-face. You are not of this country. You have come from far in the Great Wings," ships, of course. "You stayed only long enough in the Manhattan to speak to your friends the other pale-faces who move further down among the Lenni-lenape. You see we know every-thing."

"Yes," assented Christian Henry wearily.

"But one thing we do not know," continued Tschoop. "Will you answer one question before I throw your body into the forest or even into the river. It does not matter where it drifts for you do not belong to this river, nor this land nor this forest. Why did you send the young John of Rhinebeck back with the canoe? Why did you not bring him here? Did you send the young John of Rhinebeck to report to his governor, in case you did not return? The young John of Rhinebeck is of this land, this river. The governor would listen to him. Did you send the young John back to tell the governor where you had last been, in case you did not come back?"

"No," said Christian Henry.

"What did you tell him? How did you get him to go back? He is not the sort of young pale-face to leave a companion alone among the Mohicans. What did you tell him to tell the governor and your people?"

"I told him," said Christian Henry, "that I was going among friends."

"Yes," said Tschoop, inwardly delighted with this twist of irony. "But if you did not come back," he persisted, "from these *friends,* what then, what was he to say to them?"

"John Mueller was to tell them," said Christian Henry simply, "that I had found my Friend."

It is a matter of history that when Count Zinzendorf visited Shekomeko in August 1742, with that redoubtable little adventuress, Benigna, he found the beginnings of a friendly community. Christian Henry or Brother Henry was known as *Z'higochgoharo.*[69] His great stay and companion was no other than our friend Tschoop, who later became prominent as the Indian Elder Job or John Wasamapah.[70] Other "Brethren" with their families joined the settlement and fields were laid out and the business of seed-time and harvest considered. When the community became self-supporting, the Indians no longer kept contact with the traders. The whiskey and rum merchants agitated against the mission. The Brethren were accused of being Papists in disguise and in league with the French. An act against the Jesuits in 1700 was revived in New York state and received endorsement in September 1744; among other things, it enacted measures against "every vagrant preacher, Moravian or disguised Papist."[71] The following year, "Moravian missionaries did actually suffer, not only fine but imprisonment, and their work among the Indians in New York was ruined."[72]

Christian Henry Rauch finally returned to Bethlehem. The greater part of his Indian colony followed him. This caused great difficulties as the Indians at Bethlehem now far out-numbered the settlers. This led to the establishment of *Friedenshuetten* or Habitations of Peace, "at the foot of the hill to the south-east of the present Seminary for Young Ladies."[73] These cabins or groups of log-houses increased out of all proportion to the town itself and these Indians from New York and Connecticut came to be known generally as the "Bethlehem Indians."

The young man of Rhinebeck, New York had journeyed with Christian Henry to Bethlehem, however, before the Shekomeko community was dispersed. This was in the summer of 1742. John Mueller stayed at Bethlehem. He was the first to rest in the field or rather the "woods north-east of the Community House," which Count Zinzendorf consecrated on that occasion as "God's acre."[74] John Mueller's was the first funeral in the present old historic cemetery. Four years later, in the summer of 1746, there was a new disproportionate crop of little earth mounds. Victims of the small-pox had joined John Mueller in the "woods north-east of the Community House." Among these new graves of the summer of the year 1746 was that of Tschoop or Chingachgook, the Indian Elder John Wasamapah, The Last of the Mohicans.[75]

She saw Count Zinzendorf sitting in the tent.

In September, after his return from Shekomeko, Count Zinzendorf planned his last and most daring adventure. We find no mention of Benigna this time, and we may trust that her rage and chagrin at being left behind was tempered with Christian resignation. The Count first paid a visit to the King of the Oneidas, one of the Six who had met him at Tulpehocken and had exchanged tokens of peace and brotherhood on August 3rd of this same summer.[76] This time, the King and the Count met at Shamokin, the large Indian town on the Susquehanna River, and pledges were renewed and we may imagine gifts exchanged—we know at any rate that the King Shikellimy was vastly pleased with a shirt that the Count gave him.[77]

It is interesting to note that years after the Count's return to Europe, during the time of the terrors of the so-called French and Indian Wars, one of the brotherhood, the "missionary and mastersmith, Marcus Kiefer,"[78] having been given up for lost, after the outrages along the Susquehanna, was finally traced not far from his original station in the wilderness; he was safe for "he had meanwhile, been protected by John Shikellimy or Thachnechtoris, son of the famous chief, old Shikellimy."[79] This however was in the late autumn of 1755.

Let us return to September, 1742. The Count having parted with his shirt, or possibly only a shirt, now pays a visit to the famous Madame Montour at Ostonwakin.[80] We may be sure that there was a courteous exchange of civilities and we may wonder what this lady felt on thus being addressed by one of the old world, in her own language. She had been a long time in the wilderness, having broken all connection with her country and her people. It appears that she was not only satisfied with her predicament but on no condition, would she give up her way of life. She was perfectly happy, she assured her visitors. It was rather the good Count who should pause and consider; this is as far as anyone can go. Beyond, was the unpredictable and unexplored waste-land. Her own people here—she was speaking of the Indians of Ostonwakin—could persuade him to give up the idea, even if the Count would not listen to the reasoned warnings of a French—well—lady.

He had already listened to his good friends at Shamokin, he assured Madame Montour, and she need feel no responsibility for his welfare. He had already been prompted by—a Friend. He was on a diplomatic mission—this—well Friend had counselled him to proceed further. And proceed further, he did.

Wajomik is further up the river. The Susquehanna is very wide and shallow, but with unexpected currents and hidden deep wells or pits of water. (The Count's horse, on one occasion on fording the river slipped or stumbled and the Count was caught up in a hidden whirl-pool and nearly drowned.)[81]

The party, however, reached their journey's end, without serious loss or injury and "passed twenty days among the treacherous, blood-thirsty Shawanese of Wajomik, where no white man had before set foot."[82]

The Shawanese could make neither head nor tail of this excursion. And yet it was very simple, after all. They knew the pale-face. They were always after something. They wanted something. They wanted ore for their wampum, their coins were struck in silver. There was an alleged deposit of silver ore in the hills. But the remedy to all this, was only too self-evident. It might however be simpler, on the whole, if the Captain or Chief of the party died a natural death. He had certain pledges or passports from the Six Nations and Six Nations were Six Nations and the Shawanese were only one. Hence the arrangements so courteously made for the pitching of the tents.

Here is Martin Mack's story: "the tent was pitched on an eminence; one fine sunny day, as the Disciple sat on the ground within, looking over his papers that lay scattered about him, and as the rest of us were outside, I observed two blowing adders basking at the edge of the tent. Fearing that they might crawl in, I moved toward them, intending to dispatch them. They were, however, too quick for me, slipped into the tent, and, gliding over the Disciple's thigh, disappeared among his papers. On examination we ascertained that he had been seated near the mouth of their den. Subsequently the Indians informed me that our tent was pitched on the site of an old burying-ground in which hundreds of Indians lay buried. They also told us that there was a deposit of silver ore in the hill and that we were charged by the Shawanese with having come for silver and nothing else."[83]

The Shawanese however, treacherous and malignant as they were reported to be, were an off-shoot of the Algonquin or Algonkin. Our Delawares, Lenape or Lenni-lenape were another branch. The Algonquins were reputed to be the most highly developed of the North American Indians. Their mantles of feather-work have been compared to those of the Aztecs. It was the Algonquins along the north-eastern Atlantic coast who had saved the early New England colonists from famine, who taught them the various uses of the native plant and tree, notably maize or Indian corn and how to convert the sap of the maple-tree or the sugar-tree as they called it, to what we call maple-sugar. Hominy, succotash, maple-sugar and johnny-cake are all legacies of the Algonquins. Not to mention tobacco, that most civilised and civilizing of commodities. This of course was best grown and flavoured further down the coast among the Powhatans of Virginia. The Powhatans should be gratefully remembered by descendants of the original Jamestown colony which was also saved from starvation:

> . . . *the food was given, not in hate,*
> *Liking or dazzled wonder, but, it seems,*
> *As if compelled by something past all plans,*
> *Some old barbaric courtesy of man's.*[84]

In naming the Powhatans, we must inevitably recall the desperately tragic story of "the lady Rebecca Rolfe." This was Pocahontas, the child-princess whom Captain John Smith had advised the English Queen to entertain royally for she "could move her people." John Smith meets her for the last time in London, "very soon to die as caged things will." [85] But all this had happened a hundred years before Nicholas Louis, Lord of Zinzendorf and Pottendorf bowed his stately farewells to the famous Madame Montour at Ostonwakin.

There is this, however. As in Europe, the old-seed of the old-faith had been run to ground and run underground to put forth a miraculous shoot, as it were, under the fence (across the Bohemian border) in Nicholas Louis' own wild-wood, so here in the forests of the upper Susquehanna, the old faith or if you will, the old superstition of the mystery religion of the Algonquins, sees a curious flowering. For the Algonquins, like the Athenians of an older or perhaps younger Europe, were the wardens and guardians of the best of the civilizations of their time. The Iroquois on the other hand, might well be likened to the Spartans,[86] as the Iroquois had maintained distinction and independence by their weapons and their astute political confederacy. The Algonquins whose traditional body of song and poetry, it is said has much in common with the old Scandinavian Eddas, lacked the tribal organization of the Iroquois or Six Nations.[87] We have these separate members of the one family, who might be compared to the Athenians in their decadence or the Greeks of the dispersal.

The Mohicans, also Algonquins, for instance, we may venture to say, have entirely lost contact with the Shawanese. But they have this in common, even in their degradation. They have still the hidden-seed or the underground instincts of members of a great race and of a great religious body. The uninformed might imagine that Tschoop's "conversion" was a matter of mere time-serving or even of decadent delirium. I am inclined to put forward my considered theory, that the Mystery Religion of Count Zinzendorf, his actual belief in the atonement by blood and the all-importance of the *sacrifice*, struck a familiar chord in the heart of Tschoop, a descendant of a long line of initiates and priests. And now here, along the upper Susquehanna, there is an even more curious "conversion."

This comes about through no sermon or argument. I understand that *manito* is an Indian word that applies to the riddles of the supernatural, the unknown, the religious mysteries and so on. The word itself is sometimes used for serpent, as if the serpent and the supernatural power were the same thing. Or the serpent had control of super-natural energies or was controlled by them. Anyhow, I find this, introducing the story of Count Zinzendorf and the adders, in a collection of the Myths and Legends of the North American Indians.[88]

"'Who is *manito*?' asks the mystic Meda Chant of the Algonkins. 'He,' is the reply, 'he who walketh with a serpent, walking on the ground; he is a *manito*'."[89]

The editor of these Myths and Legends applies this to the story of Count Zinzendorf, saying he owed his life to the "superstition." He tells of two anonymous Indian Braves who have determined to kill the first white man they met in revenge for an injury done them; they come across the temporary bark-hut of a stranger and peering in, discover "the venerable man." He is "seated before a little fire, a volume of the Scriptures on his knees." A great king rattlesnake is curled up on the earth before the camp-fire. The Indians sneak off, defeated in their purpose, whispering that "this was indeed a man of God."[90] This is the story, stripped of the authenticity and charm of the historical version. Yet the conclusion is the same.

And Nicholas Louis goes back to Bethlehem. He had endured hunger and danger and humiliation. He would give up all idea of founding a mission among the Shawanese. But something had happened. The Shawanese said he led a charmed life, "he is under the direct protection of the Great Spirit." And through the records of the Indian troubles, we find continued reference to Paxnous, the Shawanese chief, who proved a "consistent friend" and "faithful to whatever promise he made" and most astonishing, in 1755, in those most troubled days, Paxnous or Paxinosa brought his wife to the mission at Bethlehem to be baptized.[91]

. . . his wife Erdmuth Dorothea's ancestor . . . King of Bohemia.

A certain Gregory, a nephew of the famous Rokycana, one of the Archbishops of the old-Bohemian or Protestant party, left Prague with a group of the early "Brethren" to establish a colony near Kunwald, Lititz, in north-east Bohemia. This was the estate of George Podiebrad, and this was the year 1457. The next year Podiebrad became King of Bohemia.[92]

It will be recalled that some four decades earlier, 1415, John Huss, the "Bohemian reformer who paved the way for the reformation . . . was condemned by the Council of Constance and burnt at the stake."[93] His followers were known for years simply as "the Brethren" and outside their own country as "the Bohemian Brethren." They suffered endless vicissitudes and internal division, one section represented the extreme Hussite spirit, that is you might say, the uncompromising Cromwellian or Puritan fighting spirit, the others, drawn for the most part from the universities and the titled classes, were inclined to negotiate and make temporary concessions for the sake of expediency or simply with an eye to re-establishing the old claims of the Bohemian Church, when circumstances became more favourable.

The actual old Bohemian Church is said never to have "bowed beneath the Romish yoke." They traced their origin through the Greek Church back to the primitive age of Christianity and so, I presume could claim to be as old as the so-called old-church or mother-church of Rome. At any rate, there is no question but that the Protestants of Bohemia were reformers long before the actual Reformation. It is to be noted however, that Huss was strongly influenced by John Wyclif or Wycliffe of the University of Oxford, the "fore-runner of the Reformation in England." Wycliffe escaped martyrdom because of an attack of paralysis of which he died, but the two names may well be considered together, as pre-reformation Reformers, their dates just overlap; Wycliffe of England is 1320–1384, Huss of Bohemia 1370–1415.

Frankly, I should never have had the impulse nor the patience to unravel these few threads from the tangled skein of the history of the pre-Reformation (leading on to the beginnings of the actual Reformation under Henry VIII in England and to the Thirty Years' War of the Palatinate or Ancient German Empire on the Continent) if I had not this purely personal desire to "place" Erdmuth Dorothea.

History repeats itself or life advances in a spiral, and we have George Podiebrad patronising or protecting a band of the Brethren on his estates in Lititz, in north-east Bohemia in 1457;[94] in 1722, the Austrian exile across the border in Lusatia, Saxony repeats the pattern.

He had recently married the sister of his best friend and cousin, Count Henry de Reuss. This Henry would be, I presume, Henry Count Reuss XXVII, as the nephew of the Countess Zinzendorf, who is known in the brotherhood as "Ignatius," is later listed as Count Reuss XXVIII.[95] Anyhow, Erdmuth Dorothea von Zinzendorf, but lately Erdmuth Dorothea de Reuss, enters whole-heartedly into her husband's plans[96] for sheltering and actually "adopting" this last survival of the wrecks of wars and counter-wars, this handful of persecuted Protestants from Moravia, who in the late spring of 1722 were granted temporary permission to rest in the wilderness of the Berthelsdorf forests, by the (we may imagine) somewhat sulky steward.

We may imagine that the Countess Zinzendorf led no easy life. The Count, it is said, from early childhood held long conversations and even wrote lengthy letters to his Friend and Constant Companion, his all-but visible Redeemer.[97] He would be prompted by an impulse, by inspiration or by some form of spiritual guidance, and at moment's notice, the whole household would be moved or he himself would leave this or that estate or community in the hands of his wife, while he set out on his wanderings over the continent of Europe, or on some dangerous pilgrimage to the West Indies or to America.

Erdmuth Dorothea is said to have managed the very complicated business side of the growing community of the renewed Brotherhood, as the Count, even before marriage had turned over the bulk of his not inconsiderable fortune to her. It is recorded of Erdmuth Dorothea that "she managed all the Count's manorial and domestic affairs during their thirty-four years' union," but she could not be expected to cope with the ever-increasing complications of the growing settlement of Herrnhut and the later settlement, Herrnhaag, the Enclosure or Field or Hedge of the Lord.

The name Herrnhaag later became synonymous for religious extravagance and fanaticism of any kind. Undisciplined religious hysterics and undesirable characters flocked there;[98] debts were incurred by unreliable agents and trustees, all of which, it is said, were eventually settled by the Count.[99] But the Protestant court at Dresden did finally succeed in securing the Count's banishment from Saxony.[100] For ten years he was technically exiled from Upper Lusatia. He was the butt of the eighteenth-century pamphleteers and persecution followed him, although in London, "in 1749, by an act of the British parliament, the United Brethren were recognized as an ancient Protestant Episcopal Church."[101]

Count Zinzendorf had gained the admiration and friendship of certain English families of high position. He was everywhere, the associate of Princes and Kings.

Frederick William I, King of Prussia was intensely interested in his work and persuaded him to receive consecration as a bishop; this suggestion was followed, with "the understanding that he assumed this episcopate of an ancient suppressed church as a Lutheran divine."[102]

Actually Count Zinzendorf used the title of *Ordinarius:* he referred to himself as "a retired senior, or bishop of the Brethren—*Ancien Évêque des Frères.*"[103]

It is reported that the royal commission of 1732 had actually found nothing "amiss in the new settlement," that is Herrnhut. The banishment was secured by "certain of the unfriendly class among the Protestant clergy." But whatever the rights or wrongs of his predicament, there were certainly "embarrassments." The Countess was left in charge at Herrnhut. Her life was one of painful partings and we may imagine, over-exuberant re-unions. She was not a very strong woman and she bore her husband twelve children, six boys and six girls. Three of the girls grew up, Henrietta Benigna Justina (whom we already know), Maria Agnes and Elizabeth.[104] Only one of the boys survived to maturity, that was the young Count, Christian Renatus or Christel as we have heard Andrew Frey call him.

Christian Renatus died in his twenty-fifth year, in London; his mother was not there with him. She had recovered in her day, from many shocks but from this one she did not recover. She did not wait very long before joining her Christel. The Countess died in Herrnhut in 1756.[105] We read of her that she was "tender and unwearied in her maternal duties, weak in body, but strong in understanding, of original mind and overflowing compassion."[106] There was that and very much more. She was known simply by all, of whatever station and however remotely connected with the community, as *Mother.*

III.

[The Dream][107]

Papa . . . looked round the table as if he came from another world, another country.

Papa's name was Charles Leander Doolittle. He was born in Indiana, his father had gone out from the east, by way of New York State, but they had come originally from New England.

Their name was English, from the north of England, though their most important kinsman is intimately associated with London and was persecuted when he "in defiance of the law, erected preaching-places when churches were lying in ruins after the great fire."[108]

This was Thomas Doolittel or Doolittle, his parish was Saint Alphage on the walls or Saint Alphage, London Wall. He eventually threw in his lot with the dissenters and his name is listed in ecclesiastical Church of England history as the "last of the ejected clergy."[109]

The list of his works is considerable, among them is an elaborate mystical treatise on the Holy Communion, and there are various religious poems and hymns.[110] His date is 1632–1707 and his cousin or older brother Abraham Doolittle, is somewhat earlier.[111] Their quaint name, in England, runs back into the reign of Queen Elizabeth and some time before. The spelling is not stabilized even in Thomas Doolittel's day, and his own father Antony, a glover,[112] is frankly partial to Doelittle. It is this glover and his progenitors, weaver, clothier or tailor who appear variously in the sixteenth century lists as Doelitle, Dolitell, Doollytle, Dolitle, Dolytell and so on.[113] Abraham went to America or rather to the New Settlement at the time of the great Puritan exodus. His house in the New Settlement "in the time of King Philip's war . . . was protected by a picket fort, against an attack by the Indians."[114]

We learn this from the New England Historical Register. Also that "Abraham Doolittle was of New Haven and the father of a large family."[115] He is said to have settled in New Haven, Connecticut, about the year 1640. "He was one of three appointed by the New Haven Committee, to superintend the affairs of the New Settlement."[116] This New Settlement was afterwards known as the town of Wallingford.

We are very sensible people; in us, runs a terrible integrity. It is not always a pleasant thing, it does not always make for happiness. We do not always, for example, *suffer a witch to live.*[117] We do not go out of our way to fraternize with these savages as did our mother's people—though it is true that Abraham arrived almost a hundred years before that special branch of the Pennsylvania colony which is my personal predilection. There were others of our mother's family who went back, too; we have some charming names and we have some very plebeian ones, we have a de Vinney[118] for example and we have a Schropp;[119] in our father's family there is no such suggestion of racial admixtures and cross-currents. All their names and the names of their wives are English or New English until we get to our own mother. But here they are:

Abraham Doolittle	1620	Abigail Moss
Samuel Doolittle	1665	Mary Cornwall
Jonathan Doolittle	1689	Rebecca Ranny
Samuel Doolittle	1729	Elizabeth Hubbard
Samuel Doolittle	1752	Anne Arnold
Willard Doolittle	1782	Piany Roberts
Charles Doolittle	1813	Celia Sanger
Charles Doolittle	1843	Helen Wolle

Here we are, as I say, we do not fraternize with savages nor a hundred years after our arrival, indulge in any new-fangled eighteenth-century nonsense about blood-and-wounds atonement or a root-religion common to all people. We have come a long way but we do not look back. We have put our hands to the plough. We have run a straight furrow. We have left our mark on the makers of history and the repercussions of the intellectual or spiritual power of our English New England Demos is felt around the world. We are unchanged. We are unrelenting. We are stubborn. We are independent and we are loyal. We know how deadly our strength is so we connive at peace; *thou shalt not kill*[120] is branded with the other shalt-nots on our conscience, so we would not strike because if we strike we must kill. *Don't tread on me* was one of our early local slogans, it was written on a banner with a rattlesnake erect above it, ready to strike.[121]

Don't tread on me.

We have the quality of the serpent. We slide away from the unfriendly shore. We leave England. England in time, is not so far away. It is only 300 years. These Du or Doe or De Littles had already fled from some other shore; the men were tall and grey-eyed with domed foreheads. Charles the father of our father Charles had hesitated as long as he dared; then he followed the Viking call that he imagined, was to take him to another ocean. He did not reach the Pacific. Our own father's eyes swept the horizon above the Indiana prairies. There was no sea. He did not know what he felt, he did not know what he wanted. He found what he knew he must have always known, have always wanted as his eyes rested on unswerving Polaris, as his eyes caught the momentary breath-taking wonder of the green-silver of the planet Mercury that would be visible in its icy isolation only this one second longer, as the sun sank.

He came from another world, another country. He looked at the sky as the sons of the sea must always look. His text book on Practical Astronomy was used for many years, I believe, at the Naval College of Annapolis. This book was called *Practical Astronomy, As Applied to Geodesy and Navigation.*[122] I do not remember the exact titles of his other works; his life work had to do with the variation of latitude. He gave thirty years of observation to this work. I remember the book; there was a brief concise introduction and then numberless pages of columns and columns of numbers. Here was cold and absolute beauty, here was mathematics as applied to the revolution of the earth round the sun. All I know about this "variation" is that the earth itself floats like a ship on the ocean. It sways slightly or "wobbles" as he used to explain to curious and, like myself, illiterate inquirers. "The earth does not go round and round in perfect circles," he would say, "it wobbles like a ship at sea." I was frightened for some reason, by the thought of this precarious voyaging. Fears of the sky were linked up with the usual racial subconscious fears of the unknowns. And with a personal shock, which I deal with in a later chapter of this book.

So much for our father's family. We knew very little of them. Most of that is incorporated in these pages. There was a picture of our great-uncle Bill, like a robust caricature of our own father; a Walt Whitman or Santa Claus with long, very white beard, the same high forehead, the same Egyptian over-length of limbs and that Egyptian posture, seated upright on a stiff chair. There was a beautiful daguerreotype of Alvin, who gazed out of the reflecting surface of the oval like a ghost of a young Byron, the hair flung back, the eyes clear and brimming over with some sort of inward laughter, the mouth held level but only just. There was one of our father taken at the same time, the frail seemingly irresolute mouth and chin really masked a steel-will. There was the less extravagant flow of hair but still the slight suggestion of nordic poet or musician.[123] Alvin, it was obvious was the "gifted" one, the gay one, the favourite, as we had been told. There was Aunt Rosa looking very beautiful and not as we remembered her, with an almost-stranger Uncle John Ladd who was her husband, taken at about the time of her marriage. Rosa

Ladd looked as lovely as her name, in a modest near-fashionable frock with the row of buttons that I had just remembered on our mother's dresses, and the bunched flounces at the back. There was Aunt Rosa's baby who died, but I have spoken of that picture.

There were old-fashioned books, a bible with a smooth cover and another with knobbled leather design and with pictures of the Unclean Animals and the Ark of the Tabernacle and some others that did not hold the same dramatic interest as our own Doré[124]—with the exception of the Unclean Animals which seemed to me to be so excessively clean—at least I thought it very unfair that our Easter Rabbit should be among them and a kingly Swan out of Hans Andersen. The Rabbit was a hare, I was told, and the Swan—I do not remember what explanation was forthcoming—anyhow they were not "unclean" now.

The animals in the back of "his" bible and the animals that he bought us and the bear he took us to see in a pen by an old hotel by the river, that was soon after demolished, all link up—but O, so vaguely—with a pattern of animals in the sky, a Bear again and a Swan too and some others—a Bull like the one at the fair-grounds that got a prize and a Ram, a Crab that we saw at Point Pleasant,[125] Fishes and what-not. No—you could not see the animals in the sky—there was something very frustrating about a star-map that was shown us—not by our father, I think. You could not by any feat of the imagination make a Bull or a Bear out of the points blackened for stars and the lines that ran between them.

The earth wobbles as it goes round the sun. Indeed, it wobbles very much and in strange fashion. This is June 29, 1944 and I started these notes or biographical memories back in the early days of the Battle of Britain, way back in the early forties. That is a long time ago. Now, this minute, the flying-bomb is on the way—now this minute, there is a distant crash and we are safe for this minute.

I have felt all along a deep gratitude for the place of my birth and for my people—but my people, as I have tried to show are not parochial, not conditioned by small boundaries, not shut-in by provincial barriers.

The earth wobbles as it goes round the sun. Comfort and peace came to me, in recalling the strange mystical adventures of Count Zinzendorf and in a later chapter, I go further into the spiritual or psychic sub-strata of the religious inheritance of the race, as it flowered in a personal revelation—constructed or re-invoked as between the child and the grandmother, Mamalie, our mother's mother.

Our father's mother, we did not know. Her name was Celia and some say that Celia, often written Coelia, "points to a possible origin in Latin *coela,* the heavens."[126] Be that as it may, we do know that our other grandmother grieved and did not hide her disappointment when *she found it was Charles and not Alvin,* who *had come back from the Civil War.* The child recognized some poignant tragedy and loneliness in her father's spirit—if she turned for comfort to her own mother's family, it was not for lack of loyalty. The beauty of the heavens is unbearable; Charles, after all, was a scientist.

Charles was a sea-captain, he had lost the sea but in the Indiana prairies he found the sky. In the Indiana prairies, he found the sea. He found his ship; it was the earth simply.

IV.
[Because One Is Happy][127]

. . . the music coming from our church was the voice of the Great Spirit.

I had been under the impression that this was a Christmas story but Miss Ann Hark in her delightful book about Pennsylvania, *Hex Marks the Spot,* tells this as an Easter legend. The Indians, she says, planned a sortie on the early settlement. They landed on the island, opposite the town. At dawn "on Calypso Island there was sudden stir and movement. Cautiously the Indians launched their frail canoes and dipped their paddles. The barks shot forward . . . at a signal from their leader, they prepared to disembark. But . . . suddenly the wild, unearthly strains of music rent the quiet air. In panic the marauders paused. Those strange, uncanny cadences—they came from the direction of the white men's dwelling!

"With faces blanched by terror, the intruders sat and listened. For a moment no one spoke. Then, from the lips of their leader came a hurried order. ''Tis the voice of the Great Spirit!' he whispered fearfully. 'Because we planned to harm the peaceful brethren, he is displeased! Quick—let us go before His wrath overtakes us!'"

And so, Miss Hark concludes, "the little town of Bethlehem was saved on Easter Morn by the trombones!"[128]

I will wear a cap. Already as far back as 1850, the cap was the only distinctive feature of the Moravian Sisters' dress. "Formerly, they had adopted one uniform dress; now, the only distinction is a peculiar white linen cap, not unlike three large oyster-shells, one on the crown of the head and one at each ear, worn by the females, fastened under the chin with a ribbon. Young girls wear scarlet, but after being received into the community at the age of fourteen to sixteen, pink; married women, blue; and widows, white."[129]

I do not remember these oyster-shell caps. In my day, the ribbons were not fastened under the chin but a knot of blue or pink or white was worked into the lace; the cap was more like a round lace pincushion-top or doily. These caps were worn in church by the choir and by the serving sisters. Certain old ladies wore the caps all the time—but caps were worn, at one time, pretty generally, by grandmothers or great-grandmothers.

For Mysteries were ordained.[130]

The birth or manifestation of an Avatar was almost universally associated with the winter solstice. I have come across an interesting pamphlet, *The Calendar,* since writing *The Gift.* Dr. W.B. Crow, its compiler, gives: "December 25. Christmas or Yule. Nativity of Our Lord Jesus Christ. Day also regarded as the birthday of Mithras, Osiris, and many other forms of the Saviour."[131]

He gives December 20th, the day before the winter solstice to "Quetzalcoatl. The Feathered Serpent. Aztec form of the Saviour, or according to early Spanish missionaries of St. Thomas." So it is not illogical to imagine that the ghosts or spirits of our own Lenni-lenape, the Delaware or Pennsylvania Indians, might have joined their ghost-voices to the chants of the children who prepare, toward Christmas time, as instinctive man has always prepared, ceremonies and games—and ring-games are the oldest of ceremonial dances, celebrating as they do, the circling of the moon or the planets or the apparent circling of the sun or even the appearance of the flat circle or disc which the sun-surface gives.

Look, the sun will rise again. Yes, "our" Indians would certainly have been with us. For this is a religious cycle that applies to all people and to all times. But here is Dr. Crow in his introduction to *The Calendar:* "some Buddhists celebrate the birth of Buddha on December 25th. The Persians celebrated the birth of Mithras on this day, which follows from the fact that Mithras was a

Sun God. The ancient Egyptians celebrated the birth of Horus at the Winter Solstice. They also fixed the beginning of the pregnancy of Isis, his mother, nine months before, i.e., at the Spring Equinox, which is precisely the time of the modern Catholic celebration of the Annunciation.

Bacchus was, according to the Greeks, born at the early dawn on 25th December. Jesus was born at midnight, according to sacred tradition, on the same day. Adonis, a Syrian god, was born at Christmas and mourned at the Spring Equinox, near our Good Friday. The Norse Freyr was also born at the Winter Solstice, and this was kept as a feast called Jul, from whence we get our Yule. The Druids also had a great feast about this time. The Chinese similarly celebrate the Winter Solstice."

. . . the fan-maker in London.[132] In assembling these chapters of *The Gift* during, before and after the worst days of the 1941 London Blitz, I let the story tell itself or the child tell it for me. Things that I thought I had forgotten came to light in the course of the narrative and although, for instance, I had a vague recollection of having heard of this fan-maker or having read of him, the actual fan-maker had nothing to do with our story. Yet I tried to keep "myself" out of this, and if the sub-conscious bubbled up with some unexpected finding from the depth, I accepted this finding as part of the texture of the narrative and have so far, in going over these chapters (to-day is July 2nd 1944) changed very little. Instead of tidying up the body of the narrative, I thought it better to let things stand as they were (as the story was written under stress of danger and great emotion) and where indicated, confirm certain statements or enlarge on them in these Notes.

Actually, I have been greatly indebted throughout to J.M. Levering's *History of Bethlehem, Pennsylvania, 1741–1892,* and have glanced at it from time to time. But as it is a weighty volume and I was not a serious student of the subject of the Moravian Brotherhood and its very complicated historical and psychological background, I did not delve very deep. But in recalling my own childhood, I approach the subject from a different angle, not critically but emotionally. There was a fan-maker. He gave the Bethlehem community a spinet in the very early days and it is not at all unlikely that one of old Jedediah's ancestors touched the keys of that spinet for the first time, as it was joyously acclaimed and set up in one of the assembly rooms or *Gemein*[133] houses.

Hence the spinet and the fan-maker become personal matters and of interest to me. I made an effort to track down this fan-maker and did finally find him in Bishop Levering's book. His name was William Peter Knolton of London, and later, for a few years of Philadelphia. It appears he sent the spinet over on the *Little Strength*. He himself with his wife Hannah came to Pennsylvania on a later voyage. The spinet rested in a warehouse at New Brunswick and was later conveyed to Bethlehem by wagon. It was the first musical instrument of its kind in the town though a small organ was soon to follow, and stringed instruments had been brought over by some of the members of the first Sea Congregation.[134]

Mary Ann Wood Henry has nothing to do with this spinet; her association with Bethlehem is by way of her son's wife. It is possible that the younger William Henry met Sabina Schropp because of his father's connection with General George Washington who for some time had his headquarters in the town.[135]

V.

[The Secret][136]

. . . *a lady called Mary Ann Wood.*

This Mary Ann was born 1734. She was married to William Henry;[137] it was through this William Henry that there was the de Vinney connection of which I have spoken. His mother was Elizabeth de Vinney. This was the first William Henry; his son William Henry married Sabina Schropp. It was their daughter Sabina Henry who married John Frederick Wolle, our grandfather's father. The portrait of Mary Ann Wood Henry by Benjamin West was in Philadelphia in the rooms of the Historical Society.[138] There was another Henry portrait at one time hanging on the stairs of the old Independence Hall in Philadelphia. It was by way of these Henrys that our mother was urged by Philadelphia cousins[139] to put in her *Claim for Membership in the Colonial Dames*. My mother never did this. But here is the "claim."

> *John Bevan*—Judge and Assemblyman
> *John Wood*—Judge and Assemblyman
> *William Henry*—Judge and Armorer[140]

John Bevan was born in Wales in 1646. He came to Pennsylvania in 1683.

The child is the 9th on this list as she is on the other, though the New England connection begins a little earlier.

Here are their names:

John Bevan—Barbara Ambry
Jane Bevan—John Wood
Abraham Wood—Ursula Taylor
Mary Ann Wood—William Henry
William Henry—Sabina Schropp
Sabina Henry—John Frederick Wolle
Francis Wolle—Elizabeth Weiss
Helen Wolle—Charles Doolittle

. . . accusing us of Popish practices.

We have seen in our entry on *The Last of the Mohicans* in II of the Notes, that an early law against the Jesuits was revived in New York State and used against the Moravians. Although the original Bohemian or Moravian Brotherhood had struggled for more than 700 years "for freedom and for the preservation of their primitive Christianity in character and form"[141] even before the Inquisition, the enemies of the mystical reformer Nicholas Louis von Zinzendorf, at the Protestant Court at Dresden, secured his banishment (according to his most astute detractor, Henry Rimius) partly because of various mystical doctrines and monastic rules that to them smacked strongly of Rome.

Henry Rimius in his most delightful and deadly eighteenth-century pamphleteer manner speaks of "gross and scandalous . . . Mysticism."[142] He speaks of the "*Arcana* or Secret Counsels of their Leaders"[143] and "Secrets probably known by the Adepts alone."[144] Personally, I consider these findings highly stimulating and exciting though I must confess, in my own day, there was no hint of this exoticism. We were a small community, respected and highly respectable, classed by the superficial as a body of what you might call, musical Quakers or Friends. Like the Friends, the Moravians were known as a peace-loving people and were exempt from taking certain legal oaths.[145] The history however differed in a marked manner, and their race-roots. In the very early days, there was not very much, even superficially, in common. Our grandmother would be one of the last, I imagine, to have heard even distant, dim hints that there ever was or had been any suggestion of "gross and scandalous . . . Mysticism."

German reformed people of Pennsylvania creep into this reconstructed confidence between the grandmother and the child, I presume, because there had been incriminations of the same sort in the early days against the Bethlehem community. For instance there was an active crusade against "the Count's party" in Germantown, Philadelphia, by a certain Rev. Philip Boehm who represented "the extreme Calvinism and the austere rule of the Classis of Amsterdam."[146] John Christopher Pyrlaeus, as assistant to Count Zinzendorf had been in charge of a neglected Lutheran congregation there.[147] This local clash with the extreme Calvinists was in miniature, a repetition of the more formidable struggle between the Count and the Protestant party at the court of Dresden.

. . . *Christian Heinrich Johann Seidel.*

The child through the grandmother makes a connecting link with the various Seidels of the *History.* The name is common enough, though actually, I find in Grimms' massive work on the derivation of German words at the London Library (to my surprise and delight) that the very word *seidel* does more than justify my use of it in this pattern.

I have in *The Gift,* allowed the child to follow, through the grandmother, the story of the Seidels, who reveal the secret of the *seidel* or cup, actually depicted as an urn on the personal seal of the above Christian Heinrich Johann Seidel.

My cousin Clifford Howard sent me a wax impression of this seal which I have by me, still unbroken. But he wrote in answer to my question, in a letter from Los Angeles, dated St. Afra's Day, 1938, "regarding the several Seidels mentioned in The History of Bethlehem, so far as I know, the only one among them with whom our family is connected is Charles Frederick, my great-grandfather.[148] The others were all of an earlier date than he, and if they were related to him, the relationship must have been quite distant."

The Christian Heinrich Johann Seidel, whom they called Uncle Henry, was the elder brother of the Rev. Charles Frederick Seidel whose son Henry was our own grandmother's first husband. But the grandmother, the "mamalie" and the child, reconstruct their own story and follow the clue, inspirationally, in their own way.

In any case, we have Grimms' final word for it that *seidel,* the common German word for a pint—or even a tankard or mug, is originally a *fremdwort* or foreign word, as from the Latin *situlus* or *situla.* The French *seille* and the

Italian *secchia* derive from the same source. And *situlus* or *situla* is a small vessel or bucket for holding water or other liquids, also for drawing water out of a well. And *situlus* is a *measure*![149]

Situlus is also "a vessel from which lots were drawn, a ballot-box." Our mother as a young woman, had recalled this old custom of drawing lots, when she was caught up in her own reverie, in the spring woods outside Bethlehem, while she was waiting to consult the fortune-teller. This drawing of lots is an important later motive of *The Gift*.[150]

The first Christian Seidel.

We have brief mention of the first Christian Seidel in connection with the Indian Uprising, 1755–1756. He visits another Christian, Christian Frederick Post, "the well-known, indefatigable, somewhat eccentric missionary to the Indians."[151] The *History* says, "David Zeisberger . . . went to Wyoming with Christian Seidel to see how Post fared." They found Post "keeping his lonely watch in the midst of great peril" and "Zeisberger and Seidel pushed on, far up the Susquehanna, to procure some food for the famishing little flock." Then, "having brought their few bags of corn safely to Post and the little band he was yet holding, Zeisberger and his companion continued their tour among the Indians at various places, in spite of the disturbed condition of things."[152]

Christian Frederick Post does not come into this story. However we can not resist noting this reference to him, among the list of Single Men, 1742. He could not have remained very long in that "choir" for we read, "he was thrice married. His first two wives were Indian women; his idea being that this would facilitate his efforts."[153]

He was known among the Indians as *Ahamawad*.[154]

Since writing this, I find several references to Christian Seidel and his wife Catharine in Miss Fries' *Road to Salem*. He was one of those chosen to go to the new station in the wilderness of North Carolina. "A strange kind of fever"[155] broke out before the colony was fully housed and established. This was the summer of 1759. Catharine Seidel was stricken, only a few weeks after her arrival and her marriage. As to the *first Christian Seidel,* "he did not seem very ill at first, but when hope was expressed for his recovery he shook his head, saying, 'No; life was lonely without my Catharine and I asked the Lord to take

me to Himself, and He has heard and answered'. And so it was, and his re-
mains were borne up the steep path to the little God's Acre on the hill."[156]

Gnadenhuetten. This was the first Gnadenhuetten. We will deal with
David Zeisberger more fully with the first and second Gnadenhuetten, in a
later note. We have seen in our note on *The Last of the Mohicans,* II, that the
New York and Connecticut Indians had their own settlement of cabins and
log-huts "at the foot of the hill" but the increasing number of the "Bethlehem
Indians" caused such concern and alarm among the non-Moravian Pennsylvanians of the vicinity that it was decided to move them further up the river,
about a day's journey from the town. So Friedenshuetten or Habitations of
Peace is evacuated and Gnadenhuetten, Habitations of Grace is established.
There is an interesting note in Bishop Levering's book, which contains references to both Habitations, as well as to *Wunden Eiland.* Here it is.

"Not far from where the cabins of Friedenshuetten were built, another
small structure rose in May, 1746, which although of no great importance is,
in retrospect, of some topographic interest. This was the summer-house on
the *Wunden Eiland.* This island was in the Monocacy Creek, at the foot of the
present grounds in the rear of the Young Ladies' Seminary. It is marked on the
oldest map of the locality, and a depression in the grounds reveals where the
inside channel of the stream then was. A rustic foot-bridge was constructed
across it to the island, and there many interesting social meetings, official
conferences and important interviews with Indians took place. Its name, 'the
Island of the Wounds,' meant that it was dedicated to the remembrance of the
wounds of Jesus, as then dwelt upon in certain special liturgies and hymns.
Closely connected with the buildings of Friedenshuetten, the Indian adjunct
to Bethlehem, is to be mentioned the founding of the important settlement
for these fugitive converts, up the Lehigh, at the mouth of the Mahoning
Creek, which received the name *Gnadenhuetten*—Habitations of Grace. . . .
A beginning was made with the new settlement in May, 1746, and on June 13,
after a love-feast on the *Wunden Eiland,* the first detachment of fifteen set out
for the place; some in canoes and some afoot."[157]

Cammerhof, whom they criticised for what they called antinomianism . . .
The child says, *Mamalie is talking like something in a book* and we must consult a number of books before we get this quite straight. To begin with,

Chamber's English Dictionary says antinomianism is "the belief that Christians are emancipated by the gospel from the obligation to keep the moral law—a monstrous abuse and perversion of the Pauline doctrine of justification by faith." The word is from the Greek *anti,* against and *nomos,* a law.

The young Bishop, John Christopher Frederick Cammerhof, came to the settlement, early in January 1747. His wife was with him, the "gifted and pious young Livonian baroness, Anna von Pahlen."[158] They had come from Herrnhaag, the Hedge of the Lord, of which we have spoken in our note on the Countess Zinzendorf. Though straight from what came to be known as a hot-bed of "religious enthusiasts and erratics,"[159] they both however, seem to have been equal to the rigours of a winter crossing of the Atlantic and a not very happy landing. "The ice preventing their progress up the Delaware, they went ashore there, made their way by land to Philadelphia and reached Bethlehem January 12."[160]

Bethlehem at this time was divided in sentiment regarding what Bishop Levering calls "the craze that broke out" when "followers ran away with what leaders would have kept within restrictions." He refers to "mawkish sentimentality and puerile language" and "a rage for the spectacular . . . in connection with all kinds of festivities."[161]

Count Zinzendorf himself was much criticised for a series of poems or hymns, dealing for the most part, with the mystery of love or marriage. He is said to have offended many by regarding every woman as a symbol of the Church, as literally Christ's Bride.[162] There is beauty and poetry in many of these mystical ideas but undoubtedly, the world at large, then as now, is not ready for this revelation.

There must have been many sincere and devout seekers but Bishop Levering says, "crack-brained adventurers and even imposters gravitated toward Herrnhaag, where far less restraint was applied to admission than at Herrnhut." With the coming of Cammerhof, "the spirit of the Herrnhaag extravagances . . . was brought to Bethlehem."[163]

The star and the verse-couplet quoted by the grandmother is a sample of the imagery and thought, the "language of the Herrnhaag extravagance."[164] Another inscription, *Gloria Pleura,* was in reference to the wounds and especially that of the Lord's pierced side.[165]

Bishop Levering says of Cammerhof, "in his desire to foster a genial conception of spiritual life over against the austere type of pietism, and, at the same time, to encourage a childlike constant clinging to the Saviour of sinners, as opposed to both legalism and perfectionism, he unwittingly occasioned a peculiar species of careless self-complacency in the direction of antinomianism."[166]

But criticism of Cammerhof was balanced by amazement at his "natural gifts, learning and eloquence." He threw himself with great energy into any enterprise of danger and adventure, penetrated in all seasons far into the *hinterland* of the Indian country, "although never inured to hardships, and of physique far from robust. His career of inordinate activity was brief. Already in 1751, he succumbed to the strain and died at Bethlehem."[167]

It was Pyrlaeus . . .

John Christopher Pyrlaeus arrived with two others and increased to 34 the number now in North America who had been connected with the church in Europe—32 of these were in Pennsylvania. This was late summer 1741 and Count Zinzendorf was preparing to visit the settlement. Pyrlaeus, "schoolman and musician, was a theological candidate from the University of Leipsic. He is chiefly noted as a student and teacher of Indian languages, particularly the Mohawk and Mohican dialects and left some linguistic work of interest in manuscript, which is preserved in the Moravian archives at Bethlehem. Pyrlaeus married Susan Benezet, daughter of John Stephen Benezet of Philadelphia."[168]

Pyrlaeus was called by the Indians, *Tganniatarechev,* between-two-seas.[169]

Lamb with the Banner.

"The episcopal seal of the Church has upon it a shield with the figure of a lamb carrying a cross from which is suspended a banner of victory, and around the shield is the motto: '*Vicit Agnus noster, Eum Sequamur,* i.e., Our Lamb hath conquered, Him let us follow'."[170]

This *Agnus Dei* is of course, the emblematic Lamb of God, found in the Roman catacombs, it is said, and elsewhere. It is probable that the Lamb or Ram was connected with the zodiacal spring sign. "Owing to the precession of the equinoxes at the time of the appearance of Christianity the sun was in the sign of Aries in the spring quarter."[171]

The symbol is of course common enough in Papal heraldry and in the

Episcopal embellishments of the Church of England. I have been told by an English heraldic specialist of some authority that he believes that the *Agnus Dei* as featured on the City Temple (now devastated in the London fires) was derived as from the Greek Church but he could find no authority for this. He knew nothing about my own work or research into this matter so his opinion is doubly valuable to me. The City Temple, so-called, was of course the headquarters of the English Templars.

Chambers' English Dictionary tells us that a *Templar* is "one of a religious and military order, founded in 1119 for the protection of the Holy Sepulchre and pilgrims going thither. Their extinction, 1307–14, is one of the darkest tragedies of history."

There is an extraordinary book called *L'Amour et l'occident* (with the English title *Passion and Society*) by the Swiss writer, M. Denis de Rougemont which may confirm certain details of the grandmother's story. I can not actually bring forward historical evidence to corroborate the grandmother's statement that it was the young Count, Christian Renatus, who connected his father's mysterious *Plan* with a somewhat related secret *Plan* of the suppressed Templars. But the members of the Hidden Church of the Moravians or Bohemians having been run to ground and then underground by the Inquisition, may have found other members of other oppressed and dispersed religious or political bodies and fraternized with them.

The Hidden Church or the Invisible Church according to M. de Rougement's illuminating theories, can never really be destroyed, any more than you can destroy a river that runs underground;[172] it occasionally bubbles up and breaks out in some unexpected quarter. So Arab mysticism seeped into the courtly rhetoric of the Troubadours and the Troubadours either turned Saint as in the case of Francis of Assisi or Teresa of Avila, or were, as in the case of Dante, actually "one of the Order of the Templars, which . . . was certainly associated with the Mohammedan order of the same kind, having identical rules and even an identical habit."[173]

The order of the Knights Templars was abolished by the Council of Vienna. Our young Christian Renatus, on his mother's side was a descendant of a King of Bohemia, on his father's side he had similar romantic affiliations with the old Austrian nobility.[174] He would be conditioned to understand the subtle and curious mystical ideas of the Albigensians and the Catharists, who were practically exterminated by the Inquisition, about the same time that the Knights Templars were beginning to flourish. The Knights Templars were abolished in the early 14th century.[175]

It was about this time that the Bohemian Brotherhood took a new lease of life, in its turn to be persecuted and in the person of John Huss, (1370–1415), martyred. The martyrdom of John Huss served to "intimidate the uprising hosts"[176] of the Bohemian reformation and at the same time to infuse new fervour into the scattered bands, which, though driven underground still continued their connection with the great seats of learning of Europe and England and in the person of Comenius of the 17th century, to save "the episcopate of the church from extinction."[177]

Comenius was the famous 17th century humanist and scholar, who through his diplomacy and skill, saved the "episcopate of the church." This was passed on by his grandson, Jablonsky, to David Nitschmann, one of that band of persecuted Protestants from Moravia, who, as we have already noted, in 1722 first found sanctuary on the estate of Count Zinzendorf, ten miles from the Bohemian frontier. David Nitschmann was the first Bishop of the Church after its resuscitation, and official founder of Bethlehem.[178]

Unitas Fratrum . . . the original Bohemian name was *Jednota Bratrska*. *Jednota* means association of any kind. *Unitas* was later used as a Latin equivalent. *Unitas* passed into German *Unitaet*. In the 18th century the Latin title was revived in negotiations with England. *Church of the United Brethren* is the awkward English rendering, the word "united" is superfluous as *Jednota* and *Unitas* imply one-ness or unity. *Brethren's Church* would be the simple and correct rendering of *Unitas Fratrum* but as there have been other claimants for the title, the name *Moravian Church* was generally adopted in England and America.

I have given certain details of the history of the Brotherhood in earlier notes. I repeat some of them here.

Their first evangelists in the 9th century, were Cyrill and Methodius of the Greek Church of Constantinople. "For more than 700 years their history had been one of the successive struggles for freedom and for the preservation of their primitive Christianity in character and form."[179] This was the original church of Bohemia and Moravia. The church was driven underground by the Inquisition, as we have said. But let us quote again from Bishop Levering.

"What their first evangelists, Cyrill and Methodius of the Greek Church gave them in the ninth century; what Rome deprived them of in the eleventh century, the Bohemian Reformation came so near restoring at the opening of the fifteenth century that the Papal authorities resorted to the desperate measure of burning the intrepid leader John Huss at the stake, July 6, 1415, to intimidate the uprising hosts. The subsequent contentions were partly political, partly religious."[180]

Paxnous or Paxinosa.

We first find references to Paxnous in the *History* in 1755. The story that the child and the grandmother re-invoke may have happened before that time, as Cammerhof is one of the chief characters or actors and Cammerhof died in 1751, after only five years in the settlement. Anyhow, it is the child's story and the grandmother's *Gift*, so we will trust to their intuition and check up their references when we are able, whether their dates and the historical dates agree or not. Anyhow, Bishop Levering does record of Paxnous, "when his wife, with whom he had lived faithfully for thirty-eight years—'a surprising thing,' says the record—was baptized at Bethlehem, and the Brethren expressed the hope that he would yet follow her example, 'he responded with a hearty *Kehelle*' an exclamation of concurrence."[181]

We hear of Paxnous, as I have already noted on several occasions as a "consistent friend" and "faithful to whatever promises he made."[182] David Zeisberger and Christian Seidel were "warned by Paxnous"[183] after their trip to Post at Wyoming—Wyoming, by the way, is the Wyoming Valley of Pennsylvania, not of course the later-named north-west territory. Paxnous and Abraham, the Mohican, prove helpful and loyal in diplomatic pour-parleys between various tribes and the Governor of Pennsylvania. We read that "Paxnous and Abraham had sturdily opposed all hostilities"[184] and so on. All this agrees with the grandmother's later estimate of the character of Paxnous and as their story of *The Gift* is not on record, it might have been that there had been previous meetings with Paxnous and his wife, before Cammerhof's death in 1751.

The Secret that my Christian explained to me seemed very simple.

The child could grasp the implications of the Secret through intuitive sympathy with her grandmother and the grandmother was conditioned to understand the Secret, because of the musical inheritance from her father and the psychic inheritance of her Scotch mother. But the Secret that seemed almost too obvious to the child ("it was easy to see what she was going to say") had been construed and interpreted by the Saxon lawyer, Henry Rimius[185] and his contemporaries, into almost demoniac dimensions.

Almost the "mark of the beast"[186] was on Brother Nicholas Louis and his disciples, according to Rimius and his like. Their anger was the greater as the Crown of England had sanctioned the renewed Church of *Jednota* or *Unitas*.

King George III was arranging for the transfer of certain lands in the Crown colony of Pennsylvania to be set aside for activities of the *Unitas*. And even Rimius himself sometimes gives the Devil his due in this beautifully translated series of pamphlets that have lately come into my hands. I can not reproduce the exquisite 18th century print and capitals but use the italics as Rimius indicates them.

Thus Rimius: "I am personally acquainted with some of the *Herrnhutters* or *Moravians,* and take them to be just and upright in their Dealings; but then, they are wholly ignorant of the *Arcana* or Secret Counsels of their Leaders, and only give the Name of the Society to the Undertakings of the former."[187] Again Rimius hints at "Secrets probably known by the Adepts alone"[188] and "Secrecy in respect to their Doctrines"[189] and "Secrecy in their Transactions. They had People in almost all Parts of the World . . . whom . . . they can easily bring together."[190] And all this secrecy and mystery is either a most astute and diabolic bid for world-dictatorship, according to Rimius, as spokesman for the German Protestant party at the court of Dresden, or it is "gross and scandalous . . . Mysticism."

Indeed, says Rimius, "he has the Knack of bringing over People to his Sect, not by Instructions: (for *this,* he says, *is not so much their Plan,*) but by the more prevailing Act of *Persuasion;* he captivates them, not by enlightening their Reason, but by entertaining their Imaginations and Passions, and by making Use of his Doctrine of *Blood and Wounds* as a Kind of *Opiate or Charm.*"[191]

The Gift actually was Mamalie's . . . through her own mother in whose family there was the usual Scotch legend of one of the family . . . being far-sighted or being second-sighted.

The child had heard this "story in the family" that the Editor [H.D.] finds confirmed in Clifford Howard's St. Nicholas' Day Letter of 1936.[192]

"George Augustus Weiss . . . was Grandma Wolle's older brother, born October 3, 1821. With his wife he went to the West Indies as a missionary, at the age of 28, and died there a few years later.

"There is a story in the family, that at the hour of his death Great-grand-mother Weiss was in her garden at Bethlehem and heard him distinctly call to her. The voice was so clear and unmistakably his, that she turned around in surprise and bewilderment at what she supposed was his unexpected and unexplainable return."

VI.

What It Was[193]

The carved words.

". . . two fine stones . . . were secured, to be squared for lintels over the main door-ways, front and rear. They were . . . ornamented with inscriptions which displayed the influence of Cammerhof. That on the north side read: Vater, Mutter, Lieber Mann—Habt Ehr vom Jünglings Plan. The stone on the south side contained the words *Gloria Pleura,* and had a sun-dial in the centre, while above this was a star . . . "[194]

The *History* goes on to explain in a foot-note that the first is in praise of the Holy Trinity—the Father, the Holy Spirit (the "Comforter," as mother) and the Son, the "supreme Man." *Jünglings Plan*—young men's plan—meant the organized body of young men, with their whole system and round of activity. The word *Plan,* however as used in German, was a favourite term of Zinzendorf and applied to a scheme, system, sphere or field of labor, or even an organization. *Gloria Pleura* was in adoration of the wounds, especially the pierced side.[195]

Nathanael Seidel.

Nathanael Seidel was the son of a Bohemian refugee or emigrant in Silesia, we learn from Bishop Levering and therefore "in close affinity with the native Moravians."[196] He was a member of the first Sea Congregation or Ocean Church, which had assembled at Herrnhaag, proceeded to Marienborn, "a neighbouring old castle—originally a convent—in possession of the Church under lease."[197] The original group was joined there by another contingent. These proceeded to the settlement at Heerendyk in Holland, where a final group joined them and proceeded to Rotterdam. From there, the English sloop *Samuel and James* took them to London and "English friends escorted them to their lodgings in Little Wild Street."[198]

Zeisberger.

Our first Christian Seidel is mentioned briefly in 3 pages of the more than 800 page *History*[199] and as a very minor character, almost nameless. His whole name, Christian Seidel fortunately is once given and that one mention of his name made the authentic link with the much later Seidel, who was our own Aunt Agnes' father. If it were not for Zeisberger, we would probably not have known of our "first Christian." He is the shadow or under-study of our later Christian Seidel, or he is, you might say, the over-study or spirit-double. Anyhow it is by way of Zeisberger that he comes on the scene at all: enter, "Zeisberger and his companion."[200] So let us gratefully now consider David Zeisberger.

There are more than 37 references to David Zeisberger in the *History*, some of them of great length. He is one of the giants of the pioneer movement. His father was one of the original band of Bohemian refugees who in 1722 found protection and shelter on the estate of Count Zinzendorf at Berthelsdorf. The elder David and his wife Rosina ended their days at Bethlehem. The younger David was the last survivor of the 17 persons who exactly a year before the authentic naming of the town, by Count Zinzendorf, "felled the first tree at a place selected by them as a desirable building-site, some distance from the river, aside of the 'Indian Path' that led up from the ford into the north-west trail of the mountains."[201] Three of the most vigorous members of this original party—who had their temporary winter-quarters at the Forks of the Delaware—"shouldered their axes and strolled down through the woods to the Lehigh."[202]

The *History* says this was two days before Christmas Eve. The three were "Father Nitschmann, Martin Mack, and another, probably Anton Seiffert or young David Zeisberger."[203]

Whether David Zeisberger felled the first tree or not, he was certainly present at that "love-feast they held with a frugal meal of corncake and drink of roasted rye on Christmas Eve—undoubtedly the first Christmas service in the Forks of the Delaware."[204] He died in 1808 in the 88th year of his age, after 63 years of missionary service. He would then have been 20 years of age when the first tree was felled. After some experience among the various Indian tribes of Pennsylvania and New York, he decided that no real help could be given to the "brown brethren" unless they were segregated from "the evil influence of whites."[205] In 1722, he had already succeeded in establishing his "fourth station," the scene of "his most brilliant success."[206]

Zeisberger was hand and glove with Netawetwes, on the Tuscarawas River in Ohio, "he was granted by the Grand Council a tract of land eighty miles square."[207] Here, the Bohemian Brethren or the Moravians built a beautiful model city; they called it *Schönbrunn*. The idea was to condition the Indians to farm work and co-operative trade and self-support so that they would be free of contact with the fur-traders and rum-merchants. White Eyes, a famous chief and councillor of the Delawares advised the King that this project met with the will of the Great Spirit of God. With the support of the King and the Grand Council, Zeisberger proposed to claim or reclaim the whole of that (then) far-western frontier for the original inhabitants.

Zeisberger had won the allegiance of the whole Delaware nation and he now proposed to the King and the Council that they take steps to have their territory clearly defined; "let their land, by Act of Parliament, be secured to them for ever."[208] Netawetwes, who it was said, was now 120 years old, himself proposed to sail to England and interview George III, at St. James's Palace, in behalf of his people.[209] Alas, Netawetwes and White Eyes and David Zeisberger were doomed to bitter disappointment. This far-seeing, visionary, yet wholly practical scheme was blighted, just as their earthly paradise began to show the glory of harvest. "The sides of the valley . . . were not only covered with potatoes, parsnips and beans, but also with strawberries, gooseberries, raspberries and other garden fruits."[210] But David Zeisberger who had persuaded the Delawares literally, to beat their spears into pruning-hooks, was not even to be given a hearing by the white settlers. This was 1776.

Gnadenhuetten I.

The lovely name, Gnadenhuetten had seized the child's imagination, at the beginning of the grandmother's reconstructed memory or re-invoked fantasy. The name followed close on the first mention of the Secret and at the end of the grandmother's story, the name comes back, *Gnadenhuetten!* The child did not know that *Gnadenhuetten* meant Habitations of Grace.

The Editor herself [H.D.] must consult the History to find that *Gnadenhuetten* was the new settlement of "May, 1746, at the mouth of the Mahoning Creek."[211]

Friedenshuetten, Habitations of Peace, was the name of the original Indian settlement at Bethlehem and it was here, as we have already noted, that the Mohicans had come when the law was passed in New York state against "every vagrant preacher, Moravian or disguised Papist."[212] But as the Bethlehem of the Indians increased in numbers, far out of proportion to that of the original settlers, it was decided to begin this new settlement, dedicated entirely to the Indians and their needs. We have already noted that "after a love feast on the *Wunden Eiland,* the first detachment of fifteen set out for the place; some in canoes and some afoot."[213]

This was the first *Gnadenhuetten.* The settlement was planned and constructed on the lines of the original community with Central building or *Gemeinhaus* and the various choirs. Ten years after the establishment, in the autumn of 1755, General Braddock was defeated in one of the skirmishes or battles with the French. This was the period of the so-called "French and Indian wars." The Moravians had been accused of complicity with the French because of their ever-growing affiliation with the Indians. But now that particular "slander" was to be proved groundless for all time.

A band of "French Indians"[214] fell on the *Gnadenhuetten* colony. The *Gnadenhuetten* Indians themselves were at work in the woods at some little distance but those of the Moravians, who succeeded in locking themselves in the dormitory in the attic, were burned to death. Several others were murdered as they tried to make their escape. One of the women, given up for dead, was discovered a year later to have been dragged from the flames. This was the wife of Martin Nitschmann, Susanna; Joachim, a baptized Indian brought word of this.

"She was taken first to Wyoming by the savages, and almost perished from cold on the way."[215] Then later Sarah, the wife of Abraham, the Mohican, recognized a "Moravian sister" and "threw up her hands in consternation when she saw her."[216] Another woman, Abigail, wife of Benjamin, was permitted to care for Susanna in her own hut, until she was dragged off to Tioga where it was reported "she sank into a dazed condition of deep melancholy."[217] It was again Joachim who brought this news, and mercifully soon after, the report of her death.

This very briefly, is the story of the first *Gnadenhuetten.* "So they had been killed at *Gnadenhuetten* . . ."[218]

These were the "Moravian brothers," their names are Bohemian and Saxon with a sprinkling of Danish and English: they were visionaries with the mad idea of creating a *Unitas Fratrum* in the wilderness. But they were white people slain by dark-skinned savages, true to the considered stories of our history books and legends. We do not see so much of the other side of the coin. The savages at the new *Gnadenhuetten* were white savages.

Gnadenhuetten II.

"Certain incidents" of the far west were used by a band of rangers and toughs as an excuse for the sort of outrages that our present-day newspaper and radio have made us only too familiar with. Our Aryans of the mid-west, "on the ragged border-edge of the great Revolutionary struggle,"[219] came across a band of some hundred and fifty Indians at the place named *New Gnadenhuetten.* This was one of David Zeisberger's famous farm-settlements. Certain refugees from some little distance who were in danger of starvation, were helping to reap the corn![220] What a picture of the sun and the waving grain and the light! Into the frame (these acres and miles set apart by the King of the Delawares by the express will of the Great Spirit or God, as conveyed to White Eyes, the famous chief and councillor) steps the band of "soldiers," gangsters of the then new west, toughs, flotsam and jetsam, washed up on the shores of the Indian continent.

A certain new-American, named David Williamson, looks over the fields, the distant cluster of houses or ledges, he sees nothing wrong, he shrugs his shoulders—ah—that's a way they have, the varmints, they're lying low, they're hiding something. They're waiting to summon a lot more with their devil-yowls; Indians don't reap corn, or do they? Indians don't stack wheat in sheaves, or do they? The Colonel questions some of his subordinates. They gather the soldiers together and take a vote on it.

It was easy enough to gather the men and women and children into their own barns. The men in one, the women in another, the children in a third. The Indians of new *Gnadenhuetten* were accustomed to these divisions into "choirs," now sanctioned by White Eyes and their King. The new-American was drunk with power. He lost no time in sending to ask for final orders from his superiors at Pittsburgh. He slept that night. But early in the morning, he unlocked the doors, told the Indians they were to die and again divided them.

It took some time, several hours in fact, to let the men out, "one after another to be slaughtered like cattle."[221] Then they turned to the women and children "penned up for the purpose."[222] The actual number reported slain was 90. The soldiers were rather tired. They could not follow the youth who had broken out and the young boy who later followed. It was these two who told the story. Among those of David Zeisberger's immediate circle, was his dear friend Glikkikan, it was later discovered, and six of his own native assistants; there were 24 of the women or "Indian sisters" under his immediate care and 22 small children. The soldiers set fire to the barns. They collected their scalps. They went on "to seek more victims at *Schönbrunn*."[223]

VII.

Morning Star[224]

A History of the Moravian Missions, J.E. Hutton, M.A.
The North American Indians, 1734–1808.[225]

New York (City), Bethlehem, Lititz, Philadelphia (Pennsylvania) and Salem (North Carolina) are marked on the map in red, as Home Churches supporting the stations or missions.[226]

North from New York are Shekomeko, Wechquadnach and Pachgatgoch, the Mohicans; Wajomik, Onondaga and Friedenshütten, the Iroquois; south of Salem, North Carolina are two missions to the Cherokees of Georgia, Springplace and Oochgelogy. But the blue station-names[227] cluster most thickly around the red Bethlehem; Wechquetank, Menjoagomeka,[228] Nain, Oley, Gnadenhütten,[229] Shamokin.

Then on across the state to the west, Friedensstadt, still among the Delawares, and further north-east on the Allegheny River, Goschgoschünk, Lawunakhannek, and north-west, Pilgerruh; south-west, we have Schönbrunn and another Gnadenhütten; then south again and west, Lichtenau with Salem and Goshen.

North again toward the shore of Lake Erie along the Huron River, we have a New Salem and now far afield around the edge of the lake, north in Michigan, we find New Gnadenhütten. Here the trail turns back toward the east but north-east, following presumably the track of the river and the lake St. Clair, by canoe into Canada, where Fairfield and New Fairfield are marked on the Thames River.

. . . London, from which the good ship *Little Strength,* by some called *Irene,*[230] had once sailed with Martin Presser,[231] with Christian Seidel,[232] with the "gifted Fabricius,"[233] with Susanna Nitschmann and the various other Sisters (Anna Margaret, Anna Barbara, Anna Maria, Mary Magdalene, Anna Rosina)[234] each in their turn, as well as with Father Nitschmann, on his separate journeys, and various assorted members of the English congregation and the ship officers and men, Nicholas Garrison, Thomas Gladman, Jarvis Roebuck, Notley Togood and so on, along with John Nelson (boy) John Leathes (boy) and John Newton (boy).[235]

We may learn that Captain Garrison sails his *Little Strength* for the most part to Rotterdam to meet the assemblies of the Herrnhut congregation and so cut short their voyage. We may be sure, however, that certain of the brotherhood went independently or in small groups to England and joined the *Little Strength* at one of the Channel ports. Speculation is fascinating in the extreme and we could go far afield, tracing the various experiences of these religious and political exiles, among whom were certain famous scholars, made welcome, as I have before indicated, at the seats of English learning at Oxford and at Cambridge.

There had been some trouble in the very early days of the Count's first visit, with the undesirable elements of the demoralized German Lutheran congregation of Philadelphia; they had long been without a minister and met in an old barn. The German reformed people used this meeting-house the last Sunday of each month, and here their itinerant minister, the Rev. Philip Boehm, discovered that John Christopher Pyrlaeus, as assistant to Count Zinzendorf himself, was in charge of the negelected congregation the three other Sundays. Boehm represented "the extreme Calvinism and the austere rule of the Classis of Amsterdam."[236] Boehm started an active crusade against "the Count's party." With the established German Reformed Church of Germantown, however, Zinzendorf seems to have been on cordial terms.

This local clash with the extreme Calvinists is in miniature, a repetition of the more formidable struggle between the Count and the protestant party at the court of Dresden, which had secured his banishment from Saxony. It may be noted here that Frederick William I, King of Prussia, who had professed great admiration for the Count's poetry, continued his interest after the banishment in 1736, and urged the "development of the Moravian Church on a more distinct basis."[237]

The abusive pamphleteers let loose a tide-wave of invective when the Count was made secure of the legal and ecclesiastical rights of the *Unitas Fratrum* or Renewed Moravian Church of England. These make very good reading. Here is an excerpt from an elaborate note of Rimius'. The italics and capitals are his.

"As both Pope and Popery, by the Reformation, were driven out of the Church by the Fore-Door, he by a back Door, by Stealth, under the borrowed Cover of the ancient *Moravian Church* or *Unitas Fratrum,* intends to bring them in again. And this is his Aim, we have still less Reason to doubt. He justifies their *Worship in an unknown Tongue.* He and his People, according to his own Account, pray *Ave Marys.* They addressed and invoked *Angels.* The *invocation of Saints* is pleaded for by him in his *Exposition.* Not to mention any more articles, nor those Monastic and other Institutions . . ."[238] and so on and so on.

This is a very mild sample of Mr. Rimius' invective style. He quotes chapter and verse, as from the Hymns and Sermons. I have not the opportunity now of checking up on these weighty accusations, but apparently the Church of England and the English Universities did not realise the depraved villainy of the Count or were not unduly impressed by it, for we read in the *History* that "during the period from the end of the Thirty-years' War until well into the second decade of the eighteenth century the representatives of the suppressed Church maintained frequent and cordial communication with the Church of England and particularly with the University authorities at Oxford where considerable sums of money were raised for the impoverished Brethren, scholarships were founded for their students"[239] and so on and so on. The same attitude seems to have been maintained toward the banished Count and his company when they had their head-quarters at Lindsey House in Chelsea, London.

He was a dreamer, a poet, a reformer, a man-of-the-world, a mystic, a great gentleman and an intimate friend of carpenters, wood-cutters, farmers, itinerant preachers and all women. His mysterious *Plan* was interpreted by his political enemies, as an astute political move or series of related political moves which would, it was alleged, lead in the end, even to a bid for world-power or world-dictatorship.

Says Henry Rimius (perhaps the most astute of the Count's detractors), "... they have not the Truth in View, but the execution of a favourite Plan."[240]

The Guard or Protection of the Lord, the *Huth des Herrn,* hence *Herrn-huth* or *Herrnhut* had grown in a surprisingly short time from the first few shelters constructed by Christian David the carpenter, to a community whose inhabitants numbered some 600, according to Rimius, in less than ten years. The *Herrnhuters* live said Rimius, as in a monastic institution, with certain "Dependence, Devotion, Rules"[241] enjoined on them. They are divided into classes, married men, married women, widowers, widows, maids, bachelors, children. Rimius remarks with some acidity on the "uncommon attention to the instruction of youth."[242] These people, Rimius asserts, by "the year 1740 ... had already made two hundred voyages by sea."[243]

As the Bohemians, Poles and educated Saxon members of the community were amazingly well-equipped with various European languages and dialects, and by some strange freak managed to "pick up" unknown and till then many unrecorded tongues of out-lying districts of Asia, Africa, and the Americas, it was obvious to the astute "Aulic Counsellor to His Late Majesty the King of Prussia"[244] that there was some world-wide political scheme afoot.

Though the royal commission of 1732 found nothing "amiss in the new settlement ... certain of the unfriendly class among the Protestant clergy" by means of "some officials at the court of Dresden ... secured the banishment of the Count from Saxony."[245]

Tho. Doolittel (1632–1707)
St. Alphage, London Wall.

> Dust drawne to th' life! yet dull and shortly dead
> Shall live. Death's slaine by death; Christ in my stead
> Did dye. Deare Lord! Love flames my flesh and mind;
> In thee do hope eternal life to find.
> My flesh, my soul, my all I owe to thee,
> Thy Wounds are health, thy stripes are balm to mee.

Printed by R.B. for Ralph Sympson at the *Harp* in *St. Paul's* Church-yard. (1711)[246]

In all which if thou findest any thing profitable to thy Soul, and tending to promote the work of Grace wrought in thy Heart ... give God the Glory; but where thou findest any thing that favoureth of the weakness of the Author, do not censure, but pray for him, who is willing, according to his own Talent he hath received from the Lord, to further thee in thy way to Heaven and Eternal Life.

Tho. Doolittel.

A treatise concerning the Lord's Supper: with three Dialogues, for more full information of the Weak, in the Nature and Love of this Sacrament (The four and twentieth Edition) 1 Cor. XI. 24. *This do in Remembrance of me.*[247]

London—1940–44

Editor's Notes

1. In H.D.'s "Notes," the headings are phrases that she underlined, referring back to passages in the seven chapters of the main text. In H.D.'s dedication, the phrase "brought me home" is from the poem "To Helen" by Edgar Allan Poe. See introduction.

2. Loskiel, pt. 2: 16.

3. Fries, v.

4. The epigraph to chapter 1 comes from Camille Flammarion, *Death and Its Mystery*, vol. 2, 14.

5. *HB,* 104–5.

6. Ibid., 226, 528.

7. Ibid., 489, 517–21.

8. This education, not as trivial as H.D. indicates, is described in William C. Reichel's *Bethlehem Souvenir.*

9. Wolle, 5. H.D.'s typescript misprints "Schmerseuz" for the correct "Schwerzens."

10. H.D. split this word to show root-link to "Sylvester," but later she "doubled on" it (ts. 3, GV, 21).

11. First published 1884, revised ed. 1892 (MH, 26).

12. First published 1887 (MH, 25).

13. Published 1890. The process of creating the hand-tinted plates is described in MH (26) and paraphrased by Charlotte Mandel in "Magical Lenses: Poet's Vision Beyond the Naked Eye," 301–17. "Next door cousin" Hilda earned pennies carrying the rolled-up sheets in bundles to the women who were to color them (307).

14. Jedediah Weiss (1796–1873) (MH, 8).

15. *HB,* 634.

16. Ibid., 166.

17. The "Sea Congregations" (*Seegemeine*) were groups traveling overseas together under the Moravian communal and spiritual discipline. *HB,* 167–68, lists the names of those in the second Sea Congregation.

18. AGS, 248.

19. Frey, *A True and Authentic Account of Andrew Frey.* In H.D.'s copy of Frey, on p. 23, she wrote, "Jonas Paulus Weiss" next to the paragraph beginning "After this I went to *Jonah Paul Weite.* . . ."

20. *HB*, 160, n. 6.

21. Frey, title page.

22. Ibid., 23.

23. *HB*, 294, n. 37; *LTDZ*, 284.

24. *HB*, 487–88.

25. Ibid., 488, n. 2; Reichel, *Souvenir*, 39–42.

26. *HB*, 584.

27. Letter dated "All Saints Day [November 1] 1936." Howard always dated his letters to H.D. by saints' days, not by the conventional calendar.

28. Clifford Howard letter dated "St. Afra's Day 1938." St. Afra's Day is either August 5 (*New Catholic Encyclopedia*, 1:171; Baring-Gould, 9:59) or August 7 (Butler, 8:65–67). Cf. *HB*, 662–63, 664, for information on Jedediah Weiss.

29. *HB*, 764–65, n. 3.

30. This ballad, which may contain a remnant of seventeenth-century Scottish history, is also known as "Mary Hamilton." Its title refers to the fact that the then Queen of Scotland had four ladies-in-waiting with the first name *Mary*. Mary Hamilton, seduced by the king, has murdered the infant and is sentenced to be hanged. The song's last stanza contains her final words on the scaffold:

> Last night there were four Marys;
>> Tonight there'll be but three.
> 'Twas Mary Beaton and Mary Seaton
>> And Mary Carmichael and me.

Virginia Woolf alludes to this song and these "four Marys" in her essay *A Room of One's Own* (1928).

31. MH, 8. Her full name was Mary Stables. See illustrations, pp.31, 133.

32. The epigraph to chapter 2 comes from Shakespeare's *As You Like It*, 2.1.12.

33. To carry out Zinzendorf's communal living plan, large sandstone buildings were built in the early 1740s, the Sisters' House as a residence for all single women and the Brothers' House for all single men. These still stand on Church Street in Bethlehem; the Brothers' House has become Colonial Hall of Moravian College (Hamilton, 18).

34. *HB*, 197, n. 7.

35. Ibid., 54–55, n. 15.

36. Ibid.

37. Ibid., 644.

38. Ibid., 45, n. 9.

39. Ibid., 45–46, n. 9.

40. Ibid., 643.

41. Ibid.

42. Ibid., 46, n. 9. *Menagachsink* was the Native American name for Bethlehem.

43. Zinzendorf used the Latin expression "Ecclesiolae in ecclesia" (little churches within the church) to express the independence of the three denominations that originally constituted the community at Herrnhut: the Old Church of Bohemia (the ethnic Moravian Protestants), the Lutheran Church (Zinzendorf's own denomination), and the Reformed Church (*HB*, 23).

44. AGS, vi; *HB*, 92, n. 2. Levering misprints "Ems" for "Ens."

45. Ibid., 3; *HB*, 92, n. 2.

46. John R. Weinlick in *Count Zinzendorf* describes the influence upon Zinzendorf of his Pietist grandmother, Countess von Gersdorf (60–62).

47. *HB*, 21–22.

48. Hutton, *Church*, 198. Christian David's words are from Psalm 84:3.

49. *HB*, 77–78, n. 14.

50. This translation is by H.D. She does not use any wording from *HB*, 78, n. 14, which gives "an English rendering in the same measure" of this hymn, beginning "Jesus, call Thou me / From the world to flee. . . ." Cf. the H.D. character Midget, who translates Heine in H.D.'s roman à clef *Paint It Today*, ed. and intro. Cassandra Laity (New York: New York University Press, 1992), 11.

51. *HB*, 561. Levering sets this phrase in quotation marks, apparently quoting the "Bethlehem Diary," the official anonymous record of daily events in the early community. He also summarizes the career of the Reverend John Ettwein, who came to America in 1754, as "the zealous superintendent of work among the children, the indefatigable itinerant, the commanding spirit at Bethlehem during the Revolution, and then the bishop of such extensive acquaintance and correspondence with public men" (*HB*, 278).

52. Ibid., 561.

53. Ibid., 562. The chieftain speaks "to the young ladies" because, at this last major visit of Native Americans to Bethlehem, the students of the Seminary For Young Ladies were present, and several young women delivered prepared speeches of greeting to the fifty-one *sachems*. The scene made a deep impression upon witnesses, according to the detailed account in Reichel, *Souvenir*, 98 ff.

54. Loskiel, pt. 1: 2; *HB*, 48.

55. *HMM*, 91.

56. Ibid., 92; cf. Reichel, *Souvenir*, 102 ff; Loskiel, pt. 1:27–28. Zinzendorf's own account of his having been given this fathom of wampum—i.e., a string about six feet long—is included in Reichel, *Memorials*, vol. 1, 124–25.

57. Ruth 1:16. H.D. was a lifetime incessant reader of the Bible, according to her daughter, Perdita Schaffner (interview, May 22, 1997).

58. *HB*, 153.

59. *HMM*, 86; *HB*, 142, 154.

60. This phrase is Cooper's description (413–14).

61. These are the last lines in the Cooper novel. "Lenape" is the tribal name for the Delawares.

62. I have been unable to locate the actual edition of *The Last of the Mohicans* read by H.D. James Franklin Beard's afterword to the Signet paperback states that Cooper read Heckewelder's *Account of the History, Manners, and Customs of the Indian Nations* (422). See *HB*, 40, on Rauch. Independent testimony of his presence in Shekomeko is given in "Moravians in Dutchess County," ed. F. B. O'Callaghan, 614. Abbreviated *Doc. Hist.*

63. Source unidentified. Cf. *HMM*, 86, 90.

64. Ibid., 85.

65. Ibid., 86–87. Cf. Loskiel, pt. 2:14.

66. *HB,* 142, names John Mueller as "a young man of Rhinebeck, N.Y., who had accompanied the missionary Rauch to Bethlehem" (142).

67. This language draws strongly from Rev. 21:23, 25 and 22:5.

68. *HMM,* 86, states that Tschoop was so drunk that he remembered only "one word of the sermon. The word he remembered was 'blood'. He thought about it, dreamed about it, wondered what it could mean."

69. *HB,* 242, n. 7. Cf. *MR,* 34.

70. *HB,* 154.

71. *HMM,* 94, is verified by *Doc. Hist.,* 617.

72. Cf. *HMM,* 94.

73. *HB,* 192.

74. Ibid., 142.

75. Ibid., 193.

76. Cf. *HMM,* 92. The summer of 1742 is being referred to.

77. Loskiel, pt. 1:30; *HMM,* 93.

78. *HB,* 306.

79. Loskiel, pt. 1:64; *HB,* 306–7.

80. Loskiel, pt. 1:32; *HB,* 153; Reichel, *Memorials,* 96–97.

81. Reichel, *Memorials,* 106–7; *HMM,* 93.

82. *HB,* 153.

83. Ibid., 153–54; Reichel, *Memorials,* 106.

84. Source unidentified.

85. Source unidentified. Cf. Spence, 32–36, a book owned and marked by H.D.

86. Spence describes the Algonquins as "milder than the Iroquois, and less Spartan in habits" (24) and says that "they were the most intelligent and advanced of the eastern tribes" (26).

87. Spence, 27.

88. Ibid., 114.

89. Ibid., quoting from Daniel G. Brinton, *The Myths of the New World* (New York: Leypoldt and Holt, 1868).

90. Ibid., 114–15, quoting Brinton, 131–33.

91. *HB,* 300; *LTDZ,* 220.

92. *HB,* 21.

93. Ibid., 7.

94. Ibid., 9.

95. All the male members of the house of Reuss bore the first name *Henry* and were distinguished by numbers in official records. H.D. wrote the numbers of various Henry von Reusses in her "Zinzendorf Notebook." Count Henry 28, Erdmuth's nephew, remained Zinzendorf's lifelong friend and was present at his death (AGS, 501). Cf. JA *Mys,* 115, n. 10 and n. 11.

96. *HB,* 21.

97. AGS, 4.

98. *HB,* 186–88.

99. Ibid., 270.

100. Hutton, *Church,* 255–65.

101. *HB,* 28, n. 3. Cf. Weinlick, 197.

102. *HB,* 91; AGS, 219–22.

103. *HB,* 91.

104. Verified in *Nikolaus Ludwig von Zinzendorf,* 229, 259.

105. *HB,* 281.

106. AGS, 458.

107. The source of the zodiac nursery-rhyme epigraph is unknown.

108. *Dictionary of National Biography,* 1:1142.

109. Ibid.

110. Ibid., 1:1143, speaks of Doolittel's "'A Treatise concerning the Lord's Supper,' (1665), 12mo. (portrait by R. White)," which "went through many editions."

111. O. P. Allen, "Abraham Doolittle and Some of His Descendants," says that Abraham Doolittle was born in England in 1619 (153).

112. *DNB* identifies Thomas Doolittle as a "nonconformist tutor, third son of Anthony Doolittle, a glover . . . born at Kidderminster in 1632 or the latter half of 1631" (1:1141). Allen gives the birthdate as 1630 (151).

113. *New England Historical and Genealogical Register,* index.

114. Ibid., 6:295.

115. Ibid., 6:295, 359.

116. Ibid., 6:295.

117. Exodus 22:18.

118. *Dictionary of American Biography,* 8:560.

119. MH, 5–6.

120. Exodus 20:13.

121. This motto appears on the Gadsden Flag of 1775, designed by Colonel Christopher Gadsden of South Carolina. It shows a green and black rattlesnake, coiled to strike, in the center of a bright yellow field. The words "Don't Tread on Me" appear in black capital letters under the snake. Gadsden proposed it as the flag of the commander in chief of the American navy, but Congress refused. However, the navy liked Gadsden's idea and in 1775 adopted as its first official ensign "a flag with 13 alternating red and white stripes, with a rattlesnake diagonally across eight of the stripes" and the motto beneath it (John Winthrop Adams, ed., *Stars and Stripes Forever* [New York: Smithmark, 1992], 12–13).

122. The Nimitz Library of the United States Naval Academy at Annapolis has the first (1885) and fourth (1893) editions of *A Treatise on Practical Astronomy, As Applied to Geodesy and Navigation.* Not an official textbook in courses of instruction from 1885–86 through 1904–5, it was presumably used in research or as supplementary reading (Alice S. Creighton, head of special collections, Nimitz Library, letter to the editor, July 28, 1993).

123. This description fits a photograph now at the Beinecke Library, showing Charles Leander Doolittle at about the age of 17 in his Civil War uniform, with collar-length hair and without the full beard and mustache of his later years. See p. 134.

124. The Bible illustrated by the French artist Gustave Doré was published in 1866.

125. Point Pleasant is a resort in Ocean County, eastern New Jersey, near the Manasquan Inlet, where the Doolittles sometimes spent vacations.

126. Cf. Yonge, 312.

127. The epigraph to chapter 4 is the closing stanza of hymn 753 on p. 185 in the 1891

edition of *Offices of Worship and Hymns,* a book H.D. owned. The Rev. Henry Williams identified this hymn by its meter; it is "the only hymn text to that meter out of more than 1400 texts in the 1891 hymnal" (letter to the editor, September 30, 1993). The author of the hymn is Anatolius of Constantinople, d. 458; John Mason Neale, tr., 1818–66. H.D. noted these authors in her first draft of *The Gift.*

128. Hark, 192–93.

129. Source unidentified. Portraits of Moravian pioneer women wearing these caps are shown in *HB* opposite p. 190. Myers lists cap ribbon colors (38). See also p. 143.

130. The key phrase *For Mysteries were ordained* does not appear in the third typescript of *The Gift.* It heads a section, pp. 21–23 in the second typescript of chapter 5, preceding the phrase "the keepers of the Mysteries." In that typescript it is crossed out, but evidently in revising her "Notes," H.D. forgot that she had eliminated the passage from the main text. This is the only point at which a note exists that has no correspondence to the main text. See also discrepancy in n. 10.

131. This pamphlet is not among H.D.'s books at the Beinecke Library nor at the Bryher Library in East Hampton.

132. *HB,* 171; 185, n. 2.

133. *Gemein* is a form of the German word *Gemeine,* meaning "community" or "parish." Bethlehem's *Gemeinhaus* (Community House), like a city mayor's office, was the center of activity and government during the town's earliest years. It still stands at the corner of Church and Cedar Streets, "the oldest house in Bethlehem" (*HB,* 68).

134. Ibid., 185, n. 2.

135. Ibid., 462–70.

136. The first epigraph to chapter 5 is from the Old Testament, 2 Samuel 23:15. Levering also quotes it (*HB,* 58). The second epigraph is from Shakespeare's *The Merchant of Venice,* 5.1.54.

137. William Henry was famous as the designer and manufacturer of the "Henry rifle," whose accuracy contributed to Washington's winning the Revolutionary War. Mary Ann Wood married him in 1755; they had six daughters and one son.

138. Since William Henry was "the first to recognize the genius of Benjamin West and to extend to him both moral and material help" (*DAB,* 8:561), it is natural that he and Mary Ann Wood Henry should be the subject of one of his paintings. Monica Crystal of the Historical Society of Pennsylvania reported in 1994 that Ann Wood's portrait is not on display but is in the Society's possession, having been presented on May 26, 1902, by the Jordan family, descendants of the Henrys and therefore distant cousins of H.D. (Wainwright, 111). See illustrations, p. 129.

139. These cousins are the Bells and the Jordans. H.D. mentions "Cousin Laura and cousin Emily Bell" in chapter 6.

140. As manufacturer of the "Henry rifle," William Henry became "the principal armorer of the troops" called into service during "the Indian wars which desolated the frontier from 1755 to 1760" (*DAB,* 8:560).

141. *HB,* 7.

142. *CN,* 70. After quoting several hymns by Zinzendorf dealing with sexuality and his view that "All the Souls are of the Feminine Sex," Rimius comments: "I question whether Examples are to be found of a *Fanaticism* more extravagant, & a *Mysticism* more *gross & scandalous.*" This remark is copied in H.D.'s handwritten "Zinzendorf

Notes" and appears on the last page of her novel *The Mystery* (1949–51). H.D. repaginated for each new source of data in this notebook, so the page number for the entire notebook is given here in brackets, e.g., for this passage ZN, 20 [52]. Cf. JA *Mys,* 374.

143. *CN,* 9; also noted in ZN, 2 [32].

144. *CN,* 19; ZN, 7 [38].

145. *HMM,* 42, 94–95.

146. *HB,* 95.

147. Ibid., 94.

148. Charles Frederick Seidel came to America in 1806 and settled at Bethlehem in 1817 (*HB,* 517, n. 12).

149. In Grimm (1905 edition), *seidel* is referred to as a *lehnwort,* a borrowed or naturalized foreign word, meaning "a measure for liquids and drinks; borrowed or naturalized foreign word from *situlus* . . ." H.D.'s exclamation point after "measure" links this definition with Luke 6:38, which she quotes in chapter 1: "already the measure is *pressed down and shaken together, and running over.*"

150. H.D. read the accounts of the powerful influence the drawing of lots had on pioneer Moravians' careers, such as that of Leonard Dober in the Danish West Indies (*HMM,* 21–24).

151. *HB,* 124.

152. Ibid., 304–5.

153. Ibid., 124.

154. Ibid., 242, n. 7.

155. Fries, 79.

156. Ibid., 80.

157. *HB,* 192–93.

158. Ibid., 185.

159. Ibid., 187.

160. Ibid., 185.

161. Ibid., 187.

162. *CN,* 50–51; ZN, 31 [63].

163. *HB,* 186.

164. Cf. *HB,* 189.

165. *HB,* 199.

166. H.D. misread *HB,* 186. This passage refers not to Cammerhof but to Zinzendorf. Cammerhof, however, upheld the same principles.

167. *HB,* 185. In chap. 5, H.D. mistakenly says that Cammerhof died at age 25 years. He was born on July 28, 1721, and died on April 28, 1751 (*LTDZ,* 143, 182).

169. Ibid., 242, n. 7.

168. Ibid., 70, n. 8.

170. Ibid., 5. The seal is also illustrated on this page.

171. Source unidentified.

172. Cf. *TF,* 70–71. H.D. describes the unconscious: "this unexplored depth ran like a great stream or ocean underground." See editor's introduction.

173. Rougemont, 120.

174. *HB,* 21; AGS, intro. See p. 26, n. 25, in this volume.

175. The Council of Vienna, abolishing the Order of the Knights Templars, took place in 1311–12. (*Columbia Encyclopedia,* 5th ed.), 1488.

176. *HB,* 7.

177. Cf. Ibid., 19.

178. Ibid., 21–22.

179. Ibid., 7. H.D. repeats the phrase she quoted earlier. Cf. n. 141. "Cyrill" is often spelled "Cyril"; H.D. follows Levering's spelling.

180. Ibid., 7–8.

181. Ibid., 300.

182. Ibid.

183. Ibid., 305.

184. Ibid., 340.

185. Rimius is a "Saxon lawyer" because his official title, given on the title page of *CN,* is "Aulic Counsellor to his Majesty the late King of Prussia."

186. Rev. 13:11–17.

187. *CN,* 9.

188. Ibid., 19; ZN, 7 [38].

189. *CN,* 22; ZN, 21 [53].

190. *CN,* 83; ZN, 21 [53].

191. This note comes from another pamphlet by Rimius, *A Solemn Call on Count Zinzendorf,* 3–4. H.D. copied it in ZN, 25 [57].

192. St. Nicholas's Day is December 6. The letter is in the Beinecke Library.

193. "Notes" section 6 continues notes for chapter 5, to which its underlined phrases allude. Chapter 6, "What It Was," has no notes related specifically to it.

194. *HB,* 199.

195. Ibid., 199, n. 8.

196. Ibid., 125.

197. Ibid., 106–7.

198. Ibid., 107.

199. Ibid., 305, 306, 307.

200. Ibid., 305. The "companion" is Christian Seidel.

201. Ibid., 57.

202. Ibid.

203. Ibid.

204. Ibid. This first Christmas service took place in 1740, a year before the famous Christmas eve on which Count Zinzendorf named Bethlehem and sang the Bethlehem hymn recorded by H.D. in "Notes" section 2.

205. Hutton, *Missions,* 109.

206. Ibid., 106.

207. Ibid., 107.

208. Ibid., 110.

209. Ibid., 109.

210. Ibid., 107.

211. *HB,* 193.

212. Ibid., 175; *HMM,* 94.

213. *HB,* 193. See n. 157.

214. Ibid., 311. The italics are in the original.

215. Ibid., 316, n. 5.

216. Ibid., 317, continuation of 316, n. 5.

217. Ibid., 317.

218. H.D. is quoting her own lines in chapter 5.

219. *HB*, 522.

220. *HMM*, 113–14. In order to break down the stereotype of the Native American "savage" and to connect with the World War II context, H.D. refers to the "white savages" as "Aryan," the Nazis of their time.

221. *HB*, 523. Cf. *HMM*, 113–14.

222. *HB*, 523.

223. *HMM*, 114. Cf. *HB*, 523; *LTDZ*, 537–57.

224. The epigraph to chapter 7 refers to the chapter's title, "Morning Star." It is taken from Percy Bysshe Shelley's translation of Plato's Greek that appears as the epigraph to Shelley's *Adonais: An Elegy on the Death of John Keats*. This "Notes" section does not refer directly to the contents of the seventh chapter, but, like "Notes" section 6, amplifies notes for section 5, referring to that chapter.

225. Title of chapter 6, *HMM*, 78.

226. A map in *HMM*, opposite p. 80, has a key that shows a red globe surmounted by a cross as indicating "Home Churches supporting the Mission."

227. The map key places a blue cross and globe beside "Stations or Missions no longer occupied."

228. H.D. wrote "Meniolagomeka (?)" because she couldn't read the place name. The black line of the Delaware River crosses its pale blue lettering. A magnifying glass reveals the Germanized spelling, "Menjoagomeka." *HB*, 244, mentions "Meniolagomeka."

229. "Gnadenhütten," the German spelling of "Gnadenhuetten," is used on the map in *HMM*.

230. *HB*, 166; *HMM*, 185.

231. See the list of passengers on the *Irene* (*HB*, 253–54). H.D. used *HB*, 316, as the basis of "The Death of Martin Presser," written in the winter of 1943, according to her notes on the ts.

232. Christian Seidel's name is not on the list of the second Sea Congregation, which arrived on the *Little Strength* in 1743. Perhaps H.D. is conflating him with Nathanael Seidel, a member of the first Sea Congregation, which arrived on the *Catherine* in 1742 (*HB*, 125).

233. *HB*, 319, n. 6. Fabricius was killed in the Gnadenhuetten massacre, November 26, 1755 (*HB*, 319).

234. These are first names of women members of the second Sea Congregation (*HB*, 167–68).

235. *HB*, 168.

236. In this paragraph and the next, H.D. is apparently unconscious of repeating information she gave already, early in "Notes" section 5, under the heading "*German reformed people*." See nn. 146 and 147.

237. *HB*, 91.

238. Rimius, *A Second Solemn Call*, 21–22, n. 1.

288 · Editor's Notes

239. *HB*, 19.
240. *CN*, 14; ZN, 3 [34].
241. *CN*, 8.
242. *CN*, 10; ZN, 4 [34].
243. *CN*, 31; ZN, 8 [39].
244. *CN*, title page; ZN, 1 [31].
245. *HB*, 25.

246. This poem, signed "TD," appears opposite the title page of Thomas Doolittel's *A Treatise Concerning the Lord's Supper* in the nineteenth edition, of which the Beinecke Library has a copy "Printed for Samuel Sprint, at the Bell in Little-Britain. 1697." The printing information here recorded by H.D. evidently belongs to the twenty-fourth edition.

247. *This do in remembrance of me* (Luke 22:19, KJV) are Jesus' words at the Last Supper, repeated in 1 Corinthians 11:24, the records of the early church's institution of the sacrament of Holy Communion. These words are repeated in the Communion service in the Anglican and other Christian churches. This entire paragraph constitutes the final lines of Doolittel's "The Epistle to the Reader," the preface to *A Treatise . . . ,* facing p. 1. H.D. intends it to be read as a spiritual dedication of her work as well as its coda and a message to her readers.

Works Cited

I. WORKS BY H.D.

Asphodel. Ed. and intro. Robert Spoo. Durham, N.C.: Duke University Press, 1992.

Collected Poems, 1912–1944. Ed. Louis L. Martz.[Includes *Sea Garden.*] New York: New Directions, 1983.

"The Death of Martin Presser." *Quarterly Review of Literature* 13, no. 3 (1965): 241–61.

The Gift [abridged by Griselda Ohannessian]. Intro. Perdita Schaffner. New York: New Directions, 1982.

"H.D. by Delia Alton." [Originally cataloged as "Notes on Recent Writing."] Ed. Adalaide Morris. *Iowa Review* 16, no. 3 (1986): 174–221.

Hedylus. Ed. and afterword John Walsh. [Includes "Sketch of H.D.: The Egyptian Cat" by Perdita Schaffner.] Redding Ridge, Connecticut: Black Swan Books Ltd., 1980.

HERmione. Intro. Perdita Schaffner. New York: New Directions, 1981.

Hippolytus Temporizes. Ed. and afterword John Walsh. Redding Ridge, Connecticut: Black Swan Books, Ltd., 1985.

Ion. Ed. and afterword John Walsh. [Includes excerpts from H.D.'s "Notes on Euripedes."] Redding Ridge, Connecticut: Black Swan, Ltd., 1986.

Kora and Ka. [Includes "Mira-Mare."] Ed. and intro. Robert Spoo. New York: New Directions, 1996.

Majic Ring. Ts. (1943–44). L.D. Papers, Beinecke Library, Yale University, New Haven, Conn.

"*The Mystery:* H.D.'s Unpublished Moravian Novel Edited and Annotated." Ed. and intro. Jane Augustine. Ph.D. diss., City University of New York, 1988.

Nights. Intro. Perdita Schaffner. New York: New Directions, 1934. Reprint of Darantière edition, Dijon, France, 1934, published under the pseudonym John Helforth.

Notes on Thought and Vision. [Includes "The Wise Sappho"]. Ed. and intro. Albert Gelpi. San Francisco: City Lights Books, 1982; London: Peter Owen, 1988.

Paint It Today. Ed. Cassandra Laity. New York: New York University Press, 1992. [Chapters 1–4 are in *Contemporary Literature* 27, no. 4 (1986): 444–74.]

"Séance Notes." Ts. H.D. Papers, Beinecke Library, Yale University, New Haven, Connecticut.

Tribute to Freud. Foreword by Norman Holmes Pearson. New York: New Directions, 1984.

Trilogy. Foreword by Norman Holmes Pearson. New York: New Directions, 1973.

"The Zinzendorf Notebook." Ms. H.D. Papers, Beinecke Library, Yale University, New Haven, Connecticut. H.D. did not number all pages consecutively. Citations list H.D.'s page numbers first, then in brackets the numbers consecutive from the first page.

II. WORKS BY OTHER AUTHORS

In this list a single asterisk indicates those volumes owned by H.D. that are now at Beinecke Rare Book and Manuscript Library at Yale University, New Haven, Connecticut, and a double asterisk indicates her books now in the Bryher Library, East Hampton, New York, owned by her daughter, Perdita Schaffner.

Adams, John Winthrop, ed. *Stars and Stripes Forever: The History of Our Flag.* New York: Smithmark, 1992.

Allen, O. P. "Abraham Doolittle and Some of His Descendants." *Magazine of New England History.* Vol. 3, no. 3 (July 1893), 151–88.

Baring-Gould, Rev. Sabine. *Lives of the Saints.* Vol. 9. Edinburgh: John Grant, 1914.

Butler, Rev. Alban (1711–1773). *Lives of the Saints.* Ed. and rev. Herbert Thurston and Donald Attwater. London: Burns, Oates, and Washbourne, 1926–38.

Collecott, Diana. Introduction to the British edition of *The Gift.* London: Virago, 1984.

The Columbia Encyclopedia. 5th ed. New York: Columbia University Press, 1993.

Cooper, James Fenimore. *The Last of the Mohicans.* [First published 1826.] Afterword by James Franklin Beard. New York: Signet Classic, 1962.

**Curtiss, Harriette Augusta, and F. Homer Curtiss. *The Message of Aquaria.* Washington, D.C.: Curtiss Philosophic Book Co., 1932.

———. *The Key of Destiny.* San Francisco.: Curtiss Philosophic Book Co., 1923.

Dembo, L. S., ed. and intro. *H.D.: A Reconsideration.* Special issue. *Contemporary Literature* 10, no. 4 (1969).

Deutsches Wörterbuch von Jacob und Wilhelm Grimm. Munich: Deutscher Taschenbuch Verlag, 1984. Reproduction of the first edition of 1905.

Dictionary of American Biography. Eds. Allen Johnson and Dumas Malone. New York: Charles Scribner's Sons, 1928– .

Dictionary of National Biography. Eds. Sir Leslie Stephen and Sir Sidney Lee. London: Oxford University Press, 1921–22.

The Documentary History of the State of New York. Vol. 3. Ed. E. B. O'Callaghan. Albany, N.Y.: Weed, Parsons, and Co., 1850.

DuPlessis, Rachel Blau. "A Note on the State of H.D.'s *The Gift.*" *Sulfur* 9 (1984): 178–81.

Edmunds, Susan. *Out of Line: History, Psychoanalysis and Montage in H.D.'s Long Poems.* Stanford: Stanford University Press, 1994.

Flammarion, Camille. *Death and Its Mystery.* Vol. 2, *Manifestations and Apparitions of the Dying, "Doubles," and Phenomena of Occultism.* Tr. Latrobe Carroll. New York: Century Co., 1922.

*Frey, Andreas. *A True and Authentic Account of Andrew Frey; containing the Occasion of his coming among the Herrnhutters or Moravians, his observations on their Conferences, Casting Lots, Marriages, Festivals, Merriments, Celebrations of Birth-Days, Impious Doctrines, and Fantastical Practices; Abuse of Charitable Contributions, Linnen Images, Ostentatious Profuseness, and Rancour against any who in the least differ from them; together with the Motive for publishing this Account. Faithfully translated from the German.* [London]: J. Robinson, M. Keith, and J. Jolliff, 1753.

Friedman, Susan Stanford. *Psyche Reborn: The Emergence of H.D.* Bloomington: Indiana University Press, 1981.

———. *Penelope's Web: Gender, Modernity, H.D.'s Fiction.* New York and Cambridge: Cambridge University Press, 1990.

Friedman, Susan Stanford, and Rachel Blau DuPlessis, eds. "H.D.'s 'The Dark Room'" [a complete chapter from *The Gift* with H.D.'s "Notes"]. *Montemora* 8 (1981): 57–76.

———. *Signets: Reading H.D.* Madison: University of Wisconsin Press, 1990.

Fries, Adelaide L. *The Road to Salem.* Winston-Salem: University of North Carolina Press, 1944.

Gregory, Eileen. *H.D. and Hellenism: Classic Lines.* New York: Cambridge University Press, 1997.

Guest, Barbara. *Herself Defined: The Poet H.D. and Her World.* New York: Doubleday, 1984.

Hamilton, Kenneth G. *Church Street in Old Bethlehem.* Edited and updated by Bernard E. Michel. Bethlehem, Pa.: Moravian Congregation, 1988.

Hark, Ann. *Hex Marks the Spot: In the Pennsylvania Dutch Country.* Philadelphia and New York: Lippincott, 1938.

Heckewelder, Rev. John G. E. *An Account of the History, Manners and Customs of the Indian Nations, Who Once Inhabited Pennsylvania and the Neighbouring States.* Philadelphia: Abraham Small, 1819; published under the auspices of the American Philosophical Society. New and revised edition: *History, Manners, and Customs of the Indian Nations Who Once Inhabited Pennsylvania and the Neighbouring States* (vol. XII of the Memoirs of the Historical Society of Pennsylvania) with an introduction and notes by the Rev. William C. Reichel. Philadelphia: Historical Society of Pennsylvania, 1876. Reprint. New York: Arno Press, 1971.

Hollenberg, Donna Krolik, ed. *Between History and Poetry: The Letters of H.D. and Norman Holmes Pearson.* Iowa City: University of Iowa Press, 1997.

Howard, Clifford. Letters to H.D. H.D. Papers, Beinecke Library, Yale University, New Haven, Connecticut.

Hutton, Joseph Edmund. *A History of the Moravian Church.* London: Moravian Publication Office, 1909.

*———. *A History of Moravian Missions.* London: Moravian Publication Office, 1923.

King, Michael, ed. *H.D.: Woman and Poet.* Orono, Maine: National Poetry Foundation, 1986.

Laity, Cassandra. *H.D. and the Victorian Fin de Siècle: Gender, Modernism, Decadence.* New York and Cambridge: Cambridge University Press, 1996.

*[Lavington, George.] *The Moravians Compared and Detected.* London: J. and P. Knapton, 1755.

*Levering, Joseph Mortimer. *A History of Bethlehem, Pennsylvania, 1741–1892.* Bethlehem: Times Publishing Co., 1903.

Loskiel, George Henry. *History of the Mission of the United Brethren Among the Indians in North America.* In three parts (one vol.). Tr. by Christian Ignatius La Trobe of *Geschichte der Mission der Evangelischen Brüder unter den Indianern in Nordamerika.* London: Brethren's Society for the Furtherance of the Gospel, 1794.

Mandel, Charlotte. "Magical Lenses: Poet's Vision Beyond the Naked Eye." In *H.D.,* ed. by M. King, 301–17.

Meyer, Gerhard. *Nikolaus Ludwig von Zinzendorf.* Ergänzungsband 1, *Eine genealogische Studie mit Ahnen- und Nachfahrenliste.* [Nicholas Louis von Zinzendorf. Supplementary volume 1, A genealogical study with lists of ancestors and descendants.] Hildesheim: Georg Olms Verlagsbuchhandlung, 1966.

Morris, Adalaide. "Autobiography and Prophecy: H.D.'s *The Gift.*" In *H.D,* ed. by M. King, 227–36.

———. "A Relay of Power and Peace: H.D. and the Spirit of the Gift." In *Signets,* 52–82.

Myers, Elizabeth Lehman. *A Century of Moravian Sisters.* New York: Fleming H. Revell, 1918.

The New Catholic Encyclopedia. New York: McGraw Hill, 1967–69.

The New England Historical and Genealogical Register. Vols. 1–50. Baltimore: Genealogical Publishing Co., 1972. Originally published by New England Historic Genealogical Society, Boston, 1907.

———. Vol. 6. Boston: Thomas Prince, 1852.

———. Vol. 9. Boston: Samuel Drake, 1855.

———. Vol. 47. Boston: [New England Historic Genealogical] Society, 1893.

*Offices of Worship and Hymns (with tunes). 3d ed. Bethlehem, Pa.: Moravian Publication Office, 1891.

Pearson, Norman Holmes. Foreword to *Trilogy,* by H.D. New York: New Directions, 1973.

Poe, Edgar Allan. *Poems of Edgar Allan Poe.* Ed. Dwight Macdonald. New York: Crowell, 1965.

Reichel, William C. *Bethlehem Souvenir: A History of the Rise, Progress and Present Condition of the Bethlehem Female Seminary with a Catalogue of its Pupils, 1785–1858.* Philadelphia: Lippincott, 1858.

———. *Memorials of the Renewed Church.* Vol.1. Philadelphia: Lippincott, 1870. [Contains portions of J. Martin Mack's Journal.]

*Rimius, Henry. *A Candid Narrative of the Rise and Progress of the Herrnhuetters, Commonly Called Moravians or Unitas Fratrum, with a Short Account of Their Doctrines, Drawn from Their Own Writings, To Which Are Added Observations on Their Politics in General, and Particularly Their Conduct While in the Country of Budingen in the Circle of the Upper-Rhine in Germany.* London: A. Linde, 1753.

*———. *History of the Moravians, from their first Settlement at Herrnhaag in the County of Budingen down to the present time; With a View chiefly to their Political Intrigues.* London: J. Robinson, 1754.

*———. *A Second Solemn Call on Mr. Zinzendorf, otherwise call'd Count Zinzendorf &c., the author and advocate of the sect of Herrnhuters, commonly known by the name*

of Moravians or Unitas Fratrum, to answer all and every charge against them, and to publish the promised third part of his exposition, &c., with some remarks concerning a pamphlet, intitled, An essay toward giving some just ideas of the personal character of Count Zinzendorf, &c. London: A. Linde, 1757.

*———. *A Solemn Call on Count Zinzendorf, the author, and advocate of the sect of Herrnhutters, commonly call'd Moravians, to answer all and every charge brought against them in the Candid Narrative etc., with some further observations on the spirit of that sect.* London: A. Linde, 1754.

*Rougemont, Denis de. *Passion and Society.* Tr. by Montgomery Belgion of *L'Amour et l'occident.* London: Faber and Faber, 1940. Revised and augmented ed., published under the title *Love in the Western World.* New York: Pantheon, 1956.

Schweinitz, Edmund de. *The Life and Times of David Zeisberger.* Philadelphia: Lippincott, 1870.

Silverstein, Louis H. "H.D.: A Chronological Account, Part IV, 1929–1946. Work in progress.

Smaby, Beverly Prior. *The Transformation of Moravian Bethlehem from Communal Mission to Family Economy.* Philadelphia: University of Pennsylvania Press, 1988.

Spangenberg, August Gottlieb. *The Life of Nicholas Lewis Count Zinzendorf.* Tr. with abridgment by Samuel Jackson, with an introduction by the Rev. P. La Trobe. London: Holdsworth, 1838.

*Spence, Lewis. *The Myths of the North American Indians.* London: George G. Harrap, 1914.

Sword, Helen. "H.D.'s *Majic Ring.*" *Tulsa Studies in Women's Literature* 14, no. 2 (1995): 347–62.

Wainwright, Nicholas B. *Paintings and Miniatures at the Historical Society of Pennsylvania.* Philadelphia: Historical Society of Pennsylvania, 1974.

Weinlick, John R. *Count Zinzendorf.* Nashville: Abingdon Press, 1956.

[n.a.] "Wolle Family Genealogy as far back as is known (1956)." Unpublished ts., Moravian Collection, Reaves Library, Bethlehem, Pennsylvania.

**Wolle, Francis (1889–1975). "A Moravian Heritage." Boulder, Colo.: Empire Reproduction and Printing Co., 1972.

[Yonge, Charlotte Mary]. *History of Christian Names.* Vol. 1. London: Parker, Son, and Bourn, 1863.

Zilboorg, Caroline, ed. *Richard Aldington and H.D.: The Early Years in Letters.* Bloomington: Indiana University Press, 1992.

———. *Richard Aldington and H.D.: The Later Years in Letters.* Manchester and New York: Manchester University Press, 1995.

Index

Numbers in italics refer to the illustrations

Abide with me, 173, 174, 217. *See also* hymns

Abigail (Native American, wife of Benjamin), 272

Abraham: Biblical patriarch, 88; the Mohican, 267

Account of the History, Manners, and Customs of the Indian Nations, 281n.62

adders. *See* puff-adders

Adonais (Shelley), 207, 287n.224

Adonis, 257

"Advent," 6, 7. *See also Tribute to Freud*

Advent (season on church calendar), 23

Africa, 38, 277

Agamemnon, 211

Aggie, Aunt, Aunt Agnes. *See* Howard, Agnes Angelica Seidel

Agnus Dei (lamb of God). *See* Lamb with the Banner

Ahamawad (Christian Post), 261

airplanes, 22, 110, 111, 213, 221

air raids, 27n.30, 110, 209, 215, 216, 218, 220, 221; all-clear, 223

Aladdin, 113

Albigensians, 24, 265

alchemical-poetic ritual, 13–14

Alcott, Louisa M., 43

Aldington, H.D. (married name), ix–x

Alexandria, 47

algae, 41, 229

Algonquin (also Algonkin, Native American tribe), 245, 246, 282n.86; Meda Chant of the, 247

Alice. *See* Doolittle, Alice

Alighieri, Dante, 265

Allegheny river, 274

Allentown, Pennsylvania, 45

alligator, 41, 95, 119–20. *See also* Castor and Pollux

Alphage, Saint, church of, London Wall, 251

Alton, Delia (H.D. pseudonym), 7. *See also* "H.D. by Delia Alton"

Alvin, Uncle. *See* Doolittle, Alvin

Amelia, Aunt. *See* Weiss, Amelia

Amen forever and ever (Matt. 6:13), 84

Amen-Ra, 88. *See also* Ammon-Ra

America, 19, 23, 44, 66, 68, 156, 157, 167, 180, 214, 219, 233, 249, 251, 264, 281n.51; the Americas, 277

American Revolution. *See* War of Independence

Americans: 17, 45, 48

Americans, Native. *See* Native Americans

Ammon-Ra, 84

Amos. *See* Moravian Indians

Amsterdam, Holland: Classis of, 260, 275

Anael. *See* Annael

analysis. *See* psychoanalysis

Andersen, Hans Christian, 50, 125–26, 152, 153, 254

angel, 13, 26n.27, 44, 276

Angelica (name given to Paxnous' wife), 23, 163, 171, 213, 219

"Angelic Rulers of the Heavens," 26n.27
anima (soul), 9, 10, 22, 284n.142
animals: farm, 201, 203; in constellations,
 254; large toys as early Christmas gifts,
 98–99, 105; for *Putz,* 86–87, 89; spirit
 voices of, 169; the Unclean, 254. *See also*
 dog; lion
Anna, 13, 23, 170, 223. *See also* Grace;
 Hannah; Pahlen, Anna von
Annael, 13
Annapolis, Maryland, 253, 283n.122
Annie (nursemaid in Upper Darby), 92, 94,
 96, 114, 187, 188, 190, 193, 194, 200
Annunciation, the, 257
antinomianism, 20, 155, 262, 263
Anton. *See* Moravian Indians
Apfelholzer, Mrs. (old lady with a farm), 201,
 202, 204
Aphrodite, 22. *See also* Venus
Apollo, Phoebus, 114
*Aquaria, The Message of. See Message of
 Aquaria, The*
Aquarian Age, 11, 23, 26n.23, 28n.50
Aquarius, 26n.23. *See also* zodiac
Arabian Nights, 50, 113, 160, 190
Arab mysticism, 265
Archiv der Brüder-Unität, 143
Aries, 84, 264. *See also* Ram; zodiac
Ark of the Tabernacle, 254
armour, spiritual, 215, 220
arrow that flieth by night (Ps. 91:5), 19, 177
art, 47; Christian Renatus as artist, 213; Helen
 Wolle as artist, 71. *See also* Gift (gifted-
 ness)
Arthur. *See* Bhaduri, Arthur
artists: "people who are gifted," 43
Aryans of the mid-west, 273, 287n.220
Ashmead house, Germantown, Philadelphia,
 228
Ashursts, the (neighbors in Upper Darby),
 186, 188, 190, 203
Asia, 277
Asphodel, ix, 25n.4
Assisi, Italy: Saint Francis of, 265
astronomer, 40, 96, 104, 185
As You Like It (Shakespeare), 55, 280n.32
Athene. *See* Pallas Athene
Athenians, 246

Athens, 47, 211
Atlantic ocean, 245, 263
atonement, 246
Auld Lang Syne, 66. *See also* music; songs
Austria, 234; exiled from, 248; Freud's
 homeland, 12; Zinzendorf's ancestors
 from, 12, 26n.25
"Autobiography and Prophecy: H.D.'s *The
 Gift,*" 25n.11
Avatar, 256
Avila, Italy: Saint Teresa of, 265
Aztecs, 245; Aztec form of the Savior, 256

baby, the. *See* Doolittle, Melvin
Bach: choir and festival, 19, 92, 142, 198, 223;
 Bach, Johann Sebastian, 231. *See also*
 Wolle, John Frederick (uncle)
Baines, Martie (seminary student), 60
Baltimore, 200
Baltimore, I had a girl in, 200, 201. *See also*
 music; songs
baptism of Moravian Indians, *142,* 171, 247,
 267. *See also* Morning Star; Paxnous
baroness, Livonian. *See* Livonian baroness
bateau, en ("boat" neckline of dress), 57
Battle of Britain (1940), 218, 254
Bavaria, Germany, 26n.25
beasts, 183. *See also* animals
beat their spears into pruning hooks (Isa.
 2:4), 271
bee-hive: bees, 36, 37, 154, 155, 203, 211, 222,
 230
Bees, Fred (artist), xi, *128*
Beinecke Rare Book and Manuscript Library,
 ix, xi, 26n.35, 134, 283n.123, 284n.131,
 286n.192, 288n.246
Belle, Aunt. *See* Wolle, Belle Robinson
Bell, Emily and Laura (cousins of Helen
 Doolittle), 185, 258, 284n.139
Bell House (18th century building), 68, 100
Belshazzar's feast (Dan. 5:5–30), 6
Benade, Bishop, 158
Benezet: John Stephen, 264; Susan (daugh-
 ter), 264
Benigna, Sister. *See* Zinzendorf, Henrietta
 Benigna Justina
Benjamin (Native American), 272
Berkshires, 111

Bernard, Saint (monk), 84. *See also* Saint
  Bernard (dog)
Bernese Oberland (Swiss railroad), 84
Berthelsdorf, Saxony, Germany, 62, 234, 249
Bessie. *See* Howard, Bessie
Bethany-St.John, West Indies, 130, 228
Bethlehem: in Asia Minor, birthplace of our
  Lord, 228; Christmas Hymn (*Jesu rufe
  mich*), 235, 236; "— Diary," 281n.51; "—
  Indians," 243, 262; in Pennsylvania (the
  Settlement), 2, 3, 5–8, 11, 12, 14, 16, 19, 20,
  21, 30, 61, 66, 67, 128, 133, 151, 156, 162,
  198, 199, 227, 228, 229, 230, 232, 236, 238,
  243, 247, 255, 257, 258, 261–64, 266, 267,
  269, 270, 272, 280n.43, 281nn.51,53,
  284n.133; — *Souvenir,* 279n.8, 279n.53; —
  Steel (corporation), 64, 147, 228; Native
  American name for, 280n.42; "town of
  Mary," 7
Between History and Poetry (BHP), ix, 25nn.1, 5
Bhaduri, Arthur (medium), 17, 27n.35
Bhaduri, May (mother of Arthur Bhaduri),
  221
Bible, 25nn.10, 14, 28n.39, 45, 64, 78, 94, 97,
  115, 163, 254, 281n.57; Scriptures, 247
Bible, Doré, 89, 109, 126, 190, 254, 283n.124
Big-tree (Seneca chief), 236, 237
Bill, great-uncle, 253
Black-horse hill, 205
black rose growing in your garden, 67, 76, 172,
  176. *See also* rose
Black Swan publishers, 25n.4
Blavatsky, Madame, 26n.24
blitz of London, 15, 18, 109–11, 209–23, 257.
  See also World War II
blood: atonement by, 238, 239, 246; "Blood
  and Wounds" theology, 20, 155, 240, 252,
  268, 282n.68; *made of one, 239; purchased
  with his* (Acts 20:28), 239. *See also* Cam-
  merhof; "Sifting Time, The"; Zinzendorf
bloodhounds, 44, 45, 49. *See also* dog; *Uncle
  Tom's Cabin*
Bloom, Sister Maria (Auntie Bloom, Mary
  Catherine Bloom, first cousin of Jedediah
  Weiss), 173, 174, 178
Bluebeard, 39. *See also* fairy tales
Bob, Uncle. *See* Wolle, Robert Henry
Boehm, Rev. Philip, 260, 275

Bohemia, 8, 26n.25, 65, 73, 95, 227, 246, 266,
  269; old Church of, 18, 247, 248, 265,
  280n.43 (*see also Unitas Fratrum*);
  Protestant refugees from, 234, 270, 277,
  280n.43
Bohemian: Brethren (followers of Hus), 248,
  259, 271; names, 272
bomb, 109. *See also* air raids; blitz of London
Bona Dea, 13. *See also* goddess
Bonheur, Rosa. *See Horse-fair*
"books in the running brooks," (epig. ch. 2), 55
Braddock, General, 272
Brethren, stricter, 167, 171
Brethren's House. *See* Brothers' House
bride of Christ. *See* Christ
Brotherhood, The. *See Unitas Fratrum*
brothers, 36, 37, 126
Brothers' House (Brethren's House), 9, 57, *128,*
  155, 158, 232, 280n.33
brought me home. See "To Helen"
Boy and Girl (painting), 199
Brinton, Daniel G. 282nn.86, 90
Brunelleschi doors, 83
Bryher (Annie Winifred Ellerman), 3, 209,
  211–13, 216–23; as "mother," 6, 24, 27n.34;
  Library, East Hampton, New York, xi, 5,
  26n.24, 284n.131
Buckinghamshire, 111
Buddha, Buddhists, 256
bull-rushes, 125, 126
But it shall not come nigh thee, 217
Byzantine church, 13, 211. *See also* Greek
Byron, 253

Calendar, The (pamphlet), 256
California, 122
calix (calyx), 159, 176
Calixtines, 159, 176
Callaghan, F. B., 281n.62
Calvinism, 260, 275
Calypso Island, 255
Cambridge, University of, England, 275
camera obscura, 50. *See also* imagery, photo-
  graphic
Cammerhof, John Frederick von, 9, 13, 21, 22,
  28nn.41, 45, 159, 161, 162, 163, 167, 168, 171,
  182, 213, 223, 262, 263, 264, 267; verse by,
  27n.30, 155, 269, 285nn.166, 168

Cammerhof, Mrs. John Frederick von. *See* Pahlen, Anna von

Canada, 105, 274

canal at Bethlehem, 233

Candid Narrative of the Rise and Progress of the Herrnhuetters, A, 10

candle, 28n.50, 75, 77, 150, 153, 161, 171, 172, 174, 214

candles, Moravian beeswax, 41, 46, 74, 88, 89, 90, 100, 115

Cape May, New Jersey, 200

caps: Moravian women's, 49, 149, 153, 162, 180, 255, 284n.129; Russian, 90, 96; meaning of ribbon colors in women's, 255

Captain Shanks (Native American chief), 237

Carlotta, "Aunt," 57

Carmen (opera), 59, 67, 76

carpenter from Moravia. *See* David, Christian

Castor and Pollux: alligators, 41, 85, 86, 95; stars, 85

cat, 213. *See also* H.D.

Catherine (ship), 287n.232

Catharists, 265

Cathedral, 7, 166 *See also* dream; psychoanalysis

cathedrals, Gothic, 83, 211

Catholic. *See* Roman: Catholic

Cayuga (Six Nations tribe), 237

cella, 14, 26–27n.30

Celtic lyric, 231

Chalice, 159, 169

Charleston, South Carolina, 57, 61, 68

Chastellux, Marquis Francais Jean de, 93, 228

Chelsea, London, 6, 30, 228

Cherokee (Native American tribe in Georgia), 274

Cherry, Mr. (gardener in Bethlehem), 119

Chestnut Street, Philadelphia, 195

Chevalier, 62, 160

Chicago, Illinois, 204

Chinese: mask, 212; nationality, 257

Chingachgook, 16, 237, 239, 243

Choir (*Chor,* Moravian community subgroup, not musical), 159, 232, 261, 272, 273, 280n.33; called "classes" by Rimius, 277

Christ, 9, 10, 12, 20, 25n.10, 204, 277; bride of, 263; as king, 238, 239. *See also* Jesus

Christel. *See* Zinzendorf, Christian Renatus von

Christian (given name). *See* Seidel, Henry Augustus

Christianity, 7, 8, 9, 26n.24, 248, 259, 266; Holy Trinity, 269. *See also* Church; religion; *Unitas Fratrum*

Christian Renatus. *See* Zinzendorf, Christian Renatus von

Christiansbrunn (Christian's spring), 177, 182

Christmas, 11, 61, 74, 85, 86, 87, 90, 97, 120, 152, 166, 181, 185; as birthday of many gods, 255, 257; first—service in Bethlehem, 270

Christmas eve, 100; candle service, 11, 28n.50, 88, 115; first at Bethlehem (1740), 270, 286n.204; in 1741 Zinzendorf names Bethlehem on, 11, 19, 235, 237

Christmas Oratorio (Bach), 231

Christmas tree, 35, 42, 72, 87, 90, 94, 97, 99, 111, 112, 119, 121, 215

Church, the (= the Moravian Church). *See Unitas Fratrum*

Church, Central Moravian, Bethlehem (Old Church), 41, 46, 58, 74, 100, 112, *128,* 147

Church: Church within the, 234, 280n.43; of England, 251, 264, 276; Greek, 248, 265, 266; Hidden, 157, 169, 265; inner, 170; Invisible, 157, 265; Lutheran, 280n.43; the lost, 213; Reformed, 280n.43, 287n.236; of Rome, 248, 264 (*see also* Roman: Catholic); Ocean, 269 (*see also* sea-congregations)

Church Street, Bethlehem, 37, 38, 74, 98, 99, 100, 101, 102, 105, 116, *128,* 134, 175, 176, 186, 280n.33, 284n.133

Civil War, the, 38, 44, 97, 121, 122, 228, 230, 255, 283n.123

Classis of Amsterdam, 260

Coachman, the. *See* Young Man

Cobbs creek, 185

coffres forts (strongboxes, safes), 50

Cole. *See* Henderson, Cole

Collecott, Diana, xii, 2, 25nn.1, 17

Colonial Dames, 258

Columbus, 44, 156

Comenius, Johann Amos, 266

Communion, Holy, 251, 288n.247

Community House, 243. *See also Gemein house*

concussion, 193, 194, 195. 206, 209

Connecticut, 243, 262

consciousness, 7, 51, 58, 83; stream of, 232; the unconscious, 3, 8, 24, 111, 114, 285n.172. *See also* mysticism; psycho-analysis

Constance, Council of, 248

Constantinople, Turkey, 266

Contemporary Literature xi

controls, spiritualist. *See* Kapama, Red Cloud, White Eagle

Cooke, Grace (medium), 27n.37

Cooper, James Fenimore, 16, 68, 281nn.60, 61, 62

Corfu, 6, 27n.34. *See also* Greece

Corn-planter (Seneca chief), 236, 237

Cornwall, 216

Count Zinzendorf, 281n.44

Cousin Clarence, 202, 203

Cousin Edd. *See* Wolle, Rev. Edward

Cowes, England, 229

crab, 118, 254. *See also* zodiac

Crazy Peter, 69

creating, we were, 89

Creation, The (oratorio by Haydn), 177, 230

Cretan snake goddess, 28n.50

Christel. *See* Zinzendorf, Christian Renatus von

Croce Bianca, Switzerland, ix

Cromwellian spirit (of Oliver Cromwell, Puritan leader), 248

cross, 156, 165, 213

Crow, Dr. W. B., 256

Crown of England. *See* George III

Crusaders, 9, 155, 170

crystal-lens, 43; -goblet, 180, 181; *river . . . as crystal, proceeding out of the throne* (Rev. 22:1), 180, 182

cup, 170, 175, 182. *See also* chalice

cupola of Moravian Central Church, 57, *128*, 232, 233

Cuba, 192

"Curtiss Books, The," 26nn.24, 27

Curtiss, F. Homer, M.D., 11, 26n.24

Curtiss, Harriette Augusta, 11, 26n.24

Cyrill and Methodius, Saints, 266, 286n.179

Czar Alexander, 35

Czerny (piano exercises), 70

Daniel. *See* Moravian Indians

Dante. *See* Alighieri, Dante

Darby, Upper. *See* Upper Darby

dark, seeing in the, 22, 213. *See* also second sight

"dark Mary." *See* Mary

darkness deepens (from hymn *Abide with me*), 173, 174, 217

dark-room, 50. *See also* imagery, photographic

"Dark Room" (ch.1): epigraph cited, 18; prior publication of, xii

David, Christian (carpenter from Moravia), 157, 164, 169, 180, 217, 222, 234, 277, 281n.48

Day of Judgment, 109

Dayton, Ohio, 61

Dead-House, The. *See* Mortuary

death, 5, 17, 19, 24, 35, 38, 39, 45, 69, 78, 100, 102, 104, 105, 110, 122, 148, 181, 182, 212, 213, 215, 221, 233, 272, 277

Death and Its Mystery, 18, 33, 279n.4

"Death of Martin Presser, The," ix, 287n.231

Deetie (= H.D.) *See* H.D.

Delaware (Native American tribe). *See* Lenape

Delaware river, 61, 227, 228, 237, 263; Forks of the, 233, 270; Water Gap, 42, 148

De la Ware, Lord, 233

"Delia Alton" (H.D. character in *MR*), 17, 18

delivered myself to death (epig. ch. 6), 183

Delphic oracle, 7,

Dembo, L.S., xi

Desmids of the United States, 229

Devil, 48, 119, 170

de Vinney, Elizabeth, 251, 258

Diatomaceae of North America, 71, 229

Dick. *See* Wolle, Richard

dimension: another, 77, 126, 214, 217, 221, 222; fourth, 83, 84, 231

Dis (Hades), 78

Disciple, The. *See* Zinzendorf, Nicholas Lewis, Count von

Divinity College, 62

dog, 45, 84, 116. *See also* bloodhounds; dream; myth; Saint Bernard

Doelittle, Antony, 251, 283n.112

Don't tread on me, 252, 283n.121. See also flag: Gadsden; snake

Doolittel, Thomas, 24, 251, 277, 283n.112, 288n.246

Doolittle, Abraham, 251, 283n.111

Doolittle, Alfred (half-brother) 36, 37, 122, 139, 141

Doolittle, Alice (daughter of C.L. Doolittle and first wife, died in infancy), 35, 36, 39, 40, 122

Doolittle, Alvin (uncle, died in Civil War, brother of C.L.), 39, 44, 97, 121, 253, 255

Doolittle, Charles Leander (father, Papa, the Professor), 4, 39, 44, 52, 64, 90, 91, 92, 94, 95, 101, 103, 117, 120, 121, 128, 134, 138, 139, 151, 153, 154, 166, 182, 197–202, 206, 250, 252, 255; as astronomer, 40, 96, 98, 104, 185, 253, 283nn.122, 123; buys children toys before Christmas, 98–100; takes children boating, 122–25; seen wounded, 185–94

Doolittle, Charles, senior (father of Charles Leander), 35, 252

Doolittle, Celia (mother of Charles Leander), 255

Doolittle, Edith (sister, died in infancy), 36, 37, 39, 40

Doolittle, Eric (half-brother), 36, 39, 46, 91, 95, 122, 139, 147, 148, 153, 173, 185, 186, 191–201, 203–6

Doolittle family tree, 252

Doolittle, Gilbert (older brother), 37, 40, 42, 44, 45, 46, 49, 86, 89, 91, 92, 94, 95, 96, 97, 98, 99, 100, 101, 102, 104, 105, 113, 116, 117, 118, 121, 122, 137, 139, 141, 176, 186–202, 205–6

Doolittle, Harold (younger brother), 36, 40, 45, 89, 91, 92, 96, 99, 100, 104, 105, 113, 116, 117, 118, 121, 176, 186–93, 195, 196, 198–99, 202

Doolittle, Helen Eugenia Wolle (mother, Mama, Mrs. Charles L. Doolittle, Miss Helen in ch. 2), 4, 5, 6, 7, 8, 18, 28n.50, 30, 35, 36, 37, 40, 41, 48, 49, 52, 53, 57–79, 88, 89, 91, 92, 93, 94, 97, 98, 99, 100, 101, 103, 113, 114, 115, 116, 118, 122, 127, 135, 136, 137, 138, 150, 158, 168, 172, 173, 176, 185, 186, 187, 190, 192–95, 198, 199, 201–4, 232, 251

Doolittle, Hilda. See H.D.

Doolittle, Martha (first wife of C. L. Doolittle, the Lady), 35, 36, 40, 122, 157

Doolittle, Melvin (younger brother, the baby), 90, 96, 120, 137, 138, 139, 140, 141, 185, 193, 195

Doolittle, Sara Halliwell (Mrs. Eric Doolittle), 138, 139

Doré Bible. See Bible, Doré

dragon, 220. See also monster; snake

dream: of Cathedral, 7; as creative source, 84–85; in fever, 179; Nightmare, 103–5; of Old Man with the Sleigh, 101–2, 175; of "Poet's Lady" in Trilogy, 13, 26n.26; "Princess dream," 7; of snake-bite, 14, 28n.50, 114; in Uncle Tom's Cabin, 47; waking-dream, 178; white lily, 7, 102, 175, 176, 183; Zinzendorf as dreamer, 276

"Dream, The" (ch.3): discussed, 12; prior publication of, xii

Dresden, Germany, 90, 189, 234, 249, 259, 260, 268, 275, 277

Drese, Adam (hymn-writer), 235

Druids, 257

DuPlessis, Rachel Blau, xii, 1, 2, 16, 22. See also Gift, The (text)

Dutch: language, 233, 239; people, 233, 238, 260

Easter, 36, 79, 132, 159, 181, 185, 230, 255; Rabbit, 254

Easton, Pennsylvania, 45

Economy (structure of 18th-century Bethlehem), 158, 159. See also Unitas Fratrum

Eddas, Scandinavian, 246

Edith. See Doolittle, Edith

Edmunds, Susan, 25n.5

education by Moravians, 228, 277, 279n.8. See also Seminary for Young Ladies

Egypt, 51, 109, 212

Egyptians, 38, 86, 253, 257

1892, 400-year celebration of Columbus's arrival, 44, 156

Eliza. See Uncle Tom's Cabin

Elizabethan English forebears, 48
Elizabeth Caroline. *See* Howard, Elizabeth
    Caroline
Ellerman, Annie Winifred. *See* Bryher
"Elohim," 26n.27
End of the World, 109
Engel, Emily (friend of Helen Wolle), 69, 76
England, 17, 51, 68, 95, 121, 221, 229, 232, 248,
    252, 266, 271, 275
English: Channel, 275; dictionary, 263, 265;
    language, 163, 167; names, 272; parlia-
    ment, 249, 271; people, 251, 265;
    universities, 276 (*see also* Oxford;
    Cambridge)
enthusiasm, religious, 9, 20, 21, 167, 178, 263.
    See also Cammerhof, John Frederick von;
    "Sifting Time, The"
episcopal seal. *See* Lamb with the Banner
equinox, 257; precession of the equinoxes,
    264
Erie, Lake, 274
Eskimo (people), 38, 39
Ettwein, Bishop, 236, 237, 281n.51
Euripides, 25n.4
Europe, 11, 19, 21, 23, 51, 64, 68, 92, 121, 156,
    159, 163, 167, 187, 214, 219, 227, 231, 244,
    246, 266
European: languages, 277; people, 48
Evans, Mr. (Henry Brown Evans), 91, 97, 98,
    104, 153, 185, 191–94, 196, 197, 206
evil, 21, 78, 94, 112, 166; dark wings of, 4, 168;
    influence of whites, 271
extravagances, religious, 178. *See also*
    Herrnhaag; religion; "Sifting Time, The"
Fabricius, "the gifted," 275, 287nn.231, 232
fairy tales: *Bluebeard*, 39; dancing bear, 101;
    Little Mermaid, 111; princess and ball and
    frog, 156, 158; glass-mountain, 101, 182,
    204; princess with star on forehead and
    nine swan brothers, 23, 157, 48–49, 101,
    181, 204, 219, 254; *Red Fairy Book*, 186;
    sculpture of Old Man and Old Lady, 189
"family portraits," 4, *127–44*
family seal, 25n.16, 222. *See also L'amitié passe
    même le tombeau*
fan-maker in London (William Peter
    Knolton), 15, 16, 152, 257, 258

Fanny. *See* Wolle, Frances Elizabeth
Farmer's Brother (Native American chief),
    237
fast falls the eventide (from hymn *Abide with
    me*), 173
Fate, Fates, 110, 111; three, 37
father, 9; cosmic, 11, 12; our-father, 116. *See
    also* God
Father, Mother, Dearest Man (verse). *See*
    Cammerhof, John Frederick von
fathom of wampum. *See* wampum, fathom of
Fernandez, Mr. *See* Spanish: Student
Fetters' farm, 185, 187, 205
Fetters, Mr. and Mrs. (owners of Fetters'
    farm), 205
fifth Symphony (Beethoven), 61
fir tree and pine . . . , 88. *See also* hymns
flag: American, 44; Pennsylvania, 71;
    Gadsden, with rattlesnake and motto
    Don't tread on me, 252, 283n.121. *See also*
    Lamb with a Banner
Flammarion, Camille, 18, 33, 279n.4
Florence (childhood friend), 38, 39
Florida, 41, 120
Flower farm (grounds of Observatory), 185
Flower Observatory, 90, 139, 140, 147, 148,
    153, 185, 193
flower of the grass . . . that withereth (para-
    phrase Ps. 90, 5–6; John 15:6), 60.
fortune-teller, 51, 52, 53, 62, 67, 75–79, 198,
    199, 261
"Fortune Teller" (ch. 2): prior publication of,
    xii
fortune-telling games, 53
Four Marys, The, 152, 158, 231, 280n.30. *See
    also* music; songs
France, 214
Francis, Saint, 265
Frankfort, Germany. *See* Herrnhaag
Frederick William I, King of Prussia, 249, 275
French: and Indian wars, 16, 244, 261, 272,
    284n.140; "French Indians," 272;
    language, 6, 25n.16, 30, 43, 74, 93, 159,
    195, 221, 222, 228, 239, 244; people, 195,
    238, 244
Fresh Water Algae of the United States, 229
Freud, Sigmund, 4, 5, 6, 7, 11

Frey, Andreas (Andrew), 229, 279n.19
Freyr, 257
Friedenshuetten (Habitations of Peace), 243, 262
Friedman, Susan Stanford, xii, 25nn.2, 8, 15, 27n.31
Friends, Society of (Quakers), 186; exempt from oaths, 259
Fries, Adelaide L., 227, 261

Gaia, 14, 114
Gardener. *See* Young Man
"Gareth" (Bryher). *See Majic Ring*
Garrison, Captain Nicholas, 229, 275
Gelpi, Albert, 25n.4
Gemein house (Community House), 16, 243, 257, 272, 284n.133
genealogies: of Charles Doolittle, 252; of Helen Doolittle, 258, 259
George III, King of England, 268, 271
Georgine. *See* Wolle, Georgine
Gerald. *See* Henderson, Gerald
Gerard, Chevalier Conrad Alexandre, 228
German: language, 52, 67, 70, 74, 86, 95, 154, 155, 158, 159, 167, 176, 191, 228, 232, 260, 266, 269, 271; musical tradition, 231; people, 95, 109, 154; Reformed church congregation, 259, 275
Germantown, Philadelphia, 260, 275
Germany, 26n.25, 109, 143; ancient empire of, 248. *See also* Frankfort; Herrnhaag; Herrnhut; Saxony
Gersdorf, Countess von (grandmother of Nicholas Count Zinzendorf), 234, 281n.44
Geschichte (Loskiel's *History of the Mission of the United Brethren,* 227
Gettysburg, Pennsylvania, 39, 60
Gib, Gibbie (= Gilbert), 95. *See also* Doolittle, Gilbert
Gibbon, Edward (historian), 191
Gift (poison), 70
Gift, The (text):
—abridged edition (*NDG*), x, 22, 23; "autobiographical almost," ix, 18; ch. 7 discussed, 21; dates of composition, ix, 13, 14, 15, 16, 254, 257; dedication of, 6, 30
—full-length version, 3, 10, 22, 23; "autobio-

graphical almost," ix, 1; genesis of, 4–5, 27n.34; motive in, 261; "Notes" to, ix–xi, 1, 10, 14, 15, 16, 17, 18, 20, 26nn.20, 21, 28nn.41, 50, 256, 257, 259, 261, 279n.1, 286nn.193, 204, 287nn.224, 236; prior work done on, xi; as a prophetic book, 1; relationship to *Majic Ring,* 17, 26n.28, 27nn.34, 35; third ts., ix, xi, 12, 14; Virago edition, 2, 25nn.1, 6, 17
Gift (giftedness): artistic, 1, 3, 12, 15, 20, 42–43; children "not gifted," 19, 22, 42, 51, 96, 198; loss of, 16; of Helen Doolittle, 36, 59, 68, 167, 168; of H.D. predicted, 53, 59–79, 199; of Jedediah Weiss, 36, 132, 230; spiritual, 3, 8, 13, 23, 79, 166, 167, 177, 212, 214, 232, 267; of J. Fred Wolle, 19, 42, 43, 152, 230
Gifts: of the Holy Spirit, of Vision, of Wisdom, 214. *See also* Holy Spirit; *Sanctus Spiritus*
Gil Blas, 95
glass: Claude Lorraine, 60, 74; *in a — darkly* (1 Cor. 13:12), 222; mountain, 101, 182, 204; mirror, 215, 219. *See also* fairy tales
Glikkikan (Moravian Indian), 274
Gloria Pleura. See wounds
Gnadenhuetten (Habitations of Grace) I, in Pennsylvania: 271, 272, 287n.229; Indians of, 164, 262; massacre of whites by Native Americans at, 16, 154, 157, 159, 177, 179, 181, 182, 272, 287n.233
Gnadenhuetten II, in Ohio: 17; massacre of "Moravian Indians" by whites at, 273–74
Gnostic thought, 3, 24
God, 6, 9, 12, 18, 24, 28n.52, 40, 41, 72, 89, 111, 112, 115, 161, 179, 183, 217, 223, 235, 241, 247, 272, 273; the father, 14, 114; glory to, 277; *is a jealous —* (Exod. 20:5), 180; Norse, 257; Paxnous', 169; Sun, 257; Syrian, 25. *See also* Great Spirit; Holy Spirit
goddess, 26n.28; temple to the, 114. *See also* Annael; Bona Dea; cella; Isis; Lady; Mary; Venus
God's Acre (cemetery), 243, 262
Goheen, Mr. *140*
Golden Eagle, 222
Golden Fleece, 88

Good Friday, 257
Good Peter (Native American chief), 237
Gospel, Christian, 227. *See also Power of the Gospel, The*
Grace, 13, 14, 23, 24, 168, 223, 277
grandfather. *See* Wolle, Rev. Francis
grandfather's clock, 36, 51, 90
grandmother. *See* Wolle, Elizabeth Caroline Weiss Seidel
Grange (Ashursts' neighboring home in Upper Darby), 186
Great Spirit, 72, 112, 163, 168, 223, 247, 255, 271. *See also* God; Manitou
Great War (= World War I), 173
Greece, 6, 120
Greenaway, Kate, 147
Greenwich, England, 147
Greek: language, 21, 158, 159, 168, 263; people, 245, 257; myth, 78, 85, 101. *See also* myth
Gregor's 46th Metre (hymn tune), 67, 161, 235
Gregory (nephew of Abp. Rokycana), 247
Gregory, Eileen, 25n.5
Grimm, Jakob and Wilhelm, editors: book of fairy tales, 35, 50, 85, 100, 103, 158, 200; as children's Bible, 101; dictionary by, 260. *See also* Andersen; fairy tales
Guest, Barbara, 27n.35
Guiding Spirits, 165. *See also* Paxnous; *Wunden Eiland*
gyno-poetics, 1, 2
gyno-vision, 2
gypsy. *See* fortune-teller
gyroscope, 204. *See also* imagery, photographic

Haidt, John Valentine (18th-century Moravian painter), 143
Half-town (Seneca chief), 236
Halley's comet, 11
Hallowe'en, 53, 75, 77, 112
Hannah, 13, 23, 223
Hansel and Gretel (Grimm's fairy tale), 204. *See also* fairy tales; Grimm, Jakob and Wilhelm, editors
Harding, Professor (colleague of C. L. Doolittle), 118
Hark, Ann, 255

harmony is in immortal souls . . . (epig. ch. 5), 145, 284n.136
Hartz mountains, 111
Haydn, Franz Joseph, 231
H.D. (Hilda Doolittle, Deetie, the child): *127, 137, 138, 139, 140, 141;* baptized Moravian, 17; cat-like, 213; called Deetie and Sister, 95; deceived by Ida, 201–4; feels gift is lost, 214; as "frozen," 37, 105, 110, 112, 166, 211, 215, 219, 220, 221; gratitude of, for birthplace, 254; "H.D. by Delia Alton," 4, 12, 15, 18, 19, 22; *Hermetic Definition,* 26n.27; *HER (HERmione),* x, 25n.4; *Kora and Ka,* 25n.4; *Majic Ring,* 17, 27n.34; meets man with the milkcart (a flasher?), 205; as "Midget," 281n.50; *Mira-Mare,* 25n.4; misnamed by Mamalie, 148–51; music lessons for, 186–87; named Hilda, 40; name-changes for, 172, 214, 219; *Sea Garden* (in *Collected Poems, 1912–1944*), 27n.31; sees father wounded, 184–94; *The Sword Went Out to Sea,* 27n.35; *Tribute to Freud,* 5, 6, 7, 8, 11, 24; *Tribute to the Angels,* 13, 22; *Trilogy,* 2, 12, 13, 14, 17, 22; "union" with mother, 9; *The Walls Do Not Fall,* 13; "Zinzendorf Notebook," 2, 10, 282n.95, 284–85n.142, 286n.191
H.D. and Hellenism, 25n.5, 42n.4
H.D. and the Victorian fin de Siècle, 25n.5, 42n.4
"H.D. by Delia Alton," 4, 12, 15, 18, 19, 22
"H.D.'s *Majic Ring*" (essay), 27n.34
H.D.: Woman and Poet, 42n.11
"heart of another is a dark forest," 110
heaven, 24, 255, 277
Hebrew (language), 158, 160, 168
Heckewelder, John G., 281n.62
Hedylus, 25n.4
Heerendyk, Holland, 269
Heine, Heinrich, 281n.80
Helen. *See* Doolittle, Helen Eugenia Wolle; Helen of Troy
Helen, Miss (teacher of H.D.), 38, 90, 94, 101, 112, 170
Helen of Troy, 6. *See also* "To Helen"
Helen, thy beauty is to me. See Poe, Edgar Allan; "To Helen"
"Helen" (poem by Poe). *See* "To Helen"

Helios, 114

Hellas, Greece, 6, 114

Helle, 114

Henderson, Cole (Mrs. Gerald Henderson), 221

Henderson, Gerald, 221

Hennersdorf, 234

Henry VIII, King of England, 248

Henry, Sabina (great-grandmother, Mrs. John Frederick Wolle), *130,* 153

Henry, Mary Ann Wood (wife of the elder William Henry; great-great-great grandmother), *129,* 152, 258, 284nn.136, 137

Henry, William (the elder; great-great-great grandfather), *129,* 154, 258, 284nn.136, 137

Henry, William (the younger; great-great grandfather), *129,* 154, 258

HER (HERmione), x, 25n.4

heraldry, 264

heritage: Bryher as H.D.'s, 217; Moravian, 4, 127–44. *See also* inheritance

Hermelin, Baron von, 228

Hermetic Definition, 26n.27

hermeticist, 24

Hermione. See HER

Herrnhaag, Germany (the Lord's Hedgerow, near Frankfort), 20, 21, 229, 249, 269; "— extravagances," 263

Herrnhut (the Lord's Watch, in Saxony, Germany), xii, 26n.25, 61, 68, 143, 156, 167, 229, 232, 235, 249, 250, 275, 277, 280n.43

Herrnhuters, 10, 229, 268. *See also* Moravians

Herself Defined: The Poet H.D. and Her World, 27n.35

Hesperus (evening star, in epig. to ch. 7), 207

Hex Marks the Spot, 255

himmelschlüssel. See keys-of-heaven

Hippolytus Temporizes, 25n.4

Historical Society of Pennsylvania. *See* Pennsylvania, Historical Society of

History of Bethlehem, Pennsylvania, 1742–1892, A, 16, 17, 20, 28n.45, 142, 257, 260, 262, 267, 269, 270

History of the Mission of the United Brethren, 28n.52

History of the Moravian Church, 20, 28n.45

History of Moravian Missions, A, 287nn.226, 227, 228

Hollenberg, Donna, xii, 25nn.3,5

Holy Children, 88, 121

Holy Ghost, 10, 111, 155, 163, 168, 171. *See also* Holy Spirit

Holy Spirit: as female, 1, 12, 14, 23; as Comforter, 9, 11, 22, 213; Gift of, 214; as "Mother," 9, 22; Native American, 163; unified, 168, 214. *See also Sanctus Spiritus*

Holy Wisdom, 23, 213. *See also Sanctus Spiritus;* Holy Spirit

Hope, 94. *See also* myth

Horus, 257

Horse-fair, The (painting by Rosa Bonheur), 90, 198

house, the new (in Upper Darby), 90, 147, 193. *See also* Upper Darby

house, old (in Bethlehem), 90, 187. *See also* Bethlehem; Church Street

Howard, Agnes Angelica Seidel (Aunt Aggie, Aunt Agnes, half- sister of Helen Wolle Doolittle), 4, 23, 35, 37, 61, 62, 64, 93, 96, 115, 117, *131, 135, 136, 139,* 150, 151, 152, 153, 157, 160, 163, 169, 171, 172, 173, 174, 178, 179, 214, 219

Howard, Bessie (cousin, daughter of Agnes and Will Howard), 120, *131*

Howard, Clifford, *131,* 230, 260, 268

Howard cousins, 46

Howard, Elizabeth Caroline (died in infancy), 37

Howard, William B. (Brother Will), 59, 62, 66, 121, 151

Howard, Mrs. William B. *See* Howard, Agnes Angelica Seidel

Hudson river (North river), 238

Hugo, Victor, 190–91

Huron river, 274

Hus, Jan (John Huss), 26n.25, 227, 247, 266, 267

hut in the forest (or woods), 68, 101, 111, 122, 123; burned in Gnadenhuetten massacre, 181

Hutton, Joseph Edmund, 20, 26n.20

hymnals, Moravian: 1752, twelfth appendix to, 21; 1891, 283–84n.127

"Hymn of the Moravian nuns of Bethlehem" (Longfellow), 223

hymns: *Abide with me,* 217; *fir tree and pine,* 88; *Holy Night,* 42; *Jesu rufe mich* (Jesus call thou me), 235, 236, 281n.50; played from cupola, 57, 232; in services, 36; *Offices of Worship and Hymns* (1891, H.D.'s hymn book), 283–84n.127; *Storm of Death roars sweeping by,* 107, 181, 182, 283–84n.127; of animals and spirits, 169; and Jedediah Weiss, 131

I am the light of the world (John 8:12), 41, 115

Ida (Ida Drease, housekeeper in Bethlehem), 35, 44, 45, 47, 85, 89, 92, 93, 94, 96, 98, 100, 103, 105, 113, 114, 120, 122, 176, 185, 188, 191; deceit of, 201–4

Ida (mountain), 114

Ignatius, Saint, quoted, 183

imagery, photographic, 5, 42, 49–50, 83, 101, 110, 111, 172, 279n.13

"impersonality" (in modernism), 2

Indiana, 44, 122, 250, 252, 255

Indian: guides, 105; Path, 270; skull, 94, 122; "sisters," 274; Uprising (*see* French: and Indian wars)

Indians, American. *See* Native Americans

Indians, Zeisberger Preaching to the. See Power of the Gospel

inheritance, 37, 50, 120–21, 166, 182; musical, 267; psychic, 267; racial, 255. *See also* mysticism; second sight

initiate, 7, 8, 23, 170, 214, 223, 246; initiation, 216

Innocents (Matt. 2:16), 126

Inquisition, the, 157, 265, 266

Ion, 25n.4

Ionian island, 6,

Iowa Review, xii

Irene (ship name), 275

Iroquois (Native American tribal group, also called Six Nations), 237, 246, 274, 282n.86

Isaac (biblical patriarch, son of Abraham), 88

Isis, 22, 257

Island of the Wounds, Isle of Wounds. *See Wunden Eiland*

Israel, lost tribes of, 22

Italian (language), 261

Italy, 211

Jablonsky, Daniel, 266

Jack and Jill (nursery rhyme), 95, 99

Jacobsburg, Pennsylvania, 130

James (son of "dark Mary"), 114

Jamestown, Virginia, 245

Jaquette, Pierre (Native American chief), 237

Jednota Bratrska (Czech) = *Unitas Fratrum* (q.v.)

Jenkins, Birdie (cousin, daughter of Laura Jenkins), *137*

Jenkins, Laura Rebecca Wolle (aunt, Mrs. Henry C. Jenkins), 35, 59, 90, 96, 115, *135, 136, 137,* 172, 176

Jennie, Aunt. *See* Wolle, Mrs. J. Fred

Jerome, Saint. *See* Lion of Saint Jerome

Jesuits, 242, 259

Jesu rufe mich (Jesus call thou me, Bethlehem Christmas Hymn), 235, 236

Jesus (Our Lord, Redeemer, Savior, King), 9, 10, 11, 20, 88, 159, 160, 177, 178, 181, 230, 238, 239, 256; as Friend, 242, 244, 249, 264; "all-important *sacrifice*" of, 246; called Jesus Jehovah, 237; Lord's Supper, 278, 288n.247. *See also* Christ; God; Holy Spirit

Joachim (Moravian Indian), 272

Joey (clown in Punch and Judy), 99

Johanan, Brother. *See* Zinzendorf, Nicholas Lewis, Count von

John's (shop in Bethlehem), 112

John, Uncle. *See* Ladd, John

Jordan, Viola, 11, 26n.23

Joyce, James, 27n.31

Judas, 162

Judge (magazine), 194, 204

Jupiter, 14

justification by faith, 20

K. *See* Kapama

kaleidoscope, 203. *See also* imagery, photographic

Kapama (K., spiritualist control), 17

Karnak, Egypt, 84,

Kast, Miss, *139*

keepers-of-the-Mysteries. *See* Wise Men

Kehelle, 23, *142*, 123, 267
Kent, Jack (childhood friend), 126
Kent, Mrs. (neighbor, mother of Jack and
    Teddie), 126
Kent, Teddie, 126
Key of Destiny, The, 26n.27
keys-of-heaven (*himmelschlüssel*, primula), 51,
    151
Kiefer, Marcus (Moravian missionary), 244
Kingdom (of God), 180
King: of Bohemia (Podiebrad), 73, 265; of the
    Delawares, 271, 273; of England (George
    III), 268, (Henry VIII), 248; *King of the
    Jews, Jesus of Nazareth* (Matt. 27: 37, John
    19:19), 160; of the Oneida, 243; Philip's
    War, 251; of Prussia (Frederick William I),
    249; "late — of Prussia," 277; of the
    Shawanese (Paxnous), 213; Shikellimy, 243
Kings of the Six Nations, 237
Knights Templars. *See* Templars, Knights
Knolton, Hannah (wife of William), 258
Knolton, William Peter. *See* fan-maker in
    London
Kora and Ka, 25n.4
Kunwald, Bohemia, 247
Küsnacht, Switzerland, ix

Ladd, John (uncle, brother-in-law of C. L.
    Doolittle), 97, 253
Ladd, Rosa (aunt, sister of C. L. Doolittle),
    97, 103, 104, 253
Laddie. *See* Wolle, Philip
Lady: C. Doolittle's first wife, 36; "Poet's or
    Troubadour's Lady," 13, 26nn.26, 28. *See
    also* dream
lady, old. *See* Apfelholzer, Mrs.
Lafayette, Marquis de, 158, 186, 237
Lafayette's Walk (old road in Upper Darby),
    186
Laity, Cassandra, 25nn.4, 5, 28n.50
Lake Erie, 233
lamb, lambs, 23, 87; meaning of the name
    Agnes, 170
Lamb with the Banner (*Agnus Dei*), 156, 170,
    229, 264–265
L'amitié passe même le tombeau, 6, 25n.16, 30,
    174, 181, 221, 222

L'amour et l'occident, 265
Langly, Rebecca, 230
*Last Night there were four Marys. See Four
    Marys, The*
Last of the Mohicans, The, 16, 68, 237, 238, 259,
    261, 281n.62
Latin (language), 215, 219, 229, 260
latitude, variation of, 98, 253
La Trobe, Christian Ignatius, 227
laughter (ecstatic), 169
Laura, Aunt. *See* Jenkins, Laura Rebecca Wolle
Lavington, Bishop George, 19, 28n.38
leaves were for the healing of the nations (Rev.
    22:2), 180
Lehigh River (Lecha, a fork of the Delaware),
    227, 228, 234, 237; Lenape names for, 233
Lehigh mountains, 117
Lehigh University, 4, 36, 39, 46, 47, 52, 64, 96
Leibert, Bishop, 64, 79
Leipsic, Germany, 264
Lenape (Native American tribe, also called
    Delaware), 16, 233, 238, 245, 256, 271, 274,
    281n.61
Lenni-Lenape. *See* Lenape
Leo, 89. *See also* lion; zodiac
Les Misérables (Victor Hugo), 191
Levering, Joseph Mortimer, 16, 17, 26n.20,
    27n.33, 257, 262, 263, 266, 267, 269,
    28inn.44, 51, 286n.179
life: and death, 213; endurance of the worst —
    has to offer, 219; eternal, 24, 42, 278;
    H.D.'s desire to save, 6
Life and Times of David Zeisberger, 27n.33,
    28n.45
Life of Nicholas Lewis Count Zinzendorf, 20,
    26n.25
light-of-heaven (candle), 74
lilies: calla, 79; Chinese, 93, 204; princess with,
    157. *See also* water-lilies
lily, white, 102, 175, 176, 181, 182. *See also*
    Sleigh, Old Man with the
Linden House, 47
Lindsey House, London, 228, 276
lion, 105, 200; of Saint Jerome, 84; of Saint
    Mark's, 84. *See also* animals; dog
Litz: in Bohemia, 247, 248; in Pennsylvania,
    274

Little Billy (Native American chief), 237
Little Eva. *See Uncle Tom's Cabin*
Little Mermaid, The. *See* fairy tales
Little Strength (ship), 229, 258, 287n.131;
    Moravian sisters on board listed, 275;
    officers and men listed, 275
Little Wild Street, London, 270
Little Women, 194. *See also* Alcott, Louisa M.
Liturgien (liturgies), 177
Livonia, 227
Livonian baroness, 13, 162. *See also* Pahlen,
    Anna von
Lo, I am with you alway (Matt. 28:20), 157
London, England, ix, 1, 5, 13, 15, 18, 19,
    27n.37, 109, 152, 209, 220, 221, 223, 227,
    228, 249, 250, 257, 265, 270, 274, 278;
    Library, 260, 276
Longfellow, Henry Wadsworth, 230
The Lord is risen indeed (Luke 24:34), 36
Lord of Hosts, 235
Lord with me abide (from hymn *Abide with
    me*), 174
Loskiel, George Henry, 28n.50, 227
lots, Moravian custom of drawing, 23, 65,
    162, 213, 223, 261, 285n.150
love-feast (Moravian ritual), 177, 270
Lowndes Square, London, flat at #49, 3, 22,
    211, 220
Lucerne, Lake, 84
Lucia, Aunt, 61, 63, 172, 174, 178, 180, 182
Luckenbach, Mr. (grocer), 41,
Lucy (boat), 125
Lucy (Lux, Light), 23, 172, 173, 174, 176, 179,
    180, 214
Lugano, Switzerland, viii
Lusatia, Saxony, Germany, 234, 248, 249
Lutheran congregation, 275
lynx, 105. *See also* animals

Mack, John Martin, 70, 73, 235, 245, 270
Macmullen, Miss (teacher), 101
Madonna, 78, 181
Madre, 14, 113. *See also* mother
Madrigal cycle (H.D.), 3
Magi, 77. *See also* Wise Men
magic, 112, 167
"Magical Lenses: Poet's Vision," 279n.13

magician, Indian, 162, 163
magic-lantern, 42, 83. *See also* imagery,
    photographic
Magic Ring. See Majic Ring.
Mahoning Creek, 262, 271
Maia, 14, 113, 114
Main Street, Bethlehem, 98, 100, 105, 128
Maine (state), 111
Majic Ring, 17, 26n.28, 27n.34
Mama. *See* Doolittle, Helen Eugenia Wolle
Mama-and-Papa's bed, 113
Mamalie. *See* Wolle, Elizabeth Caroline Weiss
    Seidel
Mamie (boat), 124–25
Mandel, Charlotte, 279n.13
Manhattan, New York, 241
man in the milkcart (flasher?), 205
"Manisi, Ben" (Arthur Bhaduri). *See Majic
    Ring*
Manitou (Manito), 24, 28n.52, 238, 246, 247
Man on the stairs (Reni painting of Christ),
    204
man-with-the-horse, 122–24
mar, 13
marah, 13
Maria, "Aunt," 57. *See also* Bloom, Sister
    Maria
Marienborn, Germany, 20, 21, 229, 269
Mark, Saint. *See* Lion of Saint Mark's
Market Street, Philadelphia, 200, 204
Mars, 148
Martens, Sammy (young man in Bethlehem),
    189
Martz, Louis L., xii
Mary: "Aunt," 92; "dark —" (housekeeper in
    Upper Darby), 14, 22, 29n.50, 113; great-
    grandmother Weiss, 152; "town of —," 7;
    Virgin, 7, 13, 14, 22, 111, 113, 114, 115
*Mary Beaton, Mary Seaton. . . . See Four
    Marys, The*
Marys, Four. *See Four Marys, The;* songs
massacres: Gnadenhuetten, Ohio, 48n.33;
    Gnadenhuetten, Pennsylvania, 48n.3
Mass in B Minor (Bach), 231, 232
Massa's in the cold, cold ground, 44. *See also*
    music; songs
mater (mother), 14

May. *See* Bhaduri, May
May-day party, 120
measure, 261; *pressed down and shaken together*
 (Luke 6:38), 50
medicine-man, 162, 163, 164, 167, 174, 213
medium: creative, 50; spiritualist, 17, 27n.37
Melinda (childhood friend), 38
Memorials of the Renewed Church, 28n.46
memory, 5, 50, 51, 83, 111, 114, 215, 219
mer (sea), 14. *See also* Mary; mother
Merchant of Venice (Shakespeare) quoted, 145,
 284n.136
Mercury (planet), 252
Mercy (younger sister of C. L. Doolittle, died
 in childhood), 97
Mère (mother), 14, 113. *See also* mother
Message of Aquaria, The, 11, 23, 26nn.24, 27
Methodius. *See* Cyrill and Methodius
Michael. *See* Moravian Indians
Michigan, 274
middle-ages, Guilds and Societies of, 218
Millie, Aunt, 88, 203, 204
Mimmie (Mamalie). *See* Wolle, Elizabeth
 Caroline Weiss Seidel
Minne-ha-ha (Longfellow, *Hiawatha*), 169
miracle play, medieval, 48
Miralles, Don Juan de, 228
Mira-Mare, 25n.4
Miriam, 14, 113
Mithras, 256
modernism, 1, 2
Mohammedan: Order similar to Templars,
 265; tomb, 211
Mohawk (tribe in Six Nations), 237, 238, 241,
 264
Mohican (Native American tribe), 17, 238,
 241, 243, 246, 272, 274; language, 239, 264
Monocacy river, 58, 155, 168, 262; Lenape
 names for, 234
monster, 114. *See also* dream; snake
Montour, Madame, 244, 246
Montemora, xii
moon, 13, 26n.28
Moonlight (sonata by Beethoven), 48. *See also*
 music
Moravia, 26n.25, 95, 157, 169, 180, 227, 234,
 249, 266

Moravian Archives, Bethlehem, xii, 127, 130–
 42, 144, 264
Moravian Church. *See* Unitas Fratrum
Moravian College, Bethlehem, xii, 280n.33
"Moravian Heritage, A," xi, 130, 131, 135, 136.
 See also Wolle, Francis (cousin)
Moravian Indians, 17, 68, 164, 242, 256, 273–
 274; "Bethlehem Indians," 243, 262
Moravian mission-stations in North America,
 274, 287nn.226, 227, 228
Moravians (Brethren and Sisters, church
 members), 3, 9, 15, 16, 19, 28n.52, 37, 92,
 112, 164, 165, 167, 168, 227, 236, 238, 243,
 256, 265, 267, 271; Danish, 95, 272;
 exempt from oaths, 259; German, 95;
 Herrnhuters, 10, 229, 268
Moravians Compared and Detected, 28n.38
"Moravians in Dutchess County," 281n.62
Morning Star: epig. to ch. 7, 207; called
 Indian Princess, 171, 181; Native American
 woman, Paxnous' wife, 22, 28n.46, 163,
 167, 169, 171, 173, 181, 213, 219, 247, 267;
 Morning Star, I will give him the (Rev.
 2:28), 162, 167, 223; *morning stars sang
 together* (Job 38:7), 173, 174; *thou were the
 Morning Star*, 207, 287n.224. *See also*
 Cammerhof; princess; star, stars
Morris, Adalaide, xii, 25nn.11, 12. *See also*
 Gift, The
Mortuary, The (Dead-house), 38
Moses. *See* "Princess Dream"
mother: cosmic, 11; Divine, 26–27n.30;
 Erdmuth von Zinzendorf as, 250; Holy
 Spirit as, 9, 10, 22, 25–26n.19; *mère*, 14,
 113; identified with Mary, 14, 113; phallic,
 23, 28n.50, Primal, 14, 23; psychoanalytic
 view of, 6; spiritual, 23; "union" with, 6;
 See also Bryher; Doolittle, Helen Eugenia
 Wolle; Holy Spirit
mothers, four, 231
moving-picture, 5, 80 *See also* imagery,
 photographic
Mueller, John, 241, 243, 282n.66
music: ancient manuscript of, 158–61;
 communicating with Native Americans
 through, 156, 163, 169; Church, 112, 158,
 255; *Creation*, 177; fifth Symphony, 61;

Indian songs, 172, 256; instruments, 258; Jedediah Weiss's gift for, 36, 57, *132;* J. Fred Wolle's gift for, 19, 42, 230, 231; Mama's gift for, 42, 43, 47, 48, 58, 61, 63, 154; Mama's singing criticized, 51–52; Mamalie's gift for, 167, 168, 172, 173; *Moonlight,* 48; opera, 52; *Träumerei,* 154. *See also* hymns; Pyrlaeus; songs

Mut (courage), 14, 26–27n.30, 113

Mutter (mother), 9, 14, 22, 26–27n.30, 114 *See also* mother; Holy Spirit

Mycenae, 211

My garden is under the window (line in a play), 147, 150, 169

Mysteries, the (religious), 121

Mystery, The, xvi, 285n.142

mysticism: 17, 26n.29, 101–2, 180, 263, 276; Arab, 265; Zinzendorf accused of "gross and scandalous —," 259, 268, 284n.142. *See also* Rimius, Heinrich; dream

myth, 3, 7, 37, 84, 85, 88, 94, 110; mythical method, 4; *Myths of the New World,* 282nn.86, 90; *Myths of the North American Indians,* 28n.52, 247

names: baptismal exchange of, 163; invented Indian, 169, 222, 223; Native American, for Moravians, 17, 242, 261, 264; Mamalie's confusion of, 148, 150; same, in H.D.'s family, 170; significance of, 40, 169. *See also* H.D.

Native Americans, 3, 13, 15, 16, 28n.52, 67, 68, 71, 72, 112, 227, 234, 237, 238; languages of, 158, 160, 163, 164, 165, 170, 172, 223, 233, 239, 240, 243, 244, 245, 246, 247, 255, 261, 264, 267, 273; gave names to Moravians, 17, 242, 261, 264, 270, 271, 281n.53

Nazareth: in Asia Minor, 169; in Pennsylvania, 130, 227

Nazis, 16, 287n.220

NDG (= New Directions *Gift,* abridged), x, xii, 1, 14, 22, 23

Neapolitan inlaid wood, 219

negroes. *See Uncle Tom's Cabin*

Nellie (fiancée of Eric Doolittle, song personage), 200, 201

Netawetwes (Native American chief in Ohio), 271

net of the fowler (paraphrase Ps. 91:3), 217

Nettie (childhood friend), 38

Neuville, Chevalier de la, 228

New Age. *See* Aquarian Age

New Brunswick, New Jersey, 258

New Directions (publishers), 1

New England, 167, 245, 250, 258; Historical Register, 251

New Haven, Connecticut, 251

New Jersey, 200

New Orleans, 74, 151, 179

New Year's eve, 59

New York (city), 46, 62, 66, 68, 274

New York (state), 46, 238, 242, 243, 250, 259, 262, 270

Nicholas, Saint, 23, 111, 219; feast-day, 268, 286n.192

Nicht Jerusalem, sondern Bethlehem (not Jerusalem but Bethlehem, from Bethlehem Christmas Hymn), 235, 236

Nightmare, 14, 103–5, 115

Nights, 25n.4

Nile river, 84

9th century, 176

Nisky Hill cemetery, 38, 69, 76

Nita Juanita, 78. *See also* music; songs

Nitschmann, Anna Charity (daughter of David Nitschmann, second wife of Count Zinzendorf), 232

Nitschmann, David (Bishop, Father Nitschmann), 227, 266, 270, 275

Nitschmann, Martin, 272

Nitschmann, Susanna, 272, 275

Noah's Ark animals, 98

non-Christian, 13

North America, 3, 245

North Carolina, 227, 261

North river. *See* Hudson

"Notes" (by H.D. to *The Gift*), ix–xi, 1, 10, 14, 15, 16, 17, 18

Notes on Thought and Vision, 25n.3

Observatory, Flower. *See* Flower Observatory

Observatory, the old (Bethlehem), 96, 100, 104

ocean, 200; Church (*see* sea-congregations); or great stream underground, 7, 8, 24. *See also* sea

Ohannessian, Griselda, xii

Ohio, Gnadenhuetten, 41

Old Church. *See* Church, Central Moravian

old cousin Elizabeth, 175

Old cousin Theodore [Theodore F. Wolle, cousin of Rev. Francis Wolle, son of his uncle Peter], 61, 64, 73

old house. *See* house, old

Old Hundred (chorale), 63

Old Man. *See* Sleigh, Old Man with the

old-town, 147. *See also* Bethlehem

old-witch. *See* witch

Olympus, 111

Onandaga (tribe in Six Nations), 237

Oneida (tribe in Six Nations), 237, 243

opera, 52

oracle, Delphic. *See* Delphic oracle

oracles, 216

Osiris, 256

Ostonwakin, Pennsylvania, 244, 246

Out of Line: History, Psychoanalysis, and Montage in H.D.'s Long Poems, 52n.5

Overbrook, Pennsylvania, 195

Oxford, University of, England, 248, 275

Pacific ocean, 252

Pahlen, Anna von (Anna Maria von der Pahle; Mrs. John Cammerhof), 13, 21, 22, 23, *143*, 162, 163, 167, 168, 169, 171, 174, 213, 219, 223, 263

Paint It Today, 25n.4, 28In.50

Palatinate, 248

Palestine, 47

Pallas Athene, 48

Pandora, 94

Papa. *See* Doolittle, Charles Leander; Freud, Sigmund

Papalie. *See* Wolle, Rev. Francis

Papal: authorities, 267; heraldry, 264

Papists, 242, 243, 272

Paris, France, 187

parma-violets. *See* violets

Passion and Society. See L'amour et l'occident

pathfinder, 96

Pathfinder, The (Cooper), 68

Paul, Saint, 162; Pauline doctrine, 20, 263

Paul Potter's Bull (picture), 92

Paxinosa. *See* Paxnous

Paxnous (Shawanese chief), 22, 23, 156, 157, 158, 162, 164, 166, 167, 169, 171, 181, 213, 214, 217, 247, 267

Paxnous, wife of, 163, 167, 171, 213. *See also* Morning Star

peace, 1, 3, 8, 12, 15, 23, 24, 222, 237, 243, 259; *peace on earth* (Luke 2:14), 19

Pearson, Norman Holmes, ix, xii, 1, 13, 25nn.5, 6, 26nn.23, 26

Peloponnesus, 114. *See also* Greece

Penelope's Web: Gender, Modernism, H.D.'s fiction, 2, 5, 6, 25nn.2, 8, 26n.25

Penn, John, 164

Pennsylvania, 6, 12, 44, 238, 255, 270; Historical Society of, xi, xii, 129, 258, 284n.136; settlers in, 237, 251, 258, 259; University of, 90, 91, 185, 187

Perdita. *See* Schaffner, Perdita

Persians, 256

Peter the child or Peter the stork (Andersen story), 125

pervenche (periwinkle), 74, 179

Pharoah's daughter (Exod. 2:3–10). *See* "Princess Dream"

Philadelphia: cousins, 258; ladies, 90, 93. *See also* Bell, Emily and Laura

Philadelphia, Pennsylvania, xii, 36, 38, 44, 62, 64, 90, 98, 151, 153, 185, 186, 195, 200, 204, 230, 236, 237, 258, 263, 274

Philippus (Indian medicine-man, priest), 213, 223

Phoebus. *See* Apollo, Phoebus

picture-writing, 161, 170, 239, 241. *See also* imagery, photographic

Pilate, Pontius, 160

pillar-of-cloud (Exod. 13:21), 120

pillar-of-fire, (Exod. 13:21), 120

Pine Plains. *See* Shekomeko

Pitti Gallery, Florence, Italy, 215

Pittsburgh, 62, 199, 273

Plan (Zinzendorfian term), 9, 19, 21, 24, 155, 156, 265, 268, 276

planes. *See* airplanes

play, 48, 147, 150, 169

Pocahontas ("the lady Rebecca Rolfe"), 246

Podiebrad, George, King of Bohemia, 73, 247, 248

Poe, Edgar Allan, 5

poetics, 2

poet: Byron, 253; Dante, 265; Christian Renatus as, 213; Heine, 281n.50; H.D. as Imagist, 1; Poe, 5, 25n.13, 30, 62; Shakespeare, 55, 145, 280n.32; Shelley, 207, 28n.224; suggestion of nordic, 134; Whitman, 253; Zinzendorf, 276

poetry, 47

"Poet's Lady," 26n.26. *See also* dream

Point Pleasant, New Jersey, 200, 201, 283n.125

Poland, 130, 227, 228, 231; Poles, 277

Polaris (North or pole star), 252

polar-bear, 98, 105. *See also* animals

Pollux. *See* Castor and Pollux

Polly (boat, parrot), 125

Pompeii, 215, 219

Pope, Popery: Popish practices, 154, 259; outlined by Rimius, 276

Posen, Poland, 130, 228

Post, Christian Frederick (missionary), 261

Power and Spirit, 168; union of, 214

Power of the Gospel, The (painting by Christian Schussele, also called *Zeisberger Preaching to the Indians*), 70, 90, 144, 162

Powhatan (Native American tribe), 245, 246

Practical Astronomy As Applied to Geodesy and Navigation, 253

Prague, Czechoslovakia (formerly Bohemia), 247

prayer ("pray for us"), 113–14

pre-Christian, 13

pre-oedipal, 6

pressed down and shaken together. See measure *pressed down*

Presser, Martin, 275. *See also* "Death of Martin Presser, The"

priest, Indian, 162, 164, 169, 174, 213, 223, 246 *See also* medicine-man; Philippus; shooting-star

Prince, Florence, *140*

princeps facile (a prince indisputably), 222

princess, 23, 48, 157, 158; Anna von Pahlen as, 161; Little Eva as, 47; Paxnous' wife as, 171, 181; Pocahontas as, 246. *See also* fairy tales; lilies; star

"Princess Dream," 7. *See also* dream

Promise, 171, 173, 179, 180, 212

Promised Land (Gen. 17:8), 86

Promise is redeemed and the Gift restored, 160, 171, 177, 214

Protestant: clergy, 250, 260, 275, 277; church members, 12, 19, 21, 26n.25, 234, 247, 248, 249, 259, 266, 268. *See also* Reformation

Prussia, Frederick William I, King of, 249

Prussian lawyer. *See* Rimius, Heinrich

Psyche Reborn, 27n.31

Psychic News, 27n.37

psychic thought processes, 53, 267

psychoanalysis, xii, 2, 3, 6, 7, 15

public-school, 91

Puck (children's magazine), 194, 203

Punch and Judy, 99, 187

puff-adders (blowing adders), Zinzendorf and the, 70, 245, 247. *See also* flag: Gadsden; snake

Pulaski banner, 230

Pulaski, Count Casimir, 228, 230

Purgatory, 48

Puritan, 24, 248, 251

Putz (Moravian crèche), 11, 12, 86, 87, 94, 99

putzen (to decorate), 86

Pyrlaeus, John Christopher, 155, 156, 157, 159, 161, 162, 163, 164, 165, 168, 170, 260, 275; Native American name of, 264

Python, 114, 115

Pythoness, 115

Quakers. *See* Friends, Society of

queen, 26n.28; Bessie as May-day, 120; Elizabeth I, 251; English, 246

questions by H.D., 158, 173, 217

Quetzalcoatl (the Feathered Serpent), 256. *See also* Manitou; serpent

Ram, 84, 85, 264. *See also* sheep; zodiac

Rauch, Christian Henry, 16, 17, 238, 239–243, 281n.62, 282n.66

Red Cloud (spiritualist control), 27n.37

Red Fairy Book, 186

Red Jacket (Seneca chief)

Reformation: Bohemian, 266; pre-, 248; Protestant, 234, 248, 276, 276

regents. *See* "Elohim"

Reichel, William C., 28n.45, 279n.8

religion, 7, 11, 26n.24, 156; to found a new, 8; Moravian, 4; Mystery, 121, 246; oppressed, 265; root — common to all people, 252, 256. *See also* Christianity; Jesus; mysticism; "Sifting Time, The"; *Unitas Fratrum;* Zinzendorf

Reni, Guido (Italian painter), 190

Reuss, Count Henry de (brother of Countess Zinzendorf); Count Ignatius de (nephew of Countess Zinzendorf), 248, 282n.95

Revelation, Book of, 13, 22, 180, 282n.67

Rhinebeck, New York, 239; young John of, 242, 243, 282n.66 *See also* Mueller, John

Richard Aldington and H.D.: The Early Years in Letters, 25n.5

Richard Aldington and H.D.: The Later Years in Letters, 25n.5

Richardson, Dorothy, 2

Richmond, Virginia, 61

Rimius, Heinrich (Henry), xv, 10, 19, 20, 259, 268, 286nn.185, 191; denouces Zinzendorf's purported political motives, 276–77

Rinaldo, Madame, 52, 59, 65, 66, 67, 76

rittersporn (lit. "knight's spur," larkspur), 67

Roberts, Estelle (medium), 27n.37

Road to Salem, The, 227, 261

Rokycana, Archbishop, 247

Rolfe, "the lady Rebecca." *See* Pocahontas

Roman: catacombs, 264; Catholic, 13, 26n.25, 78, 257, 259; Triumph, 47

Romanism, 234

Rome, Italy, 47, 120

Rome (Gibbon's *The History of the Decline and Fall of the Roman Empire*), 191

Rosa, Aunt. *See* Ladd, Rosa

rose, 37, 151, 165, 174, 182, 195; *Calixtines,* 176; cherokee-roses, 57; water-roses, 176. *See also black rose*

Ross, Betsy, 44

Rothe, Rev. John Andrew, 234

Rotterdam, Holland, 68, 229, 269, 275

Rougemont, Denis de, 265

ruling spirits. *See* "Elohim"

Russia, 35, 62, 90, 96

Ruth (fictionally named cousin of Helen Wolle), 62, 67, 75, 77, 78, 198, 199

S (letter), 77, 158, 169, 170, 174, 218

Sabina, Aunt, 170, 175

Sailor's Lake, 122

Saint Alphage church, London Wall, 260, 277

Saint Afra's Day, 260, 280nn.27, 28

Saint Bernard (dog), 105, 116

Saint Clair, Lake, 274

Saint James's Palace, London, 271

Saint Mark's cathedral, Venice, Italy, 84

Saint Matthew Passion (Bach), 231, 232

Saint Nicholas (children's magazine), 194, 199, 205

Saint Paul's church-yard, London, 277

Saint Thomas, Virgin Islands, 256

Salem: Massachusetts, 167, 171; North Carolina, 274

Samuel and James (ship), 270

Sanctuary. *See* Wunden Eiland

Sanctus Spiritus, 13, 170, 171, 174, 179, 214, 218

Sand Island, 177

Santa Claus, 253

Santa Sophia, 23, 213

Sarah (Native American, wife of Abraham the Mohican), 272

Saratoga, New York, 60

Savannah, Georgia, 230

Saxon: lawyer (*see* Rimius, Heinrich); names, 272; people, 277

Saxony, 12, 26n.25, 227, 234, 248, 249, 275, 277

Schaffner, Perdita, v, xi, xii, 6, 25n.4, 217, 281n.57

Schelling, Mrs. (visitor in Upper Darby), 92, 197

Schneider, Elizabeth. *See* Weiss, Elizabeth Schneider

Schneider, Fritzie (son of Mrs. Schneider, Ida's cousin), 201, 202

Schneider, Mrs. (cousin of Ida Drease, involved in deception), 201

Schönbrunn (Beautiful Spring), 271

Schropp, Sabina (wife of William Henry, the younger; great-great grandmother), 129, 251, 258

Schussele, Christian (also called J. C. Schuessele). *See Power of the Gospel, The*

Schweinitz, Brother de [one of many Zinzendorf descendents], 62

Schweinitz, Edmund de, 21, 26n.20, 27n.33

Schwerzens, Poland, 130, 228

Scotland, 133, 167, 231

Scriptures. *See* Bible

sea, the, 6, 8, 22, 61, 118, 200, 233, 277. *See also mer;* mother

sea-congregations (Ocean Church), 180, 279n.17; first, 229, 258, 269, 275, 287n.232; second, 229, 287nn.232, 234

Sea Garden, 27n.31

"Séance Notes," 27n.35

séances, spiritualist, 17, 27n.36

second sight, 133, 268, 269; Scotch legend of, 167. *See also* inheritance; mysticism

Second World War. *See* World War II

secret, 3, 24, 151, 152, 155, 156, 157, 160, 162, 178, 181, 182, 213, 267

"The Secret" (ch. 5), 18

Seed, Hidden (Zinzendorfian expression), 169

seidel (cup), 159, 169, 174, 260, 285n.149

Seidel, Agnes Angelica. *See* Howard, Agnes Angelica Seidel

Seidel, Catherine (wife of the first Christian Seidel), 261

Seidel, Charles Frederick (father of Henry Augustus), 160, 260, 285n.148

Seidel, Christian (Moravian pioneer, the first Christian Seidel), 26n.21, 154, 156, 157, 159, 160, 161, 167, 170, 261, 267, 270, 275, 287n.232

Seidel, Christian Heinrich Johann (uncle of Henry Augustus, called Henri Chevalier de Seidel in ch. 5, known as Uncle Henry), 154, 159, 160, 169, 181, 260

Seidel, "Christian." *See* Seidel, Henry Augustus

Seidel, Elizabeth Caroline Weiss. *See* Wolle, Elizabeth Caroline Weiss Seidel

Seidel, Henry Augustus (father of Aunt Agnes, called "Christian," "Henry Christian," "Christian Henry," Brother Henry), 9, 26n.21, 153, 155, 157, 158, 159, 160, 162, 167, 168, 169, 171, 172, 176, 177, 178, 222, 270

Seidel, Nathanael, 26n.21, 160, 269, 287n.232

Seiffert, Anton (Moravian pioneer), 270

Sellers, the (Quaker neighbors in Upper Darby), 186

Seminary for Young Ladies, The, 4, 35, 38, 57, 60, 61, 67, 76, 95, 98, 100, 122, 155, 168, 228, 229, 243, 262, 281n.53

Seneca (tribe in Six Nations): chiefs named, 236

Sepulchre, Holy, 265

serpent, 113, 247; Feathered (Quetzalcoatl), 256; *serpents, be ye wise as* (Matt. 10:16), 170. *See also* dream; snake

Settlement (= Bethlehem), 162; the New (= Wallingford), 251

Shakespeare, William, 55, 145, 280n.32

Shamokin, Pennsylvania, 243

Shawanese: language, 160; Native American tribe, 244, 245, 247. *See also* Paxnous

Shekomeko (Pine Plains), New York, 238, 243, 281n.62

Shikellimy: John (Thachnechtoris, son of old), 244; King, 243; old, 244

Shelley, Percy Bysshe, 207, 287n.224

sheep (in *Putz,* made by Papalie), 86–87, 89, 94, 120. *See also* Ram; zodiac

shooting-star, 148, 151, 152, 173, 212; Indian name, 169, 170, 174, 176, 178

"Sifting Time, The," ("Time of Sifting"), 3, 9, 12, 13, 18, 20, 21, 25n.10, 157, 160, 167, 171, 178, 249, 263

sift you as wheat (Luke 22:31–32), 25n.10, 180

Silesia (Protestant province near Bohemia), 269

Silverstein, Louis H., xii, 26n.27

Simon Legree. *See Uncle Tom's Cabin*

Simon Peter, 25n.10

Simple Science, 103, 104, 115

Single Brothers (Single Men), 9, 222, 261, 280n.33

Singstunden (singing-hours, Moravian ritual of group singing), 177

Sister: nickname for H.D., 41, 49, 92, 115; sisters, 22, 37, 115

Sisters: Married, 233; Moravian, 38, 41, 46, 57, 74, 115, 162, 174, 230, 232; Single, 154, 232–33, 280n.33; Widows, 233

Sisters' House, 57, 100, 232, 280n.33

Six Nations (Native American tribal group), 19, 236, 237, 254. *See also* Iroquois

slaves. *See Uncle Tom's Cabin*

Sleigh, Old Man with the, 7, 101–2, 116, 121,

175, 176. *See also* dream; supernormal experience

Smaby, Beverly, 25–26n.19

small-pox, 243

Smith, Captain John, 246

snake, 28n.50, 40, 73, 113, 114, 252, 283n.121; king rattlesnake, 247. *See also* dream; puff-adders

Snively, DeForest (child neighbor in Upper Darby), 186, 187

Snively, Doctor (neighbor in Upper Darby), 186, 187

Snively, Ethelwyn (child neighbor in Upper Darby), 186, 187

Snively, Margaret (child neighbor in Upper Darby, remained longtime friend), 186, 187

Snively, Muriel (child neighbor in Upper Darby), 186

Solemn Call on Count Zinzendorf, A, 286n.191

solstice, winter, 256, 257

songs, 43, 44, 66, 152, 158, 231. *See also* hymns; music; *Uncle Tom's Cabin*

soul, 277; *anima,* 9, 10, 22; abstract self as, 215, 217; immortal, 145; Morning Star as the, 173; psyche, 218

South, 57

South America, 52, 78

South Carolina, 283n.121

Southerner, 52

Spain, castle in, 78

Spangenberg, Augustus Gottlieb (Zinzendorf's biographer), xv, 20, 21, 26n.25, 281n.44

Spanish: language, 192; nationality, 256; Student (Mr. Fernandez), 52, 64, 66, 77

sparrow falls . . . (Matt. 10:29), 116

"sparrow hath found a house . . ." (Ps. 84:3), 235

Spartans, 246, 282n.86. *See also* Algonquin; Iroquois

spell, 42

spelling: H.D.'s, ix, 41–42, 279nn.9, 10; of "Cammerhof," 26n.20, of Doolittle, 251

Spence, Lewis, 28n.52, 247, 282n.86

spinet, 16, 152, 158, 162, 167, 257, 258

spirit guides. *See* spiritualist controls

Spirit of the Air, 111

spiritualist controls. *See* Kapama, Red Cloud, White Eagle

Spoo, Robert, x, xii, 4, 6, 25n.4

Spruce Street, Philadelphia, 185

Stables, Margaretha (mother of Mary Stables), 131

Stables, Mary. *See* Weiss, Mary Stables

star, stars, 39, 40, 97, 104, 147, 153, 174; -of-Bethlehem (flower), 69; with Cammerhof's verse, 9, 22, 155, 269; Christmas tree ornament, 89, 95, 215; at fortune-teller, 76, 77, 79; Indian symbol, 164; of the Magi, 77, 212; Polaris, 252; of our Redemption, 79; Star of the Sea (*stella maris,* 14, 22. *See also* astronomer; dream; fairy tales; princess; shooting-star

steam-car. *See* trolley

steel-mills, 61, 62, 199. *See also* Bethlehem Steel; Pittsburgh

Stein, Gertrude, 2

Stella Maris (star of the sea), 22. *See also* Mary

Stimmung (feeling, sentiment), 74

stork, 125–26

storm of death, when the (epig. ch. 40), 107, 181, 283–84n.127

Stowe, Harriet Beecher, 43

street-car. *See* trolley

Strickenhof, Livonia, 227

Stuber (photographer), 132

subconscious, 8, 23, 219, 254, 257

Sulfur 9, 1

supernormal experience, 5, 7, 27n.34, 101–2. *See also* dream; Sleigh, Old Man with the

Susquehanna river, 243, 244, 246, 261

Sweden, 111

Swenska (Delaware river), 233

Swing Low Sweet Chariot, 44. *See also* music; songs

Switzerland, ix, 214

Sword, Helen, 27n.34

Sword Went Out to Sea, The, 27n.35

Tamenund, 238

Tanglewood Tales (Hawthorne), 78, 85, 94, 101

Templars, Knights, 156, 157, 167, 170, 265–66, 286n.175

Temple, City of London, 265
tempt the Lord thy God, thou shalt not (Matt. 4:7), 161, 163
Teresa, Saint, of Avila, 265
test or try the Spirits (1 John 4:1), 162
Tganniatarechev (John Christopher Pyrlaeus), 264
Thames river: Canada, 274; England, 228
Thanksgiving, 152, 185
Thirty Years' War, 248, 276
thy people shall be my people (Ruth 1:16), 237
time: -bomb, 109; *Tempus fugit,* 104, 105; out-of-time, 222; "there shall be no —," 239
"Time of Sifting." *See* "Sifting Time, The"
Thachnechtoris. *See* King: Shikellimy
Theodore, Old cousin. *See* Old cousin Theodore
theosophists, 11, 45n.24
theosophy, 26n.24
Theus-pater, 14, 114
Thiaucourt, France, 113, 121
This do in remembrance of me (Luke 22:19; 1 Cor. 11:24), 278
thou shalt not kill (Exod. 20:13), 252
thou shalt not suffer a witch to live (Exod. 22:18), 180, 251
Töchterlein (little daughter), 95, 102, 191
"To Helen" (poem by Poe), 5, 25n.13, 30, 62, 279n.1
tongues: of flame, 163; speaking with (Acts 2: 3–4), 169; *in trees* (Shakespeare, epig. ch. 2), 55
Tootie. *See* Wolle, Francis (cousin)
Topsy, 45. *See also Uncle Tom's Cabin*
toys. *See* animals
transference, 6, 12, 25n.15. *See also* psychoanalysis
Transformation of Moravian Bethlehem from Communal Mission to Family Economy, 25–26n.19
Transit House (at Flower Observatory), 90, 96, 97, 104, 147, 185, 193
Träumerei ("Reverie" by Schubert), 154, 186
"Treatise concerning the Lord's Supper," 283n.110, 288nn.246, 247
Treatise on Practical Astronomy, As Applied to Geodesy and Navigation, 283n.122

Tree of Knowledge of Good and Evil (Gen. 2:9), 78
Tribute to Freud, 5, 6, 7, 8, 11, 24
Tribute to the Angels, 13, 17, 22, 26n.27. *See also Trilogy*
Trilogy, 2, 12, 13, 14, 17, 26nn.23, 26
trolley, 139, 185, 187, 193
trombones, 36, 57, 128, 132, 230, 231, 255. *See also* hymns; music
Troubadours: medieval, 265; "Troubadour's Lady," 26n.26. *See also* dream; Lady
Tschoop (corruption of name Job), 16, 239–43, 246, 282n.68. *See also* Cooper, James Fenimore; Wasamapah
Tulpehocken, Pennsylvania, 243
Tulsa Studies in Women's Literature, 27n.34
Turk, 190
Tuscarawas River, Ohio, 271
Tuscarora (tribe in Six Nations), 237
twins, 95. *See also* Castor and Pollux; zodiac

Unamis, 238
Uncas, 238
Uncle Tom. *See Uncle Tom's Cabin*
Uncle Tom's Cabin (performance from Stowe's book), 43–48
unconscious, 3, 8, 24, 111, 114, 285n.172. *See also* psychoanalysis
Unitaet (= *Unität*), 266. *See Unitas Fratrum*
Unitas Fratrum (*Jednota Bratska,* the Brotherhood, United Brethren, the Unity, Unity of Brethren), commonly called The Moravian Church, 3, 4, 7, 9, 10, 12, 18, 73, 155, 156, 157, 159, 163, 173, 176, 178, 180, 181, 213, 214, 223, 227, 230, 231, 247, 255, 257, 259, 273, 275, 276; as ancient Protestant Episcopal church, 248; Elders of the, 167; name translated, 266; as renewed Brotherhood, 249; as "underground" religious movement, 24, 234, 246, 265, 266, 285n.172. *See also* Moravians; "Sifting Time, The"; Zinzendorf
United Brethren. *See Unitas Fratrum*
united brotherhood. *See Unitas Fratrum*
United States, 156, 233. *See also* America
University. *See* Lehigh University

University boys, 46, 77

University ladies (Upper Darby), 91, 95, 97, 185, 195, 197, 198

University of North Carolina Press, 227

Upper Darby, Pennsylvania, 137, 138, 140, 141, 186

Vater, Mutter, Lieber Mann (verse: Father, Mother, Dearest Man). *See* Cammerhof, John Frederick von; *Mutter*

Venice, 94

Venus: goddess, 13; planet, 22

Venus de Milo, 92, 187

vespers, 177

victory, 24, 60. *See also* fifth Symphony

Victory, winged, 48

Vienna, Austria, 4, 12, 92; Council of, 265, 286n.175

Viking call, 252

Villa Verena, Switzerland, ix

violets (parma-violets), 195

Virago (publishers), xii, 2, 25nn.1, 6, 17

virgin, 115

Virginia (state), 152, 231, 245

Virgo, 89. *See also* zodiac

Vision, Gift of, 214. *See also* Gift (giftedness)

visionary experience, 5, 214; in *Uncle Tom's Cabin,* 47. *See also* supernormal experience

Wajomik, Pennsylvania, 244

Wales, 258

walking treaty, 164

Wallingford, Connecticut, 251

Walls Do Not Fall, The. See Trilogy

Walnut Street, Philadelphia, 195

Walsh, John, 25n.4

wampum, fathom of (peace treaty token given to Zinzendorf), 237, 238, 281n.56; "wampum," 240

Wanamaker's (department store), 185

War and Peace (Tolstoy), 190

War of Independence, 39, 158, 230, 237, 273, 281n.51

war of the Spirit, 163

War Trilogy. *See* Trilogy

Wasamapah, John (Tschoop, Indian Elder), 242, 243

Washington at Mount Vernon (painting), 70, 162

Washington, D.C., 117, 121

Washington, George, 158, 186, 237, 258

water: *to drink of the well* (2 Sam. 23:15, epig. ch. 5), 145, 284n.136; -lilies, 122, 124–26; -music, 177; -roses, 176; *unless you are born of — and the spirit* (John 3:5), 179. *See also* lilies

Watteville, Baron John de, 228

Way down upon the Swanee river, 43. *See also* music; songs

Weinlick, John R., 281n.46

Weiss, Amelia (great-aunt, sister of Elizabeth Weiss Wolle), 62, 67

Weiss, Anna Maria, 230

Weiss, Elizabeth. *See* Wolle, Elizabeth Caroline Weiss Seidel

Weiss, Elizabeth Schneider (mother of Jedediah Weiss), 131

Weiss, George Augustus (son of Jedediah and Mary Stables Weiss), *133,* 269

Weiss, Jedediah (great-grandfather, Mamalie's father, Old Father Weiss) 16, 35, 36, 42, 86, *131, 132,* 158, 166, 229, 230, 231, 233, 257

Weiss, Mrs. Jedediah. *See* Weiss, Mary Stables

Weiss, Mrs. John George. *See* Weiss, Elizabeth Schneider

Weiss, Jonas Paulus, 229, 279n.19

Weiss, Lewis William, 230

Weiss, Margaret Catherine (great-great-great grandmother, Mrs. Mathias Weiss), 3, 229

Weiss, Mary Stables (great-grandmother Weiss, Mrs. Jedediah Weiss), 18, *131, 133,* 152, 167, 231 *See also* second sight

Weiss, Mathias (great-great-great grandfather), 3, 229

Weiss, Mrs. Mathias. *See* Weiss, Margaret Catherine

Weite, Jonah Paul. *See* Weiss, Jonas Paulus

West, Benjamin, *129,* 152, 258

West Indies, 130, 133, 231, 249, 269

Wetterau, the, 20, 21,

what I have written I have written (John 19:22), 160

White Eagle (spiritualist control), 27n.37

White Eagle Lodge, 27–28n.37

White Eyes (Delaware chieftain and councillor), 271, 273

Whitman, Walt, 253

Widowers (choir), 233

Widows' House, 57, 70, 90, 100, 172

wife of Paxnous. *See* Morning Star

Will, Brother. *See* Howard, William B.

William Morris furniture, 197

Williams, Amery (neighbor child),

Williams family, 101, 119

Williams, Mea (neighbor child), 120

Williams, Mrs. (wife of professor, mother of Amery, Mea, and Olive), 51, 120, 151

Williams, Olive (neighbor child), 49, 120

Williams, Professor (neighbor in Bethlehem), 49

Williams, Rev. Henry, v

Williamson, Col. David (leader of massacre in Ohio), 273–74

Williamson, Mrs. (neighbor in London), 214

Willow Eddy, 57, 60

Willow Eddy (painting by Helen Doolittle), 198

wind bloweth where it listeth, 84

Wisdom, Gift of, 214. *See also* Gift (giftedness)

Wise Men (Keepers-of-the-Mysteries), 88, 121, 284n.130

witch, 23, 78, 103, 115, 171, 180, 204, 219

witchcraft, 77, 167, 171

Wolle, Belle Robinson (aunt by marriage, Mrs. Hartley C. Wolle), 37, 43, 45, 46, 47, 100, *139*, 147

Wolle, Rev. Edward (cousin Edd), 57–79, 96, *138*, 147, 152, 198

Wolle, Elizabeth Caroline Weiss Seidel (Mamalie, Mimmie, grandmother, wife of Rev. Francis Wolle), 3, 4, 9, 12, 16, 18, 19, 27n.34, 35, 36, 37, 41, 49, 51, 60, 62, 63, 71, 75, 85, 86, 92, 120, *127*, *131*, *136*, *137*, 147–82, 186, 212, 214, 217, 218, 219, 231, 255, 260, 262, 265, 267, 268–69, 271

Wolle, Frances Elizabeth (Fanny, sister of Helen Doolittle, died in childhood), 36, 37, 71

Wolle, Rev. Francis (grandfather, Papalie, father of Helen Doolittle, called Papa in ch. 2 and Brother Francis in ch. 5), xii, 4,

12, 35, 37, 38, 41, 42, 49, 51, 58, 59, 60, 62, 67, 74, 77, 85, 86, 90, 92, 95, 100, 102, 115, 119, 120, 121, 122, *134*, 151, 158, 176, 178, 179, 180, 182, 228, 229

Wolle, Francis (cousin, Tootie), xi, 37, 45, 46, 86, 120, 130, 131, 135, 136, *140*

Wolle, Georgine (cousin, daughter of Robert Wolle), 198

Wolle, Hartley Cornelius (uncle), 35, 37, 43, 49, 88, 93, 96, 97, 100, 103, 104, 116, 119, 121, *135*, *136*, 147, 152, 199

Wolle, Helen Eugenia. *See* Doolittle, Helen Eugenia Wolle

Wolle, Jennie Stryker (aunt by marriage, Mrs. J. Fred Wolle), 41, 42, 49, 90, 93, 114, 116, 117, 125, 147, 148, 173, 186, 204

Wolle, John Frederick (great-grandfather, father of Papalie), *130*, 153, 228, 258

Wolle, John Frederick (uncle, J. Fred, founder of Bach choir and festival, 19, 41, 42, 48, 96, 97, 117, 122, *135*, *136*, 172, 186, 198, 230, 231

Wolle, Mrs. John Frederick. *See* Henry, Sabina

Wolle, Laura Rebecca. *See* Jenkins, Laura Rebecca Wolle

Wolle, Peter (great-great-great-grandfather), 130, 228

Wolle, Philip (cousin, Laddie), 37, 198

Wolle, Richard (cousin, Dick), 37, 59, 120

Wolle, Robert Henry (Uncle Bob), 44, 88, *135*, *136*

Wolle, Rev. Sylvester (great-uncle), 134, 148, 228–29

"Woman's Age." *See* Aquarian Age

Woolf, Virginia, 2, 27n.31, 280n.30

World's Fair, 201, 204

"world unity without war," 3, 21,

World War II, 1, 4, 14, 17, 18, 24, 53

wounds: Jesus' side-wound (*Gloria Pleura*), 20, 21, 263, 269, 277; liturgies and Ritual of the Worship of the, 167, 168, 223; sees father's, 185–94; Wounded One (father, Jesus), 182. *See also* Jesus; Christ

"writing on the wall" (Dan. 5:24–31), 6

Wunden Eiland (Isle of Wounds), 18, 154, 155, 156, 159, 160, 162, 163, 165, 166, 167, 168, 169, 170, 172, 176, 181, 182, 213, 214, 221, 262, 272

Wunderling, Carrie (family friend), *138*
Wycliffe, John (also Wyclif), 248
Wyoming, Pennsylvania, 261, 267, 272

Yale Collection of American Literature. *See*
   Beinecke Rare Book and Manuscript
   Library
Young Man (Coachman, Gardener), 101–2,
   116, 175, 176 *See also* Sleigh, Old Man
   with the
Yule, 257

Zakenuto, 17, 27n.36
Zeige mir den Stern (show me your star, from
   Bethlehem Christmas Hymn), 67, 235,
   236
Zeisberger, David (father, the elder), 270
Zeisberger, David (son, the younger), 27n.33,
   28n.45, 154, 156, 157, 159, 161, 162, 163,
   164, 165, 167, 169, 173, 174, 178, 261, 267,
   270, 271, 273, 274
*Zeisberger Preaching to the Indians. See Power
   of the Gospel, The*
Zeisberger, Rosina (wife of the elder David,
   mother of the younger), 270
Zeu-pater, 14, 114
Zeus, 14, 114
Zilboorg, Caroline, 25n.5
Z'higochgoharo (Christian Henry Rauch),
   17, 242
Zinzendorf, Christian Renatus von (called
   Christel, the young Count, son of
   Nicholas and Erdmuth), 21, 26n.21, 156,
   157, 167, 177, 178, 213, 222, 223, 229, 230,
   265

Zinzendorf, Elizabeth von (daughter of
   Erdmuth and Nicholas), 250
Zinzendorf, Erdmuth Dorothea, Countess
   von (wife of Nicholas), 73, 247, 248, 249,
   250, 265
Zinzendorf, Henrietta Benigna Justina,
   Countess von (called Benigna, daughter
   of Erdmuth and Nicholas), 228, 237, 242,
   243, 250
Zinzendorf, Maria Agnes von (daughter of
   Erdmuth and Nicholas), 250
Zinzendorf, Maximilian Erasmus von
   (grandfather of Nicholas), 26n.25, 234,
   265
Zinzendorf, Nicholas Lewis, Count von
   (1700–1760; called Brother Johanan,
   Brother Louis, Bruder Ludwig, The
   Disciple), 8, 11, 12, 18, 19, 20, 25n.10,
   26n.25, 62, 64, 68, 73, 95, 155, 156, 157,
   164, 166, 169, 180, 227, 228, 232, 235, 237,
   242–48; 254, 259, 263, 265, 269, 270, 275,
   284n.142, 285n.166; as dreamer, poet,
   reformer, mystic, friend of all women,
   276; as Lutheran clergyman and
   Moravian bishop, 250, 280n.43; noble
   titles listed, 234; his view of sexuality,
   9, 10
"Zinzendorf Notebook," 2, 10, 282n.95, 284–
   85n.142, 286n.191
Zinzendorf's hymn. *See* Gregor's 46th Metre
zodiac: epig. ch. 3, 81; constellations of, 254;
   spring sign, 264
Zürich, Switzerland, ix
Zuydt (South river, Swedish name of
   Delaware river), 233